DATA-STRUCTURES AND PROGRAMMING

Malcolm C. Harrison

Courant Institute of Mathematical Sciences
New York University

DATA-STRUCTURES AND PROGRAMMING

Scott, Foresman and Company
Glenview, Illinois London

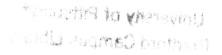

Sections 10.1 through 10.4 of the "Final Draft Report on the Algorithmic
Language ALGOL 68" by A. van Wijngaarden, ed., B. J. Mailloux,
J. E. L. Peck, and C. H. A. Koster, are used by permission of Springer-Verlag,
Berlin-Heidelberg-New York.

This book has grown out of a number of courses at the undergraduate and graduate
level given at New York University. Early versions of notes were written by Margaret
Ullman, and by Bel Wu, Barry Jacobs, Sheldon Koenig, Ronald Levenberg, William
Rutherford, Robert Dibiano, and Rosemary Wos. I am grateful for corrections and
improvements suggested by Charles Hornback and David Combs.

This revised version incorporates many corrections to the previous versions
suggested by a number of people. In particular I would like to thank James Gimpel
and J. E. L. Peck for pointing out some of my misconceptions of SNOBOL and ALGOL
68, and G. E. Hedrick, Jonathan Wexler, and Norman Buckle for their corrections to
the earlier chapters.

I would also like to thank Connie Engle, who deciphered my hieroglyphics. Her
understanding contributed much to the accuracy of this work.

PREFACE

This book is concerned with what have recently been widely recognized as some of the most important aspects of programming and programming languages: the properties of the data-objects which are manipulated by programs, and the data-structures which are used to represent them in memory. Of much less significance, comparatively, are the details of the method used to specify the program, such as the format or syntax of the language, though these can contribute significantly to the utility of a language and the ease of expression. As programs get more complicated and machines get faster, even the efficiency of execution of the program begins to decline in importance among the problems connected with getting a program completed in a reasonable time.

We will approach our concern from a number of points of view. In the first chapter, we will present a general philosophy of programming which is particularly addressed to the question of complexity. It is our view that the essential problem faced by the programmer and the programming language designer (whom we see as being increasingly indistinguishable) is that of choosing a compromise between complexity and efficiency. This compromise we feel is intimately associated with the choice of data-objects and data-structures.

In the next two chapters we consider the general properties of data-objects and data-structures. This is done from the abstract point of view, without making specific use of a particular programming language or machine.

In the following six chapters we consider some of the more important techniques for manipulating data-structures at a low level. Rather than use machine language for this purpose we have chosen to use a minor and informal extension of FORTRAN which we call XFORTRAN. This was chosen since FORTRAN is a widely known and widely implemented language, which is simple enough to have a straightforward machine-language representation and can thus be used to represent the majority of machine-language programming techniques.

The topics presented in Chapters 5 to 9 are well-established methods for string processing, expression evaluation, storage allocation, sorting, searching, and hash coding which form the common currency of programming expertise. A knowledge of these techniques is necessary to make a correct choice of data-structures when programming or designing a programming language. The first three of these chapters can also be regarded as a description of some of the more important techniques which are implicit in the newer programming languages such as PL/1.

In Chapters 10 to 14 we present some more advanced techniques using PL/1 as the programming language. These include techniques for processing data-structures which would be too complex to describe in XFORTRAN, or for which the necessary facilities are not provided. The main chapter on the use of pointers in the book is Chapter 11.

Chapters 15 onwards give outlines of a number of programming languages, with particular reference to their data-objects and data-structures. These languages illustrate some of the more interesting compromises which can be made between complexity and efficiency. No attempt has been made to give a complete definition of any of these languages, and the reader who wishes to learn to program in them should be prepared to use a manual. However, it is hoped that sufficient more important attributes of the languages have been given to enable the would-be programmer to choose the correct one.

It is suggested that the first 11 chapters could form the basis for a one-semester course on data-structures, assuming a two-semester prerequisite of FORTRAN and assembly-language programming. If the prerequisite is PL/1 and assembly language, then the material in Chapters 5 through 9 should be adapted, using 5 through 7 to illustrate the techniques used to represent a PL/1 program in machine language, and using PL/1 to specify the algorithms used in Chapters 8 and 9. A graduate course in data-structures could cover the first 14 chapters, going rather rapidly over Chapters 5 through 9. A survey course in programming languages could cover the material in Chapters 1 to 3, 10, and 15 onwards. The whole book could be covered in two semesters with a two-semester undergraduate prerequisite.

References to work listed in the bibliography are by name and date. Thus Feller (57) will refer to the work by Feller published in 1957. In the case of ambiguity, a letter will be used following the date in the reference, and in parentheses following the date in the bibliography.

Malcolm C. Harrison
New York

CONTENTS

1

INTRODUCTION

MACHINE ARCHITECTURE

In this book we will be examining methods which can be used to represent objects in the computer. For the most part, our treatment will be oriented towards the modern general-purpose computer which has dominated the computer field since its earliest days, and which is likely to play an important part for a considerable time.

To a large extent the organization of the general-purpose computer is determined by the economic balance between computer components, and as such is quite dependent on developments in technology. We will start by considering the main characteristics of the current technology, and how these are reflected in the design of modern computers.

If there were a well-established measure of computational power, analogous to the measure of information capacity given by Moore-Shannon information theory, we could measure the capability of different methods of organization of computers. Unfortunately there are only a few scattered results which seem relevant. There is clearly a minimum amount of memory for each problem, below which it cannot be solved. Winograd has shown that operations such as addition and multiplication require a certain minimum time for execution using standard transistor circuits, and it is clear that similar limits can be found, in theory at least, for all computations and any particular physical devices. On the other hand, the simplicity of the universal Turing machine shows that a very small amount of computational power combined with unlimited memory is sufficient for any computation.

Thus a particular computation or set of computations makes essential a certain amount of memory which, judging from current applications, varies from about 50,000 bits to about 5,000,000 bits. On the other hand, a universal computer can be constructed with relatively few, maybe several thousand, processing elements. The most important component in computer memory until fairly recently has been the magnetic core, which in cost is about one-tenth to one-hundredth the price of the most important processing component, the transistor. These three facts combine to force the modern computer to contain considerably more memory elements than processing elements. For example, the CDC 6600 contains about 10,000,000 cores

1

and 400,000 transistors, while the PDP-8 contains about 50,000 cores and 3000 transistors.

Another important influence on computer architecture quite different from this derives from the human preference for specifying an algorithm as a series of operations which are carried out strictly in order. Most algorithms of which we are aware are of this form, while parallel algorithms, such as those used in visual pattern recognition, appear to be carried out below our level of awareness.

The result of these two influences has been that the current general-purpose computer contains two essentially distinct units, a memory which delivers or stores *words* of 8–64 bits of information one at a time, and a serial processor which operates usually on one or two and rarely more than half-a-dozen words at once. The memory is organized in such a way that a word is referred to by a pattern of bits called an *address* which has the property that the particular word can be located quickly and with a small amount of hardware. Usually this is implemented by using the address to refer to a specific set of memory elements—in fact the word *location* is sometimes used.

Relatively small modifications have been made to this basic design since its use in the earliest computers. High-speed registers are now used as scratch-pad memory for operands and results, so that the amount of core memory use can be reduced. In some machines there is a certain amount of preprocessing of the address before it is used to calculate a memory location, permitting a certain amount of flexibility in the physical location of a word. Sometimes a number of serial processors is used, usually working on distinct problems. Recently memories have been used which permit very high data transfer rates for words with contiguous addresses, with processors which can operate on such data-streams.

At the time of writing, both the transistor and the magnetic core are in the process of being replaced by integrated circuits. Eventually this will permit a much greater degree of parallelism in computers, since it will be possible to do computations in the memory cells themselves. At present, however, the main effect of this development on machine architecture has been the availability of faster memories. This has not so far changed the basic structure of the general-purpose computer.

COMPLEXITY OF PROGRAMS

One of the most striking changes in the use of computers since their commercial development in the early 1950s is illustrated by the enormous increase in the size of programs. The early machines, with memories of the order of 4000–8000 words, were programmed in machine language, sometimes even in octal notation, without the benefit of compilers. Programs which would not fit in a straightforward way into memory had to be squeezed and pushed until they did, and much energy was expended in optimizing particular programs for particular machines, some of which had idio-syncrasies which could occupy the programmer for years. As machines became larger and faster, and cores replaced magnetic drums as main memory, programming became easier, and compilers were developed and grew in efficiency to the point at which the code they produced was comparable to that written by the capable programmer.

The main motivation for the increase in size and speed of machines was to permit the solution of larger scientific problems which were mostly numerical in nature. In some cases this simply permitted the same problem to be solved in a shorter time, or a larger problem (using larger matrices, say) to be solved in the same time. However, it also permitted the development of larger and more complex programs, thus widening the area of applications of computers considerably. Today the larger machines have of the order of 100,000 words of memory, and programs which cannot fit into this memory are common, with some programs as much as ten times this size.

The most significant property of these complex programs is that they can rarely be completely understood, even by the programmer who wrote them in the first place. In some cases it is not possible for the programmer to understand even short algorithms—in the sense that their detailed behavior cannot be predicted. In many cases it is not possible for the programmer to memorize the algorithm simply because of its size. On top of this, there are additional complexities associated with the particular way that the algorithm is implemented. The result is that the programmer is often dealing with a sprawling mass of information in the form of specifications, listings, and, if he is lucky, flow charts. This complexity is one of the major problems of programming, and will motivate much of the material in this book.

MODULARITY

The most important principle available to the programmer in his search to reduce the complexity of a program is *modularity*. Roughly speaking, we say a program is modular if it is possible to construct or analyze it in small pieces.

The notion of modularity in a program is much talked about, particularly in connection with the design of operating systems, which are often supplied by the manufacturer in a form which requires modification by the users. The importance of modularity in this instance is clear, since it is much easier to modify a system if it is divided into relatively small modules whose interaction with the other modules is simple and well defined. In that case the programmer who has to make a modification need only concern himself with those modules which are specifically related to the modification. What is less clear is that a complex system cannot be written in the first place unless it is so organized. If we have a system which requires more than one person to do the programming, the work has to be organized in such a way that the detailed decisions made by one programmer do not affect those made by others. Decisions that affect more than one programmer are made jointly or by some higher authority often called a *systems designer*. These decisions are effectively the specifications of the module being written by the programmer. It is clear that they must be well defined, and that the simpler they are the better. As the specifications get more complicated more time gets spent on them than on the programming. If they involve too many people they never get defined at all, and the project gets bogged down.

We can usefully distinguish two aspects of modularity in a system. The first is what we will call *hierarchical modularity*. We will use this term to refer to a system in which there is a single main module, called a module of level zero, which gives a relatively concise description of the algorithm, and which refers to a set of other modules, the modules of level -1, which give further details of the algorithm. In turn the modules of level -1 may refer to modules of level -2, and so on. We do not exclude the possibility that a module may refer to modules on a higher level, and in fact we will see a number of examples with such an organization. The importance of hierarchical modularity cannot be overemphasized. It is an organization which permits the system to be understood at a number of different levels, each with different amounts of detail. It is clear that this permits changes or improvements at one level without requiring that more detailed levels be completely understood. A useful addition to a hierarchically organized system is a description of the specifications of the modules at each level. This permits a newcomer to the system, whether a user, manager, programmer, or analyst, to read the modules up to level $-n$ say, together with the specifications of modules at level $-(n + 1)$.

The second aspect of modularity we will call *horizontal modularity*. We will say that a system has horizontal modularity when it is possible to understand a module at a particular level without necessarily having to understand other modules at the same level. The importance of this is that a system which has this property permits a newcomer to concentrate on a small portion of the algorithm at a particular level, without necessarily having to understand it all. To be more specific, horizontal modularity is concerned with the independence of modules at the same level. An example of a lack of independence arises when two modules interact with each other in a way which is not apparent in the modules which refer to them. A complete description of both modules would have to specify this interaction. In such a case it is necessary to understand both modules in order to properly understand either. A more subtle example of dependence occurs when a change to one module requires a change to another module on the same level, although no change is required to modules which refer to it. It is really the existence of horizontal modularity which permits a useful distinction to be made between two modules on the same level, in the sense that the description of the modules at that level is simpler when the distinction is made.

We thus envision the perfect program as being organized in modules with a structure such as that given in Figure 1.1. The arrows in the above diagram go from higher-level modules to the lower-level modules to which they refer, so we have shown one module at level zero, three at level -1, and two at level -2. Each module is described by giving its coding, together with a set of specifications which describe its effect when referred to by an arbitrary module. As a guide it seems reasonable to restrict the size of modules to about a page of code in a standard algebraic language, though to some extent this is a matter of personal preference.

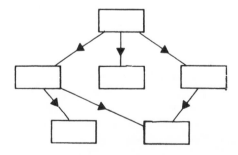

Figure 1.1

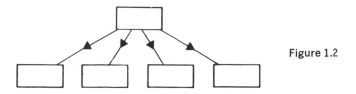

Figure 1.2

Note that in a modular structure of this idealized form we do not wish to imply that there is necessarily any correspondence between the flow of control in the program which implements the structure and the connections between modules. In some cases this is true—when, for example, a module corresponds to a procedure or subroutine— but it may be that a module does not contain executable code at all.

It is often convenient to be able to understand some aspects of a system without having to understand level zero. This is clearly the case in systems such as operating systems, in which the user is often not interested in the system supervisor, but simply in that aspect of it which affects him. In such a case he wants to be able to start with a module which is essentially in the middle of a hierarchical structure. Initially he will probably be content to understand the relationship between this module and superior modules, but later he may wish to understand how the superior modules work. In this case his investigation of the system is proceeding from level $-n$ to level $-(n - 1)$, rather than the other way round. It is really the presence of horizontal modularity which enables him to do this, since the existence of a well-defined interface between his module and superior modules means that his module is independent of other modules on the same level. Of course in practice he will find that this is only approximately true, since the interface is probably incompletely defined—in the case of an operating system, for example, which does not specify timing information. If this were included, the horizontal modularity would break down, and the description of timing would require details of the behavior of other modules on the same level.

We can point out three degenerate cases of this form of organization. The first occurs when we get a structure such as the one in Figure 1.2, in which there is one main module, and no modules below level -1. Another type of degeneracy occurs when all the modules at a particular level refer to each other in a very involved way, so that a structure which is ostensibly like Figure 1.3, where we have used dotted lines to indicate dependencies, is in reality of the form shown in Figure 1.4, with a single large

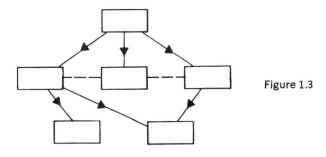

Figure 1.3

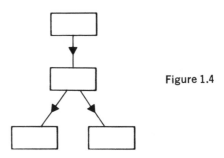

Figure 1.4

module invoked in a number of ways replacing the three original modules. The most degenerate case, the single-module program, very rarely occurs except in small programs, simply because it is almost impossible to write and to debug.

PROCEDURES AND DATA-OBJECTS

In the above discussion the main objective was to consider ways of presenting an algorithm so that it was easily understandable. Modularity was the name given to the property of being easily divided into small pieces which could be understood independently. We now wish to suggest that in the understanding process, these pieces or modules will correspond to concepts in the programmer's mind; and that the more independent the modules, the more distinct are these concepts. With this view of modularity we can see that hierarchical modularity corresponds to the ability to conceptualize the algorithm at a number of different levels, and in effect to describe the algorithm in a number of different languages with varying amounts of detail. Horizontal modularity corresponds to the independence of the notions constituting these languages.

If we look at the type of concepts which the programmer deals with, we find that they can be divided roughly into two categories: first, the objects which the program is manipulating, which we will refer to as data-objects, and second, the operations on such data-objects. We will normally expect both types of concepts to be represented by modules.

It is clear that the value of a modular organization such as we have described has been recognized implicitly in the design of many programming languages. Operation-type modules are frequently represented by various forms of subprogram, usually called *functions* or *subroutines* or *procedures*, and good programming practice prescribes that procedures:

1) will not be too long;
2) will state explicitly which quantities they use and which quantities they modify;
3) will avoid sneaky communication with other procedures;
4) will be as independent as possible.

In fact it is not an unreasonable generalization to state that one important criterion of excellence in programming is the correct selection of procedures.

Even when procedures are not explicitly used we find that the programmer usually organizes his program in a modular fashion, simply because that is the easiest way to write programs, and such programs are the easiest to debug. In fact it is impossible to write complex programs any other way. Accordingly, we consider modularity to be a property implicit in the logical connections between parts of a program rather than the explicit structure expressed by its division into procedures.

The other class of concepts, data-objects, has only relatively recently begun to receive much attention. In many scientific problems which are of a numerical nature, the data-objects are rather primitive, usually being simple vectors or matrices whose elements are numbers. However, as the area of application of computers has expanded to include problems in which the data-objects are less simple, it has become recognized that a knowledge of such concepts will play an increasingly important role in programming. In programs which have complex data-objects, a standard type of module consists of a description of the data-objects. In primitive languages this often consists of a diagram of the memory layout which is provided as informative documentation of the program rather than part of the program itself. In more sophisticated programming languages there are quite elaborate facilities provided for describing in the language the abstract properties of the data-objects.

CONCISENESS AND GENERALITY

As we have pointed out above, in large and complex programs it is important that the programmer be able to understand the algorithm, or at least that part of it with which he is concerned. Now it is clear that a significant measure of the complexity of a program is its length, in the simple sense that we would ordinarily expect a lengthy program to take more effort to write and to debug than a short one. This is not to say, of course, that all long programs will take more effort to understand, write, or debug than all short ones—this is clearly not true; but there is a correlation between length and effort required. Accordingly, one of the properties of a good program is conciseness. By the same token, one of the properties of good programming language is the ability to express complex algorithms concisely.

We will discuss two methods which can be used to make a program more concise. The first is to make use of *more powerful operations* provided either by the programming language or by the definition of new operations in terms of old. Clearly the programmer does not want to use two commands where a single one would do, but on the other hand he does not want there to be so many different commands that he can never remember them. What he wants is a small set of powerful and flexible commands, and thus we call our second method for achieving conciseness *economy of concept*. By this we mean that the number of distinct notions which the programmer has to deal with should be as small as possible. A simple example of this is found in the treatment of arithmetic operations in algebraic languages such as FORTRAN and ALGOL. Here the addition operator $+$ in fact stands for four distinct operations depending on whether its arguments are integer or real, but the use of explicit or implicit declarations effectively permits the programmer to leave out the conversion operations, and to deal with a single concept—a number. In a similar way it is possible for the FORTRAN programmer to shorten a program which deals with arrays by writing routines which process arrays of arbitrary size, rather than a routine for each different size.

EFFICIENCY

So far we have not concerned ourselves too much with questions of efficiency, either of memory or computation time. In practice this is often an important consideration, particularly in those programs, often called *production programs*, which are to be used for a considerable time when they are completed. These include the usual programs associated with operating systems, such as supervisors, input/output routines, and file management systems; and the class of utility routines such as compilers, assemblers, and loaders. In addition a large proportion of programs in most applications areas are used over and over again, and their efficiency is economically significant. In other cases a program is of no use unless it can fit in a certain amount of memory, or unless its execution satisfies certain timing requirements. Such critical requirements are often found in those situations which have to deal with critically time-dependent peripheral units such as tape units or real-time devices.

On the other hand, there is a significant number of problems in which the optimum algorithm is not known, and has to be found by writing a number of programs and trying them. We will refer to this as *experimental programming*. In such cases it is often necessary to try many different versions of the program, each one of which may only be run once or twice after it has been debugged. Economic considerations then give more importance to the effort required to write and debug the programs than to the time required to run them. In such cases modularity and conciseness are more important than efficiency. However, in most cases efficiency cannot be ignored; and unfortunately, modularity and conciseness are to some extent incompatible with efficiency.

All of these factors put certain requirements on the design of the programming language used, and the translation of the features necessary to allow a modular and concise program into an optimum machine-language program can be very complex. If we compare the machine code produced by a compiler with the machine code produced by a competent programmer, we find that the current state of knowledge of optimization can only produce comparable code for relatively simple languages such as FORTRAN. The problem of optimization in compilers is an important one which is slowly becoming better understood. For the present, the programmer usually has to make a choice about the relative importance of modularity, conciseness, and efficiency, and choose the programming language accordingly.

DATA-STRUCTURES

As the areas of application of computers have expanded, it has become apparent that one of the most important considerations in the design of a program is the way that objects are to be represented in memory. In the case of numerical calculations these objects are usually rather simple, and the simple facilities provided by an algebraic language such as FORTRAN or ALGOL 60 are found to be quite adequate. However, in other application areas it is found that the objects have a much less regular structure, and often vary dynamically in size during the computation. It is often possible to represent such objects in a number of different ways, and the choice of representation is critical. In some cases, in fact, the implementation of the algorithm is straightforward if the right representation is chosen, so that this choice becomes the most important decision in the writing of the program.

We will use the term *data-structure* to refer to the particular way in which a data-object is represented in memory. The pros and cons of different types of data-structure will be one of the major topics with which we will concern ourselves in this book. We will consider these from a number of different aspects. In the first place we will consider data-structures from the point of view of the efficiency of various operations which will occur in practical problems. This will involve both computation time and also the efficiency of use of memory. In general we will not attempt to give quantitative measures of efficiency, but will content ourselves with rather rough qualitative observations.

Second, we will consider data-structures from the point of view of the ways in which they can be described, and how operations on them can be expressed. We will do this by giving outlines of a number of programming languages, including PL/1, LISP, SNOBOL, and ALGOL 68.

Third, we will consider data-structures from the point of view of their generality. As we have mentioned previously, the complexity of large programs can be reduced by the uniform use of general-purpose modules whenever possible. This requires that the selection of data-structures be made in such a way that there be as few different types as is consistent with the efficiency required, and the operations on these data-structures be kept simple and powerful. For this reason we will be paying attention to programming languages which seem relatively inefficient but which are either very simple or very powerful.

PROGRAMMING LANGUAGES

As we have mentioned, three requirements of an ideal program are that it be modular, concise, and efficient. To a considerable extent, the degree to which a program approaches this ideal is dependent on the properties of the programming language. In practice we rarely find a single language which possesses all the required properties, and a compromise choice is necessary. We can categorize programming languages broadly as follows:

assembly language
macro assembly language
algebraic language (FORTRAN, ALGOL,...)
special-purpose language (SNOBOL, LISP,...)
"all-purpose" language (PL/1...)
extendable language (ALGOL 68...)
translator system

We will not consider assembly language seriously as a contender, in spite of the fact that most systems programming is done in assembly language. We will consider a macro assembly language as a primitive form of extendable language, which we will consider below. We will mainly be concerned with algebraic languages and special-purpose languages, both of which are currently of greatest availability. We consider the "all-purpose" language which is not extendable as a contradiction in terms, but nevertheless will consider PL/1 in some detail. The reason for this is that it is definitely superior to the algebraic languages, and as such will have a large impact on the level of knowledge of the average programmer, putting within his grasp facilities and techniques which previously required much more ingenuity on his part.

The indications are that the most satisfactory form of development of programming languages is the direction of extendable languages. In such languages only the minimum set of primitive operations will be available, but with a powerful mechanism for defining new facilities in terms of them. This may be implemented as a sophisticated form of preprocessing prior to compilation, or as an integrated part of the translation process. In any event, it is likely that the expert programmer will have some mechanism available to him for extending the features of the basic language. In these circumstances it is important for him to have a knowledge of useful external forms of language, such as the "pattern replacement" form of statement in SNOBOL, and also of the appropriate implementations. Such knowledge is best obtained at the moment by studying the special-purpose languages used to supplement algebraic languages, even though these languages will eventually turn out to be implementable in some other more general language.

2
DATA·OBJECTS

In this chapter we will consider some of the ways in which information which describes objects can be structured. We will not concern ourselves with the way that such structured information can be represented in memory, but with the abstract properties associated with the various kinds of operation which are appropriate for their manipulation.

We will use the term *data-object* to refer to that body of information which is used to represent a particular object. In algorithms dealing with this object we will suppose that no other information about it is available, so in a sense we can regard the data-object as an abstraction of the object itself.

REFERRING TO DATA-OBJECTS

When specifying an operation on a data-object, it is necessary for the programmer to have some mechanism for referring to the data-object. There are basically two ways of doing this which are provided in programming languages. One method associates with a data-object one or more *names*, and operations on the data-object are specified by referring to the data-object using one of its names. In most programming languages the association between a data-object and its name is established by a *declaration*, though this is not essential.

The second method of referring to a data-object is to write an expression which when evaluated by the program will yield the data-object which is to be manipulated. This method is not used as frequently in the more primitive programming languages except in the case of simple items such as numbers.

Accordingly we will assume that each data-object consists of a set of *names*, which may be empty, and a *value*, which may be the data-object *undefined*. Since we will want to use a name to refer to a specific value, we will suppose that the same name cannot be a name of two data-objects which have different values. This may seem unnecessarily complicated to the reader who is familiar with simple programming languages such as FORTRAN, but we introduce these notions in order to avoid making assumptions which are true in FORTRAN but not true in other languages.

To illustrate this definition of a data-object, the declarations

```
DIMENSION A(20)
real array a[1:20];
DCL A(20) FLOAT BINARY;
```

in FORTRAN, ALGOL, and PL/1 respectively can be thought of as creating a data-object whose name is A (or a), and whose value is an array with 20 elements. On the other hand, the expression

```
X+Y
```

will create a data-object with a value but no name.

In this chapter we consider the value of a data-object to be either an *atom*, which the reader can think of as including simple items such as integers or coded characters or bits; or a *collection* of other data-objects, which we will refer to as its *elements*. This is a very general assumption which enables us to talk about most types of data-object encountered in current programming languages, as well as less formal data-objects found in everyday life and the more formal data-objects used in mathematics.

For the time being we will permit only a single operation on atoms: that which tests two atoms for equal values. Otherwise we might be able to encode the whole of an arbitrary data-object into a single atom, which would defeat our purpose.

CATEGORIES OF DATA-OBJECTS

Below we will consider a very broad classification of data-objects. The aim will be to introduce in an informal way the most common forms of data-object, and give examples of the sorts of operations which are appropriate for their manipulation. We make no attempt at giving a complete categorization, or a complete set of operations.

We will start by considering two important properties of collections. First we can distinguish those classes of collections in which the elements are considered to be in no particular order from those in which order is considered significant. The first we call *sets* and the second *ordered sets*—so that we can think of a collection as a set which may or may not be ordered.

We can also distinguish those classes of collections which permit addition and deletion operations from those which do not. The first we will call *variable-size* and the second we will call *fixed-size*. There are clearly subclasses of the variable-size class which only permit additions or only deletions, but we will not distinguish these here.

The combination of these two classifications then gives us our most important categories, which we illustrate below:

fixed-size sets	fixed-size ordered sets
variable-size sets	variable-size ordered sets

The simplest of these is probably the fixed-size ordered set, which is used as the basic data-object in many programming languages, and in particular the algebraic languages such as FORTRAN and ALGOL. We will refer to such a data-object as a *vector*, and consider it in more detail below.

Variable-size ordered sets are also used widely in programming languages, in particular in those which are designed for computations on other than numeric data, such as SNOBOL and LISP. We will refer to variable-size ordered sets as *lists*. Note that this term is used sometimes to refer to a particular way of representing data-objects in memory, which we will discuss in the next chapter. However, we will reserve the use of this term to describe the abstract properties of the data-object.

Fixed-size sets are also rather simple, but have only recently started to be used in programming languages. The *structures* of PL/1 and ALGOL 68 can be thought of as fixed-size sets, as can the *records* of ALGOL W.

Variable-size sets are not provided in the majority of programming languages. However, many complex algorithms are conveniently stated in terms of sets and set operations, and their properties are well established by mathematics, in which they play a basic role. We will refer to both fixed-size and variable-size sets as simply *sets*.

OPERATIONS ON DATA-OBJECTS

In the following sections we will consider the three categories of data-object introduced above—vectors, lists, and sets—and consider some of the basic operations which we might want to use to manipulate them. We will certainly want operations which create data-objects, and which we will call *creators*. These fall into two categories—those which associate a name with the data-object, and those which do not. The first will often be found in the form of a declaration, such as, for example, the FORTRAN DIMENSION statement or the PL/1 DECLARE statement. The second is often in the form of a function or operator which will return the data-object as its value. A further distinction which can be made between creators is whether the data-object is fully specified or not. For example, it is often the case that a declaration effectively creates a data-object which has a certain size, but whose elements are not specified.

It is often necessary to provide operations which cause a data-object to cease to exist, and which we will call *destroyers*. These are usually provided to reduce the amount of memory which is required by a program, since a data-object which is destroyed can actually have its memory space used for other data-objects. However, destroyers are not absolutely necessary, as is illustrated by FORTRAN, in which all creation of data-objects is done at compilation time, and no data-objects are destroyed. In more sophisticated languages destroyers play an important role.

Perhaps the next most important type of operation is that which permits the programmer to extract part of the information in a data-object and to operate on it. We will refer to such an operator as a *selector*, which in the case of collections is in its simplest form an operator which selects an element. As we will see, the precise mechanism which is appropriate for identifying an element of a collection is highly dependent on the type of collection, and in many ways is the most critical property of the collection.

Another type of operation is that which changes a data-object. We will refer to these as *updaters*. The simplest updaters are those which simply change a single element of a collection, or perhaps remove an element or add an element. More elaborate updaters might affect a number of elements. We will find instances in which an updater can be logically replaced by the use of selectors and a creator, but the updater is preferred for efficiency.

We will also find it useful to consider *predicates*, which can be used to test a data-object for having a particular property, and miscellaneous *functions* which can be used to determine values of attributes of a data-object.

FIXED-SIZE ORDERED SETS: VECTORS

As we have mentioned above, vectors are the most common type of data-object for which facilities are provided in current programming languages. Because of their fixed size it is usual to create vectors in a single operation, so the two most common creators are:

create a vector of specified size with a specified name

create a vector with specified values as elements

There may of course be variations on these two basic operations as appropriate. Destroyers can be provided explicitly in the form:

destroy a specified vector

but are more usually provided implicitly in the structure of the program.

The most significant attribute of an ordered set, whether of fixed or variable size, is the fact that it is possible to refer to elements by their position. The usual form of selector makes use of this by permitting an element to be selected by *indexing*. This gives a selector of the form:

select the i-th element of a specified vector

It is also sometimes useful to be able to specify a subvector of elements by indices in a similar way. Other types of selector include:

select the element after the element with specified value

and analogous extensions for selecting subsections of vectors.

The usual forms of updaters for vectors are similar to the selectors, including:

change the i-th element to the specified value

and so on. A useful function is that which can give the size of a vector, although this is often logically unnecessary.

In a programming language such as FORTRAN, we find the above operations in somewhat restricted form. The DIMENSION statement is the only form of creator, effectively establishing at the time the program is translated a vector of specified length. Note that a multidimensional array in FORTRAN can be regarded as a vector whose selectors and updaters can be written in a more convenient form, and is logically replaceable by a one-dimensional array. The selector operation in FORTRAN is simply the indexing mechanism, which also provides the updater operation when used on the left-hand side of an assignment statement. There are no destroyers in FORTRAN, since an array will always keep the values last assigned to it. There is also no way of finding the number of elements of a vector in FORTRAN, though this could be added to the language without much difficulty.

In ALGOL 60 similar facilities are provided for selectors and updaters, but the main difference is in the creators and destroyers. Here vectors are effectively created at execution time rather than translation time, with a vector whose size can be specified at execution time being created on entry to the block in which it is declared, and destroyed on exit from the block. There are, in addition, *own* arrays which are not destroyed on exit or recreated on entry.

Programming languages such as PL/1, SNOBOL, and ALGOL 68 permit more control over creation and destruction of vectors, which we will be discussing in later chapters.

VARIABLE-SIZE ORDERED SETS: LISTS

The usual operation on lists include the operations given previously for vectors. However, the main difference is that a list may have updaters which change its size. In particular, there may be updaters which add new elements, or delete existing elements. As in the case of vectors, the usual way of specifying where an element should be added or deleted is by position, so we would expect updaters of the form:

delete the i-th element of the specified list

add the specified element before (or after) the i-th element of the specified list

Particular examples of these operations are updaters which add or delete elements at the beginning or end of the list. As might be expected, the function which gives the size of a list is more important than the equivalent function for vectors. We might also find updaters which add or delete in a position specified by the value of an element, such as:

delete the element of the specified list before (or after) the element with a specified value

add the specified element before (or after) the element of the specified list with a specified value

Analogous operations on subsections of lists might well be provided.

In general a new element can be added to a list at the beginning, or at the end, or in between two elements, and any element can be deleted. However, in an important class of lists there are restrictions on additions and deletions. A list in which additions and deletions can be made at only one end is called a *stack*. The addition operation on a stack is usually referred to as "push" and the deletion operation as "pop." The important property of a stack is thus that the elements are removed in the reverse order from that in which they were added—for this reason a stack is sometimes called a last-in-first-out or LIFO list.

A second class of addition-deletion-restricted lists is that in which addition occurs at one end and deletion occurs at the other. Such a list is referred to as a *queue*, or as a first-in-first-out or FIFO list. The normal usage of the word indicates one frequent use of a queue: in a situation in which information is processed in the order in which it is generated—first come, first served. We usually think of the beginning of the queue as being subject to deletions and the end of the queue as receiving the additions. Knuth (00) also uses the term "deque" to refer to those lists which can have additions and deletions at both ends, and which can be regarded as double-ended queues.

In addition to this classification of lists according to restrictions on additions and deletions, we can also classify them according to whether the selection operation is restricted or not. Once again, the usual restriction is that only the elements at one or both ends of the list can be examined. If there are no such restrictions, Laski (00) refers to the list as being "peepable." We find this type of restriction most frequently associated with stacks, queues, or deques, as we might expect. A nonpeepable stack is sometimes referred to as a *push-down* stack in analogy with the piles of plates in a cafeteria, which use Hooke's Law to ensure that just a single plate is accessible above the level of the counter. In most cases a nonpeepable list can have all its elements examined by successively deleting elements, but we regard this as a compound operation which does not make the list qualify as peepable.

In a similar way we can classify lists according to restrictions on changing the elements. Here we find that some lists are such that no changes are permitted at all, in others we find changes just at the ends, and in others all elements can be changed.

The reader should note that if we consider operations on the atoms which are other than simple tests for equality, we can construct much more elaborate structures. For instance, if we permit an atom to be an integer, we can encode into it the equivalent of the contents of a standard computer memory cell, so a peepable vector or list will give us the same logical capability as a standard computer memory.

SETS

We will not distinguish here between fixed-size sets and variable-size sets, but concentrate more on the distinction between operations on sets and ordered sets. The creator and destroyer operations are quite similar, the main differences being in the type of selectors and updaters which are appropriate. In a set there is of course no notion of position, so it is no longer possible to specify the i-th element of a set, or the element before or after an element with a specific value. We will see later that by considering an element to be a collection itself we can effectively simulate an ordered set by a set, but if we consider the elements of the set to be restricted to atoms it is necessary to resort to different types of operation. In fact it turns out that the most reasonable forms of operation are operations on sets rather than on elements of sets.

Sets are a fundamental structure of mathematics, and we will be guided by mathematical treatments in choosing operations. Normally, mathematics considers a set to be an unordered collection of distinct elements, and below we will follow this convention. Unordered collections in which elements are not assumed distinct are sometimes called *bags*, but we will not consider them here.

In order to restrict the operations to the minimum, we will initially assume that the elements of sets are restricted to atoms. In this case it does not make any sense to have a selector which selects a particular element, since we can only specify it by its value. Instead we can use a selector which selects an element at random:

select any element of a specified set

A more powerful operation can be used to select a subset of elements, as follows:

select a subset of elements of a specified set which satisfy a specified predicate

This should be regarded as a creator rather than a selector. A useful predicate is then

determine if a specified data-object is an element of a specified set

With these two operations we can construct the union and intersection of two sets. Two simple updaters can be used with sets, doing the following operations:

add to a specified set the elements of a second specified set
delete from a specified set the elements of a second specified set

These of course can be used to define the union and intersection operations also, but not too efficiently. Note that all the updaters and creators must ensure that elements are effectively not duplicated.

If nonatomic elements are permitted, an alternative way of referring to an element can be used. That is, we can represent an element as a set with two members, one of which can be treated as the identifier of the element. For example, the set:

$$\{\langle X, A \rangle, \langle Y, B \rangle, \langle Z, C \rangle\}$$

where we have written $\langle X, A \rangle$ to indicate the ordered set with elements X and A can be regarded as a set whose elements are called X, Y, and Z, and have the values A, B, and C. This suggests the use of basic operations which select or change the value of an element by referring to it by its identifier. In the case of fixed-size sets this gives effectively the "records" of ALGOL W, or the "structures" of PL/1 and ALGOL 68.

OVERLAPPING AND NONOVERLAPPING COLLECTIONS

In the previous sections we have given informally a number of the common types of operation on data-objects. However, when we consider particular programming languages it is necessary to define these operations more precisely. In most cases this does not cause too much difficulty, but in the case of update operations there is a source of difficulty which we have not considered above. This arises from the possibility that two data-objects should have elements in common, so that a change made to one by application of an updater may change the other one. In simple languages such as FORTRAN this difficulty does not usually arise, except in the case of EQUIVALENCEd variables, or subprograms with several arguments which are called with the same actual argument. In more sophisticated languages it is more of a problem.

We will say a data-object is *nonoverlapping* if it is not permitted to have elements in common with other data-objects and all its elements are also nonoverlapping. The others we will call *overlapping*. Then we can distinguish three philosophies of programming language design according to their treatment of this aspect of their data-objects.

First, we can insist that all data-objects are nonoverlapping. This implies that all creators and selectors effectively produce copies of the original data-object, so the programmer can update any data-object without the fear that other data-objects will be changed at the same time.

Second, we can permit overlapping data-objects, but restrict the set of operations in the languages so that an update operation only changes the one data-object. This can be done in a number of ways, one of which is to prohibit updaters completely, replacing them with creators. That is, instead of changing a data-object, the updaters would in fact create a new data-object with the appropriate changes incorporated into it.

Third, we can permit overlapping data-objects, and allow the programmer to manipulate them as he thinks fit, including changing elements which are common to several data-objects. This gives a general facility, of course, but requires more effort on the part of the programmer, who often has to keep track of which data-objects have parts in common. In the general case this can get impossibly complicated, but has advantages in more special cases.

GRAPHS AND TREES

A convenient way of expressing the structure of such collections is by use of *graphs*. A graph consists of a number of points, called *nodes* or vertices, which are connected by lines, called edges or sides or *arcs*. If each node in a graph is connected by arcs to every other node we say that the graph is *connected*. A particular class of graphs in which the arcs are considered to have a direction are called *directed*. An example of a connected directed graph is shown in diagrammatic form in Figure 2.1: with arrows indicating the direction of the arcs.

We can represent a collection by a connected directed graph, using the arcs to indicate the collection–element relationships, with the arrow pointing to the element.

Figure 2.1

Figure 2.2, for example, illustrates a collection with three elements where we have shown atoms as small rectangles.

It is now apparent that the nonoverlapping collections as we have defined them above correspond to directed graphs in which each node can have at most one arc entering it, and one node with no arcs entering it. Such directed graphs are called *trees*, and the node with no entering arcs is called the *root*.

Trees are useful in a number of areas as well as computer science, and there are a number of terms associated with them. By convention, they are normally drawn upside down, with the root at the top and the *branches* at the bottom. The end branches are called *terminal* branches, or *twigs*. Branches enter nodes from the top and leave from the bottom, and the arrows are sometimes left out. The nomenclature of family trees is often used to indicate the relationships between nodes, so the nodes connected to a particular node are its *children*, and it is their *parent*. The nodes which are the *descendants* of a node form a *subtree* with it as root.

In terms of directed graphs, we see that a set of nonoverlapping collections corresponds to a set of trees, as illustrated by Figure 2.3. Such a set of trees is called, not surprisingly, a *forest*. If a program is not to create data-objects which overlap, the operations must be restricted to those which do not create nontree structures.

In practice this means that operations which insert an item in a data-object must copy the item and insert the copy. Similarly a selection operation which produces a data-object, and which may be subject to subsequent modification, should construct a copy. We can thus see that many of the basic operations on nonoverlapping data-objects will require copy operations.

Let us now consider overlapping collections. There are a number of ways in which we could permit such overlap, but we will restrict consideration to that which is

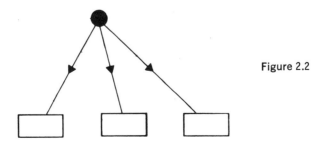

Figure 2.2

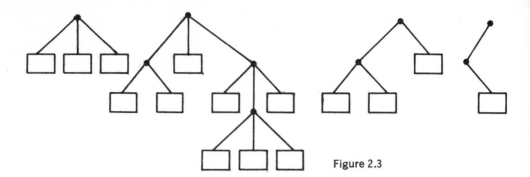

Figure 2.3

conveniently stated in terms of directed graphs. We will do this by relaxing the restriction that a node should only have a single arc entering it. When this is permitted we could find collection–element relationships described by the directed graph of Figure 2.4.

This shows four data-objects, three of which are tightly entwined by having parts in common, and the fourth of which contains the same atom in two places. These are clearly not trees, since many nodes have more than one entering arc.

In fact the directed graph shown above is a special case of the class of directed graphs, which in general cannot be drawn in such a way that all arcs end at a lower node than they start at. The above example is called a *cycle-free* directed graph. A *cycle* is a path which starts and ends at the same node, going always in the direction of the arrows, and a cycle-free directed graph is a directed graph in which there are no cycles. It is clear that a directed graph containing a cycle cannot be drawn with all arcs ending at lower nodes than they started at, and conversely that all directed graphs which cannot be drawn in this way contain a cycle. Thus we have the equivalence of the notion of cycle-free and "no upward arrows" in directed graphs.

From the point of view of our collections, a cycle-free directed graph is seen to correspond to data-objects which do not contain themselves directly or indirectly. This is a very wide class of data-objects, which are generally easier to think about and to process than the general class. Accordingly when considering operations on over-

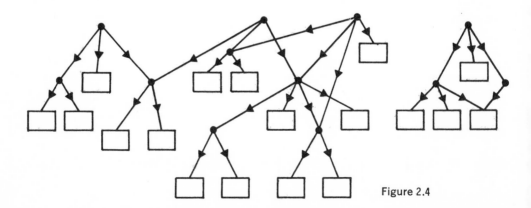

Figure 2.4

lapping data-objects, we will sometimes find it useful to distinguish the cycle-free data-objects from the remainder.

REFERENCES

A convenient way of permitting elements to be shared between data-objects uses the notion of a *reference*.

We might define a reference as any way of identifying a data-object, but this turns out to be too general for many cases. Such a definition would have to include all the ways of identifying elements of collections described so far, and all the ways of identifying collections themselves. As an example of such a reference, we might use something like "the subset of elements of the list x which are sets which contain as elements one of the elements of the vector y." Any change to the value of y would produce a very complex change in such a data-object.

Accordingly we will restrict the definition of a reference to identify a data-object which will not require reconstruction in this way. A convenient way of doing this is to restrict a reference to be the name of a data-object.

If we represent a reference as an atom which is connected by a dotted line to the node it refers to, we then get graphs such as Figure 2.5. Now it is clear that to construct

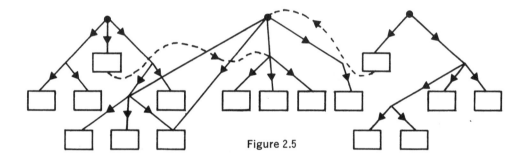

Figure 2.5

such data-objects we need some operators to deal with references. We certainly need an operator which will create a reference to a data-object, so that subsequently we can insert such a reference in a collection:

create a reference to the specified data-object

When processing data-objects which may contain references, we could interpret a graph such as that shown above as though the references were replaced by a direct collection–element arc. However, this means that we have no mechanism for selecting a reference itself.

An alternative way of regarding references is to treat them as regular atoms, and provide an operator for getting the data-object referenced:

select the data-object identified by the specified reference

EQUIVALENT DATA-OBJECTS

It is clear that the information content of each of the data-objects we have described can be expressed in a number of ways. In fact the study of the ways of representing these data-objects in a conventional computer memory will form the central theme of this book. However, it is convenient to point out some of the simpler equivalence properties between types of data-object which do not depend on the meaning of an atom. Of course, if we are permitted to interpret an atom as an integer, then we can encode all the structures into a single such integer, but this is not very interesting.

If we permit only tests for equality of atoms, we note that it is possible to represent an arbitrary ordered set in terms of ordered pairs. Thus the vector or list whose elements are atoms w, x, y, z which we can write as:

$$\langle w, x, y, z \rangle$$

can also be written as:

$$\langle w, \langle x, \langle y, \langle z, * \rangle \rangle \rangle \rangle$$

with no loss of information. Here we are supposing that the atom $*$ is an arbitrary atom which is used to indicate the absence of further items. The same representation can be used regardless of whether the elements are atoms or not. An essential operation is one which tests whether an element is an atom or not.

This property can also be generalized to sets. That is, an arbitrary set can be represented without loss of information in terms of sets with only two elements. This can be done by splitting the original set into two, then splitting those into two, and so on until there are only sets with one element each. Each such set is then paired with a distinguished atom which is not used elsewhere, making a set with two elements. In terms of trees, this is equivalent to representing the tree in Figure 2.6 in the form shown in Figure 2.7. This we call a *binary tree*, and it is clear that it contains the same information. Note that if $*$ is not a distinguished atom, and the elements of the original set are themselves sets, this will not work. It is the power of the above two observations which makes a set with two elements a powerful notion.

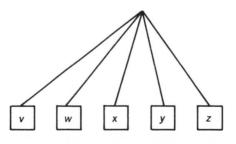

Figure 2.6

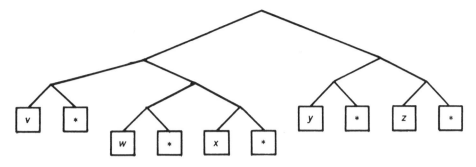

Figure 2.7

Another observation, one which appears to be of less practical significance, is the fact that an ordered set of two elements can be represented as a set with two elements. This can be done in a number of ways, perhaps the easiest being to represent the ordered pair $\langle x, y \rangle$ as the set $\{x, \{y, *\}\}$ where $*$ is once again a special atom. An alternative mechanism used in mathematics is the form $\{x, \{x, y\}\}$ which does not need a marker but appears to be messier.

It is clear that if we permit the use of integers, an arbitrary ordered set can be represented as the set of ordered pairs $\langle i, e_i \rangle$ where e_i is the i-th element. An alternative form, which loses information unless the elements do not occur more than once in the ordered set, is the set of ordered pairs $\langle e_i, e_{i+1} \rangle$. Even if the elements are distinct, this representation, though losing information, is sometimes surprisingly useful. It can be generalized if the ordered set is represented as a set of subsequences which have unique first (or last) elements.

LINEAR AND LINEARIZABLE DATA-OBJECTS

We will see in the next chapter that a very useful type of data-object is that which can be expressed in the form of an ordered set of atoms. To be more specific, suppose we consider a data-object whose collections are ordered sets. Any atom in such a data-object can then be identified by specifying its position in the collection which contains it, the position of this collection in the collection which contains it, and so on. This sequence of numbers we will call the address sequence of the atom.

We can now define an *addressing function* for a data-object containing n atoms as a function of the integers in the address sequences of the atoms onto the integers 1 to n. We will call a data-object *linear* if it has a linear addressing function. The simplest example of a linear data-object is an ordered set whose elements are atoms. The integer corresponding to the i-th element is just i, so the addressing function is

$$f(i) = i$$

In general, a tree which has the same number of branches at each level is also a linear data-object. For example, a tree of level 2 with three branches at the top level and four branches at the lower level would have an addressing function of the form:

$$f(i, j) = i + 4(j - 1)$$

or of the form:

$$f(i, j) = 3(i - 1) + j$$

There are other data-objects which have rather similar properties to the linear data-objects, in the sense that they have simple addressing functions. In fact if we are not concerned with its complexity, any data-object has an addressing function, simply by assigning the numbers 1 to n arbitrarily to the atoms of the data-object. Accordingly, we must consider the complexity of the addressing function. In practice we are concerned with both the amount of information required to specify the function, and also the time to compute it and its inverse. Note that the inverse of an addressing function may be multivalued if there is an atom which has two or more address sequences. This happens if the data-object is not a tree. Accordingly most data-objects with useful addressing functions are trees.

Without attempting to specify a particular measure of complexity, we will say that a data-object is *linearizable* if there exists a suitable simple addressing function. Most such functions are algebraic functions of the address sequence.

EXERCISES

1. For some particular programming languages, classify the data-objects and describe the operations on them.
*2. Give a formal axiomatic definition of a FORTRAN one-dimensional array and the basic operations which can be done on it. You may find it convenient to consider the state of the machine by some state variable s, and define assignment operations by their effect on s.
**3. Give a complete formal definition of the basic operations of a programming language, using the technique of Exercise 2.

3
DATA-STRUCTURES

We have so far considered abstract data-objects, without paying particular attention to the ease with which they can be represented in physical memories. Before going on to consider some of these representations in detail, let us consider the main characteristics of physical memories. We will restrict consideration to memories which satisfy our previous requirement for a low data-rate, i.e., information is extracted or inserted in essentially separate operations involving of the order of tens of bits.

We first note that if these memories are constructed out of deterministic components, their behavior will be predictable, so a reference to *any* element of a data-object will always give the same part under similar circumstances. That is, in a deterministic memory the elements of a data-object have a natural ordering, so we will find a tendency to concern ourselves with data-objects which are ordered sets rather than unordered sets.

Secondly, when we are using a general-purpose computer we have noted that there are constraints which limit the amount of memory in use at any one time to a small fraction of the total. This means that, in general, efficiency will require that whenever possible we arrange our data so that we can pick out the required element rather than having to search for it. That is, we prefer to be able, by computation, to determine where our data is, which suggests a memory organization which we can address by location.

In the next few sections we will deal with the implementation of some of the data-objects we have described on a standard addressable memory.

REPRESENTATION OF DATA-OBJECTS

We will· use the term *data-structure* to refer to the particular way in which the information in the data-object is organized in memory. There are clearly a number of possible data-structures for every data-object, distinguished by such properties as the amount of memory required and the ease with which various operations can be performed on the information. We will consider data-structures from this point of view.

In most cases the data-structure chosen to represent a data-object will be selected for its efficiency, either of memory utilization or of computation speed. However, in some cases these will be sacrificed for its ease of use.

CLASSIFICATION OF DATA-STRUCTURES

As we have pointed out previously, one of the most important properties of a data-object is the mechanism used to refer to part of the information constituting it. When we are considering conventional memories this mechanism is the construction of the address of the component, so it is convenient to classify data-structures according to the way in which such an address is constructed.

We first distinguish between two types of addressing mechanisms. An address which can be computed directly from the specification of the component we will refer to as a *computed address*. This includes most of the simpler types of addressing which is done in FORTRAN programs, including the calculation of the address of an element of an array, and the fetching of the next instruction. In some cases this calculation can be performed during compilation, such as in those cases when the indices are constant. In other cases a more elaborate calculation is necessary, such as when a variable element of a three-dimensional array is being referenced. Certainly the linearizable data-objects described in the previous chapter are appropriate candidates for using computed addresses.

The other type of address we refer to as a *link* or a *pointer*. By this we mean that the address is not computed, but is itself stored in memory somewhere. A simple example of this is the address of an argument of a subroutine in FORTRAN, which is either to be found in a register or in a memory location. In practice most address construction requires a combination of pointers and computed addresses, but in an important class of data-structures the computation is trivial and the dominant properties of the data-structure are determined by the pointers. These we will refer to as *plexes*, which we will consider in more detail below. An excellent treatment of such structures is given in Knuth (68).

COMPUTED ADDRESSES

Let us first consider some of the structures which use mainly computed addresses for locating their components. We will restrict consideration initially to those structures which can be packed conveniently into a single area of memory with contiguous addresses which we will call a *block*. The simplest structures are those for which just the address of the first word of the block is sufficient to determine the address of the various components. An example which we have already mentioned is the familiar one-dimensional *array* used in FORTRAN, which as a data-object is classified as a vector. The elements in an array require a fixed amount of memory, so the computation of the address of the i-th element is of the form $a + bi$, where a is the address of the block and b is the size of the element—this assumes that the first element is the zero-th; if if we want the first element to be number 1, we can use $a + b(i - 1)$, or $a - b + bi$.

A simple extension of this can be used for arrays of dimension two or higher, since we can regard an element of a two-dimensional array as a one-dimensional array. The (i, j)-th element of an n by m FORTRAN array, for example, can be addressed by the formula $a + (n(i - 1) + j - 1)b = a - (n - 1)b + (ni + j)b$. Here we are using the fact that the array is rectangular (has the same number of elements in each column) and the elements are of the same size. If our array is not rectangular we can either fill it out with dummy elements so that we can use the same structure, or we can utilize part of the block to contain the addresses of the columns. We will discuss the latter type of structure in the next section.

A more complex example is what we might call a triangular array, which has i elements in its i-th column. This can clearly be represented as slightly more than half the enclosing square array, but a more concise representation is possible if memory utilization is important. Calling the elements of the array a_{ij}, with i less than or equal to j, we can store the elements in the order a_{11}, a_{12}, a_{22}, a_{13}, a_{23}, a_{33}, ... Thus an n by n triangular array will have $n(n + 1)/2$ elements in it, and the elements of the $n - 1$ by $n - 1$ triangular array will occur first. Thus we will find the (i, j)-th element in the $(j - 1)j/2 + i$ position, so our addressing function will be of the form $a + b((j - 1)j/2 + i - 1)$. Once again, we can simply extend this to higher dimensions, and of course mix rectangular and triangular arrays to get wedges, tetrahedrons, and so on. Such structures are often useful when representing objects with symmetries. A simple example of this occurs when we have a symmetric matrix, which we can represent as a triangular matrix and reference a_{ji} for a_{ij} when i is greater than j.

Note that the rectangular arrays are addressed by a linear function of the indices used to reference an element, while the triangular arrays are addressed by a quadratic function. Quantities such as the dimensions of the array play the part of parameters in such functions. When these parameters are fixed we often find that they are not represented explicitly in memory, but rather their values are built into the program, as is usually the case of FORTRAN arrays. In more dynamic structures it is convenient to have these parameters variable, so we often find a data-structure specified by what is sometimes called a *dope vector*, a small block of memory, perhaps just a single word, which contains the values of the parameters and possibly a pointer to the block containing the structure. In even more dynamic situations we might find that the dope vector specifies the type of structure, or even gives the addresses of routines which can be used to operate on it. In general, we can see that the more flexibility a structure can have, the more information has to be represented explicitly in memory about its structure, the less is represented implicitly in the program manipulating it, and the less efficient is the execution of the associated operations.

We will not attempt to give a complete catalog of addressing functions, but we should point out that for many data-objects which are of fixed size, and whose elements are of fixed size, and which have some symmetry, an addressing function can be found. For example, a complete binary tree which has information only in the terminal nodes can be represented by 2^d elements where d is the number of levels in the tree, and the position of the node obtained by writing down the path from the root, writing 0 if a left branch was taken and a 1 if a right branch. The resulting sequence of 0's and 1's when interpreted as a binary number will be between 0 and $2^d - 1$, and can be used to address the corresponding element. An extension of this can be used if the tree contains information in all the nodes. Storing the root in position 1, the left son of a node which is in position i is stored in position $2i$, and the right son in position $2i + 1$. The full binary tree is then stored in the order indicated in Figure 3.1.

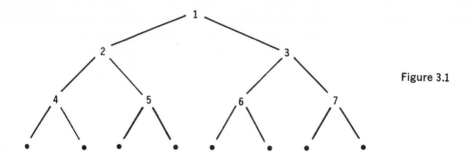

Figure 3.1

As our examples have suggested, the main use of computed addresses is for homogeneous structures, i.e., those whose elements occupy the same amount of memory. Such is the ease of use of such structures that when we have elements of differing size it is often convenient to put some or even all of the information elsewhere in memory and represent the element by a pointer to this auxiliary information.

It is also convenient to use a particularly simple form of computed addresses when we have unequal-sized elements of a data-object which can be regarded as a set rather than an ordered set: that is, when we wish to refer to the elements by name rather than by virtue of the order in which they are stored. In this case we can simply pack the elements together and note the appropriate offsets from the beginning of the block. Such data-structures are called "records" by Hoare (68), "structures" in PL/1, and "nodes" by Knuth (68), and are recognized as an important primitive type of data-structure. The computation of their address consists of simply adding the appropriate offset to the address of the block.

POINTERS

If we think of a pointer as simply an address we see that the notion is basic to programming an addressable memory. Instructions at the machine-language level use pointers as the basic way of referring to data and instructions, and this wide use permeates the implementation, if not always the external characteristics, of all programming languages.

In a higher-level programming language, we find that there are a number of reasons for using pointers. First of all, a pointer can be regarded as a universal data-structure in the sense that any data-object can be represented in such a way that all the information it contains is accessible when the pointer is given. Secondly, a pointer is of fixed size so that we can pass it around from place to place without elaborate storage allocation procedures, regardless of the data-structure to which it is referring. In particular, we can choose the size of machine registers so that they are large enough to contain pointers. In fact many machines possess registers which are precisely large enough to hold pointers, for essentially this reason. Thirdly, in most machines the amount of memory is quite limited, so that pointers are relatively small. The author knows of no machine, for example, in which an address is longer than a floating-point number, and in most machines the addresses are about half this size. This means that whenever a floating-point number is stored more than once in memory the amount of memory required could be reduced by using a pointer instead of having two copies of the number. This latter is not always easy, of course, and would often give gross execution-time inefficiencies, but the same argument can be applied to more complicated data-structures.

As we have noted in a previous section, it is usually preferable to organize data-structures in such a way that the address of an item can be computed rather than searched for, and this requires a certain homogeneity in the organization. Accordingly we find that one of the most important uses of a pointer is to permit references to a number of different data-structures to be made homogeneous. In this way we can, for example, use an array of pointers to give effectively an array of different structures and arrays. The other side of this coin, as Knuth points out, is the general philosophy of "if it doesn't fit, put it somewhere else and plant a pointer to it."

A second reason is that a data-structure in which pointers are used to indicate relationships between components of a data-object is more flexible than one in which adjacency in memory is used. This additional flexibility can be used to permit faster implementation of operations which add or delete elements, or which restructure the data-object in other ways. In particular, we frequently find that variable-size data-objects such as lists and sets are more efficiently implemented using pointers. We will discuss some such structures below.

In addition, a pointer permits a straightforward implementation of the notion of a reference, which we introduced in the previous chapter to permit overlapping data-objects.

PLEXES

We have been using the term *block* to refer to a contiguous set of memory locations. Below we will consider those data-structures which consist of a number of blocks which are associated by means of pointers. In the general case we will refer to this as a *plex*. In considering the properties of plexes we will ignore for the present the information other than the pointers which are stored in the block, and concentrate on the topology of the plex determined by the pointers.

It is clear that this topology can be conveniently described by a directed graph, in which a block is represented by a node, and a pointer connection is represented by an arc. We will sometimes use the word *node* to refer to a block of a plex.

We will not concern ourselves too much about the use of memory within a node, except to note that it is usually convenient to place the pointers in positions in which they are accessible with a minimum amount of computation. This suggests that they will either be organized in the form of an array, or occupy fixed positions relative to the beginning of the block. It is convenient in such cases to think of the arcs of the corresponding directed graphs as being labeled according to the accessing mechanism used to determine the corresponding pointer.

For example, a block such as that in Figure 3.2, which contains an array of three pointers, could be represented by the part of the directed graph shown in Figure 3.3. Similarly, a block containing two pointers in fixed positions could be represented by a

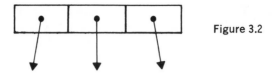

Figure 3.2

node of a directed graph with the two pointers identified by labels, as shown in Figure 3.4.

An obvious use of a plex is suggested by its representation by a directed graph. The data-objects we described in the previous chapter were also represented by directed

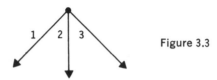

Figure 3.3

graphs, with the arcs representing the "set–membership" relation. We therefore have a straightforward representation of such a data-object by a plex in which the pointers are used to indicate the set–membership relation. Thus the block is considered to represent a collection whose elements are referred to by pointers. We have already seen an example of such a representation, namely an array of pointers used to represent a

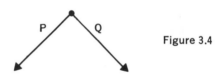

Figure 3.4

vector whose elements are not homogeneous. However, in the general case we might also want to store some of the elements of the collection in the block itself, rather than by referring to them by pointers. For example, a vector of four elements which consisted of two integers and two vectors could either have all the information packed in a single block, as Figure 3.5 shows, or it could have the integers stored in the block, and

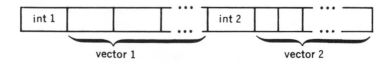

Figure 3.5

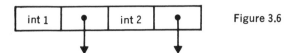

Figure 3.6

use pointers to the two vectors, as shown in Figure 3.6—or it could have all information referred to by pointer, as in Figure 3.7. The choice between these would depend on the application.

The above interpretation of a plex clearly uses the pointers to specify some or all of the set–element relationships in the data-object. In a similar way, the pointers could be interpreted as references. However, in a plex in which there is only one pointer in each node the obvious interpretation is as an ordered set of elements. The simplest kind of plexes thus use pointers to specify the "next–element" rather than the "set–element" relationship. We will consider such plexes in the next section.

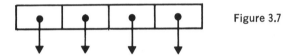

Figure 3.7

CHAINS

We will here consider those plexes in which the linkages between blocks are used simply to specify a linear ordering between the blocks. We will call these *chains*. Remember that this ordering does not mean that the blocks are consecutive in memory location.

The simplest such structure is that in which each block contains one pointer to the next block. We refer to this as a *one-way chain*. Figure 3.8 represents a one-way chain. In it we have distinguished the last block by some particular value for the pointer. This we will refer to as the *null pointer*, and in practice this will often have the value zero.

If each block in the chain contains two pointers, one pointing to the previous block and one pointing to the next block in the sequence, then we refer to the structure as a *two-way chain*. This we can represent by Figure 3.9. Once again, the terminal blocks of the chain are indicated by null pointers.

In either a one-way chain or a two-way chain it is possible to indicate the end by some other mechanism than the use of the null pointer. In this case the pointer space

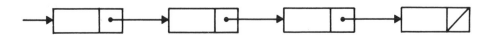

Figure 3.8

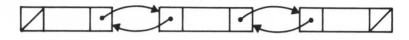

Figure 3.9

can be used to carry other information. In particular, if the terminal pointer of a chain is used to point to the other end, then we say that the chain is *circular*. It is thus possible for us to construct a circular one-way chain or a two-way chain which is circular in perhaps one or both directions.

In the majority of cases, a chain will be composed of blocks of fixed size but this is by no means necessary. If blocks of variable size are used, it will usually be convenient to allocate the pointer field at the beginning of the block or at least in a fixed position within the block.

The advantage of a chain is, of course, its flexibility. If we wish to insert another block in the chain between the second and third blocks (see Figure 3.10), then it is

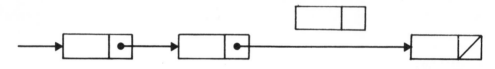

Figure 3.10

only necessary to change one pointer in the existing structure to point to the new block, and to set the pointer in the new block. This insertion would thus result in the chain shown in Figure 3.11. In a similar way, it is a simple matter to extend a chain by adding blocks at either the beginning or the end.

One of the main disadvantages of the chain is equally obvious. This is the fact that all the information in a chain is not immediately accessible. It is no longer possible, given the address of the first block, to calculate the address of an element somewhere in another block. This will require the program to trace successively through the linkages until it comes to the appropriate block, a process which though simple can be considerably time-consuming. In some cases the computation can be organized in such a way that the blocks can be processed in their natural order, such as the operation of calculating the sum of a sequence of numbers stored one to a block in a chain. However,

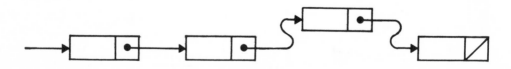

Figure 3.11

a simple problem like extracting the n-th number of the sequence would be very inefficient compared with, for instance, the simple indexing operation required to extract the n-th number of a sequence stored in successive memory location.

It will sometimes be convenient for us to refer to the chains described above as *linear plexes*. The plexes in which the pointers are used to specify more than the order of the nodes we will refer to as *nonlinear plexes*. It is clear that linear plexes can be used to implement those types of data-objects which we called linear, or which are linearizable. However, it is clear that they are most appropriate for representing the variable-size ordered sets we called lists, and particularly those with limited addition and deletion operations which do not require examination of elements not at the ends. A push-down stack, for example, is conveniently represented as a one-way chain, which can be referred to by the address of the first element. A queue can also be represented as a one-way chain, but will require an additional pointer to specify the end of the chain so that additions can be made more rapidly. This pointer should point to the last block so that a new element can be added by changing the pointer. Deletions are made at the beginning of the structure. A more convenient structure for representing a queue in some cases is a circular one-way chain referenced by a pointer to the last block added. Subsequent additions are made by insertion after this block, and deletions are of the block following the last. In a similar way we can represent double-ended queues conveniently as two-way chains or as circular two-way chains.

MULTILINKED CHAINS

In the case of the two-way chain the two pointer fields in the nodes are used to specify the order of the nodes, with the restriction that the order specified by the second pointer field is the reverse of that specified by the first. It is of course possible to use the second pointer field to specify a completely different order for the nodes. This can be done with an arbitrary number of pointer fields in each node, effectively permitting the same nodes to be on a number of different chains in different orders. In fact it is not necessary for all nodes to be on all the chains. We call such chains *multilinked*.

Multilinked chains are very useful for identifying subsets of a set. For example, the structure in Figure 3.12 shows a set of five elements divided into three subsets identified by the pointers A, B, and C.

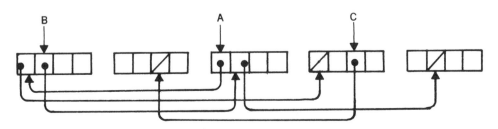

Figure 3.12

BINARY PLEXES

Another interesting class of plexes is that in which the nodes of the plex are limited to containing at most two pointers. We will call these *binary plexes.*

If both pointers in the node are interpreted as next-element pointers, then we get chains as described in the previous section. If we interpret one pointer as a set–element pointer and the other as a next–element pointer, then we get simple one-way chains whose elements are pointers to one-way chains, and thus a data-structure which is convenient for representing lists whose elements are lists. If we interpret both pointers as set–element pointers we get a plex which represents a data-object constructed out of collections which contain two elements. The fact that we can interpret a binary plex in these two ways is of course a reflection of the fact that we can represent an arbitrary collection in terms of collections with only two elements, as shown in Chapter 2.

TREES

In the cases when the directed graph is a tree we will call the corresponding data-structure a *tree structure.* Such structures have the property that one node, the root node, is not pointed to by any pointers in the other nodes, and that all other nodes are pointed to by exactly one pointer in another node.

A particularly simple but powerful form of tree structure is that in which each node contains at most two pointers. In its tree form we will refer to this as a *binary tree structure,* and we will find a number of important applications for it. When the node contains no other information except the pointers, we can illustrate a binary tree as in Figure 3.13. Some convention is necessary to indicate which nodes are terminal. A binary tree in which there is space in the node for other information is illustrated by Figure 3.14. Here we have shown terminal nodes indicated by null pointers.

It is clear that the binary tree can be used to represent arbitrary trees. In partic-

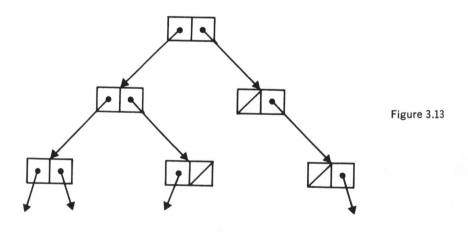

Figure 3.13

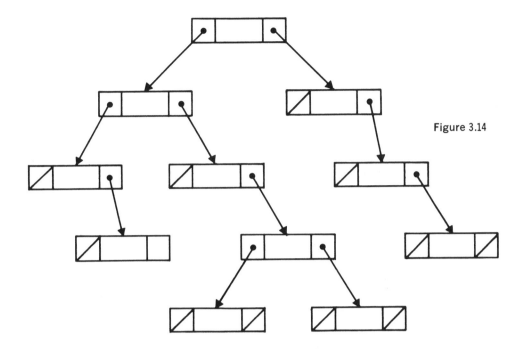

Figure 3.14

ular, the tree with information in its nodes shown above can be represented by a tree without information in its nodes. This can be done in a number of ways, but one of the simplest is by converting a node of the form of Figure 3.15 to a structure of the form of Figure 3.16. This is of course less efficient with respect to storage, and usually with respect to computation time, but permits a simpler basic form of node.

We will be discussing such structures in more detail in Chapter 11.

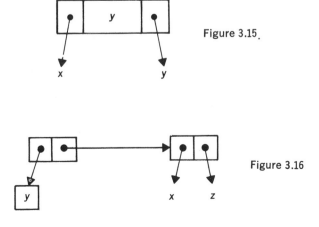

Figure 3.15.

Figure 3.16

REPRESENTATION OF SETS

As we have pointed out, physical memories are intrinsically ordered, so there is no obviously optimum representation of (unordered) sets. We could of course consider a set to be a vector or list and implement the operations in such a way that the order of the elements was not significant. However, the primitive operations on sets include:

is x an element of set a
add the elements of set b to set a
remove the elements of set b from set a

with the last two operations requiring repeated use of the first to determine if an element is in a. Thus the membership test is an important operation which must be implemented efficiently. If a set is implemented as a vector or list, the time to search for a specified element will be proportional to the number of elements in the list on average unless some special technique is used. Further, the search operation requires testing data-objects for equality, which in the case of sets is defined as "containing the same elements." The straightforward implementation of the equality test by searching for each element of one set in the other thus can take, on the average, a time proportional to the square of the number of elements in the set.

We can thus see that a straightforward implementation of a set will be very inefficient. This can be improved by sorting the elements of the sets so that a more rapid search can be carried out, and so that a test for the equality of two sets can be implemented in a time proportional to the number of elements. We will consider these matters in Chapter 8 on searching and sorting.

EXERCISES

1. Show how a two-way chain can be constructed with each node only using space for a single pointer. (Hint: fill the pointer-field with a bit-by-bit "exclusive-or" of the addresses of the nodes on either side).
2. Show how a sparse array (an array many of whose elements are zero or missing) can be represented compactly as a multilinked chain. (Hint: link together all elements in the same row).

ꓯ
PROGRAMMING IN FORTRAN

In the next few chapters we will be considering in more detail the properties of some of the data-structures which we described in the previous chapter. In particular, we will be concerned with the various ways in which the more important operations introduced in Chapter 2 can be implemented. The attempt will not be to give a complete catalog of methods for implementing these operations, but instead to give the reader a general feeling for some useful techniques.

Some of these techniques are concerned with the way in which operations can be implemented in terms of the usual machine instructions of the standard general-purpose computer. Accordingly it is necessary for the reader to have some familiarity with the machine language of at least one computer. However, in order to avoid an excessive concern with a particular machine, we will not give programs in machine language, but in a dialect of FORTRAN which we will call XFORTRAN. The examples of XFORTRAN code which we give should be regarded as a convenient shorthand form of machine language code, and not necessarily as a guide to the FORTRAN language.

In this chapter we will describe the main characteristics of XFORTRAN, which is a simple extension of FORTRAN IV. We will also discuss techniques for implementing the extensions in FORTRAN, so the reader who wishes to run the examples can do so without undue effort.

THE XFORTRAN MACHINE

As we mentioned above, we will be giving examples in XFORTRAN to illustrate various programming techniques at the machine-language level. Accordingly it is necessary for us to make certain assumptions about the main characteristics of the machine on which XFORTRAN runs.

First, we will assume that the XFORTRAN machine is a *binary* machine. We will further assume that the memory is divided into *words* which are individually address-able, and that these words are of sufficient length to specify most integers with which we will be concerned. In particular, we will assume that a word is long enough to contain the address of every word in the memory.

We will assume that at least one of the high-speed *registers* of the machine is sufficiently large to contain a word of information. There may in addition be high-speed registers which are approximately address-size, but their existence is not essential.

We will assume that the number representation is such that a positive integer is stored in standard binary notation, with the least-significant bit being at the right-hand end of the word. No assumptions will be made about the representation of negative numbers, except that the left-hand bit will be used as the sign bit. There will be no assumptions made about the form of floating-point number representation, or even whether there is any floating-point hardware at all.

We will assume that the instruction set includes addition and subtraction of word-length integers, and possibly multiplication and addition. We will also assume that the more common bit-by-bit Boolean instructions are available on words, including at least complementation and "and" or "or." We will assume that loads and stores of the contents of words whose addresses have been computed can be accomplished by indexing or instruction modification, and that jumps can also be made to computed addresses. We will assume that there is some form of shift instruction which can shift a word a number of places which has been computed. We will also assume some form of instruction to facilitate subroutine or procedure calls.

The assumptions made above include the vast majority of machines currently commercially available as potential XFORTRAN machines. In fact such machines vary from single-register 16-bit machines to multiregister 60-bit machines.

OUTLINE OF XFORTRAN

XFORTRAN is in some ways an extension of FORTRAN IV, and in other ways a restriction of it. The extensions consist of a number of additional operators to permit the programmer to have accessible most of the operations of the machine. The restrictions are assumptions which will be made about the implementation, which will permit the programmer to fake certain operations which are not strictly FORTRAN IV. However, these extensions and restrictions are reasonable ones, and the reader should not be surprised if they are consistent with the FORTRAN compiler available to him. Our description of XFORTRAN will therefore assume standard FORTRAN IV unless explicitly mentioned otherwise.

We will consider an XFORTRAN *variable* as representing a word which is assigned a fixed location in memory. An *array* will be considered a contiguous set of words also with fixed locations. The fact that the locations are fixed implies that references to these variables or arrays can be made by machine-language instructions using fixed addresses. Variables and arrays in COMMON will be represented similarly by fixed locations, but accessible to any subprogram. Arguments of a subprogram will be specified in the subprogram by the address of a variable or array, so that the subprogram can retrieve the value of the variable or any element of the array, and can also change those values. Access to such elements is done by indexing or indirect addressing, or by changing addresses in instructions in the subprogram.

We will frequently use one-dimensional arrays as arguments of subprograms without wishing to specify within the subprogram the exact size of the array. The corresponding dimension statement in a subprogram does not actually determine the size of such an array (that is done by one of the routines which invoked the subprogram), but is only used to specify that the argument is a one-dimensional array. The actual dimension specified is ignored, and in such cases we will often specify a dimension of 2.

The XFORTRAN variable, as well as taking on numerical values, can be regarded as simply containing a sequence of bits. In a similar way, the XFORTRAN array can be regarded as a sequence of bits stretching over a number of adjacent words in memory. Such bit sequences, of course, allow the storage of information within XFORTRAN in as general a way as is permitted by the computer itself. We will permit octal constants to be specified by following them with the letter B. This will specify a word with the octal constant at the right-hand end of the word, left-filled with zeros. The assignment statement

```
I = J
```

can be regarded as simply assigning to the variable I the same bit sequence as in the variable J. The standard conventions will be used to determine types of variables. However, in incomplete examples without declarations it will normally be assumed that integer variables are being used.

The Boolean bit-by-bit operations usually provided as machine instructions will be provided as the operators:

```
.A.       .O.        .N.
```

standing for the usual "and," "nonexclusive or," and "not" respectively. These will be assumed to operate on words and give words as their result. In addition, the function ISHIFT will be assumed to be available to do a circular left shift of a word a variable number of places. This will be used in the form:

```
ISHIFT(I,J)
```

to give the contents of the variable I left-shifted circularly J places. ISHIFT does not change its arguments. A negative value of J is assumed to do a right shift with sign bit extension.

We can use the above operations to permit access to parts of words. For example, the statement:

```
K = ISHIFT(I(2),-8) .A. 377B
```

will extract the second 8-bit field from the right of I(2), putting the 8 bits in the right-hand end of the word K. In a similar way the same field can be set to the value 205B by the following code:

```
I(2) = I(2) .A. .N. 177400B .O. ISHIFT(205B,8)
```

Note that we are assuming the same precedence relations between .A., .O., and .N. as between .AND., .OR., and .NOT..

In addition we will suppose that there is an additional declaration in XFORTRAN which permits us to refer to a field by name. For example, if the field used in the examples above was given the name ABC, we would be able to write the above statements as:

```
K = ABC(I)
ABC(I) = 205B
```

The field ABC can be defined by the following declaration:

```
FIELD ABC(8,16,2)
```

Here the numbers in parentheses following the name give respectively the length of the field in bits, the position of the leftmost bit of the field (with the rightmost bit of a word being numbered 1), and the number of the word in the block. These may be specified as expressions, which will be evaluated just prior to each use of the field name.

In many cases we will need to use pointers in our examples. A simple way to implement a pointer is to use an index of an array as a pointer. If the array is in COMMON this index can be used in an arbitrary subprogram. Note, however, that such an index is not an address, and so cannot be used to communicate with routines which assume addresses.

In order to provide a facility for manipulating addresses, two operations will be provided. First the function LOCF can be used to give the address of its argument. Thus

```
LOCF(I)
```

will have as its value the address of the variable I. Secondly the array MEMORY will be assumed to be predefined so that

```
MEMORY(L)
```

is the word whose address is L. MEMORY will be usable on the left-hand side of assignment statements so can be used to change the contents of a specified memory location, and can also be used in expressions to give the contents of a specified location.

USE OF FORTRAN

Most of the assumptions we have made about XFORTRAN will be true of many FORTRAN compilers. In the following sections we will consider ways of extending a regular FORTRAN compiler to permit the additional operations. Most FORTRAN compilers permit the assembly-language routines to be invoked as functions or subroutines, so we can make use of this facility to provide some of the operations.

In particular, it should be a simple matter to write machine-language functions to implement the .A., .O., .N., ISHIFT, and LOCF operations. From the point of view of execution speed and memory space, such routines and the code which invokes them will be rather poor. If possible, it is much better to modify the compiler so that it recognizes these operations and compiles in-line code. For example, the ISHIFT operation is often just a single machine instruction, but when implemented as a subprogram in assembly language requires half-a-dozen instructions. Worse than that, most FORTRAN compilers compile routines independently, so that when the invocation of the ISHIFT routine is being compiled the compiler does not know that it is a simple routine, and has to compile worst-case code. In a multiregister machine this may require code to save all the values of the registers, restoring them after returning from the routine. Even if the convention is that it is the responsibility of the called routine to ensure that no registers are changed, which gives better code in this case, the result will still require the half-dozen instructions. On the other hand, if the compiler recognizes ISHIFT, it can insert a single instruction, which can be incorporated into any optimization procedures done by the compiler.

Note that a useful gimmick with certain compilers is to implement such routines in such a way that they overwrite their calling sequences with the few instructions required to accomplish the operation. Subsequent calls then execute these instructions, and the routine is never called again.

The field operations are rather trickier to implement in regular FORTRAN, since they really require a new declaration. However, we can get a somewhat similar facility by defining two subprograms to extract or insert a field, with the field specified by values given as its arguments. Instead of specifying the length of the field, it will be more convenient to give a mask which will have as many ones in its binary representation as the length of the field. Also it will be more convenient to define the field position by the number of places it has to be shifted to the right to be in the rightmost position within the word. Thus the field we used in the previous example would be defined by the quantities 377B, 8, and 2.

When using the insertion and extraction operators it will be convenient to specify the field in as simple a way as possible. Accordingly, each field will be specified by a one-dimensional array of length 3, whose first element contains the mask, whose second element contains the position, and whose third element contains the word-number. Such a field specification can then be set conveniently by data statements at the beginning of the function or, if necessary, passed as arguments to further functions.

The insert routine can be defined as follows.

```
SUBROUTINE INSERT(I,J,K)
DIMENSION K(3), J(2)
MASK = ISHIFT(K(1),K(2))
J(K(3)) = J(K(3)).A..N. MASK .O. ISHIFT(I,K(2)) .A. MASK
RETURN
END
```

This function inserts the rightmost bits of the word I specified by the mask into the field of the array J specified by the array K. Note that the dimension statement for J merely indicates that J is a one-dimensional array, not that it is necessarily of length 2. As an example, consider the following portion of code.

```
IFLD(1) = 377B
IFLD(2) = 9
IFLD(3) = 2
...
IWD(2) = 77777777B
...
INS = 123B
CALL INSERT(INS,IWD,IFLD)
```

The reader should ascertain that this piece of code will leave IWD(2) containing the octal number 77523777B.

The extraction function is defined as follows.

```
FUNCTION IEXTRCT(J,K)
DIMENSION K(3), J(2)
IEXTRCT = ISHIFT(J(K(3)),-K(2)) .A. K(1)
RETURN
END
```

Implementation of the MEMORY pseudoarray cannot usually be done in a straightforward way with machine-language routines. However, it is usually possible to get the same effect by the use of two routines called IND and STORE. IND is a function which will give the contents of the word whose address is given as its argument, so

```
IND(I)
```

will give the contents of the word whose address is I. STORE is a subroutine which will store its first argument in the address given as its second, so

```
CALL STORE(I,J)
```

would store the value of I in the word whose address was J.

A better method for getting the effect of the MEMORY pseudoarray can be implemented in many compilers by using the LOCF function. Consider, for example, the following piece of code:

```
...
COMMON /MEMORY/ MEM,MEMORY(2)
...
MEM = 1 - LOCF(MEMORY(1))
...
1 I = MEMORY(J+MEM)
...
2 MEMORY(K+MEM) = 2 * M + 1
...
```

This assumes that the compiler makes no check on the correctness of index expressions for arrays. By initializing the value of the variable MEM to the negative of the location of the nonexistent zero-th entry in the array MEMORY, then any reference to MEMORY(L+MEM) will in fact refer to the contents of memory location L. Thus, statement 1 above assigns to I the value of the word in location J, while statement number 2 assigns to location number K the value of the expression 2*M+1. In most situations this mechanism can give considerably better code than the use of the IND and STORE operations, since the average FORTRAN compiler makes a considerable effort to optimize code concerned with array references. For example, the code

```
      DO 1 I = L1, L2
    1 MEMORY(I+MEM) = 0
```

would probably produce very respectable code for clearing a portion of memory. A second advantage of this device is that it allows storing into a location specified by an address to be accomplished by an assignment statement rather than a subroutine call.

The reader should note that some computers, such as the IBM 360 and others, have memory organized in terms of 8-bit "bytes," rather than words. In such computers an address identifies a byte rather than a word, so our XFORTRAN pointer is not the same as an address. However, in most cases this difference will not be significant.

EXERCISES

1. Find out the conventions used by the FORTRAN compiler available for your machine. These should include function and subroutine communication conventions, memory layout, and methods used for representing and accessing arrays.
2. Implement the ISHIFT, INSERT, and IEXTRCT routines in FORTRAN and assembly language for your computer.
3. Implement LOCF, IND, and STORE for your compiler.
4. Determine if any of the primitive routines can be implemented using code which modifies their calling sequences.
5. Determine if the mechanism suggested for implementing the MEMORY pseudo-array will work using your FORTRAN compiler.
*6. Modify your compiler to permit the use of a predefined MEMORY array.
**7. Design and implement modifications to your FORTRAN compiler which will permit convenient and efficient use of pointers and part-words.

5
STRING PROCESSING

In this chapter we will consider a specific type of data-object which can serve to introduce a number of the problems which we will consider in later chapters. This data-object is a form of list whose elements are restricted to be characters. We will refer to this as a character-string, or more briefly, as a *string*.

In the early programming languages, strings were not considered to be legitimate data-objects, and no operations were provided to manipulate them except in a very primitive way in connection with input and output operations. For example, FORTRAN provides Hollerith constants, and the ability to read and write strings, but no explicit operations on them; ALGOL 60 is essentially the same. However, the majority of modern programming languages provide facilities for manipulating strings, the most powerful of these is probably SNOBOL, which we will discuss in a later chapter.

Here we will be concerned with the simpler types of operations on strings, which we will illustrate by routines written in XFORTRAN. We stress once again that these routines should be regarded just as a shorthand form of machine-language routines. Such routines of course may be written by hand, or produced automatically from some higher-level language by a compiler.

STRING REPRESENTATION

We will first consider some of the more usual ways of representing a string in memory. We will regard a string simply as a sequence of "*characters*," which usually will include at least the digits, the letters of the alphabet, and a number of symbols which can be used for punctuation or as arithmetic operators. These can be simply represented in memory by assigning to each one a distinctive bit-sequence. It is apparent that n bits can be used to specify one of 2^n characters so, for instance, 6 bits can be used to represent up to 64 characters, while 8 bits can handle up to 256.

The choice of representation of strings in memory is not a trivial one, and will be given considerable attention in later chapters. In general the representation chosen depends on a large number of factors. These include questions of efficiency of use of both memory and computer time, as well as convenience for the programmer. In some cases, such as the choice of representation of strings in a particular programming language, there is no optimum solution, because it is not known to what use the language will be put. The decision often turns out to be one of personal taste as much as rigorous analysis. Here and in later chapters we will attempt to present a number of methods, together with some discussion of their advantages and disadvantages.

In this chapter we will be concerned purely with those representations of strings in which successive characters are in successive positions in memory. We will consider both packed strings, in which as many characters as possible are packed in each word, and unpacked strings, in which one character is stored in each word. If each character is represented by the same number of bits, both these representations have the advantage that the i-th character of a string can be accessed by a simple indexing operation. Accordingly, we will restrict consideration to string representations using a fixed number of bits per character.

Note that unpacked strings can be manipulated very simply in FORTRAN, since a character can be referred to using ordinary indexing operations. Accordingly, in many examples we will use a one-character-per-word representation, assuming the character to be right-adjusted in the word—i.e., at the least significant end, with the remainder of the word filled with binary zeros. In machines such as the IBM 360, which uses an 8-bit character code, and permits instructions to refer to 8-bit "bytes" as well as words, these FORTRAN programs have a straightforward implementation in machine language.

CHARACTER REPRESENTATION

It is clear that within the memory of the computer we can represent arbitrary characters, but the most useful set is that set which can conveniently be read, printed, or displayed by the peripheral equipment available on the particular computer. This often varies from machine to machine, and even from device to device on the same machine, in spite of a considerable effort within the industry devoted to establishing standards. Standard codes in use include binary coded decimal (BCD), a 6-bit code used for magnetic tapes, and EBCDIC, the 8-bit internal code used by the IBM 360 series. The one which has received the most acceptance has been the American Standard Code for Information Interchange, or ASCII. This is an 8-bit code, 7 of which are used to carry information, and the 8th of which is a check bit. A representative sample of commonly used codes is given in Figure 5.1.

The check bit in ASCII referred to above is simply a parity bit which indicates whether the number of ones in the other 7 bits is odd or even. This, of course, is redundant information which can be used to detect an error in transmission, memory, or computation which resulted in a single bit having the wrong value. It will not detect the occurrence of two errors in a character, of course, nor will it enable the error to be corrected. Codes can be designed to do these things, but their study is outside the scope of this book. However, it can be shown that codes can be designed to detect and correct any specified number of errors.

SAMPLE CHARACTER CODES IN COMMON USE FOR THE FORTRAN CHARACTER SET,
GIVEN IN OCTAL.

Character	360 EBCDIC	ASCII	6600 Display Code	External BCD	Hollerith Punch Positions
A	301	041	01	61	12-1
B	302	042	02	62	12-2
C	303	043	03	63	12-3
D	304	044	04	64	12-4
E	305	045	05	65	12-5
F	306	046	06	66	12-6
G	307	047	07	67	12-7
H	310	050	10	70	12-8
I	311	051	11	71	12-9
J	321	052	12	41	11-1
K	322	053	13	42	11-2
L	323	054	14	43	11-3
M	324	055	15	44	11-4
N	325	056	16	45	11-5
O	326	057	17	46	11-6
P	327	060	20	47	11-7
Q	330	061	21	50	11-8
R	331	062	22	51	11-9
S	342	063	23	22	0-2
T	343	064	24	23	0-3
U	344	065	25	24	0-4
V	345	066	26	25	0-5
W	346	067	27	26	0-6
X	347	070	30	27	0-7
Y	050	071	31	30	0-8
Z	051	072	32	31	0-9
0	360	120	33	12	0
1	361	121	34	01	1
2	362	122	35	02	2
3	363	123	36	03	3
4	364	124	37	04	4
5	365	125	40	05	5
6	366	126	41	06	6
7	367	127	42	07	7
8	370	130	43	10	8
9	371	131	44	11	9
+	116	113	45	60	12
−	140	115	46	40	11
*	134	112	47	54	11-8-4
/	141	117	50	21	0-1
(	115	110	51	34	0-8-4
)	135	111	52	74	12-8-4
$	133	104	53	53	11-8-3
=	176	135	54	13	8-3
blank	100	100	55	20	space
,	153	114	56	33	0-8-3
.	113	116	57	73	12-8-3

Figure 5.1

A simple example of a code which can correct any single (i.e., one-bit) error in a string of characters is the encoding shown in Figure 5.2. This shows four characters, each encoded as 3 bits, $a_1a_2a_3$, $b_1b_2b_3$, $c_1c_2c_3$, $d_1d_2d_3$. To each character encoding has been added a single parity bit h_a, h_b, h_c, h_d, which is one if the number of ones in its corresponding character is odd, and zero otherwise. Clearly if the values of $a_1a_2a_3h_a$ are not consistent with this rule, then an error has occurred in at least one of the four bits.

a_1	a_2	a_3	h_a
b_1	b_2	b_3	h_b
c_1	c_2	c_3	h_c
d_1	d_2	d_3	h_d
v_1	v_2	v_3	

Figure 5.2

By adding three other parity bits v_1, v_2, v_3, which specify the parity of the corresponding column, a one-bit error can be located and corrected. For instance, if the values of h_c and v_2 disagree with the values appearing in their row and column, and it was assumed that only one error has been made, then it would be c_2. If there were an inconsistent value in h_c alone, then the error would be in h_c. This scheme will also detect (but not locate exactly) any two errors, which will show up as one, three, or four inconsistencies, or as two row or two column inconsistencies.

CHARACTER SET EXTENSIONS

It is sometimes necessary to extend a code beyond the standard range of characters. One way to do this is simply to use more bits per character. This often requires that programs be rewritten, but in cases where the hardware is involved it is not possible to extend the code in this way. A convenient alternative is to select one of the old codes and use it as an *escape character*. The convention is then that this character and the one following it are used to represent one of the characters of the extended set. For example, the string:

```
Use $ as Escape Character
```

can be encoded in a code which only has capital letters, blank, and $ sign as:

```
U$S$E $$ $A$S E$S$C$A$P$E C$H$A$R$A$C$T$E$R
```

Here the $ sign has been used as the escape character, and the pair $$ is used to represent a $ sign. This scheme is most efficient when the extended characters are the least used.

A variant of the same scheme is preferable when there are sequences of characters in the extended set, as in the above example. This uses a selected character as a *mode changer.* When this character appears, subsequent characters up to its next occurrence are assumed to be in the extended set. Thus the above example would be encoded as:

USE $$ AS E$SCAPE$ C$HARACTER$

This is slightly more concise than the previous encoding. Of course, both these schemes can be used repeatedly to extend the character set as far as required.

A further method of extending the character set is to do just what is done in natural languages, and use words. A word is simply a sequence of characters which is delimited by a selected character, the blank. This permits the words to vary in size so that short sequences can be used to represent frequent words. The reader might note in passing that the more frequent words in natural languages tend to be shorter than the rare ones. In artificial languages used in mathematics or programming a number of characters are used as delimiters instead of just a blank. For example, in FORTRAN the string

XYZ = AB + CD

is analyzed as though the characters = and + are break characters and the sequences XYZ, AB, and CD are words which are terminated by break characters. In a later section we will give an algorithm which can analyze a string of this form.

NUMBER CONVERSION

Frequently a string contains characters representing a numerical quantity. In some situations these have no special significance, but in others it is necessary to manipulate the numerical values they represent. If the operations to be performed on the numbers are the usual arithmetic operations, it is usually more efficient to convert the string to the standard internal notation used for numerical quantities, and then use the normal arithmetic operations provided by the hardware. In some computers the hardware provides arithmetic operations on strings of coded numerical characters, and in others provides the conversion operation. In most computers, however, the internal representation of numbers is binary, and conversion operations have to be programmed.

The conversion operation is clearly simplest if there is a simple relationship between the bit pattern representing the character and the binary representation of the corresponding number. Most internal codes are chosen with this in mind. One example, used on the CDC 6000 series computers, uses a 6-bit code in which the digits $0, 1, 2, \ldots, 9$ are represented by the octal numbers $33, 34, 35, \ldots, 44$. With such a code, a single character stored in the least-significant 6 bits of a word can be converted to an integer simply by masking out the rest of the word and subtracting 33 (octal). For the sake of definiteness, we will use this code in our examples in the next few sections. A function which converts to an integer the sequence of such characters in the first N words of the array KARS can thus be written

```
FUNCTION MAKINT(KARS,N)
DIMENSION KARS(2)
MAKINT = 0
DO 1 I = 1,N
1 MAKINT = 10 * MAKINT + KARS(I) - 33B
RETURN
END
```

Very often it is necessary to write such a routine without knowing N, assuming the string of characters to contain a nondigit which will signify the end of the number. The above function can easily be adapted for this purpose by including a test within the loop.

The operation of converting an integer between 0 and 9 to a character in the above code requires addition of 33 octal. Thus a subroutine which will convert a positive integer NUMB to a sequence of characters in the above code stored one per word in the 6 least-significant bits of the array KARS can be written:

```
SUBROUTINE ITOSTR(NUMB,KARS)
DIMENSION KARS(20), KTEMPS(20)
N = NUMB
DO 1 I=1,20
KTEMPS(I) = MOD(N,10) + 33B
N = N/10
IF (N.EQ.0) GOTO 2
1 CONTINUE
I = 20
2 DO 3 J=1,I
3 KARS(J) = KTEMPS(I+1-J)
KARS(I+1) = 0
RETURN
END
```

Note that because the conversion procedure naturally produces the last character first, an auxiliary array KTEMPS is used to contain the characters produced in the reverse order before being put into KARS.

USE OF TABLES

When the processing of a string depends on the particular characters in the string, it can be very time-consuming to include code to test for the occurrence of specific characters. In some cases, such as the example of number conversion given above, there is a simple relationship which enables such tests to be simplified or eliminated.

However, in the general case this is not possible, so a more flexible technique is necessary. This usually takes the form of some sort of table, which is accessed by an index which is calculated from the character. The entry in the table then contains the information necessary for processing that character.

For example, suppose that we have a random assignment of bit patterns to characters, and wish to convert a string of coded digits to its equivalent binary number. We can do this by setting up a table whose i-th entry contains the integer whose corresponding character is coded as i. Using the previous code, for example, the 34-th (octal) entry of the table would contain 1. A function to do the string-to-integer conversion could then be written:

```
      FUNCTION MAKINT(KARS,N,KTABLE)
      DIMENSION KARS(2), KTABLE(2)
      MAKINT = 0
      DO 1 I=1,N
    1 MAKINT = 10 * MAKINT + KTABLE(KARS(I))
      RETURN
      END
```

This code is only slightly slower than the previous version on many machines, but requires an extra memory reference. However, it is clearly more flexible, since by changing the table the function will work for any code. In fact this is a simple example of what is sometimes referred to as a table-driven program.

Another illustration of essentially the same technique is appropriate when converting from one code to another. This is frequently necessary in connection with input and output operations, since the internal code used to represent characters is rarely the one used on all peripheral devices. This conversion requires a table for each direction, of course.

In some cases the code which must be executed is different for each character, or for certain sets of characters. Then the most useful form of table is a table whose entries specify the code to be executed. This is simply implemented by a table whose entries are jump instructions to the appropriate code. In FORTRAN such a table is represented by a "computed GO TO" statement.

As an example of an application of this technique, we give below a lexical scan routine. Such a routine can be used to separate a string of characters into its logical units. A lexical scan routine for the FORTRAN language, for instance, would split the statements into symbol names, key words, numbers, operators, and Hollerith constants. The simplified version we give here will recognize the following units.

1. A symbol composed of a sequence of letters or digits starting with a letter
2. A number composed of a sequence of digits or periods starting with a digit
3. An operator consisting of any single character not a letter, digit, or blank.

The routine will accept KARS containing 6-bit character codes, one per word, right adjusted. It will begin to look at character number I, and will ignore leading blanks. The function will return in I the number of the first character in the token, in J the number of the last character in the token, and in M the type of the token (values 2, 3, 4 denoting symbol, number, or operator token). The routine is written as follows.

```
       SUBROUTINE LSCAN(KARS,I,J,M)
       DIMENSION KARS(72)
       M = 1  $  J = I-1
99  J = J+1  $  KAR = KARS(J)+1        values of M = 1, 2, 3, 4 indicate
                                       routine is processing blanks, sym-
                                       bol, number, operator respectively
       GO TO (5,2,2,2,2,2,2,2,2,2,2,   computed go on to next character
     *        2,2,2,2,2,2,2,2,2,2,2,
     *        2,2,2,2,2,3,3,3,3,3,3,
     *        3,3,3,3,5,5,5,5,5,5,5,
     *        5,1,5,4,5,5,5,5,5,5,5,
     *        5,5,5,5,5,5,5,5), KAR
1  GOTO (99,24,24), M                  blank
2  GOTO (21,99,24), M                  letter
3  GOTO (22,99,99), M                  digit
4  GOTO (23,24,99), M                  period
5  GOTO (23,24,24), M                  other character
21 I = J $ M=2 $ GOTO 99              start of symbol
22 I = J $ M=3 $ GOTO 99              start of number
23 I = J $ M=4 $ RETURN               operator
24 J = J-1 $ RETURN                   terminate symbol or number
       END
```

For conciseness we have put many statements on one line, using a $ sign as separator in the above. The long computed GOTO depends on the internal character code used, so will vary from machine to machine. The one shown is for display code on the CDC 6000 series.

It should be pointed out that this routine is actually a simple implementation of what is called a finite-state analyzer, in which the state (indicated by the value of the variable M) effectively provides memory of the previous characters encountered. The action of the analyzer is simply expressed as a table. See Figure 5.3. This is a particularly simple example, because the amount of memory required is very small. If it was required to distinguish integers from real numbers, however, we would need another state, switching from one to another when a period was encountered, and terminating a real number if a second period was encountered.

OPERATIONS ON STRINGS

In the following sections we will show how a number of basic operations on strings can be implemented. As we have mentioned previously, the simple operations on a data-object are usually dependent on the particular form of data-structure used to represent it. The operations on strings which we will consider here are those which are appropriate for strings which are represented in memory as contiguous sequences of characters.

	Blank	Letter	Digit	Period	Other	
M = 1	continue	start symbol M=2	start number M=3	output operator	output operator	*Blanks*
M = 2	backup 1 character output symbol	continue	continue	backup 1 character output symbol	backup 1 character output symbol	*Symbol*
M = 3	backup 1 character output number	backup 1 character output number	continue	continue	backup 1 character output number	*Number*
M = 4	—	—	—	—	—	*State 4 is not used in memory*

Figure 5.3

We will consider concatenation, substring extraction, substring substitution, string identity, and string search. These are among the operations provided in PL/1. *Concatenation* is the name used for the operation which creates a new string from the characters of two or more other strings. *Substring extraction* refers to the creation of a string which contains the characters in a portion of another string, while *substring substitution* refers to the operation of changing part of a string. *String identity* is the operation which tests for the equality of two strings, while *string search* searches one string for the occurrence of another string within it.

UNPACKED STRINGS

We will first consider how we might implement these operations on strings which are stored with one character per word, or, more precisely, in which each character is directly addressable. In a machine like the IBM 360, which permits a single 8-bit character to be addressed, this is the most natural and efficient form of storage; but in other machines which only provide word addressing, this gives a very inefficient use of memory. However, most algorithms are simpler when individual characters can be addressed. We will write the code in XFORTRAN, and assume that a string is stored in a one-dimensional array, one character per array element.

A basic operation which we will need is a routine which can copy characters. We will define this as follows.

```
      SUBROUTINE CHMOVE(IFROM,L,ITO)
      DIMENSION IFROM(2), ITO(2)
      DO 1 I=1,L
    1 ITO(I) = IFROM(I)
      RETURN
      END
```

This copies the first L characters from IFROM to ITO. In the IBM 360 it is provided as a single machine instruction for L≤256, but in most other machines it would require a loop of instructions.

With this routine we can accomplish the substring operations mentioned above. For example, we can set the 4-th through 7-th characters of the string stored in the array I to the 8-th through 11-th of the string stored in the array J by writing

```
CALL CHMOVE(J(8),4,I(4))
```

The concatenation operation can be defined as follows.

```
SUBROUTINE CONCAT(I1,L1,I2,L2,J)
DIMENSION I1(2), I2(2), J(2)
CALL CHMOVE(I1,L1,J)
CALL CHMOVE(I2,L2,J(L1+1))
RETURN
END
```

This also makes use of the CHMOVE subroutine.

A routine to test for the equality of two substrings can be written as follows.

```
LOGICAL FUNCTION IDENT(I,L,J)
DIMENSION I(2), J(2)
DO 1 IJ = 1,L
IF (I(IJ).EQ.J(IJ)) GOTO 1
IDENT = .FALSE.
RETURN
1 CONTINUE
IDENT = .TRUE.
RETURN
END
```

This gives the result "true" if the first L characters of I are the same as those of J, and "false" otherwise. This can be used to write the search routine:

```
FUNCTION INDEX(I1,L1,I2,L2)
DIMENSION I1(2), I2(2)
I2MAX = L2 - L1 + 1
DO 1 I = 1,I2MAX
IF (IDENT(I1,L1,I2(I))) GOTO 2
1 CONTINUE
INDEX = 0
RETURN
2 INDEX = I
RETURN
END
```

This routine searches the first L2 characters of the string I2 for the string I1 of length L1. If the string is not found, **INDEX** returns the value 0, and otherwise returns the number of the character in I2 which begins the first occurrence of I1.

All these routines are trivial pieces of coding which should really be implemented in machine language for efficiency. Alternatively, the code is so simple that without too much additional programming the operations could actually be coded in-line. This would give a faster program because of the elimination of the time necessary to enter the subroutines, and possibly of the elimination of considerable amounts of code if the compiler provides sophisticated optimization techniques.

PACKED STRINGS

We will refer to those strings in which characters are stored with maximum density as *packed strings*. A computer with 32 bits per word and an 8-bit code would have 4 characters per word, while a computer with 60 bits per word could store ten 6-bit characters or seven 8-bit characters per word. The usual convention is for the first character to be stored in the most-significant or left-hand end of the word, with any empty space at the end of a word filled out with binary zeros. It is sometimes convenient for a string to be terminated by a special character which is not used for any other purpose.

When there is more than one character per addressable unit of memory, we require a different method of identifying a substring. It is usually most convenient to refer to a substring by specifying the address of the beginning of the string, together with the number of the first character and the number of characters in the string. The equivalent of the **CHMOVE** subroutine is then the subroutine **PCHMOVE** defined so that the statement

```
CALL PCHMOVE(IFROM,IF1,L,ITO,IT1)
```

would move the L characters starting at the (IF1)-th character of the string stored in the array **IFROM** into the string stored in the array **ITO** starting at the (IT1)-th character.

The **PCHMOVE** routine can be written in XFORTRAN using the **ISHIFT** routine as follows.

```
        SUBROUTINE PCHMOVE(J,J1,L1,I,I1)
        COMMON /PARAMS/ NBPW, NBPC, NCPW
        DIMENSION I(2), J(2)
        MAKI(JJ)=ISHIFT(J(JJ),ISH).A.MSK.O.ISHIFT(J(JJ+1),ISH)
     *        .A. .N. MSK
        IW = (I1-1)/NCPW
        IC = I1 - 1 - IW * NCPW
        JW = (J1-1)/NCPW
        JC = J1 - 1 - JW * NCPW
```

```
      I2 = IC + L1
      NW = (I2-1)/NCPW
      ISH = IABS(IC-JC) * NBPC
      MSK=MAKMSK(NBPW-ISH)
      IF (IC .LE. JC) GOTO 10
      JW = JW-1
      MSK = MAKMSK(ISH)
      ISH = NBPW - ISH
   10 IM = MAKMSK(IC*NBPC)
      ILM = MAKMSK((I2-(I2/NCPW)*NCPW)*NBPC)
      IF (NW.NE.0) GOTO 3
      ILM = ILM .A. .N. IM
      GOTO 2
    3 I(IW+1) = I(IW+1) .A. IM .O. MAKI(JW+1) .A. .N. IM
      IF(NW.LT.2) GOTO 2
      DO 1 M=2,NW
    1 I(IW+M) = MAKI(JW+1)
    2 I(IW+NW+1) = I(IW+NW+1).A..N.ILM
     *.O. MAKI(JW+NW+1) .A. ILM
      RETURN
      END
```

The routine MAKMSK is assumed to return a word which contains binary ones in the number of most-significant bits given in its argument, while the COMMON variables, NBPW, NBPC, NCPW are assumed to have been set to the number of bits per word, the number of bits per character, and the number of characters per word respectively. In spite of its complexity, this algorithm is not particularly efficient in a number of special cases.

A similar routine can be used to implement the basic substring identity test routine.

Both basic algorithms are considerably more complicated than the equivalent ones for unpacked strings, but they can be implemented in machine language so that they execute considerably faster, since many characters can be moved or tested for each memory reference. For short strings, or short substrings, the additional shifting and masking operations necessary with the packed strings may give slower execution times, so that in problems in which operations are mainly on single characters, unpacked strings will often be superior. Of course, packed strings are always superior with respect to memory utilization.

MORE POWERFUL STRING OPERATIONS

So far we have discussed a number of primitive operations on character strings. We found that we could do most of our manipulation using a copy operation and a test operation. Other basic operations, like concatenation and substring extraction, could be written in terms of the copy operation. However, if we attempt to do a large amount of programming using these primitive operations, we find that our code is rather cumbersome and, in a number of situations, highly inefficient.

In later chapters we will be examining in more detail a number of the major programming languages. However, at this point, we will briefly indicate what facilities are available for character-string manipulation. FORTRAN, as we have seen, does allow Hollerith constants which can be assigned to variables or arrays. In most compilers, no statements are provided for the manipulation of such strings. In ALGOL 60, character string constants were permitted, but only as arguments to procedures. No string operations were provided. In PL/1, a number of facilities are available for the manipulation of character strings. String constants and string variables of fixed and varying length (up to a maximum specified in the declaration) are permitted. Basic operations provided include concatenation and assignment with functions being available for substring extraction, assignment, and search. ALGOL 68, as defined by the draft report of January 1968, has comprehensive facilities for string variables and string manipulation. The LISP language is not basically oriented toward character string manipulation, but can be extended in this direction. The language probably possessing the most convenient features for string manipulation is SNOBOL 4. Among other things, SNOBOL permits string constants and variables and the convenient expression of the assignment, concatenation, search, and substitution operations. Operations in SNOBOL are specified quite naturally, but in a manner quite different from the functional and operational form used by more numerically oriented programming languages.

We will be discussing PL/1, LISP and its extensions, SNOBOL, and ALGOL 68 in more detail in later chapters.

AN EXAMPLE

In this section we give a complete program for editing a file in a time-sharing system. The user is presumed to be equipped with a personal terminal which he can use to type in commands to his program, in this case the editor program. The program, after executing the command, can type or display its response. The communication with the terminal is written as though it were a tape, with TAPE3 being used for input and TAPE4 for output.

The program edits the file on TAPE1 by processing it serially, writing out the modified file on TAPE2. There are commands for deleting, modifying, or inserting lines. The number of lines processed can be determined by number, or by specifying the leading nonblank characters of the line to be located. At any point in the editing process, the part of the file which has been edited is on TAPE2, the "current line" is in memory, and the unedited part of the original file is on TAPE1. After each editing operation, the new current line is typed out so the user knows where the file is positioned. Each command starts with two characters indicating the type of command, with the first character always a /. Lines starting with any character other than a slash are assumed to be lines to be inserted after the current line. The current line is written on TAPE2, and the line just typed becomes the current line. Unpacked strings are used throughout for simplicity.

The code is written as follows.

```
  PROGRAM EDT3(INPUT=100,SCRATCH=100,TTYIN=100,TTYOUT=100,
 * TAPE1=INPUT,TAPE2=SCRATCH,TAPE3=TTYIN,TAPE4=TTYOUT)
  DIMENSION IBUF(72),IOP(72),IBUF2(144)
1 REWIND 1 $ REWIND 2 $ ASSIGN 3 TO IPTTY $ IBUF(1)=777B
  GOTO 9

3 CALL WRTTY(IBUF)                        type current line, then ask
9 CALL RDTTY(IOP)                         for instructions
  IF (IOP(1).NE.1R/) GOTO 2               commands start with /
  IF (IOP(2).EQ.1RX) CALL EXIT            /X calls exit immediately
  IF (IOP(2).NE.1RR) GOTO 46             /R rewinds both files
  IF (IOP(3).EQ.1R ) GOTO 1              /R1 rewinds input file
  IF (IOP(3).NE.1R1) GOTO 47             /R2 rewinds scratch file
  REWIND 1 $ IBUF(1)=777B $ GOTO 3
47 IF (IOP(3).NE.1R2) GOTO 46
  REWIND 2 $ GOTO 3
46 CONTINUE
  IF (IOP(2).EQ.1RQ) GOTO 8              /Q rewinds files and calls
                                         exit
  IF (IOP(2).EQ.1RU) GOTO 27            /U causes original file to be
                                         updated
  IF (IOP(2).NE.1RE) GOTO 29            /E empties current line
  IF (IOP(3).NE.1R ) GOTO 30
  IBUF(1)=777B $ GOTO 3
30 IF (IOP(3).NE.1RF) GOTO 31           /EF inserts end-of-file after
  CALL WRFILE(2,IBUF)                    current line
  IBUF(1) = 77777B $ GOTO 3
31 IF (IOP(3).NE.1RR) GOTO 29           /ER inserts end-of-record
  CALL WRFILE(2,IBUF)                    after current line
  IBUF(1) = 7777B $ GOTO 3
29 IF (IOP(2).NE.1RS) GOTO 40           /S edits current line by
  DO 39 I=1,72                           substitution
  IBUF2(I) = IBUF(I) $ IBUF2(I+72)=1R
39 IBUF(I) = 1R
  ITC = IOP(3)                           search for pattern
  DO 33 I=1,72
  DO 34 J=1,30
  IF (IOP(J+3).EQ.ITC) GOTO 35
  IF (I+J.GT.73) GOTO 33
34 IF (IBUF2(I+J-1).NE.IOP(J+3)) GOTO 33
33 IBUF(I) = IBUF2(I)
  GOTO 9
```

```
35 K = I+J-2 $ IBUF(I)=IBUF2(I)              substitute for pattern of
   DO 36 II=I,72                             length J-1 starting at i
   J = J+1 $ IF (IOP(J+3).EQ.ITC) GOTO 37
36 IBUF(II) = IOP(J+3)
   GOTO 3
37 DO 38 III=II,72                           copy remaining characters
   K = K+1
38 IBUF(III) = IBUF2(K)
   GOTO 3
40 CONTINUE
   IF ((IOP(2).NE.1RC).A.(IOP(2).NE.1RD)     /C copies up to specified line
  *  .A.(IOP(2).NE.1RL)) GOTO 2              /L copies and types
   KOUNT = 0                                 /D deletes up to specified
                                             line

   DO 16 I=3,6
   IF ((IOP(I).LT.33B).O.(IOP(I).GT.44B))
  * GOTO 15
16 KOUNT = 10*KOUNT + IOP(I)-33B
15 IF (KOUNT.EQ.0) GOTO 26
   DO 10 I=1,KOUNT                           leading integer causes cards
   IF ((IOP(2).EQ.1RC).O.(IOP(2).           to be counted
  * .EQ.1RL)) CALL WRFILE(2,IBUF)
   CALL RDFILE(1,IBUF,IPTTY)
   IF (IOP(2).EQ.1RL) CALL WRTTY(IBUF)
10 CONTINUE
   IF (IOP(2).EQ.1RL) GOTO 9
   GOTO 3
26 IF ((IOP(2).EQ.1RC).O.(IOP(2).EQ.        no leading integer causes
  * 1RL)) CALL WRFILE(2,IBUF)               pattern search
   CALL RDFILE(1,IBUF,IPTTY)
   IF (IOP(2).EQ.1RL) CALL WRTTY(IBUF)
20 DO 21 I=1,50
21 IF (IBUF(I).NE.1R ) GOTO 22
   GOTO 26
22 DO 23 J=4,23
   IF (IOP(J).EQ.1R) GOTO 23
   IF (IOP(J).NE.IBUF(I)) GOTO 26
23 I = I + 1
   IF (IOP(2).EQ.1RL) GOTO 9
   GOTO 3
 2 CALL WRFILE(2,IBUF)                       anything else is inserted
28 DO 14 I=1,72                              after current line
14 IBUF(I) = IOP(I)
   GOTO 9
```

```
 27 REWIND 1 $ REWIND 2                copy scratch file back into
    ASSIGN 12 to IXT                   original
 13 CALL RDFILE(2,IBUF,IXT)
    CALL WRFILE(1,IBUF) $ GOTO 13
 12 REWIND 1 $ REWIND 2 $ GOTO 1
  8 REWIND 1 $ REWIND 2 $ CALL EXIT
    END

    SUBROUTINE RDFILE(NF,IBUF,EOF)
    DIMENSION IBUF(72)
    READ (NF,100) IBUF
    IF (ENDFILE NF) 1,2
  1 IBUF(1) = 7777B $ GOTO EOF
  2 RETURN
100 FORMAT (72R1)
    END

    SUBROUTINE WRFILE(NF,IBUF)
    DIMENSION IBUF(72)
    IF (IBUF(1).EQ.777B) RETURN
    IF ((IBUF(1).EQ.7777B).O.
  * (IBUF(1).EQ.77777B)) GOTO 1
    WRITE (NF,100) IBUF $ RETURN
  1 ENDFILE NF $ RETURN
100 FORMAT (72R1)
    END

    SUBROUTINE RDTTY(IBUF)
    DIMENSION IBUF(72)
    DO 1 I=1,72
  1 IBUF(I) = 1R
    READ (3,100) IBUF $ RETURN
100 FORMAT(72R1)
    END

    SUBROUTINE WRTTY(IBUF)
    DIMENSION IBUF(72)
    IF (IBUF(I).EQ.77777B) GOTO 3
    IF (IBUF(1).EQ.7777B) GOTO 1
    IF (IBUF(1).EQ.777B) GOTO 2
    WRITE (4,102) IBUF $ RETURN
  1 WRITE (4,103) $ RETURN
  2 WRITE (4,104) $ RETURN
  3 WRITE (4,105) $ RETURN
```

```
102 FORMAT( * *,72R1)
103 FORMAT((* END-OF-RECORD*)
104 FORMAT (* EMPTY*)
105 FORMAT (* END-OF-FILE*)
    END
```

VARIABLE-LENGTH STRINGS

In some cases it is necessary to represent strings which vary in size throughout a calculation, in which case the length of the string must be represented in memory in some way. An operation such as concatenation can be implemented with the length of the string specified explicitly as an argument of the concatenation function, or the length of the string can be stored somehow in the array with the string. There are two obvious ways of doing this: the first is to use one of the words in the array, usually the first, to specify the length of the string; the second is to use some distinguished code to mark the end of the string. The main disadvantage of the first method is that the length is usually most conveniently expressed in binary, and so cannot be treated in the same way as the characters in the string. This means that operations which require the strings to be encoded for other media require further conventions. In such cases the terminal mark is often preferred.

A string which is terminated by a special character is not quite as amenable to manipulation as that whose length is known. Of course, each operation can be preceded by a counting operation, but this would be inefficient. It is usually most convenient to extend the routines given previously so that they can detect the terminating code and act accordingly.

An important problem which arises in manipulating variable-length strings, and in general any variable-size data-objects, is that of memory allocation. If the algorithm is such that the size of the strings can be predicted fairly accurately, it is possible to allocate an amount of memory for each string which will be adequate for it to grow to its maximum size. However, even if this can be done, it will not use memory efficiently when the variation in size of the string is large. In other cases it is not possible to predict the size of strings at all, since this may depend in a complex way on the data supplied to the program, for example. Therefore, in general, it is necessary to abandon the type of memory allocation we have assumed for XFORTRAN, which is done prior to execution time. Note that this method in any case has the disadvantage that memory is allocated even for variables and arrays in subprograms which have not been invoked. In the following two chapters we will consider this problem in more detail.

STRING-MANIPULATION LANGUAGES

In this chapter we have described a number of ways in which strings can be represented in memory. The choice of representation depends on the algorithm and on the constraints under which the programmer is working. It will often be the case that no single representation is optimum for all strings in a single program, so that the programmer would like to choose one representation for some strings, and a different one for others. In addition, the allocation of memory space may vary from string to string. Some strings may be fixed in size, some may be of fixed length within a certain portion of the program, and some may vary in length dynamically throughout. It may be convenient to allocate memory for some strings prior to execution, while others will have to be allocated memory in more general ways which will be described in more detail in Chapter 7.

We can see that a seemingly simple operation such as concatenation is in such circumstances one of a rather large number of operations, the appropriate one depending on the representation of its arguments and the required representation and storage-allocation mode of its result. If we were to attempt to construct a language using the facilities provided by XFORTRAN, we would find it necessary to write a large number of routines, and the programmer would have the tedious job of selecting the correct ones. Furthermore, a small change in the format of a string would require all operations on that string to be changed also. The inevitable result is that the programmer simply abandons the preferred approach to the problem, and either writes straight in-line code, or else selects a particular data-representation which he uses uniformly regardless of efficiency. In the first case he ends up with an efficient but inflexible program which is of little use to him in his next similar programming task, and in the second with an inefficient implementation which is often of little more use.

The widely recognized solution to this problem in language design is to permit the programmer to separate the declarations which describe the representation of the data-objects from the code for manipulating them. The simplest examples of this are in FORTRAN where declarations of the type of arithmetic quantities are permitted. This enables the programmer to avoid writing things like

$$X = FLOATADD(Y, FLOAT(INTADD(I, J)))$$

when manipulating mixed integer and real expressions. This is the sort of code we would have to write to manipulate strings. The main disadvantage of this is not that it uses functional notation instead of the more familiar infix, but that so much information has to be provided for each primitive operation.

An alternative approach is to represent the data-object in such a way that its representation can be determined by the routine which executes the operation. This also permits the operation to be independent of the particular representation of the data-objects, and it has the advantage of not requiring declarations at all. However, it requires that each routine actually test each argument before carrying out the appropriate operation, which can be quite time-consuming.

OPTIMIZATION OF STRING OPERATIONS

In discussing languages for manipulating strings, we pointed out that a translator can conveniently permit the separation of data description from data manipulation. This also gives the translator information about the program which it can use to produce more efficient code. However, there are many simple examples which require considerable sophistication on the part of the translator if anything like optimum **code** is to result. Consider for example the statements

```
IF (IDENT(CONCAT(I,J), CONCAT(K,L))) GOTO 99
```

This is clearly a perfectly reasonable expression of the programmer's wishes, if not the most concise. A straightforward translation of this code would require the concatenation of the two pairs of strings followed by a loop to test for identity. This is much inferior to the code which could be produced by the human coder, who will use his knowledge of the IDENT and CONCAT operations to produce code which would not do any concatenation at all.

There are a number of solutions to this problem, one or more of which are adopted in the newer languages. The first, of course, is to build the necessary operations into the translator, and then write into the translator the algorithms for optimizing the code. In the above example there would have to be an explicit test for arguments of IDENT being calls on CONCAT. This is a very tedious approach requiring enormous amounts of code in the translator for special cases.

An alternative approach is to permit the programmer to associate with the function name a procedure which is executed before compilation, and which allows examination of the arguments of the function and construction of better code for special cases. This procedure is usually called a *macro*, and allows the programmer to tailor the translator for his own purposes to some extent. We will consider such facilities in more detail in a later chapter in connection with PL/1.

A further possibility is simply to allow selected routines to be translated as in-line code rather than subroutine calls, and then trust to the general optimization techniques of the compiler to remove superfluous code. This can be done by the use of macros also, but any significant improvement will require highly sophisticated optimization facilities in the compiler. However, it is clear that such facilities are feasible, and are beginning to appear in modern compilers.

In xFORTRAN, however, it appears that there is no possibility of constructing a convenient and efficient set of routines for string manipulation. Some improvements can be made by using a preprocessor which allows changes to be made to the program prior to compilation, but the majority of string processing in xFORTRAN will inevitably require the writing of special-purpose routines.

EXERCISES

1. Determine the internal code used for character representation on your computer, the representation of (Hollerith) character-string constants in FORTRAN, and the machine instructions useful for manipulating such strings, if any.
2. Implement a version of ITOSTR for your computer, without using an auxiliary array.
3. Implement a version of MAKINT for your computer which will convert a string of characters of arbitrary length, terminated by a nondigit, and stored one character per word, into a decimal integer.

4. Repeat Exercises 2 and 3 for octal integers.

5. Repeat Exercises 2 and 3 for packed character strings.

6. Implement the lexical scan routine for your computer, but generalized to recognize real numbers consisting of a sequence of digits, a period, and another sequence of digits.

*7. Write a set of routines (P)CHMOVE, CONCAT, IDENT, and INDEX which can manipulate Hollerith constants in FORTRAN.

*8. Implement a simple FORTRAN preprocessor. This should take as its input a FORTRAN subprogram containing statements such as:

$ABCD$ = $XYZ(12,P)$

and replace all occurrences of the string ABCD in the rest of the subprogram by the string XYZ(12,P). The $ signs are used as delimiters for the two strings, which should be permitted to contain any other characters. Note that after a replacement a statement may be eligible for a further replacement, so your program should check for this. Use the routines of Exercise 7 where possible.

*9. Proceed as in Exercise 8, but using the following form of statement to specify replacements:

REPLACE .ABCD. BY .XYZ(12,P).

with the understanding that the first nonblank character after REPLACE will be used as the delimiter character, and any sequence of characters can occur between the second and third delimiters (in this case BY). Note that this permits the result of a replacement to be itself a REPLACE statement, so your preprocessor should be prepared to recognize such situations.

**10. Proceed as in Exercise 9, but extend to permit the following features:
a) the replacing string is permitted to depend on the replaced string
b) the preprocessor is applicable not only to FORTRAN, but to arbitrary data
The design is left to the reader, but it is suggested that the implementation of a) permit statements such as:

REPLACE .ABC($1,$2). BY .$1*$2.
REPLACE .$1*X+$2. BY .DEF($1,$2).

where $1, $2,... are used to indicate the shortest strings containing as many right as left parentheses. Thus the above statements would replace ABC(A,(B+C)) by A*(B+C) and AABB*X+(X−Y) by DEF(AABB,(X−Y)).

6
EVALUATION OF EXPRESSIONS

Before considering in more detail how operations on complex data-structures can be implemented, it is necessary to get some feeling for the pattern of usage of memory in a computation. In order to do this we will consider a very basic aspect of a computation, the mechanism used to evaluate an expression.

We will use the term *expression* to refer to a portion of a computation which calculates a new data-object from old data-objects. This is a very general definition, so general in fact that it can be used to describe the whole of a computation, which can be thought of as a process which produces output which is an expression of the input. However, the evaluation of this expression usually requires the evaluation of a succession of smaller expressions, some of which require the execution of procedures which themselves require the evaluation of expressions, and so on. We will concern ourselves here with complete schemes for expression evaluation that permit efficient use of memory and processor without restricting the expressive power of the evaluation mechanism unduly.

The evaluation mechanism provided by FORTRAN is very simple. The main properties of FORTRAN from this point of view are that the components of an expression can be one-word (or two-word) blocks of memory, and functions whose arguments may be blocks of memory of arbitrary size. Values returned by functions are restricted to one-word (or two-word) blocks, while temporary storage for the calculation of the values of the functions has to be assigned before execution of the program. The major disadvantages of this evaluation scheme are that functions cannot be recursive, they cannot allocate temporary storage as it is required, and they cannot produce a variable-sized result. In fact there are a number of devices for faking these things even in FORTRAN, but they are neither efficient nor elegant.

We will mainly concern ourselves with a simple but efficient evaluation mechanism which is considerably more flexible than that used by FORTRAN. This uses a basic data-structure called a stack. The first major programming language to use such a mechanism was ALGOL, and it has proved so successful that it has been adopted by the majority of programming languages.

STACKS

We have defined a stack as a list which can have insertions and deletions at one end only. This is particularly useful for those processes which need to keep a record of their current situation while they are involved in a subordinate task, so that on completion of the task they can reestablish the situation and continue.

A stack in its simplest form can be implemented in xFORTRAN by a one-dimensional array with an index which indicates the top element. When a new element is added, this index is incremented by one, and the new value put in the corresponding location. The routine

```
SUBROUTINE PUSH(I)
COMMON /STACK/ ITOP,ISTACK(100)
DATA ITOP/0/
ITOP = ITOP + 1
ISTACK(ITOP) = I
RETURN
END
```

can be used to put its argument on the top of the stack, and the routine

```
FUNCTION IPOP(I)
COMMON /STACK/ ITOP, ISTACK(100)
ITOP = ITOP - I
IPOP = ISTACK(ITOP + 1)
RETURN
END
```

removes the top I elements and returns the last element removed as its value.

A third routine can be used to get the value of the I-th element of a stack without removing it:

```
FUNCTION IGET(I)
COMMON /STACK/ ITOP, ISTACK(100)
IGET = ISTACK(ITOP-I+1)
RETURN
END
```

The top element of the stack is referred to as IGET(1). A similar routine can be used to set the I-th element:

```
SUBROUTINE SET(I,LM)
COMMON /STACK/ ITOP, ISTACK(100)
ISTACK(ITOP-I+1) = LM
RETURN
END
```

If a number of push-down stacks are necessary then it is convenient to use the first element of the array as the index, so a stack can be specified by a single name. The routine

```
SUBROUTINE PUSH(LM,ISTACK)
DIMENSION ISTACK(2)
ISTACK(1) = ISTACK(1) + 1
ISTACK(ISTACK(1)) = LM
RETURN
END
```

can then be used to add its first argument to the stack specified by its second argument, and a similar routine

```
FUNCTION IPOP(ISTACK,I)
DIMENSION ISTACK(2)
ISTACK(1) = ISTACK(1) - I
IPOP = ISTACK(ISTACK(1) + 1)
RETURN
END
```

would remove the top I elements.

In the above routines we have assumed that the state of the stack is appropriate for the operation being performed. In some cases it will be necessary to check if the stack is empty before an element is removed, and to check that enough space is available before an element is added.

EVALUATION USING A STACK

A particularly useful application of the stack is to the evaluation of expressions. Consider the expression

$$A + B * C + D$$

We can think of the evaluation process as being composed of the following operations

> load A onto the stack
> load B onto the stack
> load C onto the stack
> remove the top two elements and replace by their product
> remove the top two elements and replace by their sum
> load D onto the stack
> remove the top two elements and replace by their sum

This will leave the value of the expression on the top of the stack. The convenience of this is that the product and sum operations are independent of their arguments. In fact we could have written the above sequence simply as

load A
load B
load C
product
sum
load D
sum

or even more concisely as

$$A \quad B \quad C \ * \ + \ D \ +$$

This latter is known as reverse Polish (or Polish suffix) notation and is, clearly, closely associated with the mechanism of evaluation using a stack. Reverse Polish notation is parenthesis-free as long as each operator has a known number of arguments, so that the expression

$$(A + B) * (-C + D)$$

would be written as

$$A \quad B + C \setminus D + *$$

where we have written $\setminus$ for the negation operator (which is unary—takes one argument) to distinguish it from the subtraction operator (which is binary—takes two arguments).

In practice this evaluation procedure must be modified to give an efficient implementation on most computers. A few computers, such as the English Electric KDF9 and the Burroughs 5000, actually have a stack implemented in hardware, so the machine language is effectively reverse Polish. However, the majority of machines have one or more fast registers in which the result of an operation is put, with the operands coming from either registers or memory locations whose addresses are constant or which have been previously computed.

SINGLE-REGISTER MACHINES

Let us consider first a machine with a single register which we will refer to as R, and an address register which we will refer to as I. Suppose we wish to write code to evaluate the expression

$$(A + B) * (-C + D)$$

and suppose that we are going to use the operations described by the straightforward reverse Polish notation:

$$A \; B + C \setminus D + *$$

where we have used $\setminus$ to indicate a unary negation operator. In fact this is not the only reverse Polish sequence we could use. The sequence

$$A \; B + D \; C - *$$

would also evaluate the expression, and would do so in less operations. However, we will not concern ourselves here with such questions, but with the actual implementation of the reverse Polish sequence.

If we use the register R as the top of the stack, and the address register I to contain the address of the second item in the stack, the following code can be used to evaluate the expression

```
R = A                              }stack A

I = I + 1                          ⎫
MEMORY(I) = R                      ⎬stack B
R = B                              ⎭

R = R + MEMORY(I)                  ⎫sum
I = I - 1                          ⎭

I = I + 1                          ⎫
MEMORY(I) = R                      ⎬stack C
R = C                              ⎭

R = - R                            }negate

I = I + 1                          ⎫
MEMORY(I) = R                      ⎬stack D
R = D                              ⎭

R = R + MEMORY(I)                  ⎫sum
I = I - 1                          ⎭

R = R * MEMORY(I)                  ⎫product
I = I - 1                          ⎭
```

Here each assignment usually corresponds to a single machine instruction. The code is quite inefficient in this form, for essentially two reasons. First, the operations are used to generate code independently of neighboring operations so that, for example, the increment I operation at the end of "sum" is immediately followed by the decrement I operation at the beginning of the "stack C" operation. Secondly, the code does not take into account the fact that an operand does not necessarily have to be on the stack. This is obviously true of the part of the code which calculates A+B, which of course can be done without using any temporary storage at all.

If we make these relatively mechanical adjustments, the code becomes:

```
R = A
R = R + B
I = I + 1
MEMORY(I) = R
R = C
R = -R
R = R + D
R = R * MEMORY(I)
I = I - 1
```

This is much more efficient, requiring nine instructions rather than the seventeen used previously. However, there is still a significant improvement which can be made by noting that there are no jumps in this code, and the only modifications to the value to I are constant increments or decrements. This means that the value of I relative of its initial value is known at all points in the above code, and so this value can be substituted, and the value of I left unchanged. The resulting code is then:

```
R = A
R = R + B
MEMORY(I+1) = R
R = C
R = -R
R = R + D
R = R * MEMORY(I+1)
```

Even if the reference to location I+1 cannot be made in a single instruction, this is still superior in the case of more complex expressions when there is more than one address register available.

A further improvement can be made if the initial value of I is a constant. In this case, all references to addresses of the form I±K, where K is a constant, can actually be replaced by references to fixed locations. The code would then become:

```
R = A
R = R+B
TEMP = R
R = C
R = -R
R = R+D
R = R*TEMP
```

If we had chosen to implement the best reverse Polish form for this expression, namely

$$A \ B + D \ C - *$$

we would have

```
R = A
R = R+B
TEMP = R
R = D
R = R–C
R = R*TEMP
```

which is in fact the optimum code for a single-register machine. In this particular example only one temporary-storage location is required, but the same techniques can be used for more complicated expressions requiring many temporaries. For example, the expression

$$(A * B + C * D) * (E * F + G * H)$$

requires two temporary locations, and could be translated as

```
R = A
R = R*B
TEMP1 = R
R = C
R = R*D
R = R+TEMP1
TEMP1 = R
R = E
R = R*F
TEMP2 = R
R = G
R = R*H
R = R+TEMP2
R = R*TEMP1
```

Note that the code reuses the same temporary when its value is no longer required, a general feature of evaluation using a stack.

MULTIPLE-REGISTER MACHINES

When there are a number of registers available, it is convenient to implement an evaluation stack so that it uses registers in preference to memory for temporaries. In such machines most operations are between registers, while memory references are simple loads or stores. Accordingly, the code to evaluate the expression given above would be

```
R1 = A
R2 = B
R1 = R1*R2
R2 = C
R3 = D
R2 = R2*R3
R1 = R1+R2
R2 = E
R3 = F
R2 = R2*R3
R3 = G
R4 = H
R3 = R3*R4
R2 = R2+R3
R1 = R1*R2
```

This uses four registers R1, R2, R3, and R4, and no memory. If more registers were required to evaluate the expression than were available, some temporary results would have to be stored away. A reasonable choice is the first stack register, since this will be required after the others. For example, if the above expressions were to be evaluated using only three registers, the instructions

```
R4 = H
R3 = R3*R4
R2 = R2+R3
```

could be replaced by

```
TEMP1 = R1
R1 = H
R3 = R3*R1
R2 = R2+R3
R1 = TEMP1
```

Note that the value of R1 is stored just prior to its use, rather than just after it becomes free, because in the general case it might be required again as a temporary.

The structure of the stack in the latter case thus consists of sequential memory locations together with a variable number of registers which are used as the top elements of the stack. The register used as the top of the stack changes as items are added to or removed from the stack. This is conveniently illustrated as a ring of registers, one marked as the top of the stack and one marked as the bottom of the stack. The registers between the top and the bottom of the stack are in use, while the others

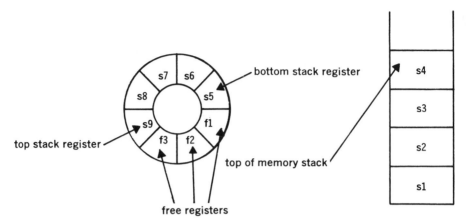

Figure 6.1

are free. With eight registers this appears as shown in Figure 6.1. Here the memory stack contains four entries, $s1$ to $s4$, and registers contain the top five entries, $s5$ to $s9$, with $s9$ being currently the top of the stack. There are three free registers $f1$ to $f3$. If the next operation requires a new register, the one next to the top of the stack, namely $f3$, will be used. If subsequent operations use $f3$, $f2$ and $f1$, and a further register is required, $s5$ would be moved into memory, and its register used. On the other hand, if subsequent operations remove items from the stack to the point that $s5$ is the top, and a binary operation is to be performed, then $s4$ must be brought into a register. The register which will be used is, of course, $f1$, so that prior to the operation the diagram will be as shown in Figure 6.2. After the binary operation $s4$ would be the top of the stack and the register which contained $s5$ would be free.

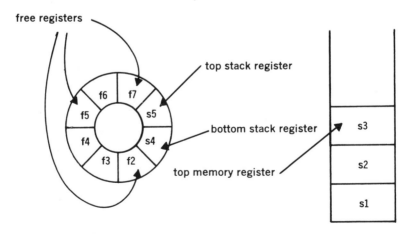

Figure 6.2

Of course, this use of registers is restrictive, in that it is not possible to save values for later use, nor is it possible to refer to a value which is not at the top of the stack. In practice this means that programmers and compilers abandon the strict stack when evaluating ordinary arithmetic or logical expressions. However, the simplicity of stack evaluation makes it a useful model, particularly when the time to execute an operation is long compared with the stack manipulation time.

LOCAL VARIABLES AND ASSIGNMENT

Most nontrivial functions are evaluated more efficiently if they permit assignments to local variables. Such operations are not simple stack operations, since they require that values which have been computed be removed from the stack to be stored elsewhere. It is not sufficient to allow such a value to remain on the stack, because subsequent assignment to the same variable will then leave both values on the stack, an unnecessary waste of space. Accordingly, it is necessary to supplement the "pure" stack evaluation procedure if we wish to permit the assignment operation.

We have already discussed one method of allocating space for variables, that used by FORTRAN. This method, which allocates fixed space prior to execution, is both inefficient and inflexible, as well as prohibiting convenient implementation of recursive functions. The other extreme is to use elaborate storage allocation procedures which will be described in more detail in a later chapter and which are very flexible, but also very time-consuming. The stack permits an intermediate mechanism which is relatively flexible and quite efficient, and which is used in the majority of modern programming languages, including ALGOL and PL/1.

The method used is to allocate space on the stack for local variables on entry to the function, and to release this space when the function terminates. This type of allocation is fast, and permits the amount of space allocated to a local variable to be calculated on entry to the function, thus allowing arrays with variable dimensions. This permits much more efficient use of memory than the FORTRAN type of allocation, not only because exactly the right amount of memory can be allocated, but also because there is no memory at all allocated for functions which are not being executed. As we will see later, it also permits simple implementation of recursive functions.

If a function is regarded as simply a generalization of the stack operations discussed above, we can see that a convenient way to implement a function is a portion of code which expects its arguments to be on the top of the stack, and which replaces them with its result. With this type of implementation, the stack usage can be illustrated by Figure 6.3. That is, on entry to the function, the arguments are on the top of the stack. The function then allocates space for local variables above this, using the values of arguments if necessary. Then the stack can be used in the standard way for the evaluation of expressions within the function, with assignments to local variables permitted in a straightforward way. When the function terminates the stack is collapsed, releasing the space occupied by local variables and arguments, and the result of the function replaces the arguments on the stack. Of course, the function can itself call other functions using precisely the same mechanism.

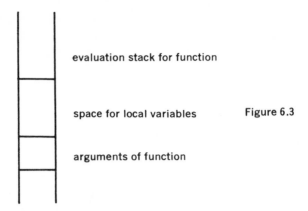

evaluation stack for function

space for local variables   Figure 6.3

arguments of function

FUNCTIONAL AND NONFUNCTIONAL EVALUATION

In fact this distinction between evaluation procedures which can be implemented purely with a stack, and those which cannot, is a very useful one. The first can be called "functional" languages, and include languages such as "pure" LISP, GPM, and TRAC, as well as a number of theoretical computational schemes such as the "lambda-calculus" and certain devices for defining "computable" or "recursive" functions. The second includes most existing programming languages, for which the assignment operation is usually considered a fundamental component. It appears that the functional languages are easier to analyze, so most theoretical work concerned with computability, or which requires the manipulation of the program itself, uses a language which does not provide assignment.

Stack evaluation as we have considered it so far is not complete, in the sense that there are expressions which cannot be computed by it. In order for it to become complete, we have to add some mechanism for allowing the current values on the stack to affect the operations executed. This can be done in a number of ways, but the most convenient is what is called a *conditional expression*. Many programming languages provide such a facility in the form

IF x THEN y ELSE z

This is an expression which is evaluated by first evaluating x, and if the result of this is "true," then evaluating y and giving this as the value of the expression; otherwise z is evaluated and taken to be the value of the expression.

A conditional expression can clearly be evaluated using a stack. The above can be implemented as:

> stack the value of x
> if the top of the stack is not "true," go to *L1*
> remove the top of the stack
> stack the value of y
> go to *L2*

L1   remove the top of the stack
stack the value of z
L2   ...

In some cases this requires a little extra care when being coded. For instance, if the stack is actually implemented as a revolving set of registers and a memory stack, then it is necessary to ensure that the registers used for the stack prior to a jump are the ones that are used for the stack at the destination. Because the stack may have been used to calculate an expression which resulted in the register and stack alignment being modified, it may be necessary to adjust the stack prior to jumps and labels. An easy way of doing this is to "normalize" the stack by simply storing the contents of the stack registers in the memory stack. This can of course be improved by more sophisticated techniques.

VARIABLE NUMBERS OF ARGUMENTS

The stack mechanism also provides a very convenient method for implementing a function which can be given an arbitrary number of arguments. All that is necessary is to establish some convention to permit the function to determine each time it is invoked how many arguments there are. A simple way of doing this is to put on the stack last the number of arguments.

A routine to square and add a variable number of arguments (with the last argument being the number of such arguments) could be written as follows

```
      SUBROUTINE SQADD
      N = IPOP(1)
      S = 0.0
      DO 1 I=1,N
      V = IPOP(1)
    1 S = S + V*V
      CALL PUSH(S)
      RETURN
      END
```

BLOCK-VALUED FUNCTIONS

There is a straightforward generalization of the reverse Polish type of evaluation described above to the case of data-objects which require more than one or two words of memory if these are of predictable size. In this case a function can expect its arguments on the stack, and determine the positions of all arguments just from the stack pointer. A trivial calculation can then determine the new value of the stack pointer, and the result of the function can be put on the stack replacing the arguments. If the programmer is concerned with execution speed rather than convenience, he can calculate the stack assignments in a similar way to that used for simple arithmetic expression evaluation, transmitting to the function the addresses of the arguments and the required location of the result. In a similar way, if the language translator can determine the size of arguments and results, it too can make stack assignments prior to execution, thus giving more efficient code.

VARIABLE-LENGTH BLOCKS

If expressions are permitted to contain data-objects represented by blocks of memory whose size cannot be determined prior to execution, then it is necessary that each variable-length data-object be represented in such a way that a function can determine its current size. This requires that a function which produces a variable-length result also should specify its size in some way. If a stack is to be used, this is conveniently done by storing the length on the stack together with the result.

There are two main differences between the use of a stack for variable-length blocks and the schemes discussed above for fixed-length blocks. The first is that a function cannot determine where its arguments are simply from the stack pointer, which we assume points to the first free stack location. If each argument carries its length last rather than first, however, the function can trace back down the stack using the length to find the start of the last argument, and hence the end of the next-to-last argument, and so on. An alternative scheme which allows the length to be put first specifies the top of the stack as being the start of the first argument, so the tracing can be done in the more natural direction.

The second difference is that with variable-length blocks on the stack it is no longer possible to assign stack locations prior to execution. This means that a stack pointer must be maintained in a register, and its value modified when stack operations are done.

MULTIPLE-VALUED FUNCTIONS

An interesting generalization of the scheme for handling functions which return blocks as their values can be used to permit functions which are multiple valued. That is, we can implement functions which not only take a variable number of arguments, but also return a variable number of results. Thus in an expression like

A + FFF(X, MMM(X,Y), Z)

the multiple-valued function MMM could return, say, three values on the stack in such a way that the function FFF would receive five arguments rather than the normal three.

To give an example of a function which receives and returns multiple values, consider the problem of removing duplicate values from a list of numbers. We will suppose that the last member of the list gives the number of values initially, and is reset on exit from the function. We could write this as a subroutine as follows:

```
SUBROUTINE KOMPRESS
COMMON /STACK/ ITOP, ISTACK(100)
N = ISTACK(ITOP)
M = 0
I = ITOP - N - 1
NM1 = N - 1
DO 1 J=1,NM1
JP1 = J + 1
DO 2 K=JP1,N
IF (ISTACK(I+J).NE.ISTACK(I+K)) GOTO 2
M = M+1
GOTO 1
2 CONTINUE
ISTACK(I+J-M) = ISTACK(I+J)
1 CONTINUE
ISTACK(I+N-M) = ISTACK(I+N)
ISTACK(I+N-M+1) = N - M
ITOP = ITOP - M
RETURN
END
```

This routine removes all but the last occurrence of duplicated numbers.

RECURSIVE ROUTINES

In a number of applications it is very convenient to be able to invoke a function or procedure within the code which defines it. At first sight this may appear to give a circular definition which will execute indefinitely. However, by ensuring that for some values of the arguments the function does not invoke itself, this circularity can be avoided. The function will keep calling itself until the arguments have these values, when it will exit without calling itself, thus terminating the chain of calls. Such routines are called *recursive*. In advanced programming projects we will find that such routines are very useful.

A standard example of a recursive routine is the factorial function defined as follows.

$$f(i) = \begin{cases} 1 & \text{if } i = 0; \\ i \cdot f(i - 1) & \text{otherwise.} \end{cases}$$

Recursive routines are illegal in FORTRAN, but if not we could implement this as follows:

```
  FUNCTION IFACT(I)
  IF (I.EQ.0) GOTO 1
  IFACT = IFACT(I-1) * I
  RETURN
1 IFACT = 1
  RETURN
  END
```

In some compilers this will be detected as a syntactic error, but even if it is not, it will not work for the following reasons. Recall that this function will be compiled so that each variable and temporary will be allocated fixed locations in memory, so we can trace the execution by looking at the values of these. If the original call of IFACT is of the form IFACT(3), then successive values of the argument of IFACT and the temporary location used to store the value of (I-1) are:

$$
\begin{array}{cc}
I = 3 & (I - 1) = 2 \\
2 & 1 \\
1 & 0 \\
0 &
\end{array}
$$

At this point the recursion will terminate, returning the value of 1 as the value of the IFACT function call in

```
  IFACT(I-1) * I
```

However, when we look up the value of I to multiply, we are actually referencing the memory location used to store the quantity (I-1) in the previous call of IFACT. Unfortunately this location still contains the value 0, rather than the intended value of 1. This is a particular case of the general problem of implementing recursive routines, namely, that a recursive call can change the values of local variables and temporaries, and illustrates why recursion is not permitted in FORTRAN.

The factorial function can be implemented much more efficiently by a simple loop. However, there do exist functions which cannot be implemented in this way. The most famous of these is Ackermann's function defined as follows:

$$
\begin{aligned}
f(i, j) &= j + 1 & &\text{if } i = 0 \\
&= f(i - 1, 1) & &\text{if } j = 0 \\
&= f(i - 1, f(i, j - 1)) & &\text{otherwise.}
\end{aligned}
$$

When defined in this way, it is apparent that there is a simple recursive implementation, and it can be shown that the amount of memory required to evaluate this function with arbitrary arguments is unbounded.

From our point of view, the important thing about recursive routines is not really that a wider class of functions can be implemented, because we can always fake the necessary mechanism, even in FORTRAN. The ability to write recursive routines does not actually increase the amount of memory available, so in fact no gain in theoretical computational power is made. However, there is a substantial gain in the descriptive power of the language if recursion is permitted.

In a later chapter we will consider the use of recursion to simplify a number of algorithms, using PL/1 as the programming language. All the languages that we will be discussing in later chapters will permit recursion. In the next section we will show how a stack can be used to implement recursive routines. In particular, we will consider methods of faking recursions in XFORTRAN, an interesting but frustrating problem.

IMPLEMENTATION OF RECURSIVE ROUTINES

As we have seen, the general problem of implementing recursive routines is that a second call of a routine before the first one has been completed may change the values of critical variables. This requires that these variables must be allocated distinct parts of memory for each invocation of the routine. That is, on entry to the routine, memory for such variables must be allocated so as not to conflict with that allocated for those variables in previous invocations. On exit from the routine, these variables are no longer required, so their memory can be released. This release is clearly done in the reverse order from the allocation, and so is conveniently implemented by a stack.

The standard way of doing this is to allocate memory for local variables on entry to a recursive routine on top of the stack, and release this space on exit. This fits neatly into the other uses of the stack which we have mentioned above. In fact, in a language such as ALGOL 60 which permits dynamic allocation of variable-sized local variables on a stack simply to save memory, the provision of recursive routines requires little extra mechanism. Certain quantities which are not explicitly defined as local variables, however, such as the return address of the function and the temporary locations used for saving information about the arguments, must also be stacked; but this provides no particular problems.

Let us consider in some detail how we might implement the factorial function recursively. In order to illustrate the technique using XFORTRAN we will have to stick closely to the attitude that we stressed above, namely, that the XFORTRAN code should be thought of simply as a shorthand form of machine language. We will permit ourselves only those forms of statement which do not imply the XFORTRAN evaluation mechanism, excluding, for instance, the CALL statement, which itself assumes a non-recursive implementation.

The code given below can be used as a recursive function. It assumes a stack specified in the usual way as

```
COMMON /STACK/ ITOP, ISTACK(100)
```

and assumes that on transferring to statement 100 the top of the stack contains the return address, and the item below the top of the stack is the argument; that is, the routine is invoked by the code:

```
      ITOP = ITOP + 1
      ISTACK(ITOP) = I
      ASSIGN 20 TO IRET
      ITOP = ITOP + 1
      ISTACK(ITOP) = IRET
      GOTO 100
   20 IRES = ISTACK(ITOP)
      ITOP = ITOP - 1
```

The routine returns to statement 20 with the top of the stack containing the result, which is removed and assigned to the variable IRES. The code is actually written as follows.

```
  100 IF (ISTACK(ITOP-1).EQ.1) GOTO 103
      ISTACK(ITOP+1) = ISTACK(ITOP-1) - 1
      ITOP = ITOP + 1
      ASSIGN 102 TO KRET
      ITOP = ITOP + 1
      ISTACK(ITOP) = KRET
      GOTO 100
  102 ISTACK(ITOP-2) = ISTACK(ITOP-2) * ISTACK(ITOP)
      ITOP = ITOP - 1
  103 KRET = ISTACK(ITOP)
      ITOP = ITOP - 1
      GOTO KRET
```

The recursive call is actually made in the statement GOTO 100. The use of the variable KRET is not significant, but is necessary because FORTRAN does not permit things like

```
      ASSIGN 102 TO ISTACK(ITOP)
```

The standard calling sequence for this function can be used if the above code is embedded in a function of the following form.

```
      FUNCTION IFACT(I)
      COMMON /STACK/ ITOP, ISTACK(100)
      ITOP = ITOP + 1
      ISTACK(ITOP) = I
      ASSIGN 20 TO KRET
      ITOP = ITOP + 1
      ISTACK(ITOP) = KRET
```

```
100 IF....
    ...
    ...
    GOTO KRET
 20 IFACT = ISTACK(ITOP)
    ITOP = ITOP - 1
    RETURN
    END
```

This will permit invocations of the usual form IFACT(IJK).

Note that with the appropriate stack operations defined, this code can be compressed somewhat to give:

```
    FUNCTION IFACT(I)
    CALL PUSH(I)
    ASSIGN 20 TO KRET
    CALL PUSH(KRET)
100 IF (IGET(2).EQ.1) GOTO 103
    CALL PUSH(IGET(2)-1)
    ASSIGN 102 TO KRET
    CALL PUSH(KRET)
    GOTO 100
102 CALL SET(2,IPOP(1)*IGET(2))
103 KRET = IPOP(1)
    GOTO KRET
 20 IFACT = IPOP(1)
    RETURN
    END
```

REENTRANT CODING

In some programming situations, in particular those associated with real-world events which can occur at undetermined times, it is useful to be able to write code which can be used by several routines simultaneously. A simple case of this is in an operating system for a large computer in which there is more than one processor with access to the memory, when it is convenient for all processors to be able to execute the same code without interfering with each other. The main requirement for this is that the code not modify itself, and that any memory that it writes into be referenced via registers which are duplicated in each process. This type of coding is called *reentrant coding*. In some cases special hardware is provided so that all data references to memory use a built-in relocation register which can be set differently in each processor, but this is not strictly necessary. Most conventional machines can be programmed reentrantly, with a small loss of efficiency.

Reentrant coding is also useful when there is only a single processor, between two jobs which use the same code, or when being used in connection with time-dependent peripheral devices such as a disk or a teletype. In the latter case it is convenient for a peripheral device to be able to signal the processor that it requires servicing by interrupting the processor and executing a transfer to a piece of code which can do the servicing. While this code is executing, a further interrupt may occur which will require the reinitiation of the interrupt servicing code, but with different initial conditions. The interrupt servicing routine should be written in reentrant code. It is clear that this could present a severe problem without appropriate hardware provisions. This often takes the form of an interrupt procedure which saves all register contents before the transfer is executed, so that on completion of the interrupt service the original program can be resumed. Alternatively the interrupt causes all subsequent interrupts to be inhibited or delayed until reenabled by the interrupt service routine after it has saved its register contents. In this latter case the code is reentrant at specified locations (those points which immediately save register contents), and only when it is prepared (after it has saved register contents).

It is not possible to write reentrant code in FORTRAN for a number of reasons, the most important one being that the standard method of compilation of a subprogram allocates local and temporary storage at fixed memory locations. Even if the code is restricted to be reentered at specified times and locations it is almost impossible for the programmer to save temporary locations. Some compilers even use self-modifying code to handle parameters, which is obviously not permissible. In some cases, however, it is possible to implement a restricted form of reentrant code by making all temporary variables arguments of a routine, always entering it in the normal way, and using an assigned GOTO as the first statement.

For example, the following code can be made to work for some compilers. It consists of a main program which executes in rotation 20 versions of the subroutine PROCESS, each of which may at times issue a call to WAIT, which returns to the main loop after storing a resumption point in M (actually TABLE(3,I) for PROCESS number I). The next time process I is entered it will take the assigned GOTO to resume at the statement after WAIT, as though there had been a normal return from WAIT.

```
      PROGRAM MAIN
      DIMENSION TABLE(3,20)
      DATA TABLE /60 * 0/
      COMMON /IRET/ IRET
      ASSIGN 1 TO IRET
    2 DO 1 I=1,20
      CALL PROCESS(TABLE(1,I), TABLE(3,I))
    1 CONTINUE
      CALL RELCP
      GOTO 2
      END
```

```
SUBROUTINE PROCESS(L,M)
DIMENSION L(2)
IF (M.NE.0) GOTO M
...
...
CALL WAIT(M)
...
...
END
```

The routine RELCP is not specified, but in a multiprogramming environment would typically give up the processor for a short period. The subroutine WAIT will have to be written in machine language and is left as an exercise for the reader. It does the following:

1. Saves its return address in the form of an assigned GOTO in its argument;
2. Jumps to the location in the main loop specified in the COMMON variable IRET.

Note that local variables of PROCESS which are saved during a call to WAIT are limited to those in the array L. Any others can be destroyed by other calls of PROCESS during a WAIT.

The above routines, being not only machine dependent but compiler dependent, represent the worst kind of programming practice, but are nevertheless interesting. It is a fairly challenging problem to extend the scheme so that a routine called by PROCESS can also issue a WAIT.

COROUTINES

Two other unorthodox uses of routine linkages are interesting in this connection. The first is referred to as a *coroutine linkage*, and occurs when two routines appear to call each other as subroutines. Neither uses a RETURN statement in the normal way, but a call of one routine by the second appears to the first as a return. It is as if we could write:

```
SUBROUTINE A              SUBROUTINE B
...                       ...
...                       ...
CALL B                    CALL A
...                       ...
...                       ...
END                       END
```

where the CALL A statement in B will return to A just after the CALL B statement.

This can easily be implemented in FORTRAN by an assigned GOTO:

```
      SUBROUTINE A                    SUBROUTINE B
      COMMON /AB/ IRESA,IRESB         COMMON /AB/ IRESA,IRESB
      . . .                           . . .
      . . .                           . . .
      ASSIGN 1 TO IRESA               ASSIGN 1 TO IRESB
      GOTO IRESB                      GOTO IRESA
    1 CONTINUE                      1 CONTINUE
      . . .                           . . .
      . . .                           . . .
      END                             END
```

The reader is invited to consider the routine COCALL such that:

```
      SUBROUTINE A                    SUBROUTINE B
      COMMON /AB/ IRES                COMMON /AB/ IRES
      . . .                           . . .
      . . .                           . . .
      CALL COCALL(IRES)               CALL COCALL(IRES)
      . . .                           . . .
      . . .                           . . .
      END                             END
```

will have the same effect as above.

Another unusual linkage which can be used in FORTRAN, and which was brought to the author's attention by James Cooke, is for a routine A which has been called by routine B to call routine B itself. This is perfectly legitimate if routine B does not execute a RETURN statement. A typical use of this is when B is a high-level control routine which is to be invoked by A when unusual circumstances arise. Note that B can have arguments in the usual way. This takes advantage of an XFORTRAN feature which is usually regarded as a deficiency, namely the static allocation of storage. It would not work in ALGOL, for instance.

EXERCISES

1. Implement a routine to compute Ackermann's function.
2. Write a set of routines which will enable recursive routines to be implemented conveniently for your FORTRAN compiler.
*3. Write a set of subroutines to implement stack operations on variable-length character strings. The following routines are suggested:

CALL LOAD(S)   load the string in array S onto stack

CALL STORE(S)   store the string on the top of the stack into the array S

`CALL CONCAT`	concatenate the two strings on the top of the stack
`CALL SUBSTR(I,N)`	extract the N-character substring starting at character I
`CALL SETSUB(I)`	change the characters starting at the I-th character of the first string to the second string
`CALL SPLIT(I)`	split the string into two after the I-th character
`CALL SEARCH(I)`	search the first string for the second string, and set I to the position of the first character if found, and zero otherwise
`CALL INSERT(I)`	insert the second string in the first after the I-th character
`CALL IDENT(L)`	set the logical variable L to true if the two strings are identical, and to false otherwise

**4. Implement a complete package of routines for character-string manipulation, including those of Exercise 3, I/O operations, conversion operations, allocation for variable-length local variables, and any other routines thought appropriate.

**5. Implement a package of routines similar to that of Exercise 4, but to manipulate variable-size vectors and matrices.

7
STORAGE ALLOCATION

In this chapter we will consider in more detail the problem of storage allocation referred to previously. In general any program which deals with data-structures which can vary in size during the execution of the program has to have some mechanism for managing the allocation of memory. The general solution is to have a set of bookkeeping routines which can supervise the use of a large block of memory, allocating a portion when requested, and keeping track of those portions which are no longer required by the program. The type of bookkeeping information depends on the pattern of use of the memory by the program, and can be considerably simplified in the case of certain types of program.

One such simple type of use has already been illustrated in the chapter on evaluation of expressions, but it is convenient to review it in this other light.

STACK ALLOCATION

This form of storage allocation can be used when blocks are freed in precisely the reverse order from that in which they were allocated. Blocks can then simply be allocated in order starting at one end of an array, and the only information that need be kept is the index of the first unused location. When a block of length N is allocated, this index will be incremented by N; when a block of length N is released, the index will be decremented by N. We refer to this type of allocation as stack allocation.

A set of functions to do this simple allocation can be written as follows.

```
FUNCTION MAKBLOK(N)
COMMON /SPACE/ MAXSP, NEXTSP, ISPACE(5000)
DATA(NEXTSP=1)
MAKBLOK = NEXTSP
NEXTSP = NEXTSP + N
IF (NEXTSP .LE. MAXSP) RETURN
CALL FULLUP
END
```

```
SUBROUTINE RELEASE(N)
COMMON /SPACE/ MAXSP, NEXTSP, ISPACE(5000)
NEXTSP = NEXTSP - N
RETURN
END
```

The routine FULLUP is called when space is exhausted, and will presumably print out an error message, and then exit.

FIXED SIZE BLOCK ALLOCATION

Another situation in which there is a straightforward solution is that in which all blocks are of the same size. This can be handled in the following way. At initialization the array which is to be used for block storage, which we will refer to as ISPACE, is split into blocks of the appropriate size. In the first word of each block is inserted a pointer to the first word of the following block with the first word of the last block being set to zero. A variable NEXTSP is then set to contain a pointer to the first word of the first block. Initially, then, all the free blocks of the appropriate size are chained together by pointers with the first block being indicated by the pointer contained in the variable NEXTSP. When a block is requested, all that it is necessary to do is to provide the contents of NEXTSP as the pointer to a free block and to reset NEXTSP to contain the pointer to the next free block in the chain. When a block is released it is added to the beginning of the chain of free blocks by setting its first word to contain the pointer currently in NEXTSP and setting NEXTSP to point to the block just released. During the course of the computation, it is not necessary that blocks be released in any particular order, so the free space chain will not necessarily specify the free blocks in the order in which they occur in memory. This storage allocation procedure is fast and efficient and can be programmed as follows.

```
SUBROUTINE SETUP(N)
COMMON /SPACE/ MAXSP, NEXTSP, ISPACE(5000)
DO 1 I=1,MAXSP,N
J = I
1 ISPACE(J) = J + N
ISPACE(J) = 0
NEXTSP = 1
RETURN
END

FUNCTION MAKBLOK(DUMMY)
COMMON /SPACE/ MAXSP, NEXTSP, ISPACE(5000)
IF (NEXTSP.EQ.0) GOTO 1
MAKBLOK = NEXTSP
NEXTSP = ISPACE(NEXTSP)
RETURN
1 CALL FULLUP
END
```

```
SUBROUTINE RELEASE (IPOINT)
COMMON /SPACE/ MAXSP, NEXTSP, ISPACE(5000)
ISPACE(NEXTSP) = NEXTSP
NEXTSP = IPOINT
RETURN
END
```

The routine **SETUP** is used to initialize the free space chained into blocks of the required length, while the routines **MAKBLOK** and **RELEASE** are used to allocate and release blocks.

An alternative form of implementation does not use a **SETUP** operation, but does stack allocation until memory is exhausted, and then changes to chained allocation.

MOVABLE BLOCKS

In the general case when blocks of different sizes are requested and released in an unpredictable order, the storage allocation problem is much more difficult. It can be considerably simplified if the blocks can be moved around by the storage allocator. This requires that the allocator have knowledge of all the places in a program from which the block is referenced, since all such references must be modified when the allocator moves a block.

A simple way of doing this is for the storage allocator to provide a pointer not to the block itself but to a word containing a pointer to the block. The allocator can then keep track of all these words, and merely modify the contents when a block is moved. This technique prohibits the programmer from writing code which assumes that blocks are stationary, and means that many references to the block have to be indirect.

We give below a set of routines for doing allocation and release of movable blocks of arbitrary size. Allocation is done in stack fashion, and a linked list is constructed at the end of available memory to keep track of those blocks which have been allocated. The data-word in this linked list is used to contain the starting address of the block, and the address of this word is delivered to the routine making the storage request. When a block is released, this word is flagged, in this case by changing the sign of the address of the block. When storage is exhausted, a compacting routine is called to move all those blocks still in use down toward the beginning of memory. List entries corresponding to released blocks are removed and linked for reuse.

The memory structure used is illustrated in Figure 7.1. A routine such as the following can be used to set up this structure initially.

```
SUBROUTINE SETUP
COMMON /BLOCKS/ BEGIN, MAX, FIRST, LAST, AVAIL
COMMON /SPACE/ SP(10000)
INTEGER BEGIN, FIRST, AVAIL
BEGIN = LOCF(SP(1))
MAX = BEGIN + 9999 - 6
```

```
FIRST = MAX + 5
LAST = FIRST - 2
MEMORY(FIRST) = LAST
MEMORY(LAST) = 0
MEMORY(LAST+1) = BEGIN
AVAIL = 0
RETURN
END
```

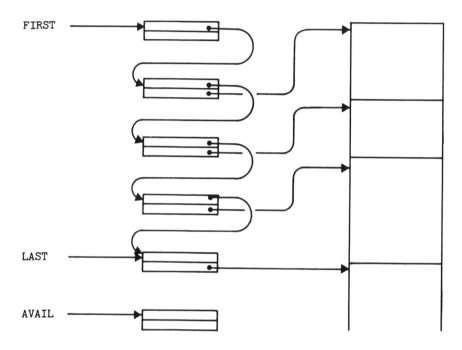

FIRST

LAST

AVAIL

Figure 7.1

Here we have assumed that the pseudo-array **MEMORY** is handled by the compiler to allow the convenient use of addresses. Any of the other schemes mentioned in the previous chapter could be used also. Note that the above routine takes 4 words from the top of the available space to initialize the block list, and 2 to be ready to be used for the next cell. **AVAIL** will be used to point to a list of free 2-word cells which can be used for new entries on the block list.

Allocation of a new block is done by the function **MAKBLOK**, written as follows.

```
FUNCTION MAKBLOK(N)
COMMON /BLOCKS/ BEGIN, MAX, FIRST, LAST, AVAIL
INTEGER BEGIN, FIRST, AVAIL
```

```
       NEXT = MEMORY(LAST+1)              get address of next available block
       MAKBLOK = LAST + 1
       IF (NEXT+N.LE.MAX) GOTO 1          test for enough space left
       CALL COMPACT                       if not, call compacting routine
       NEXT = MEMORY(LAST+1)              then test again
       IF (NEXT+N.LE.MAX) GOTO 1
       CALL PANIC                         if still not enough, call emergency
                                          routine
       NEXT = MEMORY(LAST+1)              test again
       IF (NEXT+N.GT.MAX) CALL ABORT      if still not enough, cannot proceed
     1 NEXT = NEXT + N                    get here if enough space
       IF (AVAIL.NE.0) GOTO 2             test for available cell
       MAX = MAX - 2                      if none, get space from upper
       AVAIL = MAX + 1                    memory and add to front of avail
                                          list
       MEMORY(AVAIL) = 0
     2 MEMORY(LAST) = AVAIL               add new cell to end of block list
       LAST = AVAIL                       reset last
       MEMORY(LAST+1) = NEXT              insert new value of next
       AVAIL = MEMORY(AVAIL)              reset avail to following cell
       RETURN                             return
       END
```

This will call an **ABORT** routine if there is still no space after the **COMPACT** routine and a **PANIC** routine have been used.

The **RELEASE** routine is trivial. All it does is change the sign of the address of the released block:

```
       SUBROUTINE RELEASE(L)
       MEMORY(L) = -MEMORY(L)
       RETURN
       END
```

This block will then be regarded as free by the **COMPACT** routine and the cell will be removed from the block list.

The **COMPACT** routine is the most complex, but is still relatively straightforward. It can be written as follows.

```
       SUBROUTINE COMPACT
       COMMON /BLOCKS/ BEGIN,MAX,FIRST,LAST,AVAIL
       INTEGER BEGIN,FIRST,AVAIL,PREV,THIS,FOLL
       NEXT = BEGIN                       set up for compacting loop
       PREV = FIRST
       THIS = MEMORY(PREV)
       L = MEMORY(THIS+1)
```

```
4 IF (THIS.NE.LAST) GOTO 5            check for last
  MEMORY(THIS+1) = NEXT               if it is, reset new next
  RETURN                              return
5 FOLL = MEMORY(THIS)
  L = MEMORY(THIS+1)
  IF (L.LT.0) GOTO 1
  MEMORY(PREV) = FOLL                 if this block is released, remove
                                      from list
  MEMORY(THIS) = AVAIL                and add cell to avail list
  AVAIL = THIS
  THIS = FOLL
  GOTO 4                              and look at next block
1 LL = MEMORY(FOLL+1)                 otherwise compact block
  LENGTH = LL - L
  IF (LL.LT.0) LENGTH = -LL-L
  DO 3 I=1,LENGTH
3 MEMORY(NEXT+I-1) = MEMORY(L+I-1)
  MEMORY(THIS+1) = NEXT               reset next
  NEXT = NEXT + LENGTH
2 PREV = THIS                         look at next block
  THIS = FOLL
  GOTO 4
  END
```

In the main loop, which starts at statement **4**, the variable **NEXT** contains the address of the next available memory location. The variable **THIS** contains a pointer to the cell associated with the block being processed, while the variable **PREV** contains a pointer to the previous cell, and **FOLL** is used to contain a pointer to the following cell. L is the starting address, possibly negated, of the block being processed, while LL is the starting address of the following block, also possibly negated. The difference is used to calculate the length of the block.

FIXED BLOCKS

If it is not possible for the storage allocator to move blocks, then it is inevitable that in the general case memory becomes broken into a number of available and unavailable areas. It is the responsibility of the storage allocation procedures to maintain bookkeeping information about the availability of memory in such a way that the time to allocate and release a block is minimized.

The choice of algorithms for allocation is quite wide, and there is none that is clearly best. An important problem is the fragmentation of memory, which arises when there is enough memory available for a requested block, but it is available only in the fórm of two or more blocks which are not adjacent. In order to minimize this problem it is necessary to give very careful consideration to the allocation of each block. This requires as much information as possible about the availability of memory to be accessible to the allocation routines. In particular, when a block is released, there may be neighboring available blocks, in which case it is usually best to update the bookkeeping information to reflect the fact that there is one available block rather than two, or three if both neighboring blocks are available.

In some cases it may very well be that there is a pattern in the order in which blocks of various sizes are requested and released. In the algorithms described below we will assume there is no such pattern.

RELEASE AND CONSOLIDATION

The efficient consolidation of a released block with neighboring available blocks requires that it be easy to locate the specifications of the neighboring blocks of a particular block. One way of doing this, used by Paul Abrahams for storage allocation in a PL/1 compiler, is to maintain a two-way linked list of all blocks, both used and available, in order of their occurrence in memory. When a block is released, its neighbors can be located from these pointers. A convenient way of doing this is to use the first word of each block to contain pointers to the first word of the previous and the next block in memory, as shown in Figure 7.2. If the first word also contains information

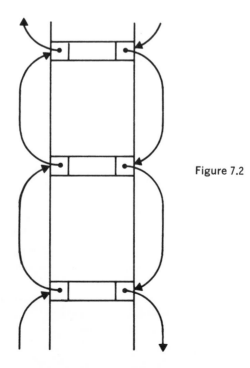

Figure 7.2

about whether the block is used or available, these tests are quickly done. Consolidation of two blocks simply requires that the first word of the first block be changed so that its "next" pointer points to the block "next" to the second, and the first word of that block be changed so that its "previous" pointer points to the first block.

An alternative scheme suggested by Knuth for doing the consolidation uses the beginning and end of each block. Both used and available blocks contain a used/available flag at the beginning and end, and the block length at the beginning. In addition, available blocks contain the block length at the end. When a block B is to be released, the first word of the following block F can be located using the length of block B, and its used/available flag examined. If it is also free, consolidation can be done by changing the length of block B to the sum of blocks B and F, and storing it at the beginning and end of the new block B. The end of the block P just previous to block B can be examined to determine if block P is available. If it is, its length is also stored at its end, which enables its beginning to be located, and consolidation done in a similar way. The advantage of this scheme is that the length of the block is often useful information to have at the beginning of a block for other purposes, but its disadvantage is that a bit at the end of a used block must be reserved for the used/available flag, and this sometimes means that a whole word is wasted.

A combination of the two schemes has much to recommend it. The beginning of each block can contain a used/available flag, the length of the block, and a pointer to the beginning of the previous block. Neighboring blocks can be found by using either the length of the block to get the following block, or the "previous" pointer.

ALLOCATION ALGORITHMS

When considering algorithms for selecting which block to allocate, or which portion of a block, two properties will concern us. The first is the time required to do the allocation and release operations on the average, and the second is the efficiency of use of memory. This latter property is of course determined by the effectiveness with which the fragmentation problem can be solved. We will look at algorithms from both points of view.

If we restrict the bookkeeping information to that which we described previously as being appropriate for doing efficient consolidation of released blocks, it is clear that we have complete information about the state of memory, even if it is not in the optimum form. It is possible to search through all of the blocks, determining the size and availability of each one, and make the allocation decision accordingly. If we are most concerned about the utilization of memory, we might choose to allocate a block from the nearest sized available block which was large enough. Knuth refers to this as the "best-fit" method. It clearly requires much searching unless additional information is maintained about the available blocks. The simplest form this can take is the use of an additional pointer in each available block to point to the next available block. This will enable the search to skip over the used blocks. When a block is released it will be necessary to search backwards in memory to find the previous available block and insert the block in the "available" list. The allocation can be speeded up by maintaining a number of available lists, one for each range of block sizes, so that the number of blocks to be looked at becomes much smaller. However, the insertion of a released block becomes slower, because the nearest available block in the same size range will be further away.

When using the "best-fit" algorithm, it will sometimes be necessary to allocate from an available block which is larger than the size requested. If it is only a little too large, it is usually better to allocate the whole block rather than split off a small block which could be allocated separately. It is generally a good policy to maintain large blocks rather than have them whittled away by a series of small allocations, which tends to aggravate the fragmentation problem. In the multilinked organization mentioned above, it is sometimes convenient to restrict the sizes of blocks to powers of 2, and link together blocks of equal size.

When it is more important to have fast allocation than efficient memory utilization, it is necessary to eliminate as much of the searching as possible, both in allocation and release. The other extreme from the "best-fit" algorithm, referred to by Knuth as the "first fit" algorithm, is then superior. As its name suggests, this allocates the requested block from the first available block which is large enough. Knuth suggests two procedures. The first one links together all the available blocks in order of occurrence in memory, and allocates by searching from the beginning of the list each time. This clearly has the tendency to allocate small blocks at the lower end of memory, and large blocks at the other, which probably accounts for its rather surprising success in memory utilization. The second algorithm is designed to shorten the searching time by starting at the block after the previous block allocated, thus not tending to cluster the small blocks at the beginning, and consequently not giving as efficient memory utilization. However, the allocation time is significantly reduced.

We give below an allocation routine which uses the first-fit algorithm using the circular search described above. Each block contains a "previous" pointer described by the field specification array **LPREV**, the block length described by **LNGTH**, and a "next available" pointer described by **NXTAV**, which might be implemented to look like Figure 7.3. The **COMMON** variable **LAVAIL** is used to point to an available block to start the search (0 if there are none available). It is assumed that the last block in

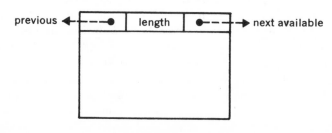

Figure 7.3

memory is a dummy one-word block marked as allocated, with the **LPREV** of the first block in memory pointing to it. The allocation routine is written as follows.

```
      FUNCTION MAKBLOK(N)
      COMMON /AVAIL/ LAVAIL,LWASTE
      FIELD LPREV(...), LNGTH(...), NXTAV(...)
      IF (LAVAIL. EQ.0) GOTO 5
    3 LAVAILP = LAVAIL                          set up for search
      LAVAIL = NXTAV(MEMORY(LAVAIL))
      KAVAIL = LAVAIL
    2 L = LNGTH(MEMORY(LAVAIL))                 get length of this block
      IF (L.GE.N) GOTO 1                        if not long enough, look at next
      LAVAILP = LAVAIL
      LAVAIL = NXTAV(MEMORY(LAVAIL))
      IF (LAVAIL.NE.KAVAIL) GOTO 2
    5 CALL PANIC                                if no suitable free block,
                                                call emergency routine,
      GOTO 3                                    and try again
    1 NXTA = NXTAV(MEMORY(LAVAIL))              found block, get next available
      IF (L.GT.N+LWASTE) GOTO 6                 if close enough fit,
      IF (LAVAIL.EQ.LAVAILP) NXTA=0             test for only one block,
      GOTO 4                                    and allocate it all
    6 LREM = L - N                              otherwise, split into two blocks
      LNGTH(MEMORY(LAVAIL)) = N                 change length of first
      LPREV(MEMORY(LAVAIL+N)) = LAVAIL          insert header information in
                                                second
      LNGTH(MEMORY(LAVAIL+N)) = LREM
      NXTAV(MEMORY(LAVAIL+N)) = NXTA
      LPREV(MEMORY(LAVAIL+L)) =LAVAIL+N         update previous pointer of next
      NXTA = LAVAIL+N
    4 NXTAV(MEMORY(LAVAILP)) = NXTA             allocate block by removing
                                                from available list
      NXTAV(MEMORY(LAVAIL)) = 0                 set next available pointer to
                                                zero
      MAKBLOK = LAVAIL
      LAVAIL = NXTA
      RETURN
      END
```

Note that the **NXTAV** field is set to zero to indicate a used block. Blocks which fit within **LWASTE** words are assumed to fit exactly.

The corresponding **RELEASE** routine is given below. Note the necessity of searching backwards through memory for the previous available block if the immediately preceding block is not available. The routine can be written as follows:

```
          SUBROUTINE RELEASE(I)
          COMMON /AVAIL/ LAVAIL,LWASTE
          FIELD LPREV(...), LNGTH(...), NXTAV(...)
          IF (LAVAIL.NE.0) GOTO 4          if no available block, build
          NXTAV(MEMORY(I)) = I             one-entry chain,
          LAVAIL = I                       set available pointer,
          RETURN                           and return
       4  IPREV = LPREV(MEMORY(I))         locate previous and next blocks
          L = LNGTH(MEMORY(I))             in memory
          INEXT = I + L
          IPNA = NXTAV(MEMORY(IPREV))
          IF (IPNA.NE.0) GOTO 1            test for previous block avail-
                                           able
          IPAV = IPREV                     not available, so search back
       5  IPAV = LPREV(MEMORY(IPAV))       for available block
          INAV = NXTAV(MEMORY(IPAV))
          IF (INAV.EQ.0) GOTO 5
          NXTAV(MEMORY(IPAV)) = I          insert this block in available
                                           list
          IF(INAV.EQ.INEXT) GOTO 2         test for next block available
          NXTAV(MEMORY(I)) = INAV          if not, complete linkage,
          RETURN                           and return
       2  LNEXT = LNGTH(MEMORY(I + L))     otherwise consolidate this and
                                           next
          LPREV(MEMORY(INEXT+LNEXT)) = I
          LNGTH(MEMORY(I)) = L + LNEXT
          INNA = NXTAV(MEMORY(INEXT))
          NXTAV(MEMORY(I)) = INNA
          IF (LAVAIL.EQ.INEXT) LAVAIL = I  check available pointer,
          RETURN                           and return
       1  IF (IPNA.NE.INEXT) GOTO 3        previous block available so
                                           test next block
          LNEXT = LNGTH(MEMORY(INEXT))     available, so consolidate all 3
          L = L + LNEXT
          INNA = NXTAV(MEMORY(INEXT))
          NXTAV(MEMORY(IPREV)) = INNA

          IF (LAVAIL.EQ.INEXT) LAVAIL = IPREV
       3  LNGTH(MEMORY(IPREV)) = LNGTH(MEMORY(IPREV)) + L
          LPREV(MEMORY(INEXT)) = IPREV
          RETURN
          END
```

OTHER CONSIDERATIONS

The algorithms we have described above use relatively little information in determining how to allocate a block. In some cases it is possible for the program requesting blocks to provide more information about its pattern of storage utilization than simply the size of the next block required. One type of information which could often be provided is an estimate of the time that the block will be required. In the extreme case a block may be required for the whole of the rest of the execution of the program. Such "permanent" blocks should clearly not be allocated using the same algorithms as the other blocks, but perhaps could be allocated in a separate area, or in stack fashion at one end of the available space. This is easily done if the requests for permanent blocks can be made before other blocks.

A further consideration in cases when blocks are being shared by many users is that the control information should not be stored in the block, where it can be destroyed. To maintain the integrity of this information, it is stored in a separate area, with the blocks identified by pointers. In the general case this is less efficient, because the release operation requires that the information describing the block be located before any modifications can be done. An improvement can be effected by passing to the user a pointer to the position in the bookkeeping tables corresponding to each block allocated. On release the user can supply this information. If it is in error, this can be detected by the **RELEASE** routine and appropriate action taken, while if it is correct, no searching will be necessary.

HARDWARE ALLOCATION

An interesting alternative to the above rather inefficient procedures is available for those machines which have address transformation hardware, such as the SDS 940, the GE 645, the IBM 360/67, and others. The interesting characteristic from our point of view is that what appears to the programmer to be a contiguous set of addresses does not necessarily represent contiguous locations in the memory. Memory is broken up into pages of between 64 and 4096 words each, and the most significant bits of each memory address generated by a program are effectively used to look up in a table the physical address of the page containing the word. This means that the dynamic allocation of storage in the form of blocks which are multiples of the page size can be handled without the fragmentation problem, since a large block can be composed of any unused physical pages. In practice the relatively large page size available on these machines restricts the usefulness of such storage allocation techniques.

A second result of the address transformation hardware is that the size of address available to the programmer can be much larger than the actual size of memory. Accordingly, the programmer can arrange to use highly noncontiguous addresses for his blocks without necessarily wasting memory, and can use the intervening address space to allow the blocks to grow or shrink dynamically. If the address space is sufficiently large, there is no essential reason for the user to reuse addresses. He can just signify to the memory management routines that certain addresses are no longer required, or that a new block of addresses is wanted. Appropriate adjustments are then made to the address lookup tables. However, this will require fast lookup hardware for a wider range of addresses than is provided in most current machines.

The primary use of these hardware facilities has been for memory allocation to users by an operating system. Dynamic management within the users' program has usually been accomplished by software techniques similar to those discussed previously. However, it seems likely that future machines and systems will be able to provide some hardware to facilitate users' problems in this area.

EXERCISES

1. Implement the **MAKBLOK** and **RELEASE** routines for fixed blocks, but store the bookkeeping information outside the allocatable space.
2. Implement storage allocation routines for blocks whose size is a power of two. (See Knuth (68) for a description of the "buddy system".)

8
SEARCHING AND SORTING

In this chapter we will consider a number of algorithms for representing a set of items in memory in such a way that retrieval of a particular item can be accomplished rapidly. In a sense this can be regarded as an extension of Chapter 3 to cover data-structures which are appropriate for representing sets. As we pointed out previously, the natural physical characteristics of conventional memory make it more suitable for representing ordered sets than unordered sets, and there are not the same "obvious" representations. Our problem is thus essentially that of representing a set as an ordered set.

We will concern ourselves primarily with the two most basic operations on a set, those of adding and removing an element. However, the techniques and data-structures will be of use in a significant number of applications, including the implementation of other operations on sets.

We will first consider a simple representation of a set in which the elements are ordered according to some property of the elements. As in a dictionary, this permits us to locate a particular item with greater ease than if the elements are not sorted. In the next few sections we will consider some of the more well-known algorithms for sorting a set of items, and later return to the searching problem.

SORTING ALGORITHMS

We will suppose that an item contains a *key* which is to be used to order the items. For the sake of definiteness, we will assume initially that these items are contained in successive locations in memory and that there is a simple comparison of two keys available which can determine which of two items should be first. Let us assume that we wish to sort a sequence of items so that their keys are in increasing order. The simplest method of doing this is to search the whole sequence for the smallest item and then to exchange it with the first position in the list. Then the list except for this smallest item is searched for the next smallest and this is exchanged with the second item on the list, etc. This algorithm is simple to program, but it does have the disadvantage that, for a sequence of n items, it requires $n(n-1)/2$ tests.

The above algorithm also has the disadvantage that it will take just as long, even if the list is in the correct order initially. An alternative algorithm, usually referred to as the *bubble sort*, does take advantage of any partial ordering. This procedure starts by comparing the first two items in the sequence. If these are in incorrect order, they are interchanged. The procedure then goes on to examine the second and third items in the sequence. In general, if the i-th and $(i + 1)$-st elements are in incorrect order, the lower one is moved upwards until it is in the correct position. Otherwise the examination continues with the $(i + 1)$-st and $(i + 2)$-nd elements until the end of the list is reached. The bubble sort is so called because an item which is too low in the order will bubble upwards to reach its correct position. In the worst case, it will require $n(n - 1)/2$ tests and exchanges, while in the best case, it will require $(n - 1)$ tests and zero exchanges.

A FORTRAN subroutine to do a bubble sort can be written as follows:

```
SUBROUTINE BSORT(A,N)
DIMENSION A(N)
DO 1 I = 2,N
IF (A(I-1).LE.A(I)) GOTO 1
S = A(I)
A(I) = A(I-1)
J = I-2
2 IF (J.LT.1) GOTO 4
IF (S.LT.A(J)) GOTO 3
4 A(J+1) = S
GOTO 1
3 A(J+1) = A(J)
J = J-1
GOTO 2
1 CONTINUE
RETURN
END
```

Alternatively, the bubble sort routine can be written to make a number of passes over the list, interchanging pairs of elements until there is a pass without any interchanges. This can be written:

```
SUBROUTINE BSORT2(A,N)
DIMENSION A(N)
K = 2
1 J = 0
DO 2 I = K,N
IF (A(I-1).LE.A(I)) GOTO 2
B = A(I)
A(I) = A(I-1)
A(I-1) = B
IF (J.EQ.0) J = I-1
```

```
 2 CONTINUE
   IF (J.EQ.0) RETURN
   K = J
   IF (K.LT.2) K = 2
   GOTO 1
   END
```

This bubbles large values downwards, rather than small values upwards.

MERGE SORT

If there is no reason to suppose that the items are already partially ordered, then a much more efficient procedure, called the merge sort, can be used. This is convenient if there is additional storage space available, able to hold half the sequence of items. The essential idea of the merge sort is that two ordered sequences of lengths m_1 and m_2 can be merged to provide a completely ordered sequence of length $m_1 + m_2$, using approximately $m_1 + m_2$ moves and less than $m_1 + m_2$ tests. This can be accomplished simply by removing at each step the smallest element of either of the two lists onto a merged list. The complete merge sort can then be accomplished by first converting the sequence of length n into approximately $n/2$ sequences, each of which is of length 2 and in which the elements are ordered. These sequences are then merged in pairs to form approximately $n/4$ sequences of length 4, etc. It is clear that the total number of comparisons required to sort a sequence of length n is then approximately $n \log_2 n$. This highly efficient sorting procedure is particularly effective for sorting very long sequences of items which have to be stored on magnetic tape, or other sequential access storage. The basic merge procedure then can take the form of merging two sequences on two magnetic tapes onto a third magnetic tape. More efficiency can be obtained if four magnetic tapes are available, and if these magnetic tapes can be written and read in the reverse direction.

To merge two vectors which are in ascending order into another vector, we can use a routine of the following form.

```
   SUBROUTINE MERGE(A,NA,B,NB,C)
   DIMENSION A(2), B(2), C(2)
   I = 1                          initialize a index
   J = 1                          initialize b index
   IJ = 0                         initialize c index
 2 IJ = IJ + 1                    determine which item to put in c next
   IF(A(I).LT.B(J)) GOTO 1
   C(IJ) = B(J)                   put b(j) in next
   J = J + 1
   IF (J.LE.NB) GOTO 2
   DO 3 II = I,NA                 if last b, copy remaining a's and return
   IJ = IJ + 1
 3 C(IJ) = A(II)
   RETURN
```

```
1 C(IJ) = A(I)                       put a(i) in next
  I = I + 1
  IF (I.LE.NA) GOTO 2
  DO 4 JJ = J,NB                      if last a, copy remaining b's, and return
  IJ = IJ + 1
4 C(IJ) = B(JJ)
  RETURN
  END
```

This merges the first NA items of the array A with the first NB items of the array B, putting the result in the array C. Note that an efficient DO loop is used to copy all the remaining items of one vector when the other vector is exhausted.

A routine which merges pairs of blocks of length L from the array A into the array C until all N items are transferred can be written using the above MERGE routine as follows.

```
  SUBROUTINE MRGPASS(A,N,C,L)
  DIMENSION A(2), C(2)
  I = 1
  L1 = L
  L2 = L
3 I2 = I + L
  IF (I2.LE.N) GOTO 1
  DO 2 IR=I,N
2 C(IR) = A(IR)
  RETURN
1 IF (I2+L.GT.N) L2 = N-I2+1
  CALL MERGE(A(I),L1,A(I2),L2,C(I))
  I = I2 + L2
  IF (I.LE.N) GOTO 3
  RETURN
  END
```

This assumes that any items following the last complete N-word block are also sorted, and its result is in the same form but with the blocks twice as large.

Using the above routine, a sorting routine can be written as follows.

```
  SUBROUTINE MSORT(A,N,T)
  DIMENSION A(2), T(2)
  L = 1
1 CALL MRGPASS(A,N,T,L)
  L = 2 * L
  CALL MRGPASS(T,N,A,L)
  L = 2 * L
  IF (L.LT.N) GOTO 1
  RETURN
  END
```

In the above algorithms, it is not of course necessary to physically move the item in all cases. Sometimes the item will require several words of memory for storage and in some cases it will require varying amounts of memory. In these circumstances, it is appropriate to represent the item simply by the key and a pointer to the rest of the item.

The merge sort described above is very efficient when it is possible to collect all the items to be sorted before the sorting operation begins. In some situations, it is necessary to sort a sequence of items and then to add a number of further items to the sequence in their appropriate position. If the application requires a sorted list to be sequential in memory, then there is no alternative but to move part of the list in order to provide room for the new element. If, on the other hand, a linked representation is satisfactory, then the new item can be inserted without moving the remaining items. However, finding the position for the insertion will on average require $n/2$ tests, where n is the number of items in the sequence. This can be improved considerably if the sorted sequence is stored as a tree structure.

BINARY TREE SORT

The binary tree sort relies on the fact that a binary tree of l levels can have $2^l - 1$ nodes. Each node can be used to store an element, so $2^l - 1$ elements can be located by tracing down l links. A sorted tree is built in such a way that both its left and right subtrees are sorted, and all those items in the left subtree occur before the item in the node, and all the items in the right subtree occur later. For example, the tree in Figure 8.1 is sorted.

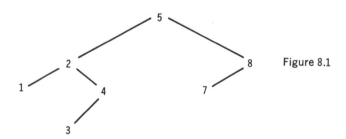

Figure 8.1

In this example, some of the subtrees contain one or zero branches. This tree has actually 4 levels, and could contain 15 items.

Inserting a new item in a sorted binary tree is straightforward. It is added as a new terminal node, whose position in the tree is obtained by tracing down the tree, taking at each node the left branch if the item is before the node item in the required order, and the right branch otherwise. For instance, the number 6 would be inserted to the right of 5, to the left of 8, and to the left of 7. A specified item in the tree can be located by a similar procedure.

The tree requires additional memory for the pointers, of course, which can be provided in the storage allocated for the item itself, or in an auxiliary array. In the following routine to sort a sequence of numbers, we will use three one-dimensional arrays, one to hold the keys, one to hold the left pointers, and one to hold the right pointers. The same index will be used to specify corresponding entries in each array. The routine is written as follows.

```
    SUBROUTINE TSORT(A,N,LL,LR)
    DIMENSION A(N), LL(N), LR(N)
    LL(1) = 0
    LR(1) = 0
    DO 1 I = 2,N
  1 CALL TINSERT(A,I,LL,LR)
    RETURN
    END
```

This routine just initializes the tree with the first item as the root, and then invokes the routine TINSERT to insert the remaining items in the tree. TINSERT is written as follows.

```
    SUBROUTINE TINSERT(A,I,LL,LR)
    DIMENSION A(2), LL(2), LR(2)
    LL(I) = 0
    LR(I) = 0
    MM = 1
    AI = A(I)
  5 M = MM
    IF (AI-A(M)) 2,3,4
  2 MM = LL(M)
    IF (MM.GT.0) GOTO 5
    LL(M) = I
    RETURN
  3 CONTINUE
  4 MM = LR(M)
    IF (MM.GT.0) GOTO 5
    LR(M) = I
    RETURN
    END
```

In the above routine an item which is equal to a node will be inserted to the right. In some cases it may be appropriate to take other action when this happens, in which case the code should be inserted after statement number 3. (One such case is when the tree is to be used to store items so that they can be retrieved, in which case arrival at statement number 3 will terminate the search.)

The efficiency of a binary tree built in this way depends to a large extent on the order in which the items were inserted. A perfectly symmetrical tree of l levels can hold 2^{l-1} items, and a new item can be inserted using l tests. However, if the tree is completely unbalanced, that is, if the entries are made in it in such an order that each node specifies at most one subtree, then we have effectively generated a table which is searched linearly, and will thus require an average of $n/2$ tests per insertion. For maximum efficiency, then, it is necessary to keep the tree as balanced as possible. In some cases this will require that the tree be reorganized, putting different nodes at the head of subtrees, and reorganizing the subtrees accordingly.

TREE STRAIGHTENING ROUTINES

The tree structures we have constructed in the above sorting algorithm are convenient for some operations such as searching but in other cases a different representation is more convenient. A common alternative form is one which permits the items to be processed in order in a convenient way. This information is of course implicit in the tree structure, but extracting it is tricky for the following reason. At each node the nodes on the left subtree come first, but before going off to process them it is necessary to record the node and the right subtree so that they can be processed later. Since this is necessary at each level, a number of pointers has to be stored.

The first algorithm we will give for this uses additional memory to keep this information. A stack is used to record each node whose left subtree is being investigated. It is written as follows.

```
      SUBROUTINE STRTN(LL,LR,L,M)
      DIMENSION LL(2), LR(2), L(2), M(2)
      I = 1                            I is current node
      J = 1                            J is next entry in L
      IM = 1                           IM is next stack entry
    3 IF (LL(I).LE.0) GOTO 1           test for left branch
      M(IM) = I                        stack node
      IM = IM + 1
      I = LL(I)                        go down left branch
      GOTO 3
    1 L(J) = I                         next node in order
      J = J + 1
      IF (LR(I).LE.0) GOTO 2           test for right branch
      I = LR(I)                        go down right branch
      GOTO 3
    2 IF (IM.EQ.1) RETURN              quit if stack empty
      IM = IM - 1                      remove node from stack
      I = M(IM)
      GOTO 1                           go to process node and right branch
      END
```

This puts the indices of the nodes in order in the array L, using the array M as a stack.

It is possible to write a straightening routine which uses the tree itself as a stack. The essential idea is that tracing down a structure which contains one-way pointers only, in such a way that the structure can be retraced, can be done by switching the pointers to point the other way after they have been traversed. In this case this means that the downward pointer in a node will be switched to point to its parent node, and will be switched back when the tree is traced upwards. A certain difficulty arises in that it is necessary to determine when tracing upwards whether it was a left branch or a right branch, and this requires another bit in each node. In fact we will implement this by using a negative backwards pointer when processing the right branch. The routine is quite involved, and is written as follows.

```
      SUBROUTINE STRTN(LL,LR,L)
      DIMENSION LL(2), LR(2), L(2)
      J = 1
      I = 1                             start with root
      IP = 0                            initialize parent
    3 IF (LL(I).EQ.0) GOTO 1            test for left branch
      LSON = LL(I)                      process left branch
      LL(I) = IP
      IP = I
      I = LSON
      GOTO 3
    1 L(J) = I                          process node I
      J = J + 1
      IF (LR(I).EQ.0) GOTO 2            test for right branch
      RSON = LR(I)                      process right branch
      LR(I) = -IP
      IP = I
      I = RSON
      GOTO 3
    2 IF (IP.EQ.0) RETURN               quit if no parent
      IF (LR(IP).GT.0) GOTO 4           test for return from left
      ME = I                            return from right branch
      I = IP
      IP = -LR(I)
      LR(I) = ME
      GOTO 2
    4 ME = I                            return from left branch
      I = IP
      IP = LL(I)
      LL(I) = ME
      GOTO 1
      END
```

The tree ordering stored in an array such as L above is quite convenient for rebuilding an unbalanced tree as a balanced tree. A tree will be balanced if each subtree contains the same number of items in each of its subtrees, so the root node should be chosen close to the middle item in the list, while the two nodes on level 2 should be close to the quarter and three-quarter points. The tree will be built correctly if the items are inserted in the tree such that every item is inserted after the items which should appear higher on the tree. Thus for 7 items the first item should be the 4-th, and the second item should be either the 2-nd or the 6-th. Both the order 4, 2, 6, 1, 3, 5, 7 and the order 4, 2, 1, 3, 6, 5, 7 can be used.

The algorithm to rebuild the tree in the above way is not trivial, and in fact is unnecessarily time-consuming, since the tree is built from the top down. It is much easier to build it from the bottom up. This can be done by first constructing a subtree with the first 3 items on it, then constructing a subtree with the 5-th–7-th items, and then joining these using the 4-th. The 9-th–15-th are treated similarly, and joined using the 8-th, and so on, till all items are exhausted. Another advantage of this algorithm is that it can be constructed from a linked representation just as easily.

THREADED TREES

The algorithms given above for straightening out a tree have the disadvantage of requiring that additional memory be available for the result. Note that a tree represented in the way we have described contains more than half its items in the form of terminal nodes, which have zero pointers in the right and left branches. In fact this means that we are using about twice as much memory as is necessary, since one bit per node would be adequate to indicate whether it was terminal or not. The remaining space we can conveniently use to describe the order of the elements. A tree in which the space for terminal pointers is used to provide additional information about the order of the nodes is called a *threaded tree*.

In the present case we are interested in using these pointers to facilitate processing the tree in the sorted order. First let us note that we have no particular problem locating the first or the leftmost item of the tree, which can be done by tracing down left branches. The difficulty arises when we wish to continue processing a higher node than the current one. This happens when we have just processed the rightmost node of a subtree, when the next node to be processed is the parent of the subtree. Thus we can thread the tree by inserting as the right pointer of every terminal node a pointer to the node which is the parent of the subtree whose rightmost element the terminal node is.

Insertion in such a threaded tree can be done by a simple modification of the routine TINSERT given previously. When tracing down the tree, the last left branch taken is from the node which will become the node immediately after the node being inserted. If we decide to store threads as negative links, then the only modification necessary to TINSERT is the insertion of the statement:

    LR(I) = −M

after statement number 2. Note that the tests for a null branch are actually done by tests for a positive rather than a nonzero pointer, so the rest of the routine can be left unchanged.

Inserting the threads in a tree already constructed is a little trickier. It can be done by a modification of the STRTN routine which uses a stack, which should be changed to insert a thread to the node on the top of the stack just before it is unstacked.

The code to process a threaded tree in order is quite simple, and can be written as follows:

```
    SUBROUTINE THREAD (LL,LR)
    DIMENSION LL(2), LR(2)
    I = 1
  3 IF (LL(I).LE.0) GOTO 1
    I = LL(I)
    GOTO 3
  1 CONTINUE
    IF (LR(I).LE.0) GOTO 2        insert code here to process node I
    I = LR(I)
    GOTO 3
  2 I = - LR(I)
    IF (I.EQ.0) RETURN
    GOTO 3
    END
```

This accomplishes no specific action as it stands, but statement number 1 will be executed for I pointing to the nodes in the correct order. Note that the threading operation is still more complex than an ordinary chain, so for fastest operation the tree should be straightened. If the tree form were no longer required this could be done by simply using one of the links in each node to specify the next item in order.

The threaded tree described above uses just the right branch of the terminal nodes to permit the tree to be traced from left to right. We call this a *right-threaded tree*. It is clear that the left pointers of terminal nodes are available for use, including other threads which may be useful. One such possibility is to use them to thread the tree in the opposite direction, giving a left-threaded tree.

RADIX SORT

The *radix sort* is a modification of the procedure used by physical card sorters, and is conveniently used when the key on which the sorting is done is relatively short, and when it consists of a sequence of symbols which can be ordered in significance. It is simply illustrated by an alphabetic sort, in which the first character is the most significant. The procedure takes the form of sorting the items first on the least significant symbol so that all items whose least significant symbol is alphabetically before those of other items are placed before such items. The result is then sorted on the second least significant symbol, then on the third, and so on. As an example, if we were to sort the sequence of numbers:

$$23, \ 27, \ 61, \ 35, \ 17, \ 51$$

after the first pass we would have:

$$61, 51, 23, 35, 27, 17$$

and after the second and final pass the correct order.

A simple implementation of this uses a chain to specify those items for which the symbols being compared are equal. We will refer to these chains as *buckets* and will maintain an array of pointers to specify the most recent item in each bucket. A subroutine to do such a sort using 64 buckets corresponding to each 6-bit portion of a 36-bit word can be written as follows:

```
      SUBROUTINE RSORT(A,N,NEXT,LBKT)
      DIMENSION A(N), NEXT(N), LBKT(64), LSAV(64)
      DO 1 I = 1,N                    initializes list
    1 NEXT(I) = I + 1
      NEXT(N) = 0
      MASK = 77B                      initialize for rightmost 6 bits
      IRSH = 0
      LBKT(1) = 1
      DO 2 I = 2,64                   initialize buckets
    2 LBKT(I) = 0
      DO 6 ICH = 1,6                  main loop
      DO 3 I = 1,64                   save old buckets in LSAV
      LSAV(I) = LBKT(I)
    3 LBKT(I) = 0                     empty new buckets
      DO 4 I = 1,64                   process each old bucket
      NXT = LSAV(I)                   first entry in old I-th bucket
    5 IF (NXT.EQ.0) GOTO 4           if empty go to next old bucket
      IBKT = IRSHIFT(A(NXT),IRSH).A. MASK
      IBKT = IBKT + 1                 calculate new bucket
      NXTNXT = NEXT(NXT)              insert at beginning of new
      NEXT(NXT) = LBKT(IBKT)            bucket IBKT
      LBKT(IBKT) = NXT
      NXT = NXTNXT
      GOTO 5                          look at next entry in old I-th
                                        bucket
    4 CONTINUE                        next old bucket
      IRSH = IRSH + 6                 next 6 bits
    6 CONTINUE
      RETURN
      END
```

This returns its result in the form of the arrays LBKT and NEXT. LBKT gives the index of the first items of each of the 64 buckets on the last pass, so the actual result is the result of linking together the chains starting at LBKT(1), LBKT(2),... etc. Note that the array NEXT is used to keep not only the result of one pass, but also the partial result of the next pass.

The radix sort can be very efficient if the keys are short, or, more accurately, if the key space is densely occupied. For example, if the numbers 1, 2, 3,..., 4096 are to be sorted starting with a random order, the routine above will accomplish this in two passes, taking about 8192 chain modifications. This is much better than the merge sort which takes of the order of $4096 \log_2 4096 = 4096 \times 12$ comparisons. On the other hand, if the 4096 numbers are only guaranteed to be below 4096^{12} the radix sort will take 12 passes, as much as the merge sort, which of course is independent of the size of the numbers.

The radix sort is fast primarily because a many-way decision is made for each number on each examination. It can be compared with a tree sort in which each tree has the same number of branches as buckets, and for which a complete tree has been constructed. Insertion on this imaginary tree takes the form of choosing the branch which contains the range into which the item falls. This imaginary tree will usually be too large to actually represent in memory, and the radix sort as we have described it allows us to simulate it in a simple and efficient way.

If we had enough memory to actually construct the above tree, it would be more efficient to allocate an address to each item according to the value of its key as an integer, and store each item in the corresponding address. A linear sweep through memory could then order the items in a time proportional to the number of possible keys.

SEARCHING TECHNIQUES

Now let us return to the original problem, that of locating a particular item of a set. This is a trivial problem when the address of the item is known, or when there is some straightforward way of calculating the address from the information we have about the item. When we are unable to arrange this, it is necessary to search the data-structure for the desired item. We will be considering below various methods for organizing the memory so that this searching process is optimized, and the various algorithms for doing the search.

As when we were discussing sorting, we will consider an item to have a key which will identify it, and we will assume that any item with the correct key is the correct item. This does not include, for instance, searching for an item whose key satisfies some condition, although many of the techniques we will be describing can be adapted for this case.

The simplest search procedure is the *linear search*, in which all the items are examined in turn until the correct one is found. This can be used when the items are stored sequentially in memory, or in a chain, but it has the disadvantage that locating a random item will require an average $n/2$ attempts where n is the number of items. If some items are not found this average will be higher. There are certain situations where this process can be very effective, however. If all items are not searched for equally often, the more frequent ones can be placed at the beginning. Also this process is so simple that it can easily be implemented in hardware, thus speeding up the search. An example of this is found in the address search in the CDC STAR machine, which looks up all addresses in a table to find out the physical memory location assigned to the block of memory in which the address lies. The top 16 entries in the table are searched in parallel, but if the block address is not found the table is searched linearly by hardware at great speed. When an address is found, it is moved to the top of the table, and the entries above it are moved down one place. Since the addresses generated by a program tend to be clustered, most addresses will be found in the top 16 entries, and little time will be spent in the linear search.

In the general case, however, there are better methods available than the linear search. If the items are sorted, for instance, retrieval can be done from n items in $\log_2 n$ tests, by using what is referred to as a binary search. In a *binary search*, the first item to be examined in the table is the item in the middle. By comparing this with the object to be found, it can be determined whether the object is in the first half of the table or the second. Subsequent tests on items at the center of the appropriate half of the table will determine which quarter of the table the particular object is in, etc.

A binary search routine can be written as follows:

```
      FUNCTION IBSEARCH(KEY,KEYT,N)
      DIMENSION KEYT(N)
      I = 1
      J = N
    5 IF (I.LE.J) GOTO 6
      IBSEARCH = 0
      RETURN
    6 L = (I+J)/2
      IF (KEY-KEYT(L)) 2,3,4
    3 IBSEARCH = L
      RETURN
    2 J = L - 1
      GOTO 5
    4 I = L + 1
      GOTO 5
      END
```

This returns the index of the item if it is found, and zero otherwise. The keys are assumed to be in increasing order. This procedure does have the disadvantage that all elements in the table must be in the correct order and so any additional insertions into the table will require resorting, a time-consuming process.

TREE SEARCHING

For the same reasons that we may want to use an ordered tree structure for more flexibility in sorting, we can also use it in situations which require insertion of new items as well as search operations. The search procedure is essentially similar to the TINSERT procedure given above. For a balanced tree the search time is proportional to $\log_2 n$

for n items, similar to the binary search. This is as we might expect, since the tree is simply a more flexible representation of the sorted list, and the tree searching algorithm is similar to the binary search.

Of course there is no reason why the tree being searched has to be limited to a binary tree. Each tree can have a number of branches analogous to the buckets used in the radix sort, and the test at each node can determine in which of the branches the item will be inserted or found. In contrast to the binary tree, which stores some items in nonterminal nodes and uses them to guide the search, the multibranch tree is best preorganized with the items being inserted in sorted chains which are pointed to by the terminal nodes.

EXERCISES

1. Given two sorted chains of integers (i.e. in which the item is the same as the key), write a routine which will construct a sorted chain containing the items which occur in either chain, including one copy of any item which occurs in both. Assume that no items occur more than once in a chain. Note that if the chain is regarded as a representation of a set, this computes the union of two sets. The routine should use the memory used by the original chains to return the result.
2. As Exercise 1, but to return the intersection of the two sets. That is, an item is included only if it occurs in both sets.
3. As Exercise 1, but to return the difference of the two sets. That is, an item is included only if it is in the first set and not the second.
4. As Exercises 1–3, but using sorted binary trees.
5. As Exercises 1–3, but using sorted threaded binary trees.
6. Write a routine which, given a sorted chain of integers, will return a sorted chain which will construct the corresponding sorted binary tree, ensuring that the resulting tree is balanced.
7. Write a routine which, given a sorted chain of integers, will return a sorted chain which will contain the integers of the original together with a specified integer. No changes should be made to the original chain.
8. As Exercise 7, but to delete an integer.
9. As Exercises 7–8, but using sorted binary trees.
10. As Exercises 7–8, but using sorted threaded binary trees.

9
HASH CODING

Hash coding is an ingenious technique which has applications in a number of areas including searching. The basic idea is that a function, called a *hashing function*, is applied to an item or its key, and the result, called a *hash code*, is used as a sort of abbreviation of the item. There are a number of ways in which such an abbreviation can be used, and we will discuss several of them below. We will first consider the application of the technique to searching, its most common use.

HASHING FUNCTIONS FOR SEARCHING

Hash codes can be used in searching problems to permit essentially the construction of a tree with an arbitrary number of branches per node. The idea is that the hash code of an item is used to specify the branch: thus to construct a tree with 100 branches from the root node, a hashing function giving values in the range 1 to 100 would be chosen. As we will see in more detail below, this is often used in the degenerate case when the tree has only one level below the root, so the hash function is essentially used to determine which bucket an item is in.

There are a number of ways of constructing hashing functions. The "ideal" is a function which results in the same number of operations on each branch. In most cases it is difficult to choose a function to account for specific differences in the amount of use of the items, so it is usually chosen to distribute the items evenly among the branches.

If we consider the key as a string of bits, and interpret it as an integer, then the hashing function is simply a function with an integer argument and integer result. A very simple function is simply the remainder after division by the number of branches:

```
FUNCTION IHASH(I)
COMMON /MAXH/MAXH
IHASH = MOD(I,MAXH)
RETURN
END
```

This is poor if MAXH is a power of 2 since it will just return the least significant bits of the key, which will give unpleasant regularities if the keys tend to end in the same way. A prime divisor is often used, or a divisor with no small factors. The latter is recommended by Lum et al., (71) whose empirical results suggest division is an excellent choice for a hash function. A simple alternative is to multiply the key by some constant, and extract some bits from the middle of the result. The following would do this:

```
FUNCTION IHASH(I)
A = I
A = A * 5555.55
IHASH = (A .A. 777B)
RETURN
END
```

This will give a number between 0 and 511. The argument is converted to floating-point to avoid overflow, multiplied by a large number which does not have a sequence of zeros in its binary representation, and then the least significant 9 bits are returned.

To avoid conversion and floating-point operations, it is sometimes appropriate to use logical operations. The following code will give a 6-bit hash code from a 24-bit key:

```
FUNCTION IHASH(I)
J = NONEQU(I,ISHIFT(I,-12))
IHASH = NONEQU(J,ISHIFT(J,-6)) .A. 77B
RETURN
END
```

Here we are using a nonequivalence function NONEQU which could be defined as

```
FUNCTION NONEQU(I,J)
NONEQU = (I .A. .N. J) .O. (J .A. .N. I)
RETURN
END
```

There are many variations on these basic forms of hash function. It is usually wise to check the performance of possible functions on a typical set of keys before choosing one.

SEARCHING ALGORITHMS

The usual use of a hashing function is not to build a tree in the sense that we have been considering a tree, but a degenerate form of a tree with only one level. In one scheme the hashing function is used to identify which of a number of linked structures the item is on. These structures may be simple linear lists, or possibly sorted binary trees of the standard form we have discussed previously.

A particularly simple implementation uses two tables. The first table contains pointers to lists of items in the second table, as illustrated in Figure 9.1.

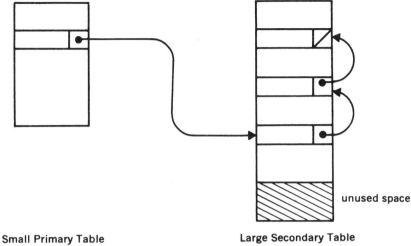

Small Primary Table   **Large Secondary Table**

Figure 9.1

To insert an item, hashing is used to generate an index into the first table. This will give a pointer to a linked list of items stored in the second table. The new item is inserted in an unused space in the secondary table, and linked to the previous list. The pointer in the primary table is then set to point to the new entry. For retrieval of an item, hashing is used to generate the index in the primary table of the appropriate list, which is then searched.

The insertion routine for this scheme can be written as follows.

```
SUBROUTINE HASHIN(KEY,INF)
COMMON /HASHTBL/ IHASHT(256)
COMMON /BIGTBL/ NEXT, INFT(1000), NEXTT(1000), KEYT(1000)
ITRY = IHASH(KEY)           compute bucket number
NEXTT(NEXT) = IHASHT(ITRY)  insert at beginning of list
IHASHT(ITRY) = NEXT
INFT(NEXT) = INF            insert in table
KEYT(NEXT) = KEY
NEXT = NEXT + 1             next free entry
RETURN
END
```

The new item is simply added to the end of the large table in the entry specified by NEXT, and the corresponding entry in the NEXTT table used to point to the beginning of the selected bucket list. Retrieval is similar except that the bucket list should be searched for the correct key.

An alternative scheme uses a single table capable of holding all items to be stored. Each entry in the table may contain an item, or may be flagged empty. To insert an item, hashing is used to generate an index into this table, and the entry is examined. If it is empty, the item is simply stored in that location. Otherwise there is a *clash*, and the item is stored in the first empty entry after that location. On retrieval, the item is found either at the hash entry, or between it and the first subsequent empty entry.

For most purposes this procedure is quite adequate, apart from requiring a sequential block of memory to be allocated large enough for all entries. However, there is a tendency for clashes to "cluster," giving inefficient performance. This can be improved by using entries which follow the hash entry by a nonlinear sequence such as

$$a, a + 1, a + 3, a + 6, a + 10, a + 15, \ldots, a + \frac{i}{2}(i + 1) \ldots$$

or simply a sequence generated by a pseudo-random number generator (for each store or search operation, the same pseudo-random sequence should be used, of course!).

We give below a hashing procedure using the clash sequence a, $a + 1$, $a + 3$, $a + 6, \ldots$. It consists of two routines, HASHIN, which inserts an item, and HASHOUT, which retrieves it. These routines were written for the CDC 6600 which uses a 60-bit word. Each routine expects two arguments, KEY, a word whose upper 42 bits will be used as the "name" of the item, and INF, a word whose 18 lower bits are used as the "value" of the item. Name-value pairs which are all zeros are not permitted, since this is used to indicate an empty entry in the table.

In each routine the DO 2 loop searches the table starting at the calculate hash address, making up to 19 further tests if the key is not found immediately. If the key is still not found and no empty entries are encountered, a simple sequential search is made by the DO 4 loop from beginning to end of the table. It is assumed that this latter will happen extremely rarely. If HASHIN finds the key already in the table, it changes the entry to contain new INF. If HASHOUT does not find the KEY, it returns a zero value for INF.

```
      SUBROUTINE HASHIN(KEY,INF)
      COMMON /HASHTBL/ LNGTHT, KITABLE(1000)
      KEY42=KEY.A.7777 7777 7777 7700 0000B $ INF18=INF.A.777777B
      KEYP = ISHIFT(KEY42,42)
      ITRY = 1 + KEYP - (KEYP/LNGTHT) * LNGTHT
      DO 2 INCR = 1,20
      IF ((KITABLE(ITRY).A.7777 7777 7777 7700 0000B)
     *   .EQ.KEY42) GOTO 1
      IF (KITABLE(ITRY).EQ.0) GOTO 1 $ ITRY = ITRY + INCR
      IF (ITRY.GT.LNGTHT) ITRY = ITRY - LNGTHT
    2 CONTINUE
      DO 4 I = 1,LNGTHT
      IF (KITABLE(I).NE.0) GOTO 4
      KITABLE(I) = KEY42.O.INF18 $ RETURN
    4 CONTINUE
```

```
  6 PRINT 100 $ CALL EXIT
100 FORMAT (* HASH TABLE FULL*)
  1 KITABLE(ITRY) = KEY42.O.INF18 $ RETURN
    END

    SUBROUTINE HASHOUT(KEY,INF)
    COMMON /HASHTBL/ LNGTHT,KITABLE(1000)
    KEY42 = KEY.A.7777 7777 7777 7700 0000B $ INF = 0
    KEYP = ISHIFT(KEY42,42)
    ITRY = 1 + KEYP - (KEYP/LNGTHT) * LNGTHT
    DO 2 INCR=1,20
    IF ((KITABLE(ITRY).A.7777 7777 7777 7700 0000B).
  *  .EQ.KEY42) GOTO 1
    IF (KITABLE(ITRY).EQ.0) RETURN $ ITRY = ITRY + INCR
    IF (ITRY.GT.LNGTHT) ITRY = ITRY - LNGTHT
  2 CONTINUE
    DO 4 I=1,LNGTHT
    IF ((KITABLE(I).A.7777 7777 7777 7700 0000B).
  *  .EQ.KEY42) GOTO 5
    IF (KITABLE(I).EQ.0) RETURN
  4 CONTINUE
  1 INF = KITABLE(ITRY).A.777777B $ RETURN
  5 INF = KITABLE(I).A.777777B $ RETURN
    END
```

An interesting improvement can be made by ensuring that the sequence of locations includes every location in the table before any one is repeated, thus eliminating the necessity for the linear search. The following scheme, suggested by Paul Abrahams, accomplishes this. First, the length of the table is constrained to be a prime number P, and the hashing function is division by P. The quotient Q and the remainder R are both used, with the search sequence being

$$R, R + Q, R + 2 * Q, R + 3 * Q, \ldots$$

all modulo P. Since P is prime, this sequence will not repeat until $R + P * Q$, that is, until all entries in the table have been examined. The actual calculation of this sequence is simpler than the quadratic sequence used above, since it requires only one addition as well as the modulo test.

OTHER USES OF HASHING

In the previous sections we have viewed hashing as a simple mechanism for producing an approximation to an addressing function for a data-object. The only property that the hashing function was required to have was that it distributed the expected data-objects uniformly in a fixed number of buckets. However, we can also regard the hashing function as an *information-compression function,* in the sense that something is known about the data-object if its hash code is known.

This view leads us to consider other properties of hashing functions. In particular, in some cases we might like to have a hashing function which preserved a particular property of the data-objects, so that some of the computations could be done with the hash code instead of the data-object itself. If the hash code is much smaller than the data-object this may give considerable improvements in the algorithm.

An interesting class of information compression functions is that in which the relationship between two data-objects is reflected in the relationship between their hash codes. In particular, we will consider below those functions which can be used to determine that a particular relationship definitely does not hold between the data-objects.

The way we can do this is as follows. Suppose we have two data-objects A and B and we want to determine if a particular relationship R holds between them. Then we seek a function H and a relationship R' such that if $R(A, B)$ holds then so does $R'(H(A), H(B))$. If then we apply the R' test to $H(A)$ and $H(B)$ and find that the R' relation does not hold, then we can say that the R relation does not hold between A and B. If on the other hand the R' relation does hold between $H(A)$ and $H(B)$ we cannot make any assumption about the R relation between A and B, and we have to do the R test explicitly. The value of this type of scheme is therefore seen to be greatest when it is likely that the R' relation will not hold.

THE EQUALITY PREDICATE FOR SETS

Perhaps the simplest example of such a test is one which can be used to determine if two sets have the same elements. If the elements in the two sets are specified in an arbitrary order, this can be a time-consuming operation if done the rigorous way. This requires that each element of each set be found in the other set, which would take of the order of n^2 operations, where n is the number of elements in the set. Even if the sets were sorted, it would take n operations.

The alternative scheme associates with each set a value called its *signature* which is computed by applying some function H to the set. In the case we are interested in the function H will give the same signature for many sets, and we will call the signatures *hash signatures.* There are a number of ways of choosing H, but a simple one is that which computes the sum of the hash codes of the elements of the set. That is, if the elements of a set S are $e_1, e_2, \ldots, e_n$ then we would have

$$H(S) = h(e_1) + h(e_2) + \cdots + h(e_n)$$

for some hash function h. The essential property of this function is that it is independent of the order in which the elements are taken, so any two sets with the same elements will always have the same signature. We can thus precede the test for equality by the much simpler test for the equality of the signatures, and only do the rigorous test in the case in which the signatures are equal.

Instead of adding the hash codes for the elements of the set, we can of course use any associative operation—that is, any operation for which

$$x \oplus (y \oplus z) = (x \oplus y) \oplus z$$

Thus we can use addition modulo some integer instead of just addition. We can also use multiplication, but this will usually give values which are too large, so multiplication modulo some appropriate integer will usually be better.

In the case when the elements of the sets are themselves sets, the hashing function h is a function of a set, so a similar scheme should be used. That is

$$h(e) = h'(x_1) \circ h'(x_2) \circ \cdots \circ h'(x_m)$$

where the elements of the set e are $x_1, x_2, \ldots, x_m$ and $\circ$ is an associative operator. The two operators $\oplus$ and $\circ$ should be different so that two sets whose elements have the same elements but in different arrangements will not necessarily give the same signature. Suitable operations might be addition, and multiplication modulo some prime.

THE SUBSET PREDICATE FOR SETS

Another interesting operation on sets which can make use of the same general principle is the subset test. That is, given two sets S_1 and S_2, to determine if S_1 is a subset of S_2. This is a more powerful test than the equality test, which can be implemented as two subset tests. Once again, if the elements of the sets are not sorted the subset test will take of the order of $n_1 n_2$ operations where n_1 and n_2 are the number of elements in the sets. If the sets are sorted the test will only take of the order of n_2 operations.

In order to improve the efficiency of the subset test we will still want to use a signature of the form

$$H(S) = h(e_1) \oplus h(e_2) \oplus \cdots \oplus h(e_n)$$

where $\oplus$ is an associative operation, but we will have to choose h and $\oplus$ so that if S_1 is a subset of S_2 then some relation exists between $H(S_1)$ and $H(S_2)$. There are a number of ways in which this can be done. One possibility is to choose h so that its values are primes, and then take $\oplus$ to be multiplication. Then we can say that if S_1 is a subset of S_2 then $H(S_1)$ will divide $H(S_2)$ exactly. This method suffers from the difficulty of doing the multiplication and division when there are a large number of elements in the sets.

A simpler method is an extension of an obvious representation of a set as a sequence of bits, with a 1 bit indicating that a particular element is present. With two such representations the subset relation can be tested for by determining if the second sequence has bits wherever the first sequence has bits. In the present case this can be generalized to make use of hashing by choosing h so that it gives values whose binary representation contains only one nonzero bit, and the $\oplus$ operation is the bit-by-bit "or" operation. Another way of writing this is

$$H(S) = 2^{h(e_1)} \oplus 2^{h(e_2)} \oplus \cdots \oplus 2^{h(e_n)}$$

where h is a hashing function which gives values which are integers between 0 and $M - 1$ for some appropriately chosen value of M, and $\oplus$ is the "or" operation. This will give a value of $H(S)$ which is not more than M bits in length.

To give a simple example, suppose we have a set whose NL elements are stored in the array LMENTS. We could use the following routine to compute the hash signature.

```
      FUNCTION IHSIG(LMENTS,NL)
      DIMENSION LMENTS(2)
      IHSIG = 0
      DO 1 I = 1,NL
    1 IHSIG = IHSIG .O. 2**IHASH(LMENTS(I))
      RETURN
      END
```

Here the hash signature is assumed to be one word in length, and the hashing function IHASH is assumed to give integers less than the number of bits in the word.

If we assume that the hash function is random, the probability of a particular bit in an M-bit hash signature being set by a particular element of a set is $1/M$. Therefore the probability that this bit is not set is $1 - 1/M$, and the probability that it is not set by any element of an n-element set is

$$(1 - 1/M)^n$$

Thus the probability that a particular bit is set is

$$1 - (1 - 1/M)^n$$

which is therefore the density of ones in the hash signature.

If M and n are large compared with one, this is approximately

$$1 - e^{-n/M}$$

For maximum information content we would expect this to be $\frac{1}{2}$, so we should choose M to be about $n/\log 2$. Of course, the larger M is, the more accurate will be the results of the test.

If we are testing to see if set S_1, with n_1 elements, is a subset of S_2, with n_2 elements, we can make some estimate of the probability of the signature test giving an affirmative answer. The probability that every element of S_1 hashes into a one-bit in the hash signature of S_2 is

$$(1 - (1 - 1/M)^{n_2})^{n_1}$$

or, using the approximation,

$$(1 - e^{-n_2/M})^{n_1}$$

The test will be most accurate when this probability is small. For an analysis of when such tests are worth making, see Bookstein (71).

ORDERED SETS

The same sort of techniques can also be applied to ordered sets.

One way of constructing the hash code corresponding to an ordered set which preserves information about the ordering is to use a hash function h on an element which is a function of the element and its position. Thus we can write:

$$h(e_i) = h(e_i, i)$$

This permits answers to questions of the form: does ordered set S contain the elements $e_1, e_2, \ldots, e_m$ in positions $i_1, i_2, \ldots, i_m$? However, it does not permit an efficient implementation of a test for a sequence of characters occurring consecutively in a specified order anywhere within the given ordered set. This of course includes the problem of determining if a word occurs in a sentence.

A more useful technique is to represent the ordered set by the set of subsequences. It is not necessary to use all subsequences, and in fact the method which seems preferable is to use all sequences of a particular length. Thus we might represent an ordered set S_1 of n elements by the $n - 1$ two-element sequences, or by the $n - 2$ three-element sequences. A test for a particular subsequence S_2 then might take the form of three tests:

1. Test S_1 for the elements of S_2.
2. Test S_1 for the two-element sequences of S_2.
3. Test S_1 for the three-element sequences of S_2.

If S_1 does not include all one-, two-, and three-element subsequences of S_2, then the sequence S_2 does not occur in S_1. Accordingly, failure of any of the three tests would constitute failure of the subsequence test.

We will refer to a subsequence of k successive elements of a string as a *k-sequence*.

Let us consider in more detail the representation of a string by its set of 2-sequences. If there are N different symbols in the alphabet, we note that there are N^2 possible 2-sequences. We will use the term *k-signature* of a string to refer to a sequence of N^k bits in which each bit is one if the corresponding k-sequence is present, and zero otherwise. If there are n symbols in the string, there will be $n - 1$ 2-sequences, so when n is small compared with N^2, the density of ones in the 2-signature is small. On the other hand, when n is large compared with N^2, we will have some 2-sequences occurring more than once, and the average density of ones will be closer to 1. As n gets very large compared with N^2, we will find that nearly all strings have all 2-sequences in them, so that most 2-signatures will be all ones. We expect to find maximum information in a 2-signature when there are equal numbers of ones and zeros, and we will expect this for a value of n approximately equal to N^2.

Unfortunately, we cannot say that strings constructed randomly from an alphabet of N symbols have 2-signatures which come from a population which is constructed randomly from an alphabet of N^2 2-sequences. In fact, there are some 2-signatures which do not correspond to proper strings at all. Thus we cannot assume a Poisson distribution of ones in 2-signatures for random strings. However, a few calculations indicate that the error in making this assumption is probably quite small, particularly in the region we are interested in where n is not too much larger than N^2. In the table below we give the numbers of ones in 2-signatures of 100 random strings chosen from a 4-character alphabet for various lengths of strings. It is seen that for $n = 16$, the average number of ones in a 2-signature is about 10.0, and the Poisson distribution would give $16(1 - e^{-1}) \approx 10.0$ also.

DISTRIBUTION OF THE NUMBER OF BITS IN 2-SIGNATURES

Length of Strings	Number of Bits in 2-Signature															
	1	2	3	4	5	6	7	8	9	10	11	12	13	14	15	16
4	1	14	85	0	0	0	0	0	0	0	0	0	0	0	0	0
8	0	0	0	8	26	40	26	0	0	0	0	0	0	0	0	0
16	0	0	0	0	0	2	2	10	21	28	21	13	3	0	0	0
32	0	0	0	0	0	0	0	0	0	0	3	8	19	33	33	4
64	0	0	0	0	0	0	0	0	0	0	0	0	1	2	30	67
128	0	0	0	0	0	0	0	0	0	0	0	0	0	0	1	99

Figure 9.2

If the strings are much longer than N^2, a 2-signature will give little information, and we should choose a 3-signature. This will be good for strings with lengths up to about N^3, while much longer strings will require a 4-sequence, and so on. What we are suggesting, therefore, is a representation of a string of n symbols by a bit string whose length is between n and nN bits.

It is clear that when an ordered set (string) is represented by its set of k-sequences, the subsequence test on the strings becomes the subset test on the sets of k-sequences. This means that we can use the hashing techniques mentioned in previous sections for implementing the subsequence test. The resulting procedure represents a string by a *hashed k-signature* obtained as follows:

For each k-sequence of the string, obtain an integer $1 \leq i \leq M$ by applying a hashing function, and set bit i of the M-bit hashed k-signature to 1. Set all other bits to zero.

This permits the representation of the string by a bit string of length M, in which each bit which is 1 indicates that one or more of a particular set of k-sequences is present in the string.

In representing a set of strings, the values of M, the number of bits in the signature, and k, the lengths of the subsequences, are free to be chosen by the programmer. Usually M will be chosen as large as possible consistent with memory restrictions, and at least as large as necessary to permit a saving in computation time. The value of k can then be chosen as large as possible consistent with maintaining sufficient ones in the signatures.

A routine to calculate the hashed 2-signature of a string of 6-bit coded characters stored one per word in the array KARS can be written as follows:

```
FUNCTION KHASH(KARS,N)
DIMENSION KARS(N)
IHASH(I) = MOD(I,31)
KHASH = 0
DO 1 I = 2,N
IPR = ISHIFT(KARS(I-1),6) .O. KARS(I)
1 KHASH = KHASH .O. (2**IHASH(IPR))
RETURN
END
```

This routine uses modulo 31 as the hashing function, and so will give a 31-bit signature as its result. Note that modulo 32 would in this case give a particularly poor hashing function, since the last 5 bits of the second character in each pair would effectively be ignored. Modifications to alter the length of the signature, or to compute 3-signatures instead of 2-signatures, are straightforward.

APPLICATIONS

Applications of the above techniques can be found in many areas. A typical example is found in a text editor, in which lines of text are to be located by searching for a specified sequence of characters. If the text is stored with the signature of each line, considerable improvements in speed can be obtained. For example, using a 40-line FORTRAN program as text, and 31-bit hashed 2-signatures, searches for specified identifiers of 4, 5, and 6 characters correctly rejected lines in 100 of the 120 tests, and identified 15 of the remaining 20 correctly. This gives an improvement by about an order of magnitude over the rigorous procedure. Results were not so good when a 2-character sequence was searched for, since this only has a 1-bit signature, but even so half the lines were rejected by the signature test. With a 45-bit signature the number of errors dropped to 40 percent of these values.

There is a simple application to the problem of information retrieval, which we can pose in the following form. Suppose we have a large number of sets of attribute-value pairs, which can be considered to be strings of coded characters or numeric quantities. The retrieval problem takes the form of requesting that all sets which have certain values for certain attributes be retrieved.

We will store the information in the following way. Consider a set of attribute-value pairs, and hash each pair into a number between 0 and $M - 1$ for some M which might typically be the number of bits in a machine word. Calculate the signature for each set. This will be an M-bit quantity. Store the sets so that sets with the same signature are linked together. Construct in memory a table giving the address of the first set with each signature. Not all possible signatures may occur, of course, so this table may be sparsely occupied, requiring a tree structure or simply a sorted list for fast lookup. The retrieval algorithm then takes the following form. Calculate the signature R of a set which contains just the required attribute-value pairs. All sets which contain these pairs will have a signature which will contain bits where R goes. All sets with such signatures are retrieved and examined.

To get some feeling of the reduction in the amount of searching which is possible by this method, suppose $M = 32$ and the number of attribute-value pairs required is 4. In the majority of cases this will generate a 4-bit signature, so only sets with these 4 bits set in their signature should be examined. This reduces the number of possible signatures from 2^{32} to 2^{28}, a gain of a factor of $2^4 = 16$ in number of signatures. With a random distribution of signatures this would also reduce the number of sets to be searched by 16 also. In fact, this distribution will not be random, so performance will usually be much better than this. For instance, if each set is restricted to P attribute-value pairs, the number of signatures will be restricted to $\binom{M}{P}$. In our example, if $p = 5$ there will be $(32.31.30.29.28)/(5.4.3.2.1)$ signatures, which is about 20,000. Of these, there will be only 29 acceptable signatures, giving a reduction by a factor of about 700.

EXERCISES

1. Implement routines for referring to elements of sparse arrays, using hashing.
2. Implement a routine which will compute a hash-code for an array of integers which is appropriate for testing two such arrays for containing the same elements. Consider the three cases
    i.   all integers are distinct,
    ii. integers may be duplicated, but duplicates are ignored,
    iii. integers may be duplicated, and the arrays considered to contain the same elements only if each integer occurs the same number of times.

10
PROGRAMMING IN PL/1

PL/1

The PL/1 language was devised by a committee of IBM users and IBM personnel around 1964, and is currently being promoted by IBM as their main all-purpose language. It is an enormous language, possessing most of the features of FORTRAN, ALGOL, and COBOL, as well as a number of additional ones.

Primitive quantities include the usual integer, real and complex numbers which can be specified with varying precision. In addition, it is possible to specify fixed point numbers with specified numbers of digits before and after the decimal point. The usual arithmetic operations are available for manipulating such numbers with automatic conversion where necessary. To the FORTRAN programmer, its significant features include recursive procedures, dynamic storage allocation, pointers, strings, and access to parts of words. In addition, it also provides facilities for file manipulation and for communication with the operating system, together with a rather powerful macro facility. In appearance, it is much closer to ALGOL than to FORTRAN, being written in a free format, with semicolons separating statements. It permits the ALGOL block structure as well as the convenience of compound statements and conditional statements.

In the discussion of the language, we will follow the official definition, rather than the version currently implemented by IBM, which at the time of writing does not permit some constructions.

STRUCTURES

The handling of partial word operations in PL/1 is handled rather elegantly by a mechanism which is derived from that used in COBOL. Rather than requiring the programmer to specify precisely the way in which information is to be packed into machine words, the programmer deals directly with the objects of his calculation and the compiler deals with the details of the relationship between these and the machine words. In order to allow the programmer the ability to consider a collection of objects as a single object, PL/1 permits the declaration of structures which are collections of objects of possibly different sizes and types and which can be referred to by name. The components of a structure will normally be allocated successive memory locations and will be of fixed size so that the compiler can generate efficient code for accessing any component.

A simple structure can be declared as follows.

```
DECLARE 1 PERSON, 2 NAME CHARACTER(10), 2 AGE FIXED,
         2 SEX BIT(1), 2 SALARY FLOAT,
         2 CHILDREN(8) CHARACTER (10);
```

This declares the structure whose name is PERSON to have five components, namely, a ten-character string referred to as NAME, an integer referred to as AGE, a one-bit string referred to as SEX, a floating point number referred to as SALARY, and a one-dimensional array of length 8, each of whose elements is a character string of length 10, which is referred to as CHILDREN. The integer component of this structure can be referred to by the name PERSON.AGE, which can be used in an expression, or can appear on the left-hand side of an assignment statement. Similarly the name of the third child would be referred to as PERSON.CHILDREN(3). In cases where there is no risk of ambiguity these could be replaced by AGE and CHILDREN(3) respectively.

The numbers appearing in the above declaration actually should be considered as indicating a hierarchy with elements at level two being components of an element at level one. By extending this hierarchy to numbers three, four, etc., we get the ability to effectively declare one structure to be a component of another structure. Thus in the declaration

```
DECLARE 1 PERSON, 2 NAME CHARACTER(10), 2 PARENTS,
         3 FATHER CHARACTER(10), 3 MOTHER CHARACTER(10);
```

the full names of all the quantities in the structure are

```
PERSON.NAME, PERSON.PARENTS.FATHER, PERSON.PARENTS.MOTHER
```

which if unambiguous could be written as

```
NAME, FATHER, MOTHER
```

The actual implementation of the structure is such that an object is packed in successive memory locations as we mentioned above, so it is perfectly natural that we should be able to refer to a substructure by name and if necessary pass it as an argument to a procedure. In this latter case, the compiler will usually find it convenient to allocate storage for the structure in such a way that a substructure begins at the beginning of an addressable location in memory. In fact, the user also has control over this storage allocation process, using the UNALIGNED and ALIGNED attributes.

It is sometimes useful to be able to use the same locations for storing any one of a number of different types of objects. PL/1 permits this using the CELL attribute, so a declaration of the form

        DECLARE 1 A CELL, 2 B FLOAT, 2 C FIXED;

would allocate overlapping storage to the quantities A.B and A.C. The CELL attribute is not currently supported by IBM implementation, however.

Operations on structures are not very extensive. As mentioned above, a structure or a substructure can be used as an argument to a procedure, but cannot be returned as the value of a procedure. An assignment statement containing similar structures on each side of the assignment operator will result in all components being assigned.

POINTERS

PL/1 provides for the use of a data type called POINTER. Although not specified in the external description of the language, it is clear that a pointer corresponds to the familiar notation of a memory address. A basic function ADDR is provided to allow the programmer to create a pointer to a variable, so the following code

        DECLARE P POINTER, (B, C) FLOAT;
        P = ADDR(B);

would assign to P the value of a pointer which can be thought of as representing the address of the data object B. Subsequent to this assignment a reference to the expression P -> A where A is any variable whose declaration is compatible with that of B could be used instead of B. In this particular example, the expression P -> C would be identical to B. The expression P -> A should be read as "A qualified by P," but in fact would be more accurately translated as "that object which looks like an A which is found at the address which is the current value of P."

Pointers can be used to refer to arrays or structures or elements of arrays or structures. Thus the expression P -> CC(5) refers to the fifth element of the array which looks like CC and is pointed to by P, while the expression P -> FIRM.ADDRESS refers to the ADDRESS field of that structure which looks like FIRM pointed to by P. It is perfectly possible to declare an array of pointers or a structure some of whose elements are pointers. In addition pointers themselves can point to pointers so that an expression such as

        P -> Q -> R

is quite legal (though not implemented at the time of writing).

STORAGE ALLOCATION

One of the most significant features of PL/1 is the fact that the user is given considerable control over the allocation of storage for variables. In FORTRAN storage is allocated prior to execution, while in ALGOL, which permits recursive routines, storage is allocated for a variable on entrance to the block in which it is declared. PL/1 admits both these modes of storage allocation, referring to them as static and automatic. In addition, however, the PL/1 programmer can declare a variable to have storage mode BASED which effectively means that storage is not allocated to the variable until the user explicitly requests it using the ALLOCATE command. Such storage will remain allocated to this variable until the user specifically releases it, using the FREE command. This means that it is possible for a procedure calculating the product of two matrices, for example, to allocate storage for the result and then to return a pointer to that array. Such a procedure could be written as follows:

```
MPROD: PROCEDURE (A,B); DECLARE (A,B) (10,10) FLOAT;
       DECLARE C(10,10) FLOAT BASED(P),
                   (I,J,K)FIXED, S FLOAT;
       ALLOCATE C;
       DO I = 1 TO 10;
       DO J = 1 TO 10;
       S = 0; DO K = 1 TO 10;
       S = S + A(I,K) * B(K, J); END;
       C(I,J) = S: END; END;
       RETURN(P);
       END MPROD;
```

Here memory is allocated to C by the ALLOCATE statement, which simultaneously sets the value of P to point to it. The form ALLOCATE C SET(P) could also be used.

In addition, PL/1 provides storage mode CONTROLLED, which is similar to BASED but in which only the most recently ALLOCATEd copy of a data-structure is accessible. FREEing a CONTROLLED data-structure makes the previously allocated copy accessible once more.

BIT AND CHARACTER STRINGS

Two types of strings are provided in PL/1, character strings and bit strings. These are of arbitrary length, but the operations permitted on them are such that they can be implemented as consecutive memory locations. Variables which are declared as containing such strings must specify a maximum length so that the compiler can assign such storage permanently to these variables throughout their existence. It is possible to declare a string as being of type VARYING, but this implies only that a length is associated with such a string rather than that the amount of memory allocated to it should vary dynamically. The logical values TRUE and FALSE are implemented as the bit strings '1' B and '0' B.

The basic string operations of concatenation, substring extraction and insertion, and string search are supplied, as well as tests for equality of two strings and lexical ordering of two strings. Examples of the use of these operations are given in the following code, which replaces all occurrence of the string 'ABC' by the string 'PQR' within the string which is the value of the variable X and assigns the result as the value of the variable Y.

```
MORE:  I = INDEX(X, 'ABC');
       IF I = 0 THEN GOTO FIN;
       X = SUBSTR(X,1,I-1) || 'PQR' || SUBSTR(X,I+3);
       GOTO MORE;
FIN:   Y = X;
```

The operator $||$ is used to signify concatenation. An alternative way of writing the same code, but using the SUBSTR operation instead of the concatenation operation is shown below.

```
MORE:  I = INDEX(X, 'ABC');
       IF I = 0 THEN GOTO FIN;
       SUBSTR(X,I,3) = 'PQR';
       GOTO MORE;
FIN:   Y = X;
```

Note that here the SUBSTR operation can be used on the left-hand side of an assignment statement and is accordingly referred to as a *pseudo-variable*.

COMPILE-TIME FACILITIES

PL/1 has quite extensive facilities for specifying changes to the text of the program prior to compilation. These can be thought of as macro facilities, which we will be considering in more detail in a later chapter. They take the form of declarations and statements which are similar to the ordinary PL/1 forms, but distinguished by being preceded by a % sign. Processing then takes the form of a scan over the text during which the compile-time statements are executed, and whose output consists of the other text scanned, with any portions which contain references to compile-time expressions having been replaced. The output from the scan is then compiled in the standard way.

Compile-time variables may take on integer or string values, which can be assigned by compile-time assignment statements similar to the standard ones. Expressions which are to be evaluated at compile time can only contain objects whose values are known at compile time, of course, such as compile-time variables, constants, and compile-time procedures. A reference to a compile-time procedure in a compile-time expression will be evaluated in a similar way to ordinary PL/1 procedure calls.

Compile-time statements include assignment, transfer, and conditional statements. Compile-time labels and DO statements are also available, as well as compile-time procedures and procedure invocations. In fact the compile-time "language" is a fairly powerful subset of PL/1, whose main restriction is that it is limited to integer and string values. It is convenient to think of this language as a PL/1 program itself, interspersed with commands to process the other text and then output it.

When processing non-compile-time text, the preprocessor will replace all occurrences of compile-time variables by their current values, converted to strings if necessary and surrounded by blanks to delimit them from surrounding text. Occurrences of compile-time procedure invocations will cause the arguments of the procedure, after being processed themselves, to be passed as strings to the compile-time procedure, which will then be executed and its result used to replace the original text. The text will be processed repeatedly until no further replacements are possible.

The power of these facilities is not widely known. We will look at some of the possibilities in a later chapter.

JOSEPHUS' PROBLEM

As an example of a very simple problem which exercises a number of interesting programming techniques and with which we can illustrate the flavor of PL/1 programs, we will consider a problem given by Knuth, and referred to as Josephus' problem. This problem is deceptively simple and can be posed as follows: The numbers $1, 2, \ldots, N$ are placed in a circle. Starting with M, every M-th number is removed from the circle, which closes up after each removal. Write a program to print out the order in which the numbers are removed. For example, if N is 5 and M is 3, the required order is 3, 1, 5, 2, 4.

There are a number of ways of solving this problem. A simple one uses an array to contain the numbers, and sets an entry to zero when the number is removed. It can be coded as follows:

```
JOSEPHUS:   PROC(N,M);
            DCL NUMB(N) FIXED;
            DO I = 1 TO N; NUMB(I) = I; END;
            NN = N; MM = M;
MORE:       DO I = 1 TO N;
            IF NUMB(I) ¬= 0 THEN DO;
               MM = MM - 1;
               IF MM = 0 THEN DO;
                  CALL PRINT(NUMB(I));
                  NUMB(I) = 0;
                  NN = NN - 1;
                  IF NN = 0 THEN RETURN;
                  MM = M;
                  END;
               END;
            END;
            GOTO MORE;
            END;
```

The disadvantage of this implementation is that it examines an entry in the NUMB array at least NM times, and in fact considerably more than this. Toward the end of the procedure most entries are zero, so the extraction time gets long.

The examination of nonexistent entries can be avoided by using a linked structure in which NUMB(I) gives the index of the next number in the circle. This can be coded as follows:

```
JOSEPHUS:   PROC(N,M);
            DCL NUMB(N) FIXED;
            DO I = 1 TO N-1; NUMB(I) = I+1; END;
            NUMB(N) = 1;
            J = N;
            DO NN = 1 TO N;
                DO MM = 1 TO M-1; J = NUMB(J); END;
                JJ = NUMB(J);
                NUMB(J) = NUMB(JJ);
                CALL PRINT(JJ);
                J = JJ;
                END;
            CALL PRINT(NUMB(J))
            RETURN;
            END;
```

It is clear that this is superior to the one previous routine because it consists essentially of two nested loops, with the assignment J = NUMB(J) being executed less than NM times.

An alternative method is similar to the first but compresses out the zeros by moving the remaining entries. This requires moving about half the entries for each removal, but permits the next removal to be located by calculating an index. The code can be written as follows:

```
JOSEPHUS:   PROC(N,M);
            DCL NUMB(N) FIXED;
            DO I = 1 TO N;  NUMB(I) = I;  END;
            J = N;
            DO NN = N TO 1 BY -1;
                J = MOD(J-1+M,NN)+1;
                CALL PRINT(NUMB(J));
                DO I = J TO NN-1; NUMB(I)=NUMB(I+1); END;
                END;
            RETURN;
            END;
```

This routine has the rather surprising property of requiring a time which is almost independent of M. In fact if we assume that each time an element is removed half the remaining elements are moved to fill in the hole, the time will be approximately proportional to $N^2/4$. This will clearly be superior to the other methods for large M. However, both previous methods can actually be considerably improved in this case by

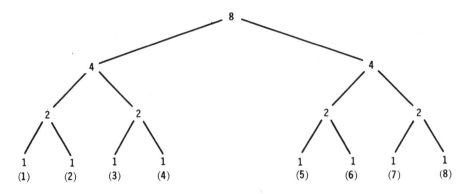

Figure 10.1

counting MOD(M,NN) instead of M places round the circle, which will eliminate complete cycles when M is larger than the number of numbers left in the circle.

A considerably better method than any of those given above uses a tree structure to store the state of the circle. The essential problem, of course, is to locate the *m*-th item in a sparse sequence as quickly as possible, and in particular without looking at each item. We can do this by using shortcuts through the sequence which contain information about how many items are being skipped. This is conveniently expressed as a tree structure whose terminals are the remaining items in the tree, and whose nodes specify how many items remain in the corresponding subtrees. For example, for N = 8 the tree in Figure 10.1 would represent the initial position. If M = 5 the first node removed would be the fifth, leaving the tree shown in Figure 10.2. The fifth item after this can be found by climbing up the tree from this zero, using the counts in the nodes to determine which branch to descend. In the above case the branch with 3 items in it is not enough, so the second item in the 4-branch will be selected, giving Figure 10.3. In fact the number of nodes which must be processed to pass M items is of the order of $\log_2$ M, so the total number of operations will be of the order of N·$\log_2$ M. This can be improved somewhat when M is larger than the number of items left in the circle, using a similar test to those described for the other algorithms. The

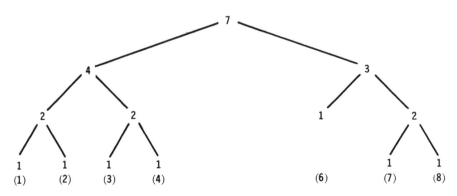

Figure 10.2

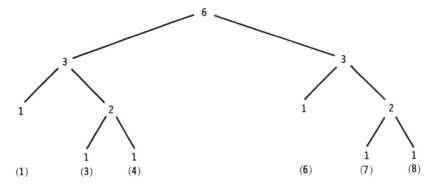

Figure 10.3

important property of this algorithm is of course the logarithmic increase with M, which is clearly superior to the others for large N and M.

A convenient compact representation of the tree can be used if it is assumed to be a full binary tree. Even if N is not a power of 2, a full binary tree with empty branches can be used. The example above with N = 8 does not require empty branches. The representation for this tree would be:

$$8 \ 4 \ 4 \ 2 \ 2 \ 2 \ 2 \ 1 \ 1 \ 1 \ 1 \ 1 \ 1 \ 1$$

In this linear representation, the left son of the i-th number in the sequence is in position $2i$, while the right son is in position $2i + 1$. This sequence is simply represented by a one-dimensional array, while the original numbers can be stored in a parallel array, initially in the form:

$$0 \ 0 \ 0 \ 0 \ 0 \ 0 \ 0 \ 1 \ 2 \ 3 \ 4 \ 5 \ 6 \ 7 \ 8$$

After the first extraction we would have:

$$7 \ 4 \ 3 \ 2 \ 2 \ 1 \ 2 \ 1 \ 1 \ 1 \ 1 \ 0 \ 1 \ 1 \ 1$$
$$0 \ 0 \ 0 \ 0 \ 0 \ 6 \ 0 \ 1 \ 2 \ 3 \ 4 \ 0 \ 0 \ 7 \ 8$$

and so on.

The algorithm can be made quite efficient by updating the nodes of the tree as the procedure crawls around it. If a particular terminal node I has just been eliminated, the following algorithm can be used to find the M-th node following.

1. Set $K = 0$
2. If $I = 1$ set $K = M - (M - K)\bmod(\text{numb}(I))$ and go to 9
3. If I is a right son, go to 6
4. If $K + \text{numb}(\text{rightsibling}(I)) \geq M$ go to 8
5. Set $K = K + \text{numb}(\text{rightsibling}(I))$
6. Set $I = \text{parent}(I)$, and set $\text{numb}(I) = \text{numb}(\text{rightson}(I)) + \text{numb}(\text{leftson}(I))$
7. Go to 2

8. Set $I = $ rightsibling(I)
9. If numb$(I) = 1$ go to 14
10. Set $I = $ leftson(I)
11. If $(K+$numb$(I)) \geq M$ go to 9
12. Set $K = K + $ numb(I)
13. Go to 8
14. Found M-th item as I.

Here the function numb(I) is assumed to give the number of items in the subtree below node I, and the functions parent(I), leftson(I), and rightsibling(I) are assumed available. In fact with the compact form of list mentioned above, parent$(I) = I/2$, leftson$(I) = 2 * I$, and rightsibling$(I) = I+1$. The details of the routine are left to the reader.

If we are only interested in the last number left in the circle, there is a simple solution to this problem which was pointed out to the author by Alan Tritter. For a given value of M it is simple to determine the position of the last number if $N = 2$. From this we can determine the position of the last number if $N = 3$, and so on. In fact, if the position of the last number for given values of M and N is $L(M, N)$, we have the relation:

$$L(M, N + 1) = (L(M, N) + M) \bmod (N + 1)$$

where we have assumed that the positions are numbered $0, 1, \ldots, N - 1$ for simplicity. Thus for example for $M = 3$ and $N = 5$ we get:

$$L(3, 1) = 0$$
$$L(3, 2) = (0 + 3) \bmod 2 = 1$$
$$L(3, 3) = (1 + 3) \bmod 3 = 1$$
$$L(3, 4) = (1 + 3) \bmod 4 = 0$$
$$L(3, 5) = (0 + 3) \bmod 5 = 3$$

as we saw earlier. This calculation is of course simple, being linear in N, independent of M, and requiring no temporary storage.

EXERCISES

1. Solve Josephus' problem using the second method, but using pointers instead of indices.
2. Solve Josephus' problem using the third method, but not moving up entries to fill up the holes until necessary. Note that this is superior to the method given when M is small compared with N.
*3. Solve Josephus' problem using the binary tree method, representing the tree using pointers.
*4. Solve Josephus' problem using the compacted binary tree suggested.

11
POINTERS AND
PLEX PROCESSING

In this chapter we will consider in more detail the data-structures which we introduced in Chapter 3, which we called *plexes*. In the general case a plex consists of a number of blocks of memory containing pointers which link them together. In previous chapters we have found such data-structures to be very useful, particularly in representing data-objects which vary in size and structure, or whose elements have to be located by searching.

The area we will be discussing below is sometimes called *list-processing*. However, this term is used by different people to mean rather different things. Knuth, for example, uses the term *list* to refer to what we call a plex, while Maurer (68) uses it to refer to what we call a chain. We have used the word list to refer to a particular type of data-object whose properties are similar to those which the normal use of the word *list* might suggest, and we will reserve the use of the term *list-processing* accordingly.

In the examples we gave of the use of plexes, we illustrated algorithms by means of routines in XFORTRAN, which we considered as shorthand for machine language. The techniques we used to write such routines become increasingly cumbersome as the algorithms become more complex. In this chapter we will consider some of the more common plex-processing techniques, illustrating them by procedures in PL/1.

NODES AND POINTERS

In PL/1, the blocks of memory of a plex, which we will call nodes, are conveniently represented by PL/1 structures. As we pointed out in the previous chapter, a structure has a name and a set of named components, which themselves can be structures, arrays, strings, or primitive objects such as numbers and pointers. This is a very powerful form of data-structure which permits us to declare very complex nodes rather easily. The natural implementation of such nodes is in a single memory block, although this is not specified in the definition of PL/1.

An important property of PL/1 is the ability to separate the declarations of the nodes from the code which processes them. Because of the ability to refer to the names of the components of the node it is possible to write this code in a form which is independent of the detailed structure of the nodes. In the examples we give below, we will usually include only the necessary components in the nodes.

Note that we could illustrate many of the procedures given below by using indices instead of pointers, as we did in the examples we gave in XFORTRAN. However, this would mean that the programmer would have to implement his own storage allocation routines, which in turn would require that the available memory be declared in such a way that it could be allocated in amounts which depended on the size of the data-structure being allocated. Thus the essential gain that we make by having an explicit pointer data-type is that decisions dependent on the relative sizes of various data-types can be hidden from the programmer, permitting a greater degree of machine independence.

We should also point out that the use of pointers instead of indices has some disadvantages. The operations permitted on pointers in PL/1 are limited to assignment and testing for equality, so operations such as testing two pointers to determine the smaller one are not permitted. This prevents us, for example, from sorting a set of pointers. In a later chapter (on garbage collection) we will find it more convenient to use indices than pointers for essentially this reason. Another disadvantage is that we cannot use a pointer to give us the equivalent of the parallel array facility that we have used previously, where an index is used to refer to corresponding items in two or more arrays. (In PL/1, *offsets* can be used for this purpose.)

In PL/1 a pointer can refer to any data-structure, so declarations of the nodes of a plex do not determine its structure completely. Any pointer in any node could be made to point to any other node, and it is the programmer's responsibility to ensure that the pointers are made to point to the appropriate types of node. In ALGOL 68 we will encounter a different type of pointer which is declared as pointing to a specific type of node. This permits the compiler to diagnose more errors than in PL/1, and also permits certain operations to be implemented more conveniently. However, the flexibility of the PL/1 pointer permits it to keep track of arbitrary nodes during the processing of a plex. In the language L[6] pointers are thought of as "bugs" which can crawl around the plex from node to node.

OPERATIONS ON PLEXES

In Chapter 2, we classified operations on data-objects as creators, destroyers, selectors, updaters, predicates, and functions, and we would expect that when the data-object is represented by a plex the most frequently used operations on the data-object would be represented by simple operations on the plex. However, it is apparent that a plex can be considered to represent a number of types of data-object, so rather than considering operations on data-objects, we will consider basic operations on plexes.

In Chapter 3, we showed that a plex could be regarded as a directed graph, with the nodes of the graph representing the blocks of memory and the arcs representing the links between blocks. We showed that two major classes of directed graphs, the cycle-free graphs, and the class of cycle-free graphs called *trees*, represent important classes of plexes.

The cycle-free plexes have the property that any operation which processes nodes in some order specified by the pointers between nodes cannot encounter the same node twice. This means that operations such as searching for a specified item, or, in fact, any operation which requires one examination of all the nodes in the plex, can make use of the fact that following a path from node to node will always lead to a terminal node.

The simplest kind of plex, the tree plex, has only one pointer pointing to each node. In addition to implying the cycle-free property, this means that each node has a unique predecessor, so that any operation which processes nodes in some order specified by the pointers will not encounter a node which has already been processed unless its predecessor has also already been processed.

In considering the operations on the various types of plex, we will not explicitly make the distinction between plexes on the basis of these properties, but on the less formal properties which make them appropriate for representing particular types of data-object. However, the reader should keep these distinctions in mind.

We will first consider those plexes which are appropriate for representing lists, and which we referred to as *chains* in Chapter 3.

BASIC OPERATIONS ON SIMPLE CHAINS

The simplest kind of chain is one in which there is one pointer per node, with the rest of the node being used to contain other information. If the pointer is used to point to another node of the same type, this specifies an order for the nodes. For example, suppose each node contained just an integer and a pointer, using the following declaration:

DCL 1 NODE BASED, 2 INT FIXED BINARY, 2 NEXT POINTER;

This could be represented as the following diagram in Figure 11.1. We could link such nodes together to form a *one-way chain* such as Figure 11.2, where we have used the NULL pointer to indicate the end of the chain, shown as a diagonal line across the pointer field.

It will usually be convenient to refer to such a chain by a pointer which points to the first node. If this pointer is P, we can see that the first integer in the chain can be referred to by the expression P->NODE.INT, or simply by P->INT if we do not have any other structures with components called INT. We can use this expression anywhere we want to use the value of the integer, and we can also use it on the left-hand side of

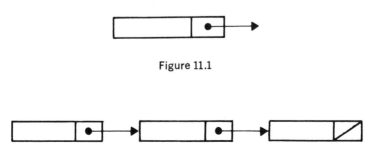

Figure 11.1

Figure 11.2

an assignment statement. Depending on the implementation, we may also be able to use it as an argument of a procedure—this is certainly possible if we declare the structure NODE to be ALIGNED, which ensures that each component of the structure starts at a word (or byte) margin. Even if the structure NODE is declared to be UNALIGNED, it is clear that the implementation could still permit substructures as arguments, but with less efficiency.

The second integer in such a chain can be referred to by an expression of the form P->NODE.NEXT->NODE.INT, or alternatively as P->NEXT->INT. Similarly we can refer to other members of the chain, though this gets cumbersome and difficult to read for much beyond the third element. Many algorithms require that the elements of the chain be processed sequentially, which can be done by moving a pointer down the chain. For example, we can initialize a pointer Q to point to the beginning of the chain by the statement Q=P, and then move it down the chain by the statement Q=Q->NEXT. At each value of Q the next element of the chain can be referred to by Q->INT.

As a simple example of a complete procedure which will return as its value the sum of the integers in such a chain, we give the following:

```
LSUM:   PROCEDURE(L);
        DCL (Q,L) POINTER, SUM FIXED BINARY;
        Q = L; SUM = 0;
NXT:    IF Q=NULL THEN RETURN(SUM);
        SUM = SUM+Q->INT;
        Q = Q->NEXT; GOTO NXT;
        END;
```

This assumes that the declaration of the node structure as given above has been given in a block enclosing this procedure definition, as we would normally expect.

The construction of simple chains of the above form is straightforward using the ALLOCATE statement to allocate a new node. Suppose that we wish to construct the chain whose values are V(1), V(2),..., V(N), for some procedure V. We can do this in two ways—either by starting with the first element of the chain, or with the last. Starting with the last element is slightly easier, so we will give this first:

```
DCL P POINTER, Q POINTER;
...
P=NULL;
DO I=N BY -1 TO 1;
    ALLOCATE NODE SET(Q);
    Q->INT = V(I); Q->NEXT = P;
    P = Q; END;
...
```

For each new value this allocates a new node to go at the beginning of the old chain, filling in the value and the pointer to the old chain. P is the pointer to the completed chain.

The other method is as follows:

```
DCL P POINTER, Q POINTER, R POINTER;
   . . .
ALLOCATE NODE SET(P);
P->INT = V(1); P->NEXT = NULL; Q = P;
DO I = 2 BY 1 TO N;
ALLOCATE NODE SET(R);
Q->NEXT = R; Q = R;
Q->INT = V(I); END;
Q->NEXT = NULL;
   . . .
```

We need an extra pointer for this method because we have to keep track of the end of the growing chain as well as the beginning and the new node. The initialization is also more complex because we can only have a pointer to the last node after we have put in the first element. Note that in the simple case we have used we can build the chain in either order, but in the general case it is usually more convenient to produce the values for the chain in either one or the other order, so it is useful to be able to have both methods available.

A chain can be "erased" by returning the memory occupied by its nodes using the FREE statement. For example, the following procedure can be used to erase the chain whose first node is pointed to by the argument of the procedure:

```
ERASE:     PROCEDURE(P); DCL(P,Q) POINTER;
      MOR: IF P=NULL THEN RETURN;
           Q = P->NEXT; FREE P->NODE;
           P = Q; GOTO MOR;
           END;
```

The pointer P will be set to NULL by this routine.

As we have pointed out, one of the advantages of linked structures is the ease with which they can be modified. In the present case the usual modifications include the insertion and deletion of elements, and operations which split a list into two or append two lists. The insertion, deletion, and split operations are usually specified by a pointer to a particular node, with the operation being concerned with the part of the chain immediately following the node. For example, a piece of code to insert a new integer I after the node pointed to by P can be written:

```
   . . .
ALLOCATE NODE SET(Q);
Q->NEXT = P->NEXT;
Q->INT = I;
P->NEXT = Q;
   . . .
```

while the code to delete the node following the node pointed to by P can be written:

```
. . .
Q = P–>NEXT;
P–>NEXT = Q–>NEXT;
. . .
```

Here the pointer Q is left pointing to the deleted node.

Splitting a chain into two can be accomplished by severing the link between two nodes. Thus if we wanted to split a chain so that the node pointed to by P was the last node in the first chain, we could write:

```
. . .
. . .
Q = P–>NEXT;
P–>NEXT = NULL;
. . .
. . .
```

which would leave the split-off part with its first node pointed to by Q. Appending two chains can be done by changing the NULL pointer in the end node of the first chain to point to the first node of the second. If a pointer to the last node is available, this is trivial, but otherwise it requires tracing down the chain testing the NEXT pointers for being NULL, similar to the code used in the ERASE procedure.

As is apparent, it is perfectly possible to construct two or more one-way chains which have nodes in common. Such a situation could be represented diagrammatically by Figure 11.3. There are a number of reasons which might make it convenient to create such a structure. It certainly permits a saving of memory, since without the common part, the information would have to be duplicated. This duplication would require more computation time and more program. In addition, any modifications to an element in one of the chains might require the modifications to be repeated for the second. In general it is useful for the programmer to be able to deal with such structures.

However, if the programmer constructs chains which have nodes in common, there is the possibility that a change to one chain will effect a change to other chains. Thus if

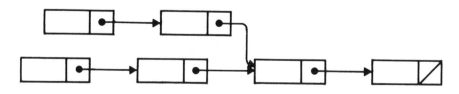

Figure 11.3

the programmer is going to change chains he has to keep track of which nodes are common. In some algorithms this is easily done, but in others it can present considerable difficulty, or even be impossible. The same remarks apply to FREEing nodes, of course. We will consider such questions in more detail in a later section, and will here address ourselves to the question of operations which do not change all the chains which have the part in common.

The usual way of doing this is to make a copy of the chain which is to be changed, and then to change the copy rather than the original. In the case of plexes which do not contain cycles, such as the simple one-way chains considered above, this is quite straightforward. A procedure which will copy a one-way chain starting at the node specified by the pointer given as its argument can be written as follows:

```
COPY:    PROCEDURE(L) RETURNS POINTER;
         DCL(L,P,Q,R,S) POINTER;
         IF L=NULL THEN RETURN(NULL);
         ALLOCATE NODE SET(R);
         P = L; Q = R;
  MOR:   Q->INT = P->INT;
         P = P->NEXT; IF P=NULL THEN GOTO FIN;
         ALLOCATE NODE SET(S);
         Q->NEXT = S; Q = S; GOTO MOR;
  FIN:   Q->NEXT = NULL; RETURN(R);
         END;
```

This will return as its value a pointer to the new copy of the chain. To change the K-th integer in a chain L to I we could use the procedure:

```
CHANGE:    PROCEDURE(L,K,I) RETURNS POINTER;
           DCL (P,Q,R,S,L) POINTER,
               (K,I) FIXED BINARY;
           ALLOCATE NODE SET(S);
           Q = S; P = L;
           DO J = 2 TO K;
              P = P->NEXT;
              ALLOCATE NODE SET(R);
              Q->NEXT = R; Q = R;
              END;
           R->INT = I; R->NEXT = P->NEXT;
           RETURN(S);
           END;
```

For example, if we had to change the third element of the chain in Figure 11.4, we would effectively produce the structure in Figure 11.5.

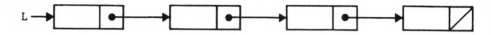

Figure 11.4

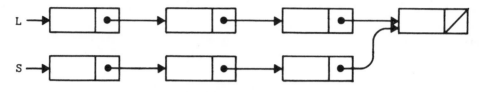

Figure 11.5

TWO-WAY CHAINS

When the processing of a chain requires that we be able to move conveniently both forwards and backwards, it is usually more efficient to use a *two-way chain*. This is similar to the one-way chain, except that each node contains two pointers, one pointing to the next node and one pointing to the previous node. If the elements of the chain are integers we might use a declaration of the following form for a node:

```
DCL 1 NODE BASED,
        2 PREV POINTER,
        2 INT FIXED BINARY,
        2 NEXT POINTER;
```

We might represent such a node by a diagram of the form of Figure 11.6, and a two-way linked chain with such nodes in the form of Figure 11.7. As in the case of one-way chains, it is usually convenient to specify such a chain by a pointer to the first node, but in the case of two-way chains we can also specify a chain by a pointer to its last node, or in fact by a pointer to any of its nodes.

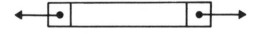

Figure 11.6

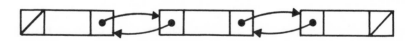

Figure 11.7

An important property of two-way chains is that it is not possible for two different chains to have nodes in common, simply because each node specifies a unique predecessor and successor. This means that a two-way chain is a distinct entity, and plays a rather different conceptual role in the mind of the programmer.

Many of the operations on two-way chains are similar to one-way chains—in fact the LSUM and ERASE procedures given above for one-way chains can be used unchanged for two-way chains if the NODE declaration is changed. Insertions of elements are rather different, however, because two pointers need to be modified, and also because it is possible to insert an element before a specified node as well as after. A procedure which will insert the integer I before the node pointed to by P can be written:

```
INSBEF: PROCEDURE(I,P);
        ALLOCATE NODE SET(Q);
        Q->INT = I;
        P->PREV->NEXT = Q;
        Q->PREV = P->PREV;
        P->PREV = Q;
        Q->NEXT = P;
        RETURN;
        END;
```

Deletion of a node can be done simply by giving a pointer to the node itself, rather than to its preceding node. The following procedure will delete the node pointed to by P;

```
DELETE: PROCEDURE(P);
        P->PREV->NEXT = P->NEXT;
        P->NEXT->PREV = P->PREV;
        RETURN;
        END;
```

The symmetry of the two-way chain is clear from this example. In these two routines, additional checks can be inserted if necessary to permit insertion before the first node and deletion of the end nodes.

CIRCULAR CHAINS

It is sometimes convenient to be able to process the items of a list continuously, with the first node of the list logically following the last. This can be done conveniently by representing the list as a chain, but not using a terminal NULL pointer, but instead using the NEXT pointer in the last node to point to the first node. The result is a structure of the form of Figure 11.8. We refer to this as a *circular one-way chain*. In a similar way we can construct *circular two-way chains*, being circular in either or both directions. The latter could be represented by Figure 11.9. Note that it is not possible for two circular chains to have nodes in common.

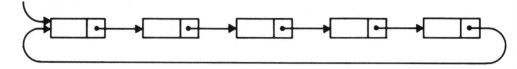

Figure 11.8

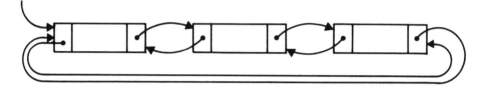

Figure 11.9

As we have shown above, circular chains have considerable symmetry in the sense that their initial node is not determined by their structure, other than the fact that it is the node pointed to by a particular pointer. In fact it is clear that the structure of a circular chain is not changed by moving the pointer round the chain, and it is perfectly possible to have more than one such pointer. A simple example of this occurs when we have a process which is producing information which is being used by a second process. We could organize the blocks of memory used to hold this intermediate information as a circular chain of the form of Figure 11.10. Here we have shown that the structure is referred to by two pointers, not just one. The first process will put a block of information in the block pointed to by NEXTIN, and then move the pointer to the next block. The other process will take information out of the block pointed to by NEXTOUT, and then move this pointer up. The important property of this type of communication is that each process only modifies one pointer, so as long as each process does not let its pointer catch up with the pointer used by the other process, the two processes can

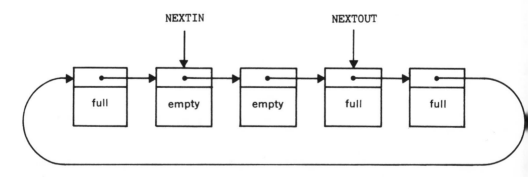

Figure 11.10

execute simultaneously. This type of structure is often found in the I/0 section of a program, where there may be two processors, one filling one block of a buffer while the other empties another block.

Sometimes the communication between two processes requires a buffer of variable length, because of its extreme variability. In this case the process inserting information in the buffer can request that a new block be allocated, which it inserts in the structure. The other process will free a block after it has processed the information in it. In this case, of course, there never will be any empty blocks, and the next block to be processed will be immediately following the last block added. We can therefore dispense with one of the pointers, and use a structure of the form of Figure 11.11. The procedure to

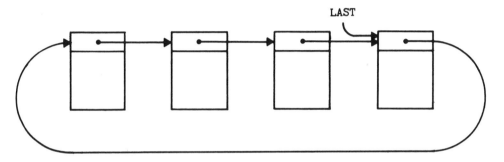

Figure 11.11

add a new block would then be of the form:

```
PUTBL: PROCEDURE; DCL P POINTER
       ALLOCATE BLOCK SET(P);
       P->BLOCK.NEXT = LAST->BLOCK.NEXT;
       LAST->BLOCK.NEXT = P;
       LAST = P;
       RETURN;
       END;
```

This assumes a declaration of the form:

```
DCL 1 BLOCK BASED, 2 NEXT POINTER, ...;
```

and assumes a global pointer variable LAST. Since PUTBL will leave LAST pointing to the block just added, normally following the call to PUTBL will be the code to fill the new block.

The code to process a block will process the block pointed to by LAST->BLOCK.NEXT, i.e., the block following LAST. Then a procedure such as the following can be used to free the block just emptied:

```
RELBL: PROCEDURE; DCL P POINTER;
       P = LAST->BLOCK.NEXT;
       LAST->BLOCK.NEXT = P->BLOCK.NEXT;
       FREE(P->BLOCK);
       RETURN;
       END;
```

This procedure leaves LAST unchanged, of course.

In some cases it is necessary for two or more processes to communicate with each other in such a way that the order of removal of information is not necessarily the same as the order of insertion. The usual case is that the blocks must be processed in precisely the reverse order—sometimes called *last-in-first-out* or *LIFO*, as opposed to the *first-in-first-out* or *FIFO* ordering used above. The LIFO processing order is easily implemented with a stack or a one-way chain, as we have seen in previous chapters. However, in the case when both LIFO and FIFO ordering are required, it is sometimes more convenient to use a two-way circular chain of the form of Figure 11.12. This has a single pointer and it is clear that the four operations:

add a new block to the beginning
add a new block to the end
process and remove the beginning block
process and remove the end block

can all be implemented without requiring all the links to be traced. A minor problem arises because of the possibility that the chain may become empty, which is not representable in the same form, so it is usual to keep one node as a dummy block, which is never used. Thus the node pointed to by Q->BLOCK.NEXT is considered to be the first node, and the node pointed to by Q->BLOCK.PREV is considered to be the last. In the empty case these would be identical, and could be checked for if necessary.

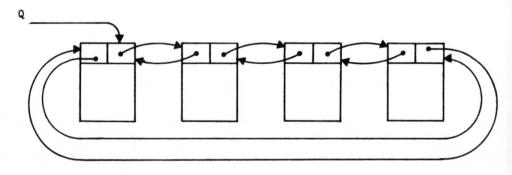

Figure 11.12

NONLINEAR PLEXES

In the following sections we will consider those plexes whose pointers specify more structure than just the order between the nodes. In Chapter 3 we called these *nonlinear plexes*, and showed that there are data-objects which cannot be represented by linear plexes in which the size of the node is fixed. If, however, we can choose the size of the nodes, we can represent some nonlinear structures very conveniently.

A simple extension of the chains described above can be accomplished in PL/1 by a simple modification of the declaration of NODE. This declaration can contain elaborate substructures and arrays of one or many dimensions. In fact it is possible in PL/1 to include arrays with variable dimensions in such a declaration, with the size of the array being determined at ALLOCATE time. Such structures would normally contain information about the size of the array, so that processing could determine the size of array used in an arbitrary node.

If the elements on the chain are of different types and structures, it is sometimes more convenient to use a standard node which contains a pointer to the element. Thus on the same chain we can store pointers to arrays or structures of arbitrary complexity.

A particularly useful form of chain is one whose elements are either simple items such as integers, or pointers to other chains. This is the basic form of structure used in LISP, which we will examine in more detail in the next section.

LISP-LIKE CHAINS

The main data-object in the LISP programming language, which we will be discussing in more detail in a later chapter, is a list which can have atoms or other lists as its elements. The standard implementation is as a chain which can have pointers to other chains as its elements. For example, a chain of the form of Figure 11.13 might be found. It is clear that in this representation a chain is identified by a pointer, and the basic operations will involve the extraction of the contents of the two fields pointed to by the pointer. These operations can be thought of as abstracting the first element of a list and that part of the list which is obtained by deleting the first element. These two basic operations are sometimes referred to as *head* and *tail*, or alternatively as *first* and *last* as well as by the functions CAR and CDR, which are the names used in LISP. We will, in addition, require operations to construct lists from their component parts. The simplest such function is that which takes a datum and a list and makes a new list, with the datum as the first element. In addition, we might require functions which

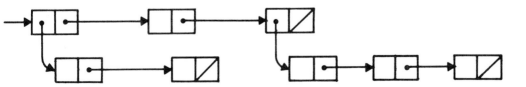

Figure 11.13

change the first element in a list or which change a list except for its first element. For testing purposes, we will require predicates which can determine if an element is an atom or a list, and which can determine if two elements are equal. We will also require a mechanism for determining if a list is empty.

A node of such a list structure could be constructed according to the following PL/1 declaration:

```
DECLARE 1 LCELL BASED,
          2 ATOM BIT(1),
          2 HD POINTER,
          2 TL POINTER;
```

This declares a structure whose name is LCELL to have 3 components, one bit called ATOM and two pointers called HD and TL. A list will actually be represented by a pointer to an LCELL, which itself may contain two other pointers which can point to other LCELLs. The ATOM bit in an LCELL is always zero to distinguish it from an atom, which will have a correspondingly positioned bit which is always one. For example, an integer on such a list would have the form:

```
DECLARE 1 LINT BASED,
          2 ATOM BIT(1),
          2 INT FIXED;
```

In this way, an item which is represented by a pointer P can either be a list or an atom, in this case an integer, and it can be determined which by testing the value of P –> ATOM. Note that this requires that the PL/1 implementation be such that structures whose initial components are the same be represented similarly in memory.

The important operation which constructs a new list from a given head and tail can be written simply as the following procedure:

```
CONS: PROC(L1,L2) RETURNS POINTER;
      DECLARE (L1,L2,L12) POINTER;
      ALLOCATE LCELL SET(L12);
      L12 –> ATOM = '0'B;
      L12 –> HD = L1;
      L12 –> TL = L2;
      RETURN(L12);
      END;
```

This returns as its value a pointer to a new LCELL which has been allocated memory within the procedure, and which contains the pointers to the head and tail given as its arguments.

The other basic operations on such a list can be written quite conveniently as in-line code. For instance, if L is a pointer to a list, then the head of the list is specified by the pointer L–>HD while the tail is specified by L–>TL. The head or tail of a list can be changed by an assignment to L->HD or L->TL, while tests can be done on lists by statements such as

```
IF L = NULL THEN ... ;
IF L1 = L2 THEN ... ;
IF L -> ATOM THEN ... ;
```

In the above list organization only one type of atomic item is used, the integer. In general it will be useful to be able to store other types of atoms on a list, such as real numbers or coded characters. If such items are put on lists in such a way that it is necessary to be able to distinguish between them, then each atomic item should contain flags to indicate its type. A declaration such as:

```
DECLARE 1 LINT BASED,
         2 ATOM BIT(1),
         2 TYPE FIXED,
         2 INT FIXED;
```

where the TYPE field for each LINT would contain some value to distinguish it from, for instance, a real atom of the form

```
DECLARE 1 LREAL BASED,
         2 ATOM BIT(1),
         2 TYPE FIXED,
         2 REAL FLOAT;
```

which would have a different value of TYPE. In the case when it is necessary to replace an integer in a list by a real, it is also appropriate to make all these atomic forms consistent with each other. One way to do this is to use the CELL attribute, as follows:

```
DECLARE 1 LATOM BASED,
         2 ATOM BIT(1),
         2 TYPE FIXED,
         2 DATUM CELL,
           3 INT FIXED,
           3 REAL FLOAT;
```

In fact by carrying this a little further we can arrive at a single form of cell capable of specifying a list, a real, or an integer. This would be declared as follows:

```
DECLARE 1 LCELL BASED,
         2 ATOM BIT(1),
         2 INF CELL,
           3 LIST,
           4 HD POINTER,
           4 TL POINTER,
```

```
3 LATOM,
  4 TYPE FIXED,
  4 DATUM CELL,
    5 INT FIXED,
    5 REAL FLOAT;
```

A list built from such nodes would contain complete information about its structure and contents. On most machines which use a whole word to store a floating-point number, such a node would usually require two words, which would be rather inefficient when used simply to contain a bit and two pointers.

A rather more efficient use of memory can be obtained by representing an item not simply by a pointer, which requires that information about the type of the item be kept in the word pointed to, but by a pointer and type information. The declaration would be of the form:

```
DECLARE 1 ITEM
         2 TYPE FIXED(1),
         2 REF POINTER;
```

while a node would have the form:

```
DECLARE 1 NODE BASED,
         2 HD LIKE ITEM,
         2 TL LIKE ITEM;
```

Here an item is a structure, so if we have a structure L declared LIKE ITEM, we can test it by statements such as:

```
IF L.TYPE = LISTF THEN ... ;
IF L.TYPE = INTF  THEN ... ;
```

where LISTF and INTF are preset integers used for flagging lists and integers. The head and tail of L can be referenced as L.REF–>HD and L.REF–>TL. However, these are now structures rather than pointers, so their use is somewhat more restricted. In particular, there is no way of writing the CONS procedure with this representation. We would like to have written:

```
CONS: PROC(L1,L2) RETURNS ITEM;
      DCL (L1,L2) LIKE ITEM;
      DCL L12 LIKE ITEM, N12 LIKE NODE BASED(P);
      ALLOCATE N12;
      N12.HD = L1; N12.TL = L2;
      L12.TYPE = LISTF; L12.REF = P
      RETURN(L12);
      END;
```

but PL/1 does not permit a structure to be returned as the value of a procedure. In this case there is no reason for this, since the structure occupies at most 2 words, and in the vast majority of machines only 1 word. In fact there is probably a way of faking it in many compilers by using some sort of CELL declaration.

TREES

The one-way chain whose elements are pointers to one-way chains, as described above, can also be regarded as a plex whose nodes have two pointers. This is a natural structure for representing a binary tree. It is obvious that a generalization of this structure can be used to represent a tree with an arbitrary number of branches. Perhaps the simplest way to represent a tree in PL/1 is to use a structure with n pointers to represent a node which has n immediate descendants. Thus the portion of a tree shown in Figure 11.14 could be represented by the structure shown diagrammatically in Figure 11.15. This node could be declared:

```
DCL 1 NODE3 BASED,
        2 BR1 POINTER, 2 BR2 POINTER, 2 BR3 POINTER;
```

If the program can be written in such a way that the number of branches in each sub-tree is always known, this would be adequate. However, if the program has to deal with subtrees which have arbitrary number of branches, it is necessary to indicate this in some way within the node. This can be done by using an extra field NBRS to hold the number of branches, giving a declaration for a three-branch node such as:

```
DCL 1 NODE3 BASED, 2 NBRS FIXED BIN,
        2 (BR1,BR2,BR3) POINTER;
```

A zero value of NBRS could be used to indicate a terminal node, so a tree which had

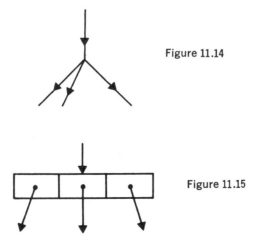

Figure 11.14

Figure 11.15

integers as its terminal values could have a declaration such as:

    DCL 1 NODE BASED, 2 NBRS FIXED BIN, 2 INT FIXED BIN;

Note that we are once again using the assumption that the implementation permits an expression such as P->NODE.NBRS to be used even when P points to a structure declared as a NODE3.

An alternative to the use of a structure as a node is the use of an array of pointers. That is, we might declare a node with three branches as:

    DCL BRANCH3(3) POINTER BASED;

or perhaps as:

    DCL 1 NODE3 BASED, 2 NBRS FIXED BIN, 2 BRANCH(3) POINTER;

Both of these forms permit a branch to be specified by an index, which is useful in some situations. However, it is necessary to declare each size of node separately, which is cumbersome and also prevents the use of nodes with arbitrary numbers of branches. An improvement on these forms of declarations can be made using the self-referencing structure provided in PL/1, which permits a declaration of the form:

    DCL 1 NODE BASED, 2 NBRS FIXED BIN,
     2 BRANCH(NBRANCHES REFER(NBRS))POINTER;

When a structure like this is ALLOCATEd, the current value of the variable NBRANCHES will be used to set both the value of NBRS and also the size of the array BRANCH.

As we saw in the chapter on data-objects, we can regard a node of a tree as a list whose elements are the nodes which are its immediate descendants. Accordingly any of the chains which we have discussed above can be used to represent a tree. For example, the tree in Figure 11.16 has an obvious representation using simple one-way

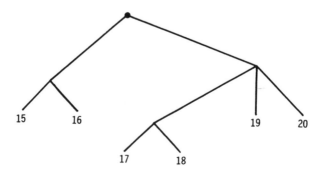

Figure 11.16

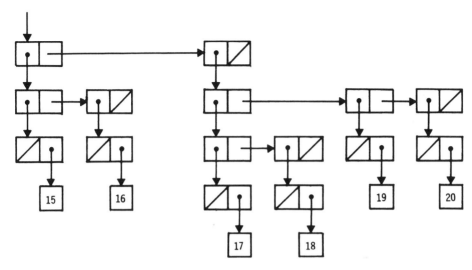

Figure 11.17

chains as Figure 11.17 shows. The links in this structure are in fact pointers to the left son of a node, and its right sibling. In practice it is often appropriate to change the terminology used in the nodes, to something such as:

```
DCL 1 NODE BASED, 2 LSON POINTER, 2 RSIB POINTER;
```

Note that a NULL value of LSON in the above example is used to indicate a terminal branch whose value is pointed to by RSIB. Alternatively we could use an extra field in the node to specify whether it was terminal or not. This would give us declarations such as:

```
DCL 1 NODE BASED, 2 TERM BIT(1), 2 (LSON,RSON) POINTER;
DCL 1 TNODE BASED, 2 TERM BIT(1), 2 INT FIXED BIN;
```

which would permit terminal nodes which were integers.

In an analogous way we can use two-way or circular chains to represent nodes of trees.

In some cases we want to be able to store information in the nonterminal nodes of a tree, rather than just the terminals. An example of this is the type of tree used for sorting which we discussed in a previous chapter. It is straightforward to allocate another field for this purpose in any of the tree structures we have described. For example, the procedure which inserts an integer in a sorted binary tree could be written:

```
TINSERT: PROCEDURE(I,R) RETURNS POINTER;
         DCL 1 NODE BASED, 2 INT FIXED BIN,
              2 (LT, GE) POINTER;
         DCL (R,P,PP,Q) POINTER;
```

```
                ALLOCATE NODE SET(Q);
                Q ->NODE.INT = I;
                Q->NODE.LT = NULL;
                Q->NODE.GE = NULL;
                PP = R;
         NXT:  P = PP;
                IF I GE P->NODE.INT THEN DO;
                    PP = P->NODE.GE;
                    IF PP ¬= NULL THEN GOTO NXT;
                    P->NODE.GE = Q;
                    END;
                ELSE DO;
                    PP = P->NODE.LT;
                    IF PP ¬= NULL THEN GOTO NXT;
                    P->NODE.LT = Q;
                    END;
                RETURN(Q);
                END;
```

Here I is the integer to be inserted, and R is a pointer to the root of the tree, which is assumed to have at least one integer (in the root node). A pointer to the new node is returned as the value of TINSERT.

COMMON SUBSTRUCTURES

In a number of cases the operations that we wish to do on data-objects will involve the reordering, replacing, deleting, and inserting of elements, and it is useful to be able to do these operations without copying whenever possible. One of the reasons a plex is chosen in preference to some other structure is to reduce the amount of such copying. The result is that it frequently happens that a plex is pointed to by more than one pointer. In simple algorithms this causes no particular trouble, and in fact can have quite beneficial effects in some cases. However, in complex algorithms, or when we are trying to provide high-level facilities for manipulating data-objects, there are a couple of serious problems.

The first we can call the *side-effect problem*. It occurs when two plexes have a part in common, and an operation on one plex changes the common portion. If the programmer knows in detail how such a change affects the second plex and takes account of it, there is no serious damage apart from the increased complexity of the program which generally results when the interaction increases between parts of a program. However, when the plexes are subject to changes which are not known in detail to the programmer, this is not possible. This may occur when the exact state of the internal structures cannot be predicted without effectively running the program, as in the case when the structures are highly dependent on the data. It can also occur when the internal structures are subject to reorganization by the system, and the changes are not known to the programmer.

The second we can call the *erasure problem*. If a substructure is common to two plexes, and one of the plexes becomes unnecessary so its memory is to be returned to the storage pool, there must be some mechanism which will prevent the common part being returned until the second plex becomes unnecessary also. This is sometimes called the *responsibility problem*.

A simple solution to the first problem is to provide operations which construct new plexes from old ones, but not to provide any means for changing existing plexes. This is the method used in LISP, which provides the CONS function as the standard list construction function, and warns the user that use of the functions which change lists, usually known as RPLACA and RPLACD, should be used with care.

The second problem is more difficult, since there is no way of avoiding it short of avoiding common structures completely. There are two generally accepted ways of solving this problem, which we will refer to as the *garbage collection method* and the *reference count method*. The first, garbage collection, is used in LISP and in ALGOL 68, both of which we will be describing in more detail in later chapters. The essential idea is that the programmer does not do any erasure of plexes at all, but allows the system to determine which parts are no longer required and to automatically reuse the memory. This is done by organizing the system in such a way that it has access to all variables or temporary results which refer to plexes. When the system runs out of memory, the system traces down all these plexes and marks those words which are used. The assumption is made that other words in the free-space area not on any of these plexes will not be required by the further execution of the program, so this area is then swept, and those words which are not marked are assumed available and collected for further use.

The second method, the reference count method, is used in SLIP, which we will be describing in more detail later in this chapter. The essential idea of this method is to maintain a count in any node which can have a number of pointers referring to it. When a node is freed its reference count is reduced by one, since one of its references is being removed. If this operation reduces the count to zero, that node is no longer referenced and all the nodes it points to can be freed. In general this method might be expected to be rather inefficient, since every operation which puts an entry on a list or removes an entry has to modify the reference count. However, it has the advantage that the erasure procedure is fairly continuous compared with the garbage collection method which spends a considerable time in the garbage collection phase during which no other computation is done. We will describe this procedure in more detail in the next section.

SLIP

SLIP is a list-processing system written originally in FORTRAN. Its data-structures are circular two-way chains representing lists whose elements are either word-size items or pointers to other lists. The system consists of a package of routines for manipulating these lists, including routines for creation and destruction of lists, insertion and deletion of elements, as well as rather complex routines for processing lists and their sublists. Compared with other list-processing systems SLIP is rather primitive, but has been widely used because of its availability.

The most interesting aspect of SLIP is the mechanism used to permit destruction of lists which are no longer required. Because a list is represented by a two-way chain, the node preceding a given node is determined, so two distinct chains cannot have nodes in common. However, a list can be an element of more than one list, and the destruction of such a list can cause problems.

The reference count mechanism used to accomplish this is as follows. The first node in each chain, called the head, is not used to contain data, but is used to keep a count of the number of pointers which are currently referencing it. The primitive operations for inserting and deleting elements which are lists update this count, and the memory is only released when this count goes to zero.

We will give below an outline of an implementation of SLIP in PL/1. For the SLIP node we will use a structure of the form:

```
DECLARE 1 SCELL BASED,
        2 LNKL POINTER, 2 LNKR POINTER,
        2 ID FIXED BINARY,
        2 DATUM CELL, 3 INT FIXED, 3 RE REAL,
        3 CH CHAR(4), 3 SUBL POINTER;
```

The basic SLIP functions could then be written

```
  ID: PROCEDURE(NAME);
      RETURN(NAME -> SCELL.ID);
      END;
LNKL: PROCEDURE(NAME) RETURNS POINTER;
      RETURN(NAME -> SCELL.LNKL);
      END;
LNKR: PROCEDURE(NAME) RETURNS POINTER;
      RETURN(NAME->SCELL.LNKR);
      END;
```

Use of such primitives is bound to give rather inefficient code, as well as not making the most of PL/1. Instead we can refer to the fields directly as part of the structure. Thus for a cell identified by the pointers P and Q, we can use statements such as

```
P -> LNKL = I;
P -> ID = 3;
```

as well as

```
P -> LNKL = Q -> LNKR;
J = P -> INT * 35 + Q -> RE;
```

Thus for SLIP at least PL/1 provides a much superior parent language than FORTRAN.

Since storage allocation and collection in SLIP uses the reference count method, the operation of putting a list on another list should increase its reference count, and erasing it should simply reduce its reference count by one, releasing the space only when the count is zero. Either we can let PL/1 do the storage allocation, or we can do it explicitly in the code.

If PL/1 does the storage allocation, we can create a SLIP cell by the statement:

```
ALLOCATE SCELL SET(NAME);
```

and erase a list by the procedure:

```
ERASE: PROCEDURE(P) RECURSIVE;
       DCL(P,Q,L) POINTER;
       P -> COUNT = P -> COUNT-1;
       IF P->COUNT ¬=0 THEN RETURN;
       L = P -> LNKL;
 NEXT: Q = P -> LNKR; FREE P -> SCELL;
       IF P = L THEN RETURN; P = Q;
       IF P -> ID = SUBL THEN CALL ERASE(P->SUBL);
       GOTO NEXT;
       END;
```

This differs from the original implementation of SLIP, in which the individual cells of a freed list are left linked until ready to be reused. A procedure to insert an integer to the left of a particular element can be written:

```
NXTLFT: PROCEDURE(I,P) RETURNS POINTER;
        ALLOCATE SCELL SET(NEW);
        NEW -> INT = ID; NEW -> ID = 0;
        NEW -> LNKL = P -> LNKL;
        NEW -> LNKR = P; P -> LNKL -> LNKL -> NEW;
        P -> LNKL = NEW; RETURN(NEW);
        END;
```

Similar functions can be written for insertions to the right, and insertions of sublists.

In practice it would be more efficient to write one's own storage allocation routines without using the ALLOCATE and FREE statements, which are really much too general unless the PL/1 implementation is able to recognize that all objects being allocated are the same size.

PLEXES CONTAINING CYCLES

In most of the operations we have discussed above it has not been of great significance whether the plex being processed contained cycles or not. Simple operations such as inserting or deleting nodes are done in much the same way in both cases. However, there are some operations in which the presence of cycles is of great significance. One such operation is that which searches a plex for a node satisfying a specified property. Unless care is taken, once such a search encounters a cycle it can continue indefinitely. Another such operation is that which makes a copy of a plex, which can run into the same trouble.

The general procedure for avoiding this type of problem is to mark the pointers in some way when they are processed, so that on encountering a marked pointer the appropriate action can be taken. For example, in searching a simple circular chain the pointer to the initial node can be recorded, and the search terminated with failure if this node is encountered before the correct node is found. A more elaborate procedure is necessary for nonlinear plexes, the processing of which will be discussed in more detail in the chapter on recursive programming.

In general, the search procedure for a nonlinear plex can be accomplished with the aid of a single mark bit for each node. However, the copy operation is more complex. In this case we can process the nodes in the plex in some systematic fashion, making a copy of each node and filling in the pointer in the node which points to it. If the plex is a tree there will be only one pointer to the node, but if not there may be others which will be encountered later in the processing. In this case it is necessary to know not only that the node is already copied, but also where its copy is located, so that the pointer to the original copy can be used. If this is not done, each time the node is encountered a fresh copy will be made, giving a less concise plex, and one which is not identical in structure to the original. In some cases this does not matter too much, but if the plex contains a cycle, the process will not terminate.

The usual solution to this problem is to mark each node when it is copied, and also maintain some record of its new location. A convenient way of doing this is by using space in the node to point to the location of the copy, if necessary removing other information temporarily until all the nodes are copied. Some such techniques will be described in the chapter on garbage collection.

EXERCISES

*1. Implement SLIP in PL/1.
*2. Write a routine which will test for two binary trees having the same information in corresponding positions in the nodes, without using more than one additional bit in each node.
*3. Write a routine which will test for two binary plexes having the same information in corresponding positions in the nodes. Note that such plexes may contain cycles. You may use additional data-structures as necessary.

12
RECURSIVE PROGRAMMING

In this chapter we will consider a number of programming techniques which use recursion. In previous chapters we have mentioned some of these, and also have shown how recursive procedures can be written in a low-level language. Here we will be more concerned with the use of recursion to simplify the programming task, and will make use of the recursive facility available in PL/1.

Recursive programming is a very natural form of programming in those problems in which the data-objects are easily defined recursively. A tree is a clear example of such a structure, and a list is another. It is usual to find that languages for processing trees or lists have some facility for permitting recursion. The lack of such a facility has an adverse effect on the ease of use of the language, as for example in the usual FORTRAN implementation of SLIP.

On the other hand, we find that a number of iterative algorithms can also be stated using recursion instead of iteration. In general, the mechanism for implementing recursion is more complex than that for iteration, so it is usually preferable to restrict recursion to those situations which are considerably simplified by its use. It is, however, interesting to note that at least one programming language, LISP, allows the user to write recursive routines but translates them prior to execution into their iterative equivalent when possible.

Another property of recursive programs should be mentioned. It can be shown that a language which possesses the facility for defining functions in terms of conditional expressions and functional composition with recursion is computationally complete in the sense that any computable function can be computed by this means. That is, if conditional expressions and recursion are permitted, assignment statements and transfers can be eliminated without any loss of theoretical power. In practice, of course, this is not advisable, but in some cases a language without assignments and transfers is preferable. In particular, it appears that certain problems which require the analysis of a program are more tractable if that program does not use assignments or transfers.

TREE PROCESSING

As we have mentioned, trees are prime candidates for recursive processing because they are essentially recursive structures themselves and tend to be used in such a way that their subtrees are to be processed in the same way as the tree itself. As an example, let us take a tree which represents the algebraic expression:

$$A * - B + C$$

There are a number of trees which can be used to represent this expression, including the one in Figure 12.1. The first uses a form of tree in which information is placed in the node itself, while the other two only contain information at the terminal nodes. The first requires more information per node, but the second two require more nodes. The only difference between the second two is the order of the branches in the subtrees. The last one uses the convention that the leftmost branch always contains an operator. This is convenient for those operations in which the subtree is processed in a way which depends primarily on the operator, which is then found in a standard position.

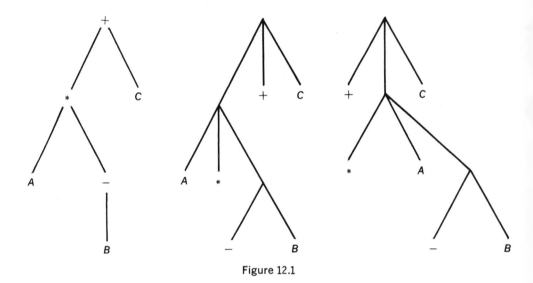

Figure 12.1

As examples of procedures which we might want to apply to a tree which represents an expression, we might mention:
a) print the expression,
b) evaluate the expression,
c) differentiate the expression,
d) generate machine code to evaluate the expression.
In addition, there are a number of procedures which are necessary for manipulating expressions, but for which the most appropriate structure is not a tree, but a list. These include:
e) multiply two expressions,
f) substitute one expression for a variable in another,
g) simplify an expression.

A list is usually preferred to a tree for these operations because the most convenient form for many expressions is a sum of terms, each of which is a product of expressions. The terms in an expression and the factors in a term can be expressed more concisely as a list. For example, the expression:

$$A + B + C$$

would be represented by the tree in Figure 12.2, while the list equivalent would be Figure 12.3.

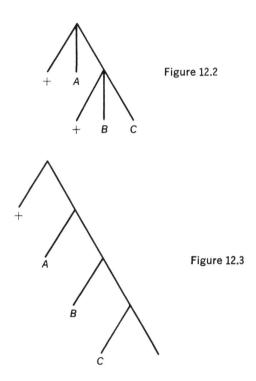

Figure 12.2

Figure 12.3

GENERAL TREE-PROCESSING PROCEDURES

Rather than give specific routines for doing particular operations on trees, we will attempt to illustrate them in a more general way by giving skeleton routines which can be modified as appropriate. In most cases these routines will not be correct PL/1, since for clarity and flexibility we have left out a number of declarations—in particular RETURNS declarations. In other cases it may be desirable for a function to return a structure, which is not legal in PL/1.

First of all we will consider binary trees without information in the nodes, and we will suppose that we have functions BRANCH1 and BRANCH2 for extracting pointers to the two subtrees, and a predicate function TERMINAL for testing if a subtree is a terminal node. A simple procedure for processing such a tree then takes the form:

```
TRPROC: PROC(TR) RECURSIVE;
        DCL TR LIKE BTREE;
        IF TERMINAL(TR) THEN DO;
            CALL TERMPROC(TR); RETURN; END;
        CALL TRPROC(BRANCH1(TR));
        CALL TRPROC(BRANCH2(TR));
        RETURN;
        END;
```

Here the two branches of a tree are processed in the same way as the tree itself, with the first branch being processed before the second. When a terminal node is reached, it is processed by the procedure TERMPROC. This type of procedure is appropriate for printing a binary tree, using a TERMPROC which inserts the printed representation of the terminal node in a buffer and incrementing the buffer pointer.

A more general procedure can be obtained if the two branches are processed by different routines. If the tree is being used to represent a list, it will often be the case that just the procedure used to process the first branch will be different from TRPROC. We will be examining this case in more detail later.

If the processing of the tree requires the result of processing the subtrees, we can use procedures which return values. The following is fairly general:

```
TRPROC: PROC(TR) RECURSIVE; DCL TR LIKE BTREE;
        IF TERMINAL(TR) THEN RETURN(TERMPROC(TR));
        RETURN(BRPROC(TRPROC(BRANCH1(TR)),
                  TRPROC(BRANCH2(TR))  ));
        END;
```

For example, this procedure can be used to build a list of terminal elements in the tree if TERMPROC returns a list just containing one item, its argument, and BRPROC is a function which appends two lists and returns the result. By writing BRPROC so that it only appends those items in its second argument which are not contained in its first, this procedure can be made to produce a nonredundant list.

In the above procedures the attribute LIKE is used to define one data-structure to be similar to one previously defined. In these examples, as in many other cases, this permits critical definitions of data-structures to be collected in a single place in the program.

GENERAL PROCEDURES FOR LABELED BINARY TREES

If the binary tree has information in the node, then the procedures become:

```
TRPROC: PROC(TR) RECURSIVE;  DCL TR LIKE LBTREE;
        IF TERMINAL(TR) THEN DO;
            CALL TERMPROC(TR);  RETURN;  END;
```

```
CALL LBLPROC(LABEL(TR));
CALL TRPROC1(BRANCH(TR));
CALL TRPROC2(BRANCH2(TR));
RETURN;
END;
```

and:

```
TRPROC: PROC(TR) RECURSIVE; DCL TR LIKE LBTREE;
        IF TERMINAL(TR) THEN RETURN(TERMPROC(TR));
        RETURN(BRPROC(LABEL(TR),
                      TRPROC1(BRANCH(TR)),
                      TRPROC2(BRANCH2(TR))  ));
        END;
```

These process the elements in this order: label, first branch, and second branch; but it is clear how it can be changed to accommodate other orders.

In the case of labelled trees, it is often the case that the function used to process the tree depends on the label. In general, such a procedure can be written as follows:

```
TRPROC: PROC(TR) RECURSIVE; DCL TR LIKE LBTREE;
        IF TERMINAL(TR) THEN RETURN(TERMPROC(TR));
        RETURN(BRPROC(LABEL(TR),
                      TRPROC1(LABEL(TR),BRANCH1(TR)),
                      TRPROC2(LABEL(TR),BRANCH2(TR))  ));
        END;
```

Here the label is given as an argument to BRPROC, TRPROC1 and TRPROC2, which can examine it and act accordingly.

An example of such a process is a function which evaluates an algebraic expression in the form of a tree structure with the label being an operator. In the simplest case, permitting only the binary arithmetic operators $+$, $-$, $*$, and $/$, this can be written:

```
EVAL: PROC(TR) RECURSIVE;  DCL TR LIKE LBTREE;
      IF TERMINAL(TR) THEN RETURN(NUMB(TR));
      RETURN(BRPROC(LABEL(TR),
                    EVAL(BRANCH1(TR)),
                    EVAL(BRANCH2(TR))  ));
      END;
```

Here NUMB will return the number specified by the terminal, which may be a constant or a variable. BRPROC will examine its first argument, which is the operator, and return the appropriate function of its other two arguments, which are the numerical values of the expressions represented by the branches of the tree.

An alternative way of writing the general function given above is in the form:

```
TRPROC: PROC(TR) RECURSIVE;  DCL TR LIKE LBTREE;
        IF TERMINAL(TR) THEN RETURN(TERMPROC(TR));
        RETURN(APPLY(FUNC(LABEL(TR)), TR));
        END;
```

Here the responsibility of processing the branches of the tree is given to the function associated with the label. APPLY is a function whose first argument is a procedure and whose value is given by applying the procedure to its second argument. This type of procedure is usually more convenient when some operators will not require a branch to be processed at all. This is the case, for instance, when evaluating an expression which involves unary operators, for which the second branch is not used. The previous TRPROC would require that the procedure TRPROC2 examine the label, and return immediately if it corresponded to a unary operator, all of which is unnecessary.

GENERAL PROCEDURES FOR PROCESSING LISTS

A data-object which has been organized as a list usually tends to have more than two items per list, and often has considerably more. It also is not usually restricted to a fixed number of items per list.

A simple form of procedure which is appropriate for a list consists of applying some procedure to each element of the list in turn. If the list is sequential in memory, the most convenient form of this is an iterative loop, in PL/1 a DO loop:

```
LPROC: PROC(L);  DCL L LIKE SEQLIST;
       DO I = 1 TO LENGTH.L;
           CALL ELPROC(L.ELS(I));
           END;
       RETURN;
       END;
```

This type of procedure is usually appropriate when the element processor ELPROC is producing its result in some global variables, or when it is changing the list element. Simple examples of this are input/output routines for lists.

It is somewhat easier to categorize procedures for processing chains. We will assume the lists are represented by binary trees, with the left branch being an element, and the right branch being the rest of the list. As usual, we will refer to these as the head and tail of the list. Processing each element of such a list can be done by an iterative routine in the following way:

```
LPROC: PROC(P);
       DCL(P,PP) POINTER;
       PP = P;
```

```
NEXT:  IF PP = NULL THEN RETURN;
       CALL ELPROC(PP->LIST.HD);
       PP =·PP->LIST.TL;
       GO TO NEXT;
       END;
```

Alternatively it can be written recursively as follows:

```
LPROC:  PROC(P) RECURSIVE;
        IF P = NULL THEN RETURN;
        CALL ELPROC(P->LIST.HD);
        CALL LPROC(P->LIST.TL);
        RETURN;
        END;
```

This is somewhat more concise, and at first sight more complex, but after a little practice such recursive routines become easy to understand, and very easy to write. A straightforward recursive implementation will usually be more inefficient in PL/1, but there is no reason why the recursive routine should not be transformed into an iterative one by the compiler.

The above routine is actually a particular case of the following rather general routine for processing a list:

```
LPROC:  PROC(P) RECURSIVE;
        IF TERMINAL(P)
           THEN RETURN(TERMPROC(P));
        RETURN(LPROCB(HDPROC(P->LIST.HD),
                      TLPROC(P->LIST.TL)  ));
        END;
```

This routine returns the result of processing the list, so can be used as a function, as can the procedures TERMPROC, LPROCB, HDPROC, and TLPROC. This procedure LPROC could be used to give a similar result to the previous one by making HDPROC the same as ELPROC, TLPROC the same as LPROC, and LPROCB and TERMPROC dummy routines which calculate nothing and return NULL.

A more complicated use of the above type of routine is to print a list using the usual parenthesis notation. The procedure LPROCB should be a dummy routine, and TLPROC should be the same as LPROC. However, the procedure TERMPROC should print a right parenthesis since it is invoked at the end of a list, and the procedure HDPROC should be written as follows:

```
HDPROC:  PROC(P) RECURSIVE;
         IF TERMINAL(P) THEN RETURN(PRATOM(P));
         CALL PRNT('(');
         RETURN(LPROC(P));
         END;
```

Here the procedure PRATOM has the job of formatting the external representation of a nonlist item, while the procedure PRNT is used to output a left parenthesis before invoking LPROC to print the items in the list. In fact the print procedure is HDPROC, which uses LPROC when its argument is actually a list. Both LPROC and HDPROC may be called recursively.

If the list is to be processed in the reverse order, a simple modification can be made to the above routine. This requires that the calls to the procedures HDPROC and TLPROC should be interchanged. This will result in the first element of the list being processed after the rest of the list, and since the rest of the list is processed by the same procedure, this will mean that the second item is processed next to last, and so on.

NONFUNCTIONAL PROCESSING

The general procedures we have described for processing trees and lists have been constructed mainly as functions of the substructures only. However, an important class of procedures requires that the result of processing a substructure be a function of all the processing done up to that point. An example of this is the print procedure described in outline previously, which essentially used global variables in which to place its result. There is a simple alternative way of doing this type of processing without using global variables which we will now describe.

The technique is to use a second argument for all the substructure-processing functions, and to pass the accumulated result of the previous processing as this second argument, the first argument as usual being the substructure itself. The function can then return the result of processing the substructure as a function of both the substructure and the result of the previous processing. To give an example, suppose we wish to reverse the elements of a chain. We can do this iteratively as follows:

```
     REV:  PROC(L);
           DCL (L,LL,LLL) POINTER;
           LL = L;   LLL = NULL;
    NEXT:  IF LL = NULL THEN RETURN(LLL);
           LLL = CONS(LL->LIST.HD,LLL);
           LL = LL->LIST.TL;
           GOTO NEXT;
           END;
```

The recursive version we can write as a function of two arguments, the first being the chain to be reversed and the second being initially NULL:

```
  REVERS:  PROC(L,LLL) RECURSIVE; DCL(L,LLL) POINTER;
           IF L = NULL THEN RETURN(LLL);
           RETURN(REVERS(L->LIST.TL,CONS(L->LIST.HD,LLL)));
           END;
```

We can then define a function of one argument to do a reverse as:

```
REV: PROC(L); DCL L POINTER;
     RETURN(REVERS(L,NULL));   END;
```

Note that the symbol LLL actually plays the same part in both the iterative and the recursive version of the procedure. In the iterative version it is a local variable, while in the recursive version it is an argument, but in both it is used to accumulate the partially reversed chain.

PROCEDURES ON TWO STRUCTURES

There are, of course, many more types of procedures which take two arguments, so we will not attempt to categorize them, but instead merely illustrate a few typical ones. One important procedure is the predicate which tests two structures for equality. An example of such a procedure for binary trees without labels is:

```
EQUAL: PROC(T1,T2) RECURSIVE; DCL(T1,T2)LIKE BTREE;
       IF TERMINAL(T1) THEN RETURN(EQTERM(T1,T2));
       IF TERMINAL(T2) THEN RETURN('0'B);
       IF EQUAL(BRANCH1(T1),BRANCH(T2)) THEN
          RETURN(EQUAL(BRANCH(T1),BRANCH(T2)));
       RETURN('0'B);
       END;
```

Here the procedure EQTERM is assumed to be available to test for the equality of two terminal branches of a tree. This procedure uses recursion to keep place in the trees while testing the first branches for equality. This can also be done by a push-down stack, and somewhat more efficiently, but the code will be much less concise.

Another simple but interesting example is a procedure which appends two chains by making a copy of the first and tacking the second onto its end. This is the way that an append operation is done in a language which discourages the modification of lists, such as LISP. The procedure is written as follows:

```
APPEND: PROC(L1,L2) RECURSIVE;  DCL(L1,L2) POINTER;
        IF L1 = NULL THEN RETURN(L2);
        RETURN(CONS(L1->LIST.HD,APPEND(L1->LIST.TL,L2)));
        END;
```

This results in a sequence of recursive calls, one for each item in the chain L1. The last call returns merely L2, since its L1 is NULL. The second to last call returns the chain obtained by CONSing the last item of the original L1 with L2, and so on.

A PATTERN-MATCHING ALGORITHM

Some procedures which at first sight appear ideally suited to recursive implementation turn out to be quite difficult to program. One such procedure is a very important algorithm for pattern matching, which we find occurring in the syntax analysis phase of translators, and also as a basic operation on character strings. We will find much use for this operation in the SNOBOL programming language in a later chapter.

The problem is to write a procedure which will determine if a subsequence of a sequence of items matches a pattern. A pattern is either a single item or a sequence of pattern elements, while a pattern element is any one of a list of patterns. Thus the pattern $(A\ B)$ matches the subsequence AB, the pattern $((A\ B)(C\ D))$ matches any of the subsequences AC, AD, BC, BD, while the pattern $(((A\ B)(C\ D))\ E)$ matches either of the subsequences ABE or CDE. This is clearly a recursively defined structure, so we expect there to be a corresponding recursive procedure to do the pattern match.

The difficulty arises in the following way. If the pattern is $(((A\ B)(A\ B\ C))\ D)$, which matches ABD or $ABCD$, and the sequence is actually $ABCE$, the first attempt at a match will match $(A\ B)$ and then look for a D. A D will not be found next, so the procedure will have to back up to try the next alternative to the pattern element previous to the D. This alternative in this case is the second item $(A\ B\ C)$, which will also match, and will also fail when the following D is looked for. Backing up this time will require going to the third alternative, which does not exist, so the match is started again for the whole pattern starting this time at the second letter in the sequence $ABCE$. In fact the match fails, of course. The difficulty lies in the backing-up process. Just because a match succeeds with one alternative does not imply that later in the sequence a failure will not occur. If it does, the next alternative will have to be tried. This means that we cannot simply assign a procedure to a list of alternatives and let it report success or failure to the higher-level procedure which invoked it, because *it may have to try again*. This means that some record will have to be kept of the next alternative. This cannot be done by ordinary local variables because they lose their values when the procedure is terminated, so it has to be done outside the procedure, or the usual recursive list-processing technique has to be abandoned.

We give below an interesting and simple recursive procedure for doing the pattern match operation. This consists of a procedure MATCH written as follows:

```
MATCH: PROC(S,P); DCL(S,P) POINTER;
       IF TERMINAL(P) THEN IF MTCH(S->LIST.HD,P)
          THEN RETURN(CONS(S,NULL));
          ELSE RETURN(NULL);
       RETURN(MATCHANY(S,P->LIST.HD,P->LIST.TL));
       END;
```

which if P is not terminal invokes the procedure MATCHANY which does all the work. If P is terminal the problem is trivially handled by a primitive procedure MTCH. MATCHANY takes three arguments; the first is the sequence S which is to be matched starting with the first item and which is represented by a chain. The second is a chain of alternative patterns, any of which can be used to match the first items of S, and the third is the chain of remaining pattern elements to be matched in succession. Thus the procedure MATCHANY will try to match the beginning of S with any of the alternatives in its second argument. After each such match, it will continue the match attempt with all the items in its third argument, in sequence. It is written as follows:

```
MATCHANY: PROC(S,APL,RPL) RECURSIVE; DCL(S,APL,R,RPL) POINTER;
          IF APL = NULL THEN RETURN(NULL);
          IF TERMINAL(APL) THEN RETURN(MATCHTERM(S,APL,RPL));
          IF TERMINAL(APL->LIST.HD)
             THEN R = MATCHTERM(S,APL->LIST.HD,RPL);
          ELSE R = MATCHANY(S,APL->LIST.HD->LIST.HD,
             APPEND(APL->LIST.HD->LIST.TL,RPL));
          IF R = NULL THEN RETURN(MATCHANY(S,APL->LIST.TL,
             RPL)); ELSE RETURN(R);
          END;
```

Here APL is either a terminal item or a chain, possibly empty, of alternative patterns, each of which may itself be either an item or a chain of pattern elements. MATCHANY first tests APL for being the empty chain NULL, in which case the match has failed, and NULL, signifying failure, is returned. If APL is a single terminal item, the result of applying the procedure MATCHTERM is returned. Otherwise APL is a chain of alternatives, and the next IF and ELSE statements determine if there is a match starting with the first of these alternatives, and set R accordingly. This is the crux of the algorithm and we will return to it below. If this attempt fails, there is no match starting with the first alternative of APL, so MATCHANY is invoked again with this alternative removed from its APL.

Let us now examine how R is set. If the first element of APL is a terminal, then the procedure MATCHTERM, which we will give below, can be used to determine if there is a match starting with it. Otherwise the first element of APL is a chain of pattern elements which must be matched in succession. The way this is done is by invoking MATCHANY again, but with the first of these pattern elements as its APL and the remainder added to the front end of the old RPL as its RPL. Thus in each case MATCHANY is called with all the pattern elements in its RPL that it needs to satisfy after satisfying any member of its APL.

Now let us look at MATCHTERM. This is only invoked with a terminal as its second argument, and it can be written as follows:

```
MATCHTERM: PROC(S,T,RPL) RECURSIVE; DCL(S,T,RPL,R) POINTER;
           IF ¬MTCH(T,S->LIST.HD) THEN RETURN(NULL);
           IF RPL= NULL THEN RETURN(CONS(S,NULL));
           R=MATCHANY(S->LIST.TL,RPL->LIST.HD,RPL->LIST.TL);
           IF R=NULL THEN RETURN(NULL);
                     ELSE RETURN(CONS(S,R));
           END;
```

If the terminal does not match the first item in S, then NULL is returned indicating failure. Otherwise if there are no more pattern elements in RPL, then success is assured, and S is returned to indicate where the match occurred. If there are more elements in RPL, MATCHANY is called to continue the match starting with the next item of S. The result of this determines the result of MATCHTERM. Note that the result of MATCH is actually a chain of those S sequences whose first element actually participated in the match. A change to MATCHTERM can easily return other information if appropriate.

AN ITERATIVE PATTERN-MATCHING ROUTINE

It is of course possible to convert any recursive routine into an iterative routine if a stack can be used. In the case of the pattern-matching routine given above, this is very instructive, because the recursive version is conceptually clearer than the iterative version, which is rather difficult to follow. We will start from the following version of MATCHANY:

```
MATCHANY: PROC(S,APL,RPL) RECURSIVE; DCL(S,APL,RPL,R) POINTER;
    NXTA: IF APL=NULL THEN RETURN(NULL);
          IF TERMINAL(APL) THEN RETURN(MATCHTERM(S,APL,RPL));
          R=MATCHANY(S,APL->LIST.HD->LIST.HD,
                  APPEND(APL->LIST.HD->LIST.TL,RPL)  );
          IF R=NULL THEN DO; APL=APL->LIST.TL; GOTO NXTA; END;
          ELSE RETURN(R);
          END;
```

This is similar to the previous version except for the removal of the test for TERMINAL(APL->LIST.HD), which is not essential, and also for the replacement of the recursive invocation of MATCHANY by the DO...END; compound.

The next step is to replace the call of the MATCHTERM procedure by the actual code. This is done by replacing

```
        RETURN(MATCHTERM(S,APL,RPL))
```

by the code

```
        DO;
        IF ¬MTCH(APL,S->LIST.HD) THEN RETURN(NULL);
        IF RPL=NULL THEN RETURN(SUCCESS);
        S=S->LIST.TL; APL=RPL->LIST.HD;
        RPL = RPL->LIST.TL:   GOTO NXTA;
        END;
```

In this the invocation of MATCHANY has been replaced by the assignments to S, APL, and RPL, and the jump to NXTA. The code for the MATCHANY routine at this point is then:

```
MATCHANY: PROC(S,APL,RPL) RECURSIVE; DCL(S,APL,RPL,R) POINTER;
    NXTA: IF APL=NULL THEN RETURN(NULL);
          IF ¬TERMINAL(APL) THEN GOTO COMPL;
          IF ¬MTCH(APL,S->LIST.HD) THEN RETURN(NULL);
          IF RPL=NULL THEN RETURN(SUCCESS);
          S = S->LIST.TL;   APL = RPL->LIST.HD;
          RPL = RPL->LIST.TL;   GOTO NXTA;
   COMPL: R = MATCHANY(S,APL->LIST.HD->LIST.HD,
                    APPEND(APL->LIST.HD->LIST.TL,RPL) );
          IF R ¬= NULL THEN RETURN(R);
          APL = APL->LIST.TL;   GOTO NXTA;
          END;
```

This version is now simply recursive and merely returns NULL or SUCCESS rather than details of the match.

The final step is to remove the recursion by using a stack. This takes the form of replacing the call of MATCHANY and changing the form of RETURN. The result is:

```
MATCH: PROC(S,P);   DCL(S,P,APL,RPL) POINTER;
       IF TERMINAL(P) THEN DO;
           IF MTCH(S->LIST.HD,P) THEN RETURN(SUCCESS);
           ELSE RETURN(NULL); END;
       APL = P->LIST.HD;   RPL = P->LIST.TL;
 NXTA: IF APL=NULL THEN GOTO FAIL;
       IF ¬ TERMINAL(APL) THEN GOTO COMPL;
       IF ¬ MTCH(APL,S->LIST.HD) THEN GOTO FAIL;
       IF RPL=NULL THEN RETURN(SUCCESS);
       S = S->LIST.TL;   APL = RPL->LIST.HD;
       RPL = RPL->LIST.TL;   GOTO NXTA;
COMPL: CALL STACK(S); CALL STACK(APL); CALL STACK(RPL);
       RPL = APPEND(APL->LIST.HD->LIST.TL,RPL);
       APL = APL->LIST.HD->LIST.HD;
       GOTO NXTA;
 FAIL: IF ¬ UNSTACK(RPL) THEN RETURN(NULL);
       CALL UNSTACK(APL);   CALL UNSTACK(S);
       APL = APL->LIST.TL;
       GOTO NXTA;
       END;
```

The routines STACK and UNSTACK save and restore the values of their arguments on a stack. The UNSTACK routine is also used to return false if the stack is empty, which happens if all possibilities have been tried and have failed. The stack actually contains a record of the successful matches if the routine as a whole is successful. In practice the string S being matched would probably be represented sequentially rather than as a chain, but this change is straightforward.

The main deficiency of the routine as given above is the use of the APPEND routine. Rather than append the two chains it is quicker to keep a pointer to the stack which has just been used to save RPL, and set APL to APL->LIST.HD->LIST.TL. This pointer will have to be stacked and unstacked also, and the code to set RPL to RPL->LIST.TL will have to be extended by a test for RPL being NULL, in which case the stack pointer should be used to extract more RPL. The appropriate changes are left to the reader.

EXERCISES

1. Given a tree representation of an arithmetic expression, write a procedure to print it out in reverse Polish notation.
2. Write a procedure to differentiate an arithmetic expression represented as a tree.
3. Write a procedure which when given a chain whose elements are chains will return a similar chain but with all its elements reversed, and all the elements of its sub-chains reversed.
*4. Complete the iterative pattern-matching routine described in the text.

13
GARBAGE COLLECTION

In this chapter we will concern ourselves with a problem which arises in the design of programming systems which make considerable use of pointers, and which we have introduced previously in connection with pointer processing. The problem is that of determining when a data-structure is no longer required, so that its memory space can be released automatically. The general technique, as we have mentioned, is for the system, when it runs out of space, to trace down all structures which may be accessed by the program, mark them as to be saved, and release the memory used by the rest. This technique is used by all the programming languages which will be described in Chapters 15–19, though not in PL/1.

In considering algorithms for doing garbage collection, we will assume that the relevant structures are linked block structures in which the positions of all pointers within the blocks are known to the garbage collector. We will assume also that the structures which have to be saved are known at all points at which the garbage collector may be invoked.

MARKING ALGORITHMS

The marking mechanism requires that each block can be flagged as being available or in use. In the case of blocks consisting of a number of words, this can usually be done quite simply by using a bit in the bookkeeping information associated with each block, which is usually kept in the first word of the block. However, when the blocks being allocated are just single-word blocks, it is usually not convenient to allocate a bit in the word itself for this purpose, since many of the operations which are provided by the hardware work on all bits. It is of course possible to represent a floating-point number by only 31 bits instead of the 32, and mask out one bit when doing floating-point arithmetic, but it is usual to use a *bit table* in which successive bits are taken to correspond to successive words in the area used for single-word allocations. This involves a small amount of additional memory, and is quite efficient in execution time.

Algorithm One

In the case of tree structures, the marking process is recursive rather than iterative, and is usually implemented using a stack. For ease of illustration we will write it as a recursive procedure. Suppose our structures are constructed out of binary nodes containing two pointers and one-dimensional arrays containing an arbitrary number of pointers. We can write a procedure to mark a binary node given a pointer to it as follows.

```
MARKB: PROCEDURE(P) RECURSIVE;  DCL P POINTER;
       IF BMARKED(P) THEN RETURN;
       CALL MARKBN(P);
       CALL MARK(P->BNODE.LEFT);
       CALL MARK(P->BNODE.RIGHT);
       RETURN;
       END;
```

and a procedure to mark a vector as follows:

```
MARKV: PROCEDURE(P) RECURSIVE;  DCL P POINTER;
       DCL N FIXED;
       IF VMARKED(P) THEN RETURN;
       CALL MARKBL(P);
       N = P->VECT.LNGTH;
       DO I=1 TO N:  CALL MARK(P->VECT.ITEM);  END;
       RETURN;
       END;
```

In each case a routine (MARKBN or MARKBL) is used to mark the block used for the structure, and then the routine MARK is called to mark its components.

The routine MARK will have to distinguish whether its argument contains a pointer, and what type of structure is pointed to. For the purposes of illustration, we will assume that there are predicates available for this purpose. The routine can then be written as follows.

```
MARK: PROCEDURE(I) RECURSIVE;  DCL I LIKE ITEM;
      IF BTREE(I) THEN DO;  CALL MARKB(I.PTR);
                            RETURN;  END;
      IF VECTOR(I) THEN DO; CALL MARKV(I.PTR);
                            RETURN;  END;
      RETURN;
      END;
```

Note that as the procedures process the tree, each item is checked for being the type of structure which contains a pointer to another structure. In some cases a structure may be restricted to contain references to only certain other types of structure. The routine can then invoke the relevant marking routine itself, rather than the general routine MARK. This gives a more efficient marking algorithm, as well as a more concise representation.

The type of structure referred to by a pointer can be determined in several ways. If space is available in the object pointed to, bits in standard positions in the first word of the block pointed to can be used to specify the type of structure. For large blocks this is quite reasonable, but once again it is not convenient for one-word blocks used to store floating-point and similar quantities. An alternative scheme puts the flags in the same word as the pointer, which leaves the block pointed to free. This however has the disadvantage of requiring more memory, since these flags are duplicated whenever the pointer is used. However, it does permit rapid determination of the type of an object without any additional memory references, and so is usually a little faster in most applications.

An efficient way of determining the type of a structure is possible if all structures of the same type are allocated memory from the same area. In this case the type of a structure can be determined by noting into which area the pointer is pointing. This is efficient from the point of view of both speed and memory space, but puts restrictions on the storage allocation algorithm.

Algorithm Two

A problem with the above algorithm is that it requires memory for the stack, which can be awkward since this may grow quite large. In fact there is no absolute necessity to use a stack at all. Whenever it comes to a branch point, the above marking algorithm uses the stack to save pointers it wants to trace later. Alternatively, it could just choose to trace one such pointer, and then repeat the whole algorithm until all branches are marked. It can do this because a branch previously marked can be tested and ignored when it is encountered subsequently.

This procedure is clearly inefficient, and the following modification of it is preferable. Allocate a small fixed amount of memory for the stack, which is used as in Algorithm 1 until exhausted. At this point, trace single pointers until the algorithm backs up to remove some pointers from the stack, which then becomes usable again. As above, this algorithm is executed repeatedly until all pointers are traced.

For details of this and other similar algorithms, see Knuth (68).

Algorithm Three

If no space is available for a stack, an algorithm due to Schorr and Waite (67) can be used. This essentially uses the same technique for processing a tree as that used in the tree-straightening routine given in Chapter 8. That is, as the algorithm moves down the tree, the pointers are reversed. These reversed pointers permit the algorithm to return up the tree without using a stack, and are reset on the way.

Algorithm Four

In the general case, the collection of memory blocks which have been freed by the marking procedure is straightforward, and we will not discuss it in detail. Any of the organizations mentioned in the chapter on storage allocation can be adapted for this purpose. In fact the bookkeeping associated with the collection is simpler when garbage collection is used, since a linear scan of all memory blocks can be used to link them together. However, garbage collection is possible only when we know the location of pointers. If we know the location of all quantities which are dependent on the location of blocks within memory, it is possible to move blocks if all pointers referring to them are modified accordingly. It is therefore natural that systems which provide garbage collection also do stack-type storage allocation, compacting used blocks when memory is exhausted. In what follows we will address ourselves to this problem.

A marking algorithm which is sometimes useful when compaction is to be done chains together all active pointers to a block. This algorithm effectively uses a single bit in the pointer field and a bit in each block to be used for marking. These bits are initially zero. We will suppose that the marking bit is the first bit in the block, so that a block pointed to by 4 pointers might appear as in Figure 13.1. If we suppose that only the first 3 pointers to the block occur on structures to be saved, the diagram after marking will have been transformed as shown in Figure 13.2. That is, the block will have its mark flag set, and the first pointer-sized field within the block will point to one of the pointers which used to point to the block, which itself will point to another, and so on. The last such pointer will contain the original contents of the first pointer field of the block, which we assume does not contain a pointer to another block.

The algorithm for doing this type of marking is very simple. When a pointer is found to point to a block, the contents of the pointer and the first pointer field of the block are interchanged, and the mark bit set to one. This builds a chain of pointers which specify all the "active" references to a block, the chain ending when the mark bit in the pointer field is zero. The inactive references do not get on the chain, and will not be referred to any more.

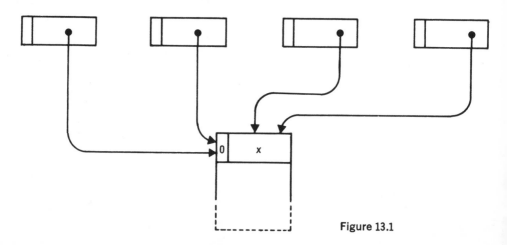

Figure 13.1

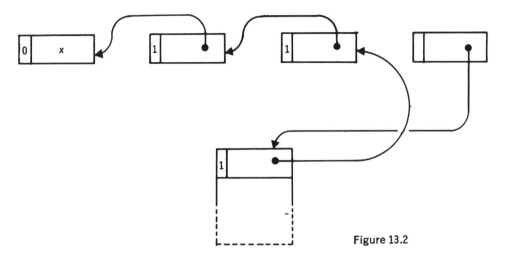

Figure 13.2

COMPACTION ALGORITHMS

For the sake of simplicity, we will assume initially that there is space in each block to store its new address.

Algorithm One

Compacting can be done by working from one end of the memory, and moving each used block into an empty space close to the other end of memory. The procedure terminates when no such empty space exists for a particular block. When a block is moved, it can be marked accordingly, and its new address inserted in a standard position in the old block. There is considerable scope for choice in deciding where to put a block to be moved, the object being to move as many blocks at one end of memory as possible. This is rather similar to the block allocation problem in the first place, but more information is available on which to base the decision. Of course if all the blocks are the same size there is no problem, and all the holes can be filled perfectly. After moving as many blocks as possible, a linear scan of all blocks can be made, examining each pointer. If a pointer is found to point into a block which has been moved, it is modified to point to the new position of the block.

Algorithm Two

If marking Algorithm Four is used, compaction is similar except that after a block is moved the chain of references is traced, and the pointers put back, now pointing to the new block position. The previous contents of the first pointer field of the block are then restored. Note that in tracing down a chain of references, some references may be in blocks which themselves have been moved, so the corresponding positions in the new blocks should be changed.

Algorithm Three

The main disadvantage of the above algorithms is that, if the blocks are of differing sizes, there will usually be "holes" which are not large enough to contain a block which is a candidate for moving. What we would prefer to do is to move all blocks down so that they are adjacent, with no holes left at all. This simplifies the bookkeeping problem considerably. However, with the above algorithms, moving a block could destroy information in a block which had been moved previously. This difficulty can be removed by splitting the compaction pass into two passes. In the first pass, a pointer in each block is set to point to its new position, and all pointers are adjusted accordingly. In the second pass, the blocks are actually moved to their new locations. This algorithm is essentially the one given in Bobrow (67).

Algorithm Four

If some blocks do not have enough free space in them to contain a pointer to their new location, Algorithm 3 will not work. This is often the case for small blocks such as binary nodes. In this case a mixture of Algorithms 1 and 3 can be used, as follows:

1. Compact small blocks into holes, posting new addresses in old addresses.
2. Calculate and post in larger blocks the new addresses of those blocks which are to be moved.
3. Adjust pointers to point to new addresses.
4. Move larger blocks to new locations.

Note that this algorithm is most conveniently implemented if the type of each block can be determined by a linear scan through memory in both directions.

Algorithm Five

A neat algorithm due to Stephanie Brown (unpublished) uses the bit table to adjust the pointers. This in effect divides the bit table produced by the marking algorithm into segments, and associates with each segment the total number of unmarked bits in all previous segments. If complete compaction is used, leaving no holes, this table contains enough information to adjust any pointer. This is done as follows: given a pointer to address p, determine the number n of unmarked bits in the bit table corresponding to words before p, and change the value of the pointer to $p - n$. The number n is easily computed as the number of unmarked bits in the same segment as p and before it, plus the number of unmarked bits in previous segments. The algorithm then takes the form

1. Move all blocks to fill holes completely, keeping them in the same order.
2. Adjust all pointers according to the bit table.

This algorithm is particularly good if there is an instruction which counts the number of one-bits in a word, in which case a segment of the bit table is conveniently chosen to be a word. The representation of data-structures is best chosen so that a linear scan from beginning (i.e. compacted) to end of memory is sufficient to determine the type of blocks. If this is not possible, a supplementary bit table can be used to keep this information.

Algorithm Six

A simple algorithm assumes that the area of memory available for storage of linked block structures is divided into two. When one part of the memory is used up, those structures which are to be saved are copied to the other area, which is assumed to be empty. Further calculations then use the second area until it is full, when the process is reversed. Although this appears to use memory very inefficiently, the regularity of the use of the extra portion of memory makes it quite convenient for systems which do automatic paging of portions of memory in and out of core, or for systems which can tolerate a program requesting more memory for a short period. Many modern machines provide a cheap low-speed core which can be used quite conveniently for this purpose also.

A copying routine for the above garbage-collection algorithm can be written in a number of ways. The most straightforward uses a recursive procedure to process the structures to be saved, written in such a way that it copies the terminal blocks first. For a simple binary tree it might be written informally as follows:

```
COPYREL: PROC(T) RECURSIVE;  DCL NEWT LIKE ITEM;
         IF MARKED(T) THEN RETURN(NEWLOC(T));
         IF TERMINAL(T) THEN DO;
             NEWT = COPYTERM(T);
             CALL MARK(T,NEWT);
             RETURN(NEWT);
             END;
         NEWT = MAKNODE(2)
         CALL MARK(T,NEWT);
         CALL INSERT(NEWT,COPYREL(HD(T)),COPYREL(TL(T)));
         RETURN(NEWT);
         END;
```

Here each structure is marked after it is copied, and its new location posted in its old location. Before copying a structure, it is checked to see if it has been copied already. If it has, a reference to the new location is returned. Otherwise, it is tested to see if it is a terminal structure, i.e. one not containing any pointers. If so, it is copied, marked, its new location posted, and a reference to its new location returned. Otherwise its constituents are first copied, the new references used to construct a copy, the old structure marked, and the reference to the new copy returned. Note that by allocating space for a two-entry node by MAKNODE and marking it before invoking the recursion, circular structures can be handled by this routine.

Algorithm Seven

An alternative routine can be written to work from the top of the structure without using recursion. This essentially does the following: the first block is copied and marked and its new location posted in its old location; then those blocks it points to are copied and marked, their new locations posted, and the pointers adjusted accordingly. Any block referred to which is marked simply has its pointer adjusted to point to the new location. This process is then repeated for any blocks which have been copied until no new blocks are copied, when the process is complete. Note that this method requires that every block copied carry with it some indication of whether it contains pointers or not. This can be provided by an additional table, in the simplest case just a bit table, which can be used by the copying routine to flag each block as it is moved.

Let us consider how we might write such a routine for data-structures made up of linked lists and one-dimensional arrays whose items have the form

```
DCL    1 ITEM CELL,
       2 IND, 3 TYPE FIXED BINARY(7), 3 REF FIXED BINARY(23),
       2 INT FIXED BINARY(31),
       2 REAL FLOAT BINARY(31),
       2 CH CHARACTER(4);
```

where the type of object pointed to by an index in REF is specified by TYPE. It can be written as follows.

```
GCOLL:  PROCEDURE(ASPACE,MARKA,BSPACE,BPTR,NEXTB);
        DCL ASPACE(MAXA) LIKE ITEM;
        DCL BSPACE(MAXB) LIKE ITEM;
        DCL MARKA(MAXA) BIT(1); DCL BPTR(MAXB) BIT(1);
        DCL(NEXTB,NX,I,J,N) FIXED BINARY;
        BSPACE(1) = ASPACE(1);   BPTR(1) = '1'B;
        NEXTB = 2;   NX = 1;
MORE:   IF ¬BPTR(NX) THEN GOTO NXT;
        I = BSPACE(NMX).REF;
        IF MARKA(I) THEN GOTO MKD;
        IF BSPACE(NX).TYPE = NOTPTR THEN GOTO NXT;
        IF BSPACE(NX).TYPE = MRKWRD THEN DO;
            BSPACE(NEXTB) = ASPACE(I);   BPTR(NEXTB) = '0'B;
            MARKA(I) = '1'B;   ASPACE(I).REF = NEXTB;
            NEXTB = NEXTB + 1;   GOTO MKD;   END;
        IF BSPACE(NX).TYPE = MRKLST THEN DO;
            BSPACE(NEXTB) = ASPACE(I); BPTR(NEXTB) = '1'B;
            BSPACE(NEXTB+1) = ASPACE(I + 1);
            BPTR(NEXTB+1)='1'B;
            MARKA(I) = '1'B;   ASPACE(I).REF = NEXTB;
            NEXTB = NEXTB+2;   GOTO MKD;   END;
```

```
    IF BSPACE(NX).TYPE=MRKVCT THEN DO;
        N = ASPACE(I);
        BSPACE(NEXTB)=N; BPTR(NEXTB)='0'B;
        DO J=1,N;
                BSPACE(NEXTB+J) = ASPACE(I+J);
                BPTR(NEXTB+J) = '1'B;  END;
            MARKA(I) = '1'B;  ASPACE(I).REF = NEXTB;
            NEXTB = NEXTB+1;  GOTO MKD;  END;
MKD: BSPACE(NX).REF = ASPACE(I).REF;
NXT: NX = NX+1;  IF NX LT NEXTB THEN GOTO MORE;
    RETURN;
    END;
```

The item in ASPACE(I) is assumed to specify a structure which will contain all structures which have to be saved. The bit array MARKA is used in parallel with the array ASPACE to mark those blocks which have been moved, and the bit array BPTR is used in parallel with BSPACE to indicate those items which contain a pointer. The global variables NOTPTR, MRKWRD, MRKLST, MRKVCT are assumed to contain the values of the TYPE field of an ITEM which does not point to anything, which points to a word which itself does not contain a pointer, which points to the first of two ITEMs which specify a binary node of a list, and which points to the first item of a vector, respectively. A vector consists of a sequence of ITEMs with the first item containing the number of items in the vector. Note that this routine also can handle circular structures without any modification, because it relocates each block as soon as it is encountered.

EFFICIENCY

The efficiency of the various algorithms for doing garbage collection varies with the amount of memory which is recovered. If garbage collection only recovers a small amount of memory, it will only be a short time until a further collection is necessary. As memory fills up, therefore, the efficiency of garbage collection as measured by the average amount of computation necessary to free a word, increases. In fact, if precautions are not taken, a program which runs out of memory will invoke the garbage collector repeatedly, recovering no memory at all. Even if this situation is detected, the increasing ineffectiveness of the garbage collection as memory fills up can result in virtually all computation time being spent in garbage collection. It is possible to devise very simple algorithms for which garbage collection can free a single word, which is sufficient to enable the calculation to proceed, but as soon as a second word is required, garbage collection will again be necessary, once again only releasing a single word. An example of such an algorithm is

```
AGN: X = CONS(Y,CDR(X));  GOTO AGN;
```

which can require and release a single word indefinitely.

The majority of garbage-collection algorithms take a time which can be written approximately in the form $an + bm$, where n is the number of words available, m is the number of words saved, and a and b are constants. Since the number of words recovered is $n - m$, the computation per word recovered is $(an + bm)/(n - m)$, which clearly gets large as m approaches n. Some garbage collection algorithms will terminate the run if insufficient memory is recovered, so avoiding this inefficiency. In modern machines which do multiprogramming, this often is simply an indication to the user to increase the amount of memory which the program requests from the operating system. With more sophisticated operating systems which can handle requests for more memory dynamically, the garbage collector can issue such a request when insufficient memory is recovered.

The memory requirements of a program which uses garbage collection is rather tricky to determine, particularly if it must be done dynamically. There is clearly a lower limit to the amount of memory which any program requires in order to finish, but this amount depends on the details of the program and its data, and it can be shown that it is not computable for all programs, so we have to resort to trial and error. If we were to choose the exact amount of memory, then it would be very likely that the program would run inefficiently as it approached its limit, so as a general rule we would probably want to allocate 10 percent more. However, if we wished to allocate memory dynamically, as in one of the more flexible multiprogramming systems, it is clear that we would probably not want to allocate the maximum amount of memory all the time. A reasonable procedure might be for the garbage collector to request 20 percent more memory whenever less than 20 percent of the available space was released, and to give up 20 percent of memory whenever garbage collection yielded more than 50 percent. This would tend to stabilize if the program itself had regular memory requirements, with the amount of memory being between 25 percent and 100 percent more than the minimum requirement. Slow fluctuations in this requirement would be accounted for without persistent wide discrepancies.

GARBAGE COLLECTION AND LANGUAGE DESIGN

In later chapters we will be describing in more detail a number of programming languages which provide garbage-collection facilities. Here we will discuss in general terms some of the considerations which affect the decision of whether to provide garbage collection or not. To be specific, we will consider how garbage collection might be provided in PL/1. The standard version of PL/1 does not provide garbage collection, of course, but requires that the programmer explicitly FREE a structure, or have it automatically freed on exit from the block in which it is declared.

The data-structures which have been allocated by an ALLOCATE statement will be the ones which would be subject to garbage collection. These are either CONTROLLED or BASED storage mode. Other variables, of STATIC or AUTOMATIC mode, are allocated either fixed space or space on a stack, respectively, and would be unaffected by the garbage collector.

In order to provide the type of garbage collection we have been talking about it is necessary for the system to keep track of all pointer variables which are currently active, i.e. declared within currently activated blocks of code. This includes pointers which may occur in arrays or structures, so the system must provide some mechanism for identifying which fields contain pointers. This can be done in a number of ways.

In the case of pointer variables, or arrays whose elements are pointers, it is straightforward to use a flag to indicate that they should be traced, or to allocate them in a space which was separated from the other variables. Temporary variables must also be marked for use by the garbage collector; this is a little trickier, because it is usual to allocate these dynamically on the stack. This requires the use of either a dynamic stack-marking scheme or static allocation for pointer temporaries.

In the case of structures some of whose fields contain pointers, the most straightforward scheme is to keep a *map* with each structure showing the location of the pointer fields. During the marking phase these maps will be interrogated in order to locate the pointer fields. A more efficient way of doing this is to store the "type" within each structure, and then compile code to process each type of structure in the appropriate way.

Note that the marking process would be considerably more efficient if, in addition to knowing where a pointer was, the system also knew what sort of object was pointed to. Without this knowledge there must be identifying information associated with every data-structure which is accessible via a pointer which will describe its map. In the case of the more complicated structures this is not too inefficient, but in the case of a pointer to a floating-point quantity it may require another word, or another addressable unit of memory. This is the main reason that garbage collection in PL/1 would be so inefficient. As we will see in later chapters, ALGOL 68 insists that the type of object referred to by a pointer is specified in the declaration of the pointer, which permits a much more efficient scheme for garbage collection. In fact ALGOL 68 does not have a FREE statement, but relies purely on its garbage collector.

LOCAL AND PARTIAL GARBAGE COLLECTION

From a language-design point of view, one of the main objections to garbage collection is the severe constraints which appear to be put on the whole language. In general, we find that the type of objects has to be marked, and we have to treat pointers specially so that their values are always accessible to the garbage collector. We cannot, for example, permit a program to store away a pointer in an integer variable temporarily, because the garbage collector will then not mark what it points to. The source of this problem appears to be that pointer variables which we normally would like to think of as being local variables are in fact forced to be global as far as the garbage collector is concerned. In this section we will consider a scheme similar to that used in a LISP system by Arnold Rochfeld which permits the garbage collector to be used locally.

The idea of this scheme is that, when a routine is entered, it records the address of the next available location to be allocated by the allocator. The garbage collector compacts storage, so all locations above this address are available. The routine than executes normally, getting space from the stack-type allocator in the usual way. When the routine terminates, the compacting garbage collector is invoked, but only to collect within the memory which has been allocated since the current routine started to execute. The pointer variables used by the current routine are used by the garbage collector for marking, together with any arguments or global variables whose values may have been changed by the routine. Marking is discontinued when a pointer refers to a location outside the space allocated to the current routine. Those structures which must be saved are compacted, and the routine continues.

The advantage of this scheme is that the garbage collector is used only when the routine is prepared for it, so that it is not necessary for the routine to maintain its pointers in the correct form at all times. That is, we have restricted the information required by the garbage collector to that which can be explicitly supplied by a single routine.

Below we give an example of a routine which uses this type of garbage collection. Just before the routine terminates the area of memory which has been allocated is copied to an adjacent area of memory space, and then the structures which are to be saved are copied back into a compacted form. The routine can be written as follows:

```
EXMPL: PROC(L1);   DCL(L1,L2,L3) LIKE ITEM;
       DCL NXT FIXED;
       NXT = NEXTAVAIL;
       . . .
       . . .
       . . .
       NUSED = NEXTAVAIL-NXT;
       DO I = NXT TO NEXTAVAIL;
          SPACE(I+NUSED) = SPACE(I);   END;
       NEXTAVAIL = NXT;
       CALL CLBITBL(MARK(NEXTAVAIL),NUSED);
       L1= COPYOFFSET(L1,NXT,NUSED);
       L2 = COPYOFFSET(L2,NXT,NUSED);
       LGLOBAL = COPYOFFSET(LGLOBAL,NXT,NUSED);
       RETURN(L2);
       END;
```

In the above routine the result is L2, which therefore must be saved. LGLOBAL is an example of a global variable whose value has been changed by the routine, and the argument L1 has also been changed, so both must be saved also. The index of the first available element in SPACE on entry to the routine is kept in the global variable NEXTAVAIL, which is stored in NXT. At the end of the routine, the cells used from SPACE are then NXT to NEXTAVAIL-1, which are copied to the next part of SPACE. NEXTAVAIL is then reset, and the structures being saved are copied by COPYOFFSET. The routine CLBITBL is invoked to clear a bit table used in the copying routine.

The routine COPYOFFSET copies its first argument into the available space starting at NEXTAVAIL, but assuming that all indices above its second argument actually refer to locations which are higher by the value of its third argument. Every block copied is marked in a bit table, and its new location stored in the cell it was originally in. A modified version of the routine GCOLL can be used for COPYOFFSET.

The use of this type of garbage collector requires that each routine which is going to call the garbage collector keep some sort of record of the structures it wishes saved. A simple way of doing this is for it to pass references to such structures to the garbage collection routine, as we have done above. However, this is only possible when the routine itself knows which global structures it has modified. In complex routines such as interpreters, arbitrarily complex routines may be invoked, and these routines may modify global structures without the knowledge of the routine which invoked them. In this case, it is convenient for such routines to have available to them a list to which they can add any global variables they modify. That is, we require that each routine do one of the following:

a) establish on entry a new garbage-collection area and a new global list, and call the garbage collector on completion, saving and compacting any structures which may be used by higher-level routines, including any structures on the global list; or

b) add to the most recent global list references to structures referred to from outside the most recent garbage collection area which have been changed.

The global list referred to above can be organized as a stack because of its first-in-last-out character, but this requires further interaction with the storage allocator, so we will assume that it is a linked list which can be allocated space in a straightforward way. One difficulty which may arise is that the same global structure may be modified several times before garbage collection, so that the global list could contain duplicates. This can be avoided by flagging any item put on the global list, and testing each new item before putting it on to check that it was not flagged.

A further difficulty is that a routine may modify a structure which is global not only to the most recent area, but also to the area before that, so this structure must be saved by both garbage collections. We can do this by requiring that any entries on the global list which are global to the previous area also should be added by the garbage collector to the global list. This will require that each global list also specify the bounds of the previous area.

Accordingly, we will keep the following information:

a) a global variable START which will contain the index of the first location in the current area;

b) a global variable NEXTAVAIL which will contain the index of the next available location on the stack;

c) a global variable SAVELIST which will point to a list of items outside the current area which might have been modified by the current routine;

d) a global variable PREVSTART which will contain the value of START for the previous area;

e) a global variable PREVSAVE which will contain the value of SAVELIST for the previous area.

At the beginning of the routine, we will have the following code.

```
DCL(PRST,PRSAV) FIXED;
PRST = PREVSTART;
PREVSTART = START;   START = NEXTAVAIL;
PRSAV = PREVSAVE
PREVSAVE = SAVELIST;   SAVELIST = 0;
```

which will effectively establish a new area. The local variables PRST and PRSAV are used to store the previous values of PREVSTART and PREVSAVE for restoring on exit.

The form of SAVELIST depends on what sort of items we are going to put on it, but in the general case we might find it convenient if the form can handle arbitrary items, whether actually in the SPACE array or not. The most convenient form in this case is to make SAVELIST an ordinary linked list whose elements are pointers to the global items. The use of standard PL/1 pointers rather than indices into SPACE permits all items to be referenced. We will suppose that all items to be saved are put on SAVELIST by the routine. At the end of the routine, the following routine can then be invoked.

```
LGCOLL: PROCEDURE;
          NUSED = NEXTAVAIL - START;
          DO I = START, NEXTAVAIL;
              SPACE(I+NUSED) = SPACE(I);
              MARK(I+NUSED) = '0'B;
              END;
NXTSAV: IF SAVELIST = 0 THEN GO TO FIN;
          P = SPACE(SAVELIST);
          SAVELIST = SPACE(SAVELIST+1);
          CALL COPYREL(P->ITEM);
          GOTO NXTSAV;
   FIN: START = PREVSTART;   SAVELIST = PRESAVE;
          RETURN;
          END;
```

so a routine will terminate with the code

```
CALL LGCOLL;   PREVSTART = PRST;   PREVSAVE = PRSAV;
RETURN(LL);
END;
```

The routine COPYREL can be written using similar code to GCOLL as follows.

```
COPYREL: PROCEDURE(L);
           DCL (NX,NEXTA,I,J,N) FIXED BINARY;
```

```
       NEXTA = NEXTAVAIL;   NX = NEXTAVAIL;
       SPACE(NEXTAVAIL) = L;   MARK(NEXTAVAIL) = '1'B;
       NEXTAVAIL = NEXTAVAIL+1;
 MORE: IF ¬MARK(NX) THEN GOTO NXT;
       I = SPACE(NX).REF;
       IF I LT START THEN GOTO NXT;
       I = I + NUSED;
       IF MARK(I) THEN GOTO MKD;
       IF SPACE(NX).TYPE = NOTPTR THEN GOTO NXT;
       IF SPACE(NX).TYPE = MRKWRD THEN DO;
          SPACE(NEXTAVAIL)=SPACE(I);MARK(NEXTAVAIL)='0'B;
          MARK(I) = '1'B;   SPACE(I).REF = NEXTAVAIL;
          NEXTAVAIL = NEXTAVAIL+1;   GOTO MKD;   END;
       IF SPACE(NX).TYPE = MRKLST THEN DO;
          SPACE(NEXTAVAIL)=SPACE(I);  MARK(NEXTAVAIL)='1'B;
          SPACE(NEXTAVAIL+1)=SPACE(I+1);
          MARK(NEXTAVAIL+1)='1'B;
          MARK(I) = '1'B;   SPACE(I).REF = NEXTAVAIL;
          NEXTAVAIL = NEXTAVAIL+2;   GOTO MKD;   END;
       IF SPACE(NX).TYPE = MRKVCT THEN DO;
          N = SPACE(I);
          SPACE(NEXTAVAIL) = N;   MARK(NEXTAVAIL) = '0'B;
          DO J = 1,N;
             SPACE(NEXTAVAIL+J) = SPACE(I+J);
             MARK(NEXTAVAIL+J) = '1'B;   END;
          MARK(I) = '1'B;   SPACE(I).REF = NEXTAVAIL;
          NEXTAVAIL = NEXTAVAIL+N+1;   GOTO MKD;   END;
  MKD: SPACE(NX).REF = SPACE(I).REF;
  NXT: NX = NX+1;   IF NX LT NEXTAVAIL THEN GOTO MORE;
       RETURN(SPACE(NEXTA));
       END;
```

This routine is actually incomplete because it does not test for its result being outside the previous garbage-collection area. If it is, then a reference to it should be added to PREVSAVE. This is difficult because it requires testing the magnitude of a pointer, which is not actually allowed in PL/1, and so will be faked. The corrective code should be inserted just before the RETURN.

In many situations this garbage-collection procedure will be quite satisfactory. The PL/1 programmer writing routines for manipulating algebraic expressions, for instance, will be able to invoke the garbage collector at the end of those routines which involve considerable calculation, and which seem likely to generate a number of temporary lists which are used and then no longer required. Such routines can often be written without changing any global structures, so the number of entries on SAVELIST can be kept down. Of course, the more the programmer knows about the characteristics of the garbage collector, the more efficient he will be able to make his program; and he will quite easily be able to avoid the grosser inefficiencies. We will normally only invoke the garbage collector when there is the possibility of releasing a considerable proportion of the memory allocated, so we expect this procedure to be quite efficient. However, because it does only local garbage collection, there will be inaccessible structures in previous areas which would not be collected by this method, but would be by the global methods. We therefore expect this method to require more memory.

In the case when the program's behavior is less predictable, such as when procedures of unknown characteristics are used as arguments to other procedures, there are problems with a local garbage collector. These arise mainly because of the possibly large number of global variables which may be modified. For instance, suppose we are writing an interpreter which will execute a program in the form of one of the linked data-structures. This will require assignments to the variables referred to by the structure, so a natural operation which will frequently arise is that this structure will have to be changed. As we have described it, the algorithm will then require that each modification cause an entry to be made on SAVELIST. This is time-consuming in itself, and becomes even more so if the size of SAVELIST is kept down by not duplicating any entries, which requires searching SAVELIST before any entry is made.

EXERCISES

**1. Implement a set of routines which will provide garbage collection for the PL/1 programmer. Note that this will require that all variables which may point to collectable structures should be accessible to the garbage collector. This requires that when such a variable becomes active, a reference to it should be placed on a chain, and removed when the variable is no longer active. Note also that the garbage collector must know the structure of the plexes being processed.

*2. Write a compacting garbage collector for binary nodes and vectors of pointers using an appropriate combination of the marking and compacting algorithms described.

19

THE USE OF MACROS

INTRODUCTION

In this chapter we will consider the use of facilities which are provided in some programming languages for preprocessing the text of the program prior to its translation and execution. That is, the programmer provides not only the text of the program, but also the specifications of how it should be preprocessed. If the preprocessing facilities are powerful enough, this effectively permits the programmer to specify his own programming language. In practice the specification of a complete translator is not straightforward, so the facilities provided for the preprocessing pass are usually restricted to those operations, which can be simply specified by the programmer. Such facilities are usually called *macros*.

The first use of macros was in conjunction with assembly languages rather than higher-level languages, and much of the knowledge accumulated about their usefulness has been derived from this experience. However, it has been recognized for some time that similar facilities can be very useful for high-level languages. In particular, as we mentioned in a previous chapter, PL/1 possesses a macro facility, and we will use this for the examples in this chapter. The full capability of macro facilities is not generally recognized. It seems that in more advanced programming languages, macros, or an extension of macros, will play a much larger part. In Chapters 18 and 19 we will describe two languages which have much more sophisticated preprocessing abilities, BALM and ALGOL 68.

We can consider macro facilities from two points of view. The first is from the point of view of the type of processing done by the macro. In the simplest case this consists of simply a replacement operation, in which a portion of the text is replaced by a different portion of text which may include pieces of the original. At first sight this is a very primitive and weak form of process, but, in fact, if the resulting text is processed repeatedly until no further change occurs, it can be shown that this permits replacement of a piece of text by any text which can be computed from it. However, the use of such a primitive facility to do complex replacements is more an exercise for the student of computability than for the anxious programmer, so its use is usually limited to the simpler types of replacement.

More complex preprocessors permit more than simple replacement. The piece of text to be replaced is actually considered to be an argument of a procedure. This procedure may be written in a fairly powerful language permitting substantial calculations on the text to be expressed conveniently. In PL/1 such a facility is available, with the language available for processing the text being a subset of the standard PL/1 statements.

We can also consider macro facilities from the point of view of the type of use made of them by the programmer. A very simple application is to use macros to make up for the deficiencies of a particular translator which does not produce optimum code. For instance, a program may often be written in a more flexible way by replacing certain fixed parameters in the code, such as the dimension of an array or the maximum length of a string, by variables which are initialized at the beginning of the program and referenced later. A good compiler will be able to notice that this variable is not changed, and thus replace it by its value in subsequent code, with considerable improvement in code produced in a number of situations. If the compiler does not do this, a preprocessor can be used to do the replacement. This is actually an example of a case where a little information about the program, in this case the information that a particular variable is constant, can eliminate a considerable amount of code from the compiler.

Another use with the same objective (that of producing faster code) but which is not necessarily to be blamed on the compiler, is to permit in-line code to be inserted for a procedure call. This may produce a program which requires more memory but will execute faster because the code which invokes the procedure will not be executed. In some cases the compiler will be able to optimize the resulting code so that the memory required is also less. An example of this is a short procedure which is invoked in the middle of a DO loop. The occurrence of the procedure in the loop would necessitate the loop counters and indices being stored in memory before the invocations, and retrieved afterwards. With in-line code there would be a good chance that this would not be necessary. In some cases the procedure may just consist of a couple of instructions when written in line. A further possibility is that a procedure may be able to permit more argument types and results if expanded as in-line code. An example of this in PL/1 is the use of a procedure to deliver a structure as its result, which is not possible otherwise.

Another use of macros is in the construction of large programs, when the provision of a number of macros used by all programmers on the project can have the effect of producing a uniformity of code, eliminating individual idiosyncrasies which can render a program unintelligible. This technique in effect provides an extended language for the programmer. If the macros contain information which is not to be used by the programmer except via the macros, a change to the basic data-structures or array sizes can be made simply, and without the programmer's knowledge. This technique is widely used to provide a flexible interface between the user program and the operating system, so that the system can be changed with a minimum of inconvenience to the user.

MACRO FACILITIES IN PL/1

PL/1 has facilities for self-modification prior to compilation which take the form of a separate scan over the whole of the program text under control of certain macro statements. After processing the resulting text is compiled in the normal way.

These facilities permit the use of distinguished variables referred to as *macro variables*, which may take on integer or character-string values, and whose values can be changed by assignment statements executed prior to compilation. When the scan encounteres an occurrence of a macro variable in the program it is replaced by the current value of the macro variable.

The scan is normally sequential, but conditional and unconditional transfer macro statements can change it. During the scan, any macro statement encountered is "executed" immediately. Any nonmacro statement is searched for occurrences of macro variables which are replaced by their values, after which the statement is simply copied to the output for later compilation.

One clear use of the PL/1 macro facility is to incorporate parameters whose values require considerable computation as constants rather than variables in the text. This has the effect of reducing storage space for parameters, and of eliminating code to initialize their values, but perhaps the most important is the effect on the code referencing to such parameters. For instance, a statement such as

```
I = K * TABLE(L,M,N)
```

requires a fair amount of code for its execution, while if K is a macro variable which has been given the value zero, the statement would become

```
I = 0 * TABLE(L,M,N)
```

which could be translated by a good compiler as though it were $I=0$. The reader can find many such examples.

Another simple case is the expansion of a DO loop. Instead of writing

```
DO I = 1 TO 100;
Z(I) = X(I) + Y(I);
END;
```

the programmer could write

```
%DECLARE I FIXED;  %I = 1;
%LAB: Z(I) = X(I) + Y(I);
%I = I+1;  %IF I <= 100 %THEN %GOTO LAB;
%DEACTIVATE I;
```

This uses I as a macro variable which is eligible for substitution in the execution time text. At expansion time the text will be passed over 100 times, with I having the values 1, 2,..., 100, giving the code

```
Z(1) = X(1) + Y(1);
Z(2) = X(2) + Y(2);
    ...
Z(100) = X(100) + Y(100);
```

In fact the code produced has blanks inserted to act as separators before and after the value of I. The same result can be obtained by:

```
%DCL I FIXED;
%DO I = 1,100;
Z(I) = X(I) + Y(I);
%END;  %DEACTIVATE I;
```

As well as using macro variables which take on numerical values, they can also have character strings as values. A simple application of this is to change variable names. If **AA** was used in a piece of code instead of BB, then

```
%DECLARE AA CHARACTER;  %AA = 'BB';
:::
%DEACTIVATE AA
```

will change all occurrences of **AA** recognizable as variables to BB. Note that the string BB is substituted, not 'BB'.

The above features allow the substitution at expansion time of a macro variable. Later versions of PL/1 also allow the use of expansion-time functions or procedures. That is, if a procedure is declared as an expansion-time procedure, a reference to it in the execution-time text will be replaced by the result of executing the procedure with the arguments specified. As a simple example, suppose we have a program which requires repeated declaration of a particular form of structure, such as

```
DECLARE 1 NODE; 2 LEFT POINTER, 2 RIGHT POINTER;
```

we might use the expansion-time procedure:

```
% NODE: PROCEDURE(NAME);
        DECLARE NAME CHARACTER;
        RETURN ('DECLARE 1' ‖NAME‖
                ', 2 LEFT POINTER, 2 RIGHT POINTER');
% END;
```

This would have the effect of replacing

```
NODE(A); NODE(B);
```

by

```
DECLARE 1 A, 2 LEFT POINTER, 2 RIGHT POINTER;
DECLARE 1 B, 2 LEFT POINTER, 2 RIGHT POINTER;
```

which is a very useful feature.

Arguments of expansion-time procedures are scanned to detect occurrences of other expressions to be expanded. This expansion is done before the procedure is invoked, and any necessary conversion of parameter types done in the usual way. It is thus possible to embed expansion-time procedure calls in the same way as execution-time procedures. This allows the use of an expression such as

```
A = MSUM(X,MSUM(Y,Z))
```

to produce in-line code. In addition, the expansion-time procedure has the ability to examine its arguments and produce code which is optimum for those arguments.

We can regard PL/1 macro facilities as being provided by the execution of an expansion-time program whose input and output is the text of the execution-time program. In PL/1 this expansion time program has similar facilities to the execution-time program. That is, it has variables, assignment statements, transfers, conditional statements, loops, and procedures. Some of the more sophisticated features, such as arrays and structures, pointers and files, block structure and internal procedures, are not available, but these are less necessary at expansion time than at execution time.

The main disadvantage of PL/1 macro facilities is that an execution-time statement can only be modified by substitution of a variable, or of a procedure call. If we want to use the macro facilities to seriously extend the language, we find that we are forced into a language notation which is functional in form.

CONDITIONAL EXPRESSIONS

As an example of how we can use macros to increase the expressive power of a language, we will consider how we can use them to implement conditional expressions in PL/1. This language feature, which is provided in a number of other programming languages such as ALGOL, permits the use of a construction such as:

```
IF x THEN y ELSE z
```

as an expression, as well as a statement. If we wished to write something like:

```
A = B + IF X THEN Y ELSE Z + C;
```

in PL/1, we could write

```
A = B + X * Y + ( ¬X) * Z + C;
```

but this would not work if the value of the conditional expression was a pointer, say. In general, it would be necessary to construct a procedure like the conditional part. This might appear something like the following:

```
COND: PROCEDURE;
      IF X THEN RETURN(Y) ELSE RETURN(Z);
      END;
      A = B + COND + C;
```

Here we have defined a function procedure COND with no arguments which will return as its value the value of the conditional expression. What we will consider below is how the PL/1 macro facilities can do this translation for us, so that the programmer can produce the above code by writing:

```
A = B + IFX(X,Y,Z) + C;
```

First we note that the most natural way of translating this expression is to use a macro IFX, which will replace IFX(X,Y,Z) by some suitable form. If we could write:

```
A = B + BEGIN; IF X THEN RETURN(Y);
               ELSE RETURN(Z);   END + C;
```

in PL/1 our job would be much easier, but unfortunately there is no way in PL/1 of constructing an expression which contains statements. This is a clear example of the deficiencies of the technique used to design PL/1, to which macros were added as an afterthought rather than as an original part of the language. In this case we are forced to use the macro IFX to insert code in a different place. We will do this by adding code to a macro variable to be inserted elsewhere in the same block.

The following compile-time statements should be put at the beginning of the deck containing the conditional expressions:

```
%IFX: PROCEDURE(X,Y,Z) RETURNS(CHARACTER);
   DCL(X,Y,Z) CHARACTER;
   IFXX = IFXK+1;
   ENDB='COND'| |SUBSTR('ABCDEFGHIJKLMNOPQRSTUVWXYZ',IFXK,1)| |
   ':PROCEDURE; IF'| |X| |
   'THEN RETURN('| |Y| |'); ELSE RETURN('| |Z| |
   '); END;' | | ENDB;
   RETURN(SUBSTR(ENDB,1,5));
   %END;
   %DCL ENDB CHAR; %ENDB='END';
   %DCL IFXK FIXED; %IFXK=0;
   %DCL IFX ENTRY(CHAR,CHAR,CHAR)RETURNS(CHAR);
```

The macro variable IFXK is used to keep a count of the number of uses of the macro IFX, and to construct the names CONDA, CONDB,... of the procedures created to evaluate the conditional expressions. The declarations of these procedures will be added to the beginning of the macro variable ENDB, which should be used instead of END at the end of the appropriate blocks. ENDB will be replaced by the code to declare the new procedures followed by the normal END. The IFX macro will just return the name of the procedure constructed.

MATRIX MANIPULATION

We will consider below how we can use the PL/1 macro facilities to permit us to manipulate matrices in a fairly convenient fashion. PL/1 actually permits matrix addition and assignment, but the statement:

```
A = B * C;
```

where A, B and C are all two-dimensional arrays does not do the matrix multiplication according to:

$$A_{ij} = \sum_k B_{ik} \cdot C_{kj}$$

but element-by-element according to:

$$A_{ij} = B_{ij} * C_{ij}$$

We will want to do the former, and will want it to work for any correct combination of matrix sizes.

The notation we will use will be functional notation of the form:

```
ASSIGN(A,MSUM(B,MPROD(C,D)));
```

which will be translated to mean:

$$A = B + C * D.$$

We will use the fact that if ASSIGN is a macro, its arguments will be scanned for macros which will be expanded first. Thus in this case the macro MPROD will be expanded first, giving its result as the argument of MSUM, which will then be expanded to give its result to ASSIGN. Thus the actual code produced will first multiply C and D, putting the result in some temporary matrix T. Then the code to add B and T will be executed, and the result put in a temporary. The assignment will be done last.

The two tricky problems that we will have to solve are the allocation of temporaries and the determination of the sizes of the matrices. The simplest way to do this is probably to use the PL/1 ALLOCATE and FREE statements for allocation of temporaries, and the DIM function to determine the size of a matrix. To get an easy implementation we will declare a number of temporary arrays BASED in the block in which the matrix manipulations will be done. This can be of the form:

```
DCL (TA,TB,TC,TD,TE) (IMAX,JMAX) FLOAT BASED;
```

We will use a macro variable ISTK to keep a pointer to the last temporary used;

```
%DCL ISTK FIXED INITIAL(0);
```

The code will be added to the macro variable C, which will be returned as the value of ASSIGN.

We will just give two macros, for MPROD and ASSIGN, to illustrate the general technique. They are written as follows.

```
%MPROD: PROCEDURE(X,Y);
        ISTK = ISTK + 1;
        C = C || 'IMAX=DIM('| |X| |',1);
               JMAX=DIM('| |Y| |',2);
               ALLOCATE T'| |SUBSTR('ABCDE', ISTK,1) | |';
               KMAX=DIM('| |X| |',2);
               DO I=1,IMAX;
               DO J=1,JMAX;
               S = 0.0;
               DO K=1,KMAX;
               S = S + '| |X| |'(I,K) * '| |Y| |'(K,J);
               END;
               T'| | SUBSTR('ABCDE',ISTK,1) | |'(I,J) = S;
               END;
               END;';
        RETURN('T'| | SUBSTR('ABCDE',ISTK,1)));
        %END;

%ASSIGN: PROCEDURE(X,Y);
        DCL SAVE CHARACTER;
        C = C| |X| |'='| |Y| |';';
        DO I=1,ISTK;
        C = C| |'FREE T'| |SUBSTR('ABCDE',I,1)| | ';';END;
        SAVE = C;
        C = '';
        RETURN(SAVE);
        %END;
```

A more elegant implementation would only declare the correct number of temporaries. The above code of course will only work as long as the number of temporaries required is not greater than the number declared. Also it is relatively easy to add to the above routines the code to check the dimensions of the matrices for consistency.

It is also possible to improve the code somewhat by doing more of the calculations at compile time, and in particular the calculations of the sizes of the matrices. This can be done by modifying the matrix declarations in the code proper so that macro variables get assigned with values specifying the sizes. An extension of the stack-type mechanism then can be used to keep the sizes of the temporaries.

A more potent objection to the above scheme is that it produces grossly inefficient code for simple operations such as:

$$A = B + C,$$

which of course needs no temporaries. The code produced would require allocation of an array to hold $B + C$, and then separate code would be used to do the assignment. This can be improved by cleverer coding, but it is not simple.

EXERCISES

1. Using the PL/1 macro facilities, implement a form of the LIKE facility so that an occurrence of

    DCL A LIKE(B);

    following an occurrence of

    DEFLIKE(B, FIXED BINARY(31));

    will transform the declaration to

    DCL A FIXED BINARY(31);

*2. Use the PL/1 macro facilities to permit a convenient use of the garbage collection facilities described in Example 1, Chapter 13.

*3. Implement a set of debugging tools for PL/1. Suggested facilities include a printed trace of procedures entered, of variables referenced or modified, and a count of the number of iterations of loops.

15
LISP

INTRODUCTION

The LISP language, developed by McCarthy about 1959 and implemented in 1960 by a group under him at M.I.T. is basically a list-processing language whose data-structures are binary trees. It was designed with a view to the manipulation of programs as data, so the basic LISP language is very simple. However, it is derived from one of the theoretical models used for investigating computability, and has considerable power. This simple language, sometimes referred to as pure LISP, has been extended to make a more useful programming language, but without losing any of this power and including pure LISP as a subset. The external form of the language has repelled a generation of programmers because of its unfamiliar appearance, but many of those who have persevered have become ardent enthusiasts. It has achieved the position of being the most widely used language for research in artificial intelligence.

LISP DATA-STRUCTURES

The LISP data-structure can be thought of as a simple one-way chain in which the items themselves may be lists, or may be numbers or symbols which we will refer to as *atoms*. We discussed such structures and their advantages and disadvantages in a previous chapter. The notation used there for lists is the same as that used in LISP for specifying constants, and we will review it here for convenience.

We will first consider a subset of LISP lists, which we will call *proper lists*. In LISP, a proper list can be considered to be an ordered set of objects, with each object being either a basic element, called an atom, or another list. In this section we will discuss two methods of representing lists on paper; an external representation, and an internal representation. The external representation is used for input and output of lists by the LISP system, and the internal representation will be used to indicate the way in which lists are actually stored within the computer.

Associated with each atom is a print name which is used for input and output. Initially we will introduce just those atoms which have names beginning with a letter, and defer discussion of other types of atoms until later. We shall also see later that atoms may have a considerable substructure of their own, but for the time being we will consider this to be represented simply by the print name.

The external representation of an atom is simply its print name, so A17, XY, SPADE, UNBOUNDEDSEQUENCEOFLETTERS all represent atoms. We will represent the internal structure of these atoms by a rectangular block with a pointer to the print name, as shown in Figure 15.1. A proper list of two atoms, A and B, is represented externally by (A B) and internally as in Figure 15.2. The block with the diagonal line actually represents the atom NIL, so the list (A B) can also be represented by Figure 15.3. A proper list of two elements, the first of which is the list above, and the second of which is the atom C, is represented by Figure 15.4. Other examples are shown in Figure 15.5. The reader should note carefully the difference between A and (A), and between (AB), (A (B)), and ((A) B).

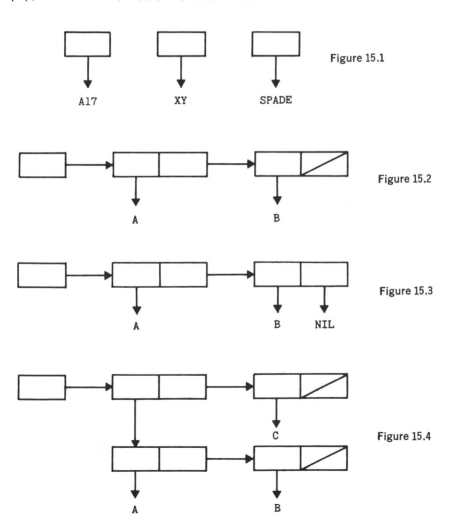

Figure 15.1

Figure 15.2

Figure 15.3

Figure 15.4

(C (AB))

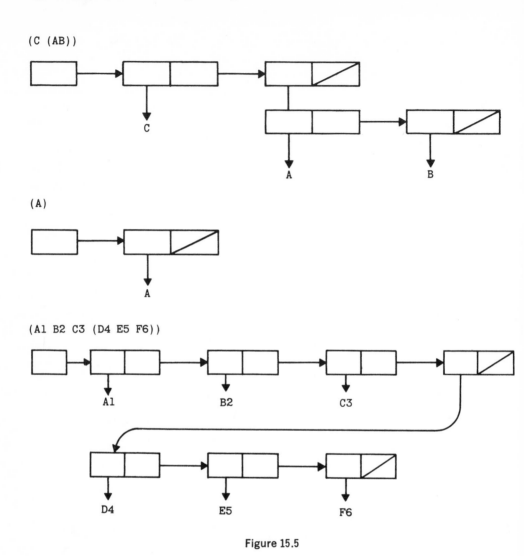

(A)

(A1 B2 C3 (D4 E5 F6))

Figure 15.5

The notation given above gives an external representation corresponding to all lists which have NIL as the only atom in the right half of a block of the form of Figure 15.6.

For example, there is no way of writing what is shown in Figure 15.7 in the external representation; it is certainly not (A B). Accordingly a notation is required to allow an arbitrary atom to be used as well as NIL. This notation is usually called *dot notation*.

Figure 15.6

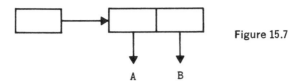

Figure 15.7

We define a more general structure than a proper list, called simply a *list*. A list is:

(1) an atom, or
(2) $(S_1 \cdot S_2)$ where S_1 and S_2 are both lists, or
(3) an abbreviation of (2) above.

We can think of (2) as defining a mechanism by which we can construct a list from two others, or conversely, a mechanism for splitting any list not an atom into two other lists. If the lists S_1 and S_2 are represented internally by Figure 15.8, then the list formed by (2) above is represented by Figure 15.9. Thus we see that the internal representation of Figure 15.10 corresponds to the list $(A \cdot B)$, and that of Figure 15.11 corresponds to $(A \cdot (B \cdot NIL))$.

By using the internal representation of proper lists and lists, we see that those lists which have the dot followed by no atom other than NIL can be represented as proper

Figure 15.8

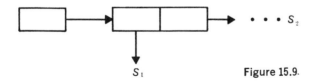

Figure 15.9.

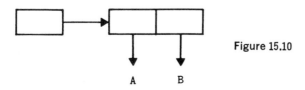

Figure 15.10

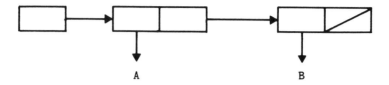

Figure 15.11

lists, and that all proper lists can be represented as lists. We thus have the equivalences:

```
(C (A B))          (C · ((A · (B · NIL)) ·NIL))
(A)                (A · NIL)
(A1 B2 C3 (D4 E5 F6))   (A1·(B2·(C3·((D4·(E5·(F6·NIL)))·NIL))))
```

We will use list notation as the abbreviation for dot notation given in (3) above whenever it is possible, and in general will only use dot notation when it cannot be avoided. Combinations of list and dot notation will be allowed, so the last example above can be written also as (A1 · (B2 · (C3 · ((D4 E5 F6) · NIL)))).

BASIC LISP FUNCTIONS

The five basic functions in LISP are CAR, CDR, CONS, ATOM, and EQ. CAR is a function of a single list, and has as its value the first element of the list. CDR is similar, but having the list without the first element as its value. CONS is a function of two lists, giving as its value the list formed by adding the first list to the front of the second, so that it becomes the first element of the resulting list. We have the following examples:

```
CAR:   (A · B)          A
CAR:   (A B)            A
CAR:   ((A B)(C D))     (A B)
CDR:   (A · B)          B
CDR:   (A B)            (B) = (B · NIL)
CDR:   ((A B)( C D)) ,  ((C D))
CONS:  A, B             (A · B)
CONS:  A, NIL           (A)
CONS:  (A), (B)         ((A) B)
```

It is essential that these examples be fully understood before proceeding. It may be found helpful to consider the effect of applying the functions to the internal representation of the lists above.

The other two functions are predicates: that is, they take on the values true or false depending on certain properties of their arguments. ATOM is a function of one argument, giving the atom T as its value if the argument is an atom, and NIL otherwise.

EQ is a function of two arguments, giving the value T if both are the same atom, and NIL otherwise. The following examples illustrate their use:

```
ATOM:  A             T
ATOM:  (A)           NIL
ATOM:  (A · B)       NIL
  EQ:  A, B          NIL
  EQ:  B, B          T
  EQ:  (B), B        NIL
```

A frequently used function, though not a primitive, is NULL, which is defined so that NULL(X) is equivalent to EQ(X,NIL).

THE STRUCTURE OF THE LANGUAGE

The basic operations in LISP are those executed by the functions CAR, CDR, CONS, ATOM, and EQ described above. The LISP language provides facilities for describing complex processes in terms of these basic operations, and it is convenient at this point to describe its overall structure. It is similar in many ways to ALGOL and PL/1, allowing functions to be defined in terms of statements and expressions, which themselves are written in terms of variables.

A variable in LISP can be thought of as having an atom or a list as its value. A function of a variable or variables is an expression, as is a function of an expression or expressions. This is similar to the facility provided by FORTRAN and ALGOL which allows the use of expressions such as:

```
F(FF(X),FFF(FFFF(Y),Z))
```

where F, FF, FFF, FFFF are functions, and X, Y, and Z are variables. As we shall see later, a slightly different notation is used in LISP, but the difference is of little significance.

The second form of expression permitted in LISP is a conditional expression. This has no parallel in FORTRAN, but is similar to the ALGOL form:

```
if ... then ... else ...
```

This is a very powerful form of expression: in fact it can be shown that the set of functions defined using composition and conditional expressions includes all computable functions.

The third form of expression has no direct equivalent in either FORTRAN or ALGOL. Its nearest relation is the ALGOL block, in that it allows local variables, and contains statements which may assign values to such local (as well as nonlocal) variables. The difference is that on exiting from the LISP block, it is assigned a value, just like any other expression. The statements allowable within the block include assignment statements, jump statements, and exit statements, as well as conditional statements similar to those found in ALGOL.

Functions may be defined in LISP in much the same way as in ALGOL. They may have arguments, and the expression defining the function may make reference to the arguments or to free variables. The standard mode of argument transmission is analogous to the ALGOL call-by-value feature, but the call-by-name facility is also available. Functions may be recursively defined.

THE LISP EXPRESSION

A LISP program consists of a number of functions defined as expressions involving variables. A LISP expression takes one of the following forms:

(1) an atom,
(2) a list of the form

$$(f\, e_1\, e_2\, \cdots\, e_n), \qquad n \geq 0,$$

where e_i are the arguments, and f is either an atom representing a function, or a list which actually is a function definition.

It should be noted that each of the above forms is expressible as a list, one of the most important qualities of LISP. An atom can be used to represent a variable, a constant, or a function name. The second form of expression represents the list obtained by applying the function to the expressions as arguments, with the usual method of evaluation being that the arguments are evaluated before being given to the function.

In order to give some examples, we will suppose that the atoms X, Y, and Z are variables which have the values (A B), ((C D)(E F)), and G respectively. Then the following expressions have the values shown:

```
(CAR X)                       = A
(CDR Y)                       = ((E F))
(CONS (CAR X) Y)              = (A (C D) (E F))
(ATOM Z)                      = T
(EQ(CDR(CDR(CAR Y))) NIL)     = T
(EQ X (CONS(CAR X)(CDR X))    = NIL
(EQ (ATOM Y) NIL)             = T
```

Certain functions are applied to their arguments in nonstandard ways. One such function is COND, which occurs in the form (COND $(p_1\, e_1)(p_2\, e_2)\cdots(p_n\, e_n)$), $n > 0$, where the p_i and e_i are expressions. It is referred to as a *conditional expression*. It is evaluated by evaluating p_1 first, and if its value is not NIL, then the value of e_1 is taken as the value of the expression. Otherwise p_2 is evaluated, and the value of e_2 is returned if p_2 is not NIL, etc. If all p_i evaluate to NIL, the expression is considered to be undefined.

Examples of conditional expressions are:

```
(COND  ((ATOM Z)  X)
       (T Y))                                    = (A B)
(COND  ((EQ Y NIL)  NIL)
       ((ATOM Y)  (CONS Y NIL))
       (T (CAR Y)))                              = (C D)
(COND  ((ATOM Z)(COND ((EQ (CAR X) NIL) NIL)
                      (T (CONS T NIL))))
       (T T)                                     = (T)
```

In the above examples it should be understood that evaluation of the expressions consisting of the atom T or the atom NIL results in T or NIL respectively. That is, T and NIL may be regarded as constants, or alternatively as variables having themselves as values.

There is also a function, namely QUOTE, for referring to a list itself, rather than a variable standing for a list. Thus (QUOTE X) has the value X, (QUOTE (A B)) has the value (A B), and (QUOTE (CAR X)) has the value (CAR X). Note the difference between the following:

```
(QUOTE (CAR X))    = (CAR X)
(CAR X)            = A
```

Thus QUOTE is used to prevent its argument being evaluated. Using this feature, we have the following additional examples:

```
(EQ (CAR X) (QUOTE A))          = T
(EQ (CAR(CAR Y)) (QUOTE C))     = T
(EQ (ATOM Z) (QUOTE (ATOM Z)))  = NIL
```

In those cases where ease of programming or speed of execution dictates the use of assignment statements and jumps, the PROG function can be used. The expression has the following form:

$$(\text{PROG } (x_1\ x_2\ \ldots\ x_n)\ s_1\ s_2\ \ldots\ s_m)$$

where $x_1 \ldots x_n$ are to be considered local temporary variables, and $s_1 \ldots s_m$ are either atomic labels, or commands in the form of expressions which are evaluated but whose values are ignored. The commands will usually be assignment commands of the form:

```
(SETQ XI e)
```

where e is an expression, or jumps of the form:

```
(GO e)
```

where e is an atomic label, or termination commands of the form:

```
(RETURN e)
```

where e is an expression. Conditional commands are written by using COND.

An example using PROG is the following expression which gives the last element of the proper list **X**:

```
(PROG (XX)
    (SETQ XX  X)
    LOOP
    (COND((NULL(CDR XX))(RETURN (CAR XX))))
    (SETQ XX (CDR XX))
    (GO LOOP)    )
```

This has one local variable, **XX**, one label, LOOP, a conditional exit command, two assignment commands, and a transfer command. Note that the conditional command need not be satisfied by any branch, and that the next command is executed if not. The RETURN command terminates the PROG, giving the value of its argument as the value of the PROG.

The functions PROG, SETQ, RETURN, and GO should be regarded as additions to the basic LISP vocabulary. SETQ, RETURN and GO are properly regarded as pseudo-functions, in that they are executed for their action rather than their value.

As well as providing a large number of functions for manipulating lists, some of which we will mention later, the system provides rudimentary facilities for calculating with numerical quantities. These include the ability to write integers, real numbers, and octal numbers in the usual notation, and the usual arithmetic functions. As in the case of all functions in LISP, functional form must be used, so that $A * B + C$ must be written:

```
(PLUS (TIMES A B) C)
```

which is rather cumbersome. The arguments to functions like PLUS and TIMES can be either octal, integer or real, with type testing and conversion being done at execution time. This of course is highly inefficient, but quite convenient.

THE LISP FUNCTION

A LISP program consists usually of a number of function definitions, with each function being specified by a name, a list of arguments, and the corresponding expression of the arguments. However, in LISP we want to have the ability to create, manipulate, and apply functions during the execution process, and we will require several different types of function. It is therefore convenient to use the following convention for specifying a function: an expression e involving the arguments $x_1 \ldots x_n$ will be used in the form

(LAMBDA $(x_1 \ldots x_n)$ e)

to denote a function. For example, the function which gives the second sublist of a list can be written

(LAMBDA (X) (CAR (CDR X)))

and it can be used to replace

(CAR (CDR Z))

in some expressions by the equivalent

((LAMBDA (X) (CAR (CDR X))) Z)

The usual method of using complex functions is to associate them permanently with a name, as described below.

The LISP system accepts commands in the form of doublets. Each doublet consists of two lists, the first list being a function, and the second a list of arguments. The system forms an expression from the doublet by affectively CONSing the first list with the list formed by prefixing QUOTE to the beginning of each argument, and then evaluates it. For example, the command

CONS ((A B) (C D))

will be transformed by the system into the expression

(CONS (QUOTE (A B)) (QUOTE (C D)))

which will then be evaluated and printed as ((A B) C D). Note that commands to the system are treated differently from expressions occurring within a function definition.

A LISP deck consists of a number of commands requesting, among other things, function definitions and executions. The function used to define a function varies with the implementation and the computer. We will suppose that it is called DEFN, and it takes two arguments, the name of the function, and the expression defining it. As an example, the function above could be defined by the command

DEFN (SECOND (LAMBDA (X) (CAR (CDR X))))

The command

SECOND (((A) (B) (C)))

would then evaluate to (B).

Using this form of function definition, it is possible to use the function name in the defining expression itself. Such recursive definitions are widely used in LISP. They are frequently used to specify repetitive procedures, as an alternative to program loops as used in more conventional languages like FORTRAN or ALGOL. For example, the function LAST which gives the last sublist in a list can be defined by the command

```
DEFN (LAST (LAMBDA (L)
           (COND ((EQ (CDR L) NIL) (CAR L))
           (T (LAST (CDR L)))  )))
```

If it is necessary for a program to use a function which is written recursively, without making a permanent definition within the system, a form of function analogous to the LAMBDA notation is available. The function LAST could be written

```
(LABEL LAST (LAMBDA (L)
            (COND ((EQ (CDR L) NIL) (CAR L))
            (T (LAST (CDR L)))  )))
```

in the middle of a program, and the definition would only be in effect during the evaluation of the expression in which it was involved. Such usage is rare.

The functions CAR, CDR, CONS, ATOM, EQ, QUOTE, COND, LAMBDA, LABEL, and DEFN form the central core of LISP. It can be shown that these features can be used to calculate any computable function. The many other features in LISP systems are added for additional convenience or efficiency, and include many more functions, and usually a compiler and an assembler.

Before giving an example of a complete LISP program, there is another thing that should be mentioned. The reader should note that the basic functions of LISP allow for construction of new lists, but not for erasure of old ones. One of the major advantages of LISP over other list-processing languages is the complete absence of such housekeeping chores in the programs, due to the use of automatic garbage collection, which we have discussed previously.

LIST STORAGE IN THE MACHINE

A real understanding of LISP requires an understanding of the way in which LISP lists can be stored in the computer. The mechanism has been suggested already by the form of the internal representation of a list given previously.

A list is stored in the computer as a set of machine words, which need not be in successive locations in memory. These words are associated by virtue of the fact that each word may contain the addresses of two other words.

To be more specific, we will suppose that the word is divided into two halves. We will refer to such a halfword as an *element*, and note that an element can be regarded as specifying the list which starts with the word pointed at by the element. The internal representation of the list ((A B) C), for instance, is shown in Figure 15.12, and is represented in the machine by four words. It is referenced by a halfword element. The

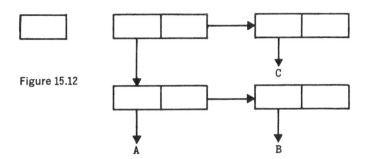

Figure 15.12

elements containing pointers to the atoms A, B, C, and NIL may contain descriptor bits which indicate that these are pointers to atoms or these bits may be in the words pointed to. In fact most atoms are represented in the machine as lists also, as we shall see below.

We can now describe how LISP functions actually operate. Their arguments and values are halfword elements which specify lists. The function CAR, for instance, is given one halfword element as its argument, and returns the halfword element contained in the most significant half of the word pointed to by the argument. The function CDR does similarly, but returning the least significant halfword element. CONS is given two elements which it packs in one word which it stores in a free location in memory, and returns a halfword element pointing to this location.

OPERATIONS ON LISTS

In addition to the set of basic operations on lists which we have described above, LISP provides a number of other routines which are of considerable power. These can actually be written in terms of the basic operations, and so do not provide any facilities which are not otherwise available, but are provided as built-in functions for efficiency.

A useful operation is that which tests two lists for being equal. A simplified version of this which works for nonnumeric atomic elements only can be defined:

```
DEFN (EQUAL LAMBDA (X Y)
          (COND
          ((ATOM X) (EQ X Y))
          ((EQUAL (CAR X) (CAR Y)) (EQUAL (CDR X) (CDR Y)))
          (T F)   )))
```

To extend this to atomic elements which are numbers we can replace the function EQ by a function which will test two numbers for having the same value. The built-in version of EQUAL normally provided by the LISP system is so defined. Note that this version of EQUAL will not work for circular lists, or lists which contain references to any part of themselves, since the recursion will not terminate.

Another useful operation is that which appends two proper lists. This is done by building a new list by adding on to the front of the second list the elements of the first list, in the reverse order. This can most conveniently be written as a recursive routine as follows:

```
DEFN (APPEND (LAMBDA (X Y)
             (COND
             ((NULL X) Y)
             (T (CONS (CAR X) (APPEND (CDR X) Y)))  )))
```

Note the use of recursion to process the elements of X in the reverse order.

A further set of functions which can be used in many different ways are those functions which have functions as their arguments. One such function is the MAPCAR function, which will apply the specified function to the elements of a list, and construct a list with these values as its result. It can be written as follows:

```
DEFN (MAPCAR (LAMBDA (L FN)
             (COND
             ((NULL L) NIL)
             (T (CONS (FN (CAR L)) (MAPCAR (CDR L) FN))) )))
```

A similar function is the function MAPLIST, which is the same as MAPCAR except it applies its functional argument to the whole list, written as follows:

```
DEFN (MAPLIST (LAMBDA (L FN)
             (COND
             ((NULL L) NIL)
             (T (CONS (FN L) (MAPLIST (CDR L) FN)))   )))
```

By an appropriate definition of the functional argument, MAPLIST can be made to have the effect of MAPCAR, so although MAPCAR is probably more useful, MAPLIST is more general.

A still more general list-processing function can be written as follows:

```
DEFN (GENMAP (LAMBDA (L OP FN FTERM)
             (COND
             ((NULL L) (FTERM))
             (T (OP (FN L)
                    (GENMAP (CDR L) OP FN FTERM)  ))  )))
```

This function can clearly be used instead of MAPLIST if the function FTERM gives NIL and OP is the CONS function. It can also be used to sum the elements of a list by writing:

```
(GENMAP L (FUNCTION PLUS) (FUNCTION CAR)
          (FUNCTION (LAMBDA() O))  )
```

FUNCTION is used instead of QUOTE when specifying functional arguments, for reasons explained later. Note that a further generalization of GENMAP can be made by replacing the termination test by another functional argument TERM, and writing the first test of the COND above as:

```
((TERM L) (FTERM L))
```

A different form in which the map-type functions can take is the function MAP, which is similar to MAPLIST except it returns no value, but simply applies the function to the successive lists. It is written as follows:

```
DEFN (MAP (LAMBDA (L FN)
          (COND
          ((NULL L) NIL)
          (T (PROG2 (FN (CAR L)) (MAP (CDR L) FN)))  )))
```

Here PROG2 is a function which returns its second argument, and which is used simply to evaluate two expressions. The main use of the MAP function is with a pseudofunction as its functional argument. For example, the following expression will print out the elements of the list L separately:

```
(MAP L (LAMBDA(X)(PRINT(CAR X))) )
```

Here we are assuming the availability of a general-purpose PRINT function which will print out its argument in a reasonable way. Such a function is normally provided in a LISP system.

ATOMS AND PROPERTY LISTS

We have seen that an atom is represented by a halfword element which may be one of several different forms. First, it may point to a list, called the *property list* of the atom, which will contain information associated with the atom, such as its name. All the atoms we have used so far, like X, CAR, and ABC, are of this form. Second, it may point to a word which does not contain two halfword elements, but perhaps a pointer and some flags.

When the LISP system reads a list from the input medium, it associates atoms beginning with a letter or consisting of a special character like +, with a property list. The same property list is used for all occurrences of the same atom.

The structure of the property list of an atom is quite flexible, and is initially made up to contain only a few pieces of information. This varies according to the way in which LISP is implemented, but the structure in Figure 15.13 is not untypical. The structure on the right is the abbreviation we have been using for the atomic structure shown on the left. The name associated with the atom is stored in coded alphanumeric form in z. In the course of computation the property list may be modified by insertions or deletions shown as ellipses (...).

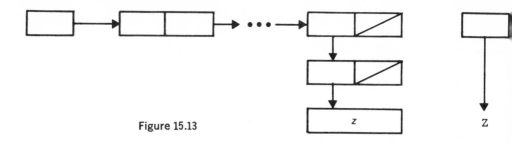

Figure 15.13

Numerical and alphanumeric atoms have the form shown in Figure 15.14 where the full word contains an integer, floating-point, octal or alphanumeric constant, and the word pointing to it contains flags to distinguish the mode of constant as well as to indicate that it is a pointer to a full word rather than a list word, shown here by an *.

The input routine behaves differently for numerical atoms, in the sense that each numerical atom is stored in a unique full word, since there is little to be gained from keeping a single copy of each number. This convention would be destroyed anyway as soon as any arithmetic calculations were done, since the system could not check for each new numerical atom produced in the course of computation.

THE INTERPRETER

As we pointed out previously, one of the important characteristics of LISP is the fact that program and data are indistinguishable. The same routine is used to read both, and it converts them into the same internal representation. An expression in the form of a list is actually executed in this form by operating on it with a set of routines collectively known as the interpreter, the main routines being EVAL and APPLY.

The variables of a LISP program are represented by atoms, so the interpreter must have some mechanism for assigning values to atoms, and for returning such values. There are a number of interesting schemes for doing this. The one we will describe below is that used in the original implementation, and in a later chapter we describe an alternative.

In LISP 1.5, a variable can be given a value (bound) in a number of ways. The most usual one uses an *association list* (*a-list*) which consists of a list of variables paired with values. The value of a variable kept in this way is extracted by searching the list for the variable, and getting the associated value. This mechanism is used for dummy variables of a function, and local variables of PROGs, so that any occurrence of such a variable requires this search operation. This is not too inefficient when there are only a few variables, but otherwise is rather time-consuming. However, it has some advantages in a number of rather tricky situations, as we will see later.

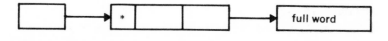

Figure 15.14

A second possibility is for variables to have values put on their property lists. This is often more efficient, since the property list is usually shorter than the *a*-list, and is of course instantly accessible simply by tracing down the atom. In LISP 1.5 two kinds of property list bindings are used, one for constants and one for functions. The first uses the APVAL property, and allows atoms like NIL and T to have permanent values, thus acting like constants. In looking up the value of a variable, the property list is searched for an APVAL before the *a*-list. The second uses four properties to describe the four different kinds of function. These are SUBR, FSUBR, EXPR, and FEXPR. A SUBR binding is used for a machine-coded function which requires its arguments to be evaluated, while an FSUBR binding is used for a machine-coded function which expects a list of unevaluated arguments. An EXPR binding is used for a LAMBDA expression which requires evaluated arguments, while an FEXPR binding is used for a LAMBDA expression which expects a list of unevaluated arguments. When looking up the value of a variable which is used as a function name, the interpreter searches for such bindings first. The DEFN function described above actually puts the LAMBDA expressions on the property lists using the EXPR property.

EVAL

EVAL may be regarded as the opposite of QUOTE, which prevents its arguments from being evaluated. For example, consider the situation in which X is bound to Y, and Y is bound to Z. Then the LISP expression (QUOTE X) will have the value X, the expression X will have the value Y, and the expression (EVAL X A) will have the value Z if A is the current *a*-list. As a more complicated example, if X is bound to

    (LAMBDA (X) (CONS (CDR X) (CAR X)))

and Y is bound to

    (QUOTE (P · Q))

then the value of the expression

    (QUOTE (CONS X (CONS Y NIL)))

is simply

    (CONS X (CONS Y NIL))

while that of

    (CONS X (CONS Y NIL))

is

    ((LAMBDA (X) (CONS (CDR X) (CAR X))) (QUOTE (P · Q)))

and that of

```
(EVAL (CONS X (CONS Y NIL)) A)
```
is

```
(Q · P)
```

The availability of a function within a programming language which can evaluate an expression of the language is a very powerful feature possessed by very few programming languages. Although not too useful for the simpler routine programming jobs, this feature will become increasingly useful for more sophisticated tasks. The most striking example is that of a program which learns from experience. A number of programs have this capability in a restricted way, perhaps the most successful being Samuel's checker playing program which adjusts its parameters depending on its success. However, such programs do not alter their own structure in a radical way. To do so requires the program to have the ability to manipulate itself as data and to execute the altered program. In LISP, there is no difference between program and data, so it is eminently suited for such problems. Of course, this identity between program and data is only maintained while the program is stored as a list. Most LISP systems contain a compiler which translates the list form into machine language, thus destroying the equivalence, but giving a faster running program by up to two orders of magnitude.

The LISP system executes commands by transforming them into expressions and evaluating them by using EVAL, so it is really EVAL which specifies the syntax and semantics of LISP. The definition of EVAL should be consulted for reference purposes in otherwise ambiguous situations.

THE OPERATION OF EVAL

In this section we will give the algorithm for EVAL. First we note that an expression in LISP is either an atom, which is interpreted as either a constant or a variable, or else it is a list of the form

$$(f\ a_1\ a_2\ \cdots\ a_n)$$

where f is either the name of a function or an expression representing a function, and the a_i are arguments, usually in the form of expressions.

The EVAL algorithm can be written as follows.

```
eval(x, a): local variables fn, args, fn2;
if x is an atom then
        if x is a constant then return x
        elseif x has an AVPAL, return its value
        elseif x is bound on a, return the value
        else print diagnostic and exit;
fn = car(x); args = cdr(x);
```

if fn is an atom, and it has an FSUBR binding, execute the specified code with
   arguments args and a and return the result;
if fn is an atom, and it has an FEXPR binding fn2 then return apply (fn2,
   list(args), a);
otherwise return apply(fn, evlis(args,a),a);

The function APPLY is invoked by EVAL when it finds that it has to apply a function to its arguments. The third argument of APPLY is the same a-list which was given
to EVAL. The APPLY algorithm is as follows.

apply(fn,args,a): local variable fn2;
if fn is an atom then
      if fn has a SUBR binding, execute the specified code with the elements of
         args as arguments, and return the result;
      elseif fn has an EXPR binding fn2, return apply(fn2,args,a)
      else return apply(eval(fn,a),args,a);
if car(fn) is LAMBDA then
      return eval(caddr(fn), pairlis(cadr(fn),args,a));
if car(fn) is LABEL then
      return apply(cadr(fn),args,pairlis(list(cadr(fn)),list(caddr(fn)),a);
return apply(eval(fn,a),args,a);

Here cadr(fn) is short for car(cdr(fn)), and pairlis binds the arguments by creating
an extended a-list.
   It is clear from the mechanism used for evaluating a function that the expression
defining the function can contain references to variables other than the arguments of
the function. Such variables are called free variables, and will have the values specified
by the highest-level binding at the time of evaluation of the function. Often such free
variables will be arguments of higher-level functions, or global variables whose values
are at the highest level, that of the set of doublets comprising the program itself.
   The operation of the PROG feature is fairly straightforward. The local variables
are bound to NIL. The statements are then executed by evaluating them as though they
were expressions, and then ignoring their value. SETQ merely effects a change in the
bound value of the appropriate variable and GO will cause resumption of evaluation at
the expression following the specified label. When a RETURN statement is encountered,
its argument is evaluated, the bindings of the local variables are removed, and the value
of the PROG is returned.
   It should be noted that the use of SETQ is not limited to within a PROG, as GO and
RETURN are. SETQ simply resets the current binding of its first argument (which it
implicitly QUOTEs) to the value of its second argument, and can be used elsewhere to
change the value of any variable. Thus SETQ can be used to reset a free variable, or
even an argument of a function. For example, LAST could be defined

```
DEFN (LAST (LAMBDA (X) (PROG ( )
LOOP (COND ((NULL (CDR X)) (RETURN (CAR X))))
      (SETQ X (CDR X)) (GO LOOP)     )))
```

Note that ( ) is identically equivalent to NIL. The above definition illustrates a difference between FORTRAN and LISP, in that the definition above does not alter its argument, but rather the value of the variable which initially was set to the value of the argument. (This is similar to the "call-by-value" feature of ALGOL.)

There are a number of ways of writing a LISP interpreter, all giving rather similar results. The one given above is essentially identical to the one used in the original LISP 1.5 implementation, with a few simplifications and omissions as noted below. First, let us consider a number of properties of this interpreter. In an expression of the form

$$(f \; a_1 \; a_2 \; \cdots)$$

f can be any of the following.

1. an atom with an FSUBR on its property list
2. an atom with an FEXPR as its property list
3. an atom with a SUBR on its property list
4. an atom with an EXPR on its property list
5. a LAMBDA expression or LABEL expression
6. an expression whose value is any of 3, 4, 5, or 6.

The ramifications of these possibilities are quite complicated to see, but it is clear that a function can be used as an argument to another function if passed as a quoted LAMBDA expression, or as a quoted atom with the function bound on the atom's property list. However, note that such a function will not be treated properly if it is an FSUBR or FEXPR.

The omissions we mentioned above are concerned with the evaluation of an expression with the wrong a-list. This occurs in its most annoying form when a function f_1 containing references to free variables is passed as an argument to another function f_2, within which it is applied. If the local variables of f_2 are the same as the free variables of f_1, these local variables will be used instead. This is usually avoided by using a special quote operator FUNCTION for passing f_1, which evaluates to

(FUNARG f_1 a)

where a is the a-list then in force. APPLY recognizes this form, and uses the attached a-list for its evaluation, rather than its own a-list.

COMPILERS

So far we have described LISP as an interpretive programming system, and it is true that the interpreter determines the essential features. However, any reasonable amount of serious programming in LISP requires considerable machine time, and the efficiency of the system then becomes important. Accordingly, most LISP systems provide facilities for compiling the LISP definition of a function into machine code, so that it becomes essentially indistinguishable from a machine-language function built into the system. Indeed, some recent LISP systems are based on the existence of a compiler, rather than an interpreter. An assembler is often provided also to allow functions to be written directly in assembly language.

The compiler and assembler in LISP are ordinary functions, available to the programmer at any point in his program. This extends still further the effectiveness of the LISP system in being able to execute data, or equivalently, to manipulate program.

Compilation of LISP functions is relatively simple. Dummy arguments and local variables usually become locations on the stack, and can be addressed directly using an index register as a stack base. Basic LISP functions are most appropriately compiled as open code, with the exception of CONS which is usually a little longer and may be compiled as a subroutine call. Other machine-language functions of type SUBR can be compiled as subroutine calls, with arguments being passed via the stack. Functions which are undefined at compilation time can be compiled as calls to a linking routine which will examine the function to determine its type and to carry out the appropriate action. In the case that the function is a machine-language SUBR, the linking routine can replace the instructions which called it with instructions to call the SUBR directly.

The functions QUOTE, COND, PROG, SETQ, GO, RETURN, and LAMBDA require special treatment by the compiler, in that they cannot be compiled as simple subroutine calls. However, two general cases also cause problems: the use of free variables, and the use of programmer-defined FEXPR's and FUSBR's. The free variable problem arises when a function refers to a free variable which is an argument or local variable of a higher-level compiled function. This variable has been compiled as a stack location and so is not accessible as a free variable. The usual solution to this situation is to declare the variable to be of a special type so that references to it are compiled to refer to a special cell rather than the stack. An alternative solution is to compile all functions to use special cells for all variables.

Compiling expressions involving FSUBR's or FEXPR's is a more difficult problem. The semantics of these expressions are determined by the definition of the FSUBR or FEXPR itself. Thus the compiler has to be provided with translation procedures for all FSUBR's that may be encountered. In theory, the compiler could analyze FEXPR's sufficiently to compile references to them, but in practice this is not done.

A convenient mechanism which can be used for the compilation of expressions involving FSUBR's and FEXPR's is to associate with each a function which will translate the expression into a form which is acceptable by the compiler. This can be thought of as replacing FSUBR's and FEXPR's with macrodefinitions, which are applied prior to compilation. For example, let us consider the case where the programmer would like to write

```
(PUT X = B * B - 4 * A * C)
```

instead of the more cumbersome LISP equivalent

```
(SETQ X (DIFF (PROD B B) (PROD 4 (PROD A C))))
```

By defining PUT as:

```
(PUT (LAMBDA (L)
     (EVAL (TRANSL L)))))
```

where TRANSL is a function which translates infix notation into LISP-type notation, the interpreter is able to handle the more convenient notation. However, in order to compile such an expression, the compiler has to be able to do such a translation, or alternatively has to have available to it a routine which could do such translation. Thus we could associate with the atom PUT a macro simply defined as

```
(PUTM (LAMBDA (L)
      (TRANSL  L)))
```

which the compiler can use to do the translation.

The scheme mentioned above can be generalized somewhat. The effect of expanding FSUBR's as macros is to produce an expression containing only SUBRs and LAMBDA expressions augmented by the basic FSUBR's QUOTE, COND, PROG, etc. It is therefore possible to expand such macros even when the expression is not to be compiled. Such expansion can properly take place when the function is being defined. Thus instead of using DEFN to establish function definitions, we can use the function DEFNEXP defined as

```
(DEFNEXP (LAMBDA (ATM EXPR)
         (DEFN ATM (EXPAND EXPR))  ))
```

where EXPAND is a function which will expand the macros in the definition.

The function EXPAND mentioned above is rather similar in many respects to both the compiler and the interpreter. It expands an expression consisting of a function and its arguments by examining the function for having a macro binding. If it has, the macro is applied to the argument list. Otherwise EXPAND is applied to each of the arguments, so that they are replaced by the expanded forms.

As an example of the use of the function EXPAND, consider the LISP function LIST defined as

```
(LIST (LAMBDA (L)
      (EVLIS L)))
(EVLIS (LAMBDA (L)
       (COND ((NULL L) NIL)
             (T (CONS (EVAL (CAR L))(EVLIS (CDR L))))  )))
```

The corresponding macro definition is

```
(LIST (LAMBDA (L)
      (COND ((NULL L) (CONS NIL NIL))
```

```
(T (CONS (QUOTE CONS)
         (CONS (EXPAND (CAR L))
               (LIST (CDR L))  )  ))  )))
```

This definition uses EXPAND to allow expansion of the individual arguments of LIST. For example, the expression

```
(LIST X (CAR Y)  Z)
```

would expand to

```
(CONS X (CONS (CAR Y) (CONS  Z  NIL)))
```

since X, (CAR Y), and Z would be found by EXPAND to require no further expansion. On the other hand, the expression

```
(LIST X (LIST  Y)  Z)
```

would expand to

```
(CONS X (CONS (CONS Y NIL) (CONS Z NIL)))
```

since EXPAND would find that (LIST Y) could be expanded also.

LISP EXTENSIONS

The LISP 1.5 programming language has a number of remarkable properties, which have made it a prime choice for writing complex programs. In particular, it has become very popular among workers in the Artificial Intelligence area, and at the time of writing is probably the most widely used language for such applications. In addition, its ability to treat programs as data has made it a useful vehicle for designing experimental special-purpose languages. However, even the most enthusiastic LISP users admit that the language has its shortcomings.

The usual criticisms leveled as LISP include:

1. The necessity of writing every expression in fully-parenthesized functional form, which is unfamiliar to the majority of programmers, and is difficult to read and lengthy to write even for the practiced LISPer.

2. The inefficiency of execution. This is more obvious for those systems which do not have a compiler, but even for those that do, the LISP language has properties which make it difficult to compile efficient code. The main reason for this is that the language was originally designed to be interpreted rather than compiled, and permits the meanings of expressions to vary in a highly dynamic way. When an interpreter is used, decisions about the type of object an expression represents can be postponed without undue loss of efficiency. A clear example of this is arithmetic in LISP in which each number carries with it an indication of its type, and execution-time tests and conver-

sions are performed. When compiling arithmetic expressions, the type of a variable is not known to the compiler, so execution-time tests are still necessary.

3. The restricted set of data-types. The LISP programmer is provided with a limited set of objects, and these objects are represented in a standard way in memory which is beyond his control. For some programs this relieves him from tedious programming details which are essentially unimportant to his algorithm, but in many cases gives rise to enormous inefficiency. In other cases he is driven to simulate a more convenient data-structure by a list which is not only inefficient but also requires additional programming.

A number of attempts have been made to remove these shortcomings. Some of these merely consist of a preprocessor to allow the programmer to use a more convenient language which is then transformed into standard LISP. This has the advantage of providing the flexibility of LISP without the mass of parentheses. The most ambitious attempt was the LISP 2 project, which used a preprocessor, but also added declarations to permit more efficient compiled code, and a number of new data-types. The resulting system was extremely complex and ran into severe implementation difficulties.

In a later chapter we will describe a less ambitious attempt to remove some of these deficiencies, which was implemented by the author and his colleagues at the Courant Institute at New York University. The objectives of the design of this system, called BALM, was to improve the form of the language and to provide additional data-types; that is, points 1 and 3 mentioned above. During the implementation, it became apparent that the translator could be written in the language itself, and could be made sufficiently flexible to permit the user to extend or to modify the form of the language itself. As mentioned in the introduction, this seems to be the most attractive way of implementing a general-purpose language, and has received much attention recently.

16
SNOBOL

INTRODUCTION

The SNOBOL programming language developed at Bell Telephone Laboratories in 1962 is a very powerful and sophisticated language for manipulating character strings. It has evolved through a number of versions, the current version SNOBOL 4 being by far the most powerful. With the character string as the basic data structure of the language, the designers felt free to abandon the standard form of operator and functional notation used as the basis for most algebraic languages, and chose instead a convenient and powerful form of command structure appropriate for dealing with character strings.

The most important innovation of SNOBOL was that it recognized the fact that subparts of a string are more conveniently recognized by their content than by their position. To give a simple example, consider the problem of locating a particular sentence in a body of text. This can be conveniently done by expressions such as "the sentence which starts with..." or "the sentence which contains the phrase...." To save searching we could sometimes localize the region where this sentence might be found, such as by specifying the page or even the line number. However, we would very rarely wish to specify a sentence by giving the number of the first and last character. Having identified the sentence in the test, the most frequent operations would be to save it for further analysis or to modify the text by changing either the sentence or other textual material nearby.

SNOBOL permits this type of operation by allowing the user to specify what is referred to as a pattern. In the simplest case, this may consist of a sequence of characters which may be constant or may be a string which is the value of an expression. In addition, SNOBOL provides a number of pattern variables and pattern functions each of which will match a particular class of strings. Patterns can be concatenated to produce other patterns. In fact, in SNOBOL 4 a pattern is just as much a basic data object as is a string.

BASIC STATEMENT FORMS

A statement in SNOBOL 4 consists of five parts: a *label*, a *string reference*, a *pattern*, a *replacement part*, and a *goto part*. One or more of these parts may be left out, giving rise to a number of different statement forms built from the same basic skeleton. String assignment, for instance, is done simply by using the string reference and replacement parts of the statement so that the statement

    AB = 'ABC'

assigns to the string variable AB the string consisting of the three characters 'ABC'. On the other hand, a statement to search the string AB for an occurrence of the substring 'BC' and to replace that substring with the string 'BCBC' would be written as follows:

    AB   'BC' = 'BCBC'

By using the pattern ARB we can write a statement which will search the string AB for any sequence of characters preceded by the string 'X' and followed by the string 'Y' by the following statement:

    AB   'X'   ARB   'Y' = 'YX'

This will delete any intervening strings and interchange the strings 'X' and 'Y'. In a similar way, we could have used BAL instead of ARB to match any string which was balanced with respect to parentheses. If the particular string which matches a pattern is required for further computation, the pattern can be followed by a period and a string name. Any successful match for the statement will then assign the specific strings found to the associated variables. Thus, if we wished to save the string which matched ARB in the example given above, we would write simply

    AB   'X'   ARB . S   'Y' = 'YX'

If it is necessary for a pattern to contain a reference to a particular string matched earlier in the same pattern, then the first pattern should be assigned to a variable using a dollar sign instead of a period. This has the effect of making the assignment to the string variable as soon as the first part of the pattern is recognized rather than waiting until the end of the statement.

Each statement (and in particular any statement which contains a pattern which is to be matched) can either succeed or fail. This is taken advantage of by permitting the goto field to contain information describing where a computation is to resume if the statement succeeds or fails. A simple illustration of this is the following statement which changes all the occurrences of the string 'AB' in the string which is the value of the variable Y, replacing each with `'PQR'`

```
MORE   Y   'AB' = 'PQR'   : S(MORE)
```

Here, each time the pattern match succeeds, the AB found is changed to `'PQR'` and the transfer specified by an S (for succeed) is taken. When the pattern match fails there are no AB strings left and the next sequential statement will be executed. In a similar way, a label preceded by the letter F will specify a transfer which is to be taken on failure. It is possible to specify unconditional transfers by just putting a label in the goto field, as well as specifying a two-way transfer containing labels for both success and failure.

VARIABLES AND DATA-TYPES

The form of the SNOBOL language is clearly chosen to give convenient operations on strings. Since its development in 1962, the language has been generalized and expanded, and a considerable number of additional data-types are now provided. These include integers, real numbers, arrays, patterns, unevaluated expressions, and code. In addition, there is a facility for programmer-defined data-types which gives a facility somewhat analogous to that provided by structures in PL/1, but with a less efficient use of memory.

Unlike most languages, but similar to LISP, a variable in SNOBOL does not have a type associated with it, so any data-object can be assigned to any variable without any implied conversion. This has some advantages, including the ability to write procedures which will work for a variety of data-types, thus permitting a certain compression of code in some situations. However, this means that the type of an expression cannot, in general, be determined at translation time, but has to be postponed until execution time. This implies that each data-object must carry with it information about its type, thus necessitating a less efficient use of memory than otherwise could have been used, as well as considerably less efficient code which must contain tests for the type of data-object. The programmer is provided with the ability to determine the type of a data-object.

EXPRESSIONS IN SNOBOL

Apart from the unusual form of statement, the components of a SNOBOL program are written in the usual notation. An expression in SNOBOL contains constants, variables, prefix operators, infix operators, and function invocations. An expression containing more than one operator is analyzed according to the precedence of the operators, and parentheses can be used to modify this precedence in the usual way. The only unusual aspects of the syntax are that infix operators must have a space on each side, prefix operators should not be followed by a space, and the left parenthesis which precedes the arguments of a function must follow the function name without any intervening spaces.

The most basic operation on strings in SNOBOL is concatenation, which is implied when two string expressions are adjacent without any intervening operator. Thus the statement:

```
S = 'ABC'  X  'PQR'
```

will assign to S the string which is the result of concatenating the string 'ABC', the value of the variable X, and the string 'PQR'. Thus the concatenation operator is like an implied infix operator, which has a precedence which is lower than the conditional assignment operators . and $, but higher than the arithmetic operators.

The other basic string operations are those which extract or change substrings. As we have shown, these operations are provided in a highly sophisticated way by the use of patterns and the special form of the SNOBOL statement. This means that reference to a substring as the component of an expression is not permitted directly, but must be achieved by first extracting the substring in a separate statement. Alternatively, a function can be defined by the user to accomplish a substring extraction operation.

A number of functions on strings are provided in the SNOBOL system. The function IDENT takes two strings as arguments, returns the null string if they are identical, and fails otherwise. There is also a function called REPLACE which takes three arguments, all strings, and returns as its value the first string with all the characters in the second string replaced by the corresponding characters in the third string.

The usual arithmetic operations are permitted on integer and real numbers, but mixed integer and real expressions are not permitted. Strings containing digits only can also be used in integer arithmetic expressions, with execution time conversions being performed. For example:

```
A = 5; B = '10'; C = A + 2 * B;
```

will assign the integer 25 to the variable C. This conversion from strings to integers can also be done in reverse, so:

```
A = 5; B = 'XYZ'; C = A B;
```

will assign the string 5XYX to C.

Arrays of arbitrary size and number of dimensions are permitted in SNOBOL. Storage for such arrays is allocated dynamically, so the statement:

```
A = ARRAY('4,5')
```

will allocate space for an array of 4 rows and 5 columns, and assign the resulting data-object to the variable A. However, the array is not permanently associated with the variable A, as it would be in FORTRAN or PL/1. It is more appropriate to think of an array in SNOBOL as a pointer to the memory block used to store the array elements, and the variable A will contain the value of this pointer after the assignment. The subsequent assignment:

```
B = A
```

will then assign this same pointer to the variable B, so that A and B can be regarded as names of the same array.

Elements of an array are referred to in the usual way. The expression $A\langle i, j\rangle$ where i and j are expressions which can yield integers is used to refer to an element of the two-dimensional array which is currently assigned to A. This array reference can be used where a value is expected, such as an element in an expression, or where a name is expected such as on the left hand side of an assignment.

SNOBOL maintains a record of the names of all variables and labels at execution time, and permits the user to use strings as names. The indirection operator $ is used for this purpose. For example:

```
A = 'XX'
$(A 'Y') = 'PQR'    :($('Z'  A))
```

will assign the string 'PQR' to the variable XXY, and then control would transfer to the label ZXX. It is clear that this facility is relatively inefficient, since it requires the variable to be looked up in a symbol table for each reference. However, it does permit some very elegant programming, as we will see in a later example. For instance, as an alternative to an array whose elements are referenced by

```
A<1>, A<2> ... A<n>
```

we can use variable names

```
A1, A2 ... An
```

calculated as $('A' I), with the advantage that not all elements need be generated if not required. Of course, there is no restriction to the use of integers in generating names, and we will more frequently find that names not involving integers will be used with the indirection operator.

Note that a variable constructed at execution time by the $ operator may not have been used elsewhere in the program, so SNOBOL must be able to create variables at run time.

PATTERNS

The most interesting object in SNOBOL, and that which gives the language much of its expressive power, is the pattern. A string can be used as a pattern, but the most interesting patterns are those which can match more than one string. The basic operations on patterns are concatenation and alternation. Patterns are concatenated using the same notation as concatenation of strings, the only difference being that if either component is a pattern the result is a pattern. A pattern which is the result of concatenating two strings or patterns $p1$ and $p2$ will match any string which consists of a string which matches $p1$ followed by a string which matches $p2$. The alternation of two patterns $p1$ and $p2$, written $p1 \mid p2$ is a pattern which will match any string which will match either $p1$ or $p2$.

These two basic operations permit the construction of a number of patterns, but these are essentially restricted to alternations of strings. More flexibility is obtained by the addition of a small number of patterns and functions which yield patterns as their value. The most useful of these are:

ARB	matches an arbitrary string
LEN(i)	matches an arbitrary string of length i
SPAN(s)	matches the longest string which contains only characters in the string s
POS(i)	matches the null string immediately following the i-th character
ARBNO(p)	matches any string which consists of a sequence of strings each of which matches the pattern p.

A number of other such patterns are provided. It should be noted that these patterns cannot be constructed simply as the concatenation or alternation of other patterns. However, a more general mechanism is available for the construction of such patterns, which uses the data-type referred to as an *unevaluated expression*.

The difficulty with the above type of patterns lies in the fact that it can match an unlimited number of strings, so some other mechanism is necessary to specify it other than listing all the strings explicitly. The use of unevaluated expressions permits all the alternatives of a pattern to be computed when they are required. An unevaluated expression is specified by the prefix operator ∗ so the statement

```
PP = '' | P *PP
```

will assign to PP the pattern which will match either the null string or a string which matches P followed by a string which matches PP. That is, the value of PP is the same as that of ARBNO(P). When PP is used as a pattern, the first attempt at a match will use the null string. Next the pattern P ∗PP will be tried, so if a P is found the pattern ∗PP will be looked for. This is an unevaluated expression, so it is first evaluated, giving '' | P ∗PP. This procedure continues, reevaluating ∗PP each time it is encountered. Note that the assignment

```
PP = '' | P PP
```

will not give the same result, since the previous value of PP will be used to construct the new value, whereas we really want to define PP recursively. In a similar way we can get the effect of SPAN('ABC') with the assignment

```
SPABC = ANY('ABC') *SPABC | ''
```

Note that this only attempts to satisfy SPABC with the null string when it has failed to find an occurrence of 'ABC', thus always matching the longest sequence of 'ABC's.

The pattern ARB could be defined by

ARB = '' | ANYCH *ARB   or   ARB = '' | LEN(1) *ARB

where ANYCH is defined as an alternation of all characters. These definitions are of course much less efficient than the predefined versions.

The patterns which specify a particular position in the string being searched can be defined with the aid of the *cursor position operator*. This prefix operator assigns to its argument, which must be a variable name, the current value of the cursor, the pointer to the current position in the string being searched. For example, the pattern 'ABC' @Y will match the string 'ABC' and will assign the number of the next character in the string to the variable Y. This permits the pattern POS(I) to be written as

@Y *EQ(Y,I)

When encountered during a pattern match, this will assign the current value of the cursor to the variable Y, and then test this value against the value of I. If these are not equal, the pattern will fail. Otherwise the result will be the null string, which will match.

As we will see later, it is possible for the user to define his own functions, and these functions can yield patterns as their values, thus permitting convenient implementation of patterns with more specific uses.

PROGRAMMER-DEFINED FUNCTIONS

The most important characteristics of programmer-defined functions in SNOBOL are similar to those of LISP. That is, they can have arguments which are usually passed by value, local variables, global variables, and can return any type of data-object as their value. Of course, these similarities are not apparent from the syntax, which is quite different.

A function is defined by executing the function DEFINE with arguments which specify the name of the function, its dummy variables, its local variables, and the label of the first statement of the function. When the function is invoked, the current values of the dummy and local variables are saved, the variables are assigned their new values, and then computation is continued at the first statement of the function. The function terminates by transferring to one of the fictitious labels RETURN, FRETURN, or NRETURN. For example, the following statements would define the function MAKARR which takes a string as its argument, separates it into a number of substrings by searching for commas, and returns as its value an array whose size is the number of such substrings, which are stored as its elements:

```
        DEFINE('MAKARR(S)P,N')        :(NST)
MAKARR  P = 0
        N = 1
MAKARR1 S = POS(P) BAL ',' @P        :F(MAKARR2)
        N = N + 1                     :(MAKARR1)
```

```
MAKARR2 MAKARR = ARRAY(N)
        N = 1
MAKARR3 S BAL . MAKARR<N> ',' =         :F(MAKARR4)
        N = N + 1                       :(MAKARR3)
MAKARR4 MAKARR<N> = S                   :(RETURN)
*
*
NST        ...    ...
```

If the above code is executed, the DEFINE statement will establish the function whose name is MAKARR and which takes one argument referred to as S, two local variables P and N, and which is defined by the statements starting at MAKARR. After executing DEFINE, the next statement executed will be that after the label NST. The reader should note the technique used to count the commas in the statement MAKARR1, using the cursor position operator to avoid looking at the same portion of the string again. Storage is allocated for the array by the statement at MAKARR2, and it is this array which is returned as the value of the function after filling in all the substrings. There is a certain inefficiency in the code above, since the string S is actually searched twice for commas. A further inefficiency arises because of the method used to implement the storage of new strings in the standard SNOBOL, which is unnecessarily cumbersome as we will see later. From the point of view of the above example, it simply means that the substrings of S should not be extracted by deletion as in statement MAKARR3, but rather by the use of the cursor position again. Thus we might substitute:

```
        P = 0
MAKARR3 S   POS(P)   BAL. MAKARR(N) ',' @P   :F(MAKARR4)
```

Alternatively, we could extract the strings on the first pass, and keep them somewhere until we could allocate the correct size of array. For example, we could write:

```
        DEFINE('MARKARR(S)P,N,M')              :(NST)
MAKARR  P = 0
        N = 1
MAKARR1 S POS(P) BAL . $('TEMP' N) ',' @P :F(MAKARR2)
        N = N + 1                             :(MAKARR1)
MAKARR2 $('TEMP' N) = S
        MAKARR = ARRAY(N)
        M = 1
MAKARR3 MAKARR<M> = $('TEMP' M)
        M = LT(M,N) M + 1                     :S(MAKARR3)F(RETURN)
*
*
NST        ...    ...
```

This uses the variables TEMP1, TEMP2,... to store the substrings. These are not local variables, so care will be necessary in using this routine.

Another interesting solution to this problem uses a recursive function to effectively generate an unlimited number of local variables:

```
        DEFINE('MAKARR(S,P,N)SS')           :(NST)
MAKARR  S POS(P) BAL . SS ',' @P            :F(MAKARR1)
        MAKARR = MAKARR(S,P,N + 1)
        MAKARR<N + 1> = SS                  :(RETURN)
MAKARR1 MAKARR = ARRAY(N+1)
        MAKARR<N + 1> = S                   :(RETURN)
```

This routine should be called initially with zero values for P and N, but this is conveniently done in SNOBOL simply by calling it with only one argument. The default for arguments not supplied is the null string, which will work just as well. Note that this version only makes one pass over the string, does not use computed variable names, and does not use any global variables. It is also shorter than the others, but may be less efficient because of the number of function calls it uses.

A function may of course return any kind of object as its value, including a pattern. An interesting example is the following function which returns a pattern which will match any permutation of the characters in the string given as its argument:

```
        DEFINE('PERM(S)S1')                 :(NST)
PERM    PERM = FAIL
NEXTP   S  LEN(1) . S1 =                    :F(RETURN)
        PERM = S1 PERM(S) | PERM            :(NEXTP)
```

This actually constructs a pattern which specifies explicitly all possible permutations of the characters in S. This will be grossly redundant if some of these characters occur more than once, since no tests are made for repeated patterns. A more serious objection is that this function can generate enormous patterns very easily, a string of 6 characters generating a pattern with 120 characters in it. Note that the effect of the statements:

```
        S = 'ABCDEF'
        ... PERM(S) ...
```

can be obtained by the statements:

```
        S = 'ABCDEF'
        PERM = ANY(S) $ Z *REMOVE('S',Z) (IDENT(S) | *PERM)
        ... PERM ...
```

where REMOVE is defined by:

```
        DEFINE('REMOVE(A,B)')               :(NST1)
REMOVE  $A  B =                             :(RETURN)
```

Note that REMOVE returns the null string as its value.

AN EXAMPLE

We give below a complete SNOBOL program which formats paragraphs of text, right-justifying lines so that the rightmost characters of the lines are in column 72. The input is assumed to be a deck of cards with carriage control characters in column 1, and text punched in columns 2 through 72. A paragraph is assumed to begin when a blank card is followed by a card with columns 1 through 5 containing blanks, and is assumed to consist of a series of "words" separated by blanks. Lines ending in a colon, or followed by a line with a nonblank column 2 are assumed to introduce formatted information, which will not be changed by the program. The paragraph is assumed to continue after such formatted information.

The program adjusts the text by collecting the lines of a paragraph, or of a portion of a paragraph, into a single string. It then replaces all strings of more than one blank by a single blank, and inserts two more blanks after a period followed by a blank. It then splits this into lines of less than 72 characters, and inserts blanks so that the line is exactly 72 characters long.

The output is written on the PUNCH file in 72 characters per card, with the first character a carriage control character.

```
*
* PROGRAM TO REFORMAT PARAGRAPHS OF TEXT
*
NEXT     LINE = TRIM(INPUT)  :F(END)
         IDENT(LINE)  :S(AFTERBL)
HEADING  PUNCH = LINE  :(NEXT)
* FOUND BLANK LINE
AFTERBL  PUNCH = LINE
         LINE = TRIM(INPUT)  :F(END)
         IDENT(LINE)  :S(AFTERBL)
         LINE POS(0) '     ' NOTANY(' ')  :S(STARP)F(HEADING)
* LINE WITH 5 BLANKS AT BEGINNING AFTER BLANK LINE ASSUMED
* TO BE START OF PARAGRAPH
STARTP   PARA = ''
MOREP    LINE POS(0) SPAN(' ') =
         PARA = PARA LINE ' '
         PREV = LINE
         LINE = TRIM(INPUT)  :F(END)
         IDENT(LINE)  :S(ENDP)
         LINE (POS(1) NOTANY(' ')  :F(ENDP)
* LINE IN PARA ENDING WITH : ASSUMED TO INTRODUCE FORMATTED TEXT
         PREV ':' RPOS(0)  :F(MOREP)
* PRINT PARAGRAPH
ENDP
* REMOVE MULTIPLE BLANKS
         P = 5
```

```
REMBLKS PARA POS(P) BREAK(' ') . X ' '↑ P (SPAN(' ') '')
.          = X ' '                          :S(REMBLKS)
* ENSURE 3 BLANKS AFTER PERIOD
        P = 0; P3B = '.   '
PERIOD  PARA POS(P) BREAK('.'). X '.'↑ P ' ' = X P3B :S(PERIOD)
NEXTL   PARA POS(0) ARB . X ' ' ARBNO(NOTANY(' ')) . Y POS(72)
.          = Y                              :F(LASTS)
        PARA POS(0) SPAN(' ') =
        X = TRIM(X)
        N = 72 - SIZE(X) :(MOREBL)
INSAGN  PTR = 0
MOREBL  EQ(N,0) :S(QUIT)
        X POS(PTR) ARB . Y NOTANY(' '). Z ' '↑ PTR = Y Z ' '
.                                          :F(INSAGN)
        N = N - 1 :(MOREBL)
QUIT    PUNCH = ' ' X :(PNEXTL)
LASTS   PUNCH = ' ' PARA
* BLANK LINE ENDS PARAGRAPH
        IDENT(LINE) :S(AFTERBL)
* NON-BLANK LINE AFTER : ASSUMED FORMATTED
SPEC    PUNCH = LINE
        LINE = TRIM(INPUT) :F(END)
        IDENT(LINE) :S(AFTERBL)
        LINE POS(1) ' '  :S(SPEC)
        LINE POS(0) ' '  :F(SPEC)
* PARAGRAPH STARTS AGAIN IF COL 1 NON-BLANK
        PARA = :(MOREP)
   END
```

IMPLEMENTATION OF SNOBOL

There are a number of very sophisticated features in SNOBOL which significantly affect its implementation. If we compare SNOBOL with PL/1 for instance, we find that SNOBOL requires dynamic storage allocation with garbage collection, all data-objects require execution-time type flags, and variables and labels must be accessible by names computed at execution-time. It is clear that each data-object will have to contain sufficient information for execution time type tests, but also to tell the garbage collector which memory cells should be saved, including those cells used in structures referenced through pointers. Thus such information as the length of an array, and the type of each item of an array must be kept. The use of computed names requires that a table of names be available at execution time, and furthermore requires that each item of the language be looked up in this table just before use, since it could have been changed by an assignment to a variable with a computed name. The freedom with which values of variables can be changed restricts the amount of optimization which can be done, since even the most innocuous statements could be changed just before execution in this way.

However, if we assume that the major applications of SNOBOL will be those which involve a considerable amount of string manipulation, the most significant implementation decisions concern the representation of strings and patterns. As we suggested in a previous chapter, the choice of representation for character strings depends to a great extent on the sort of operations which will be most used. String modification is done more efficiently with a linked representation, except in the special case of fixed-length string operations such as those provided in PL/1. However, operations such as pattern search are somewhat more efficiently done with a sequential representation. In the case of SNOBOL, the basic operation of pattern search is so powerful that the majority of algorithms can be implemented with a minimum amount of string modification. It is therefore a reasonable choice for strings in SNOBOL to be implemented sequentially.

As well as blocks of memory in which are stored character strings, we will also need structures which represent patterns. Basic pattern elements are strings, elementary patterns such as ARB, and functions such as LEN. These can be combined using the basic concatenation and alternation operators. A pattern in its most general form is a succession of pattern elements each of which may be an alternation of patterns. As soon as a match is found for one alternative, the next item which is looked for is the pattern element following. This is inherently a branching process, and as we will see below, a pattern is most conveniently represented by a tree structure.

The run-time symbol table required to implement the indirection facility is best constructed using hashing and linking techniques. Since arrays can have elements of any data-type they are clearly best represented as arrays of pointers.

It is apparent from the discussion above that the internal representation of SNOBOL more closely resembles a list-processing system rather than a string processor. In fact the storage allocation and garbage collection mechanism required by SNOBOL is quite similar to that used in LISP. The main difference is that storage for strings requires the ability to handle blocks of memory of unlimited size just as dynamically as one-word blocks are handled. Such a storage allocator is also used in the extended version of LISP described in a later chapter.

PATTERN MATCHING

A pattern in SNOBOL consists of a number of pattern elements, which are concatenated in the sense that the pattern which will match any string which consists of the concatenation of substrings, each one of which is matched by the corresponding pattern element. Each pattern element can itself have alternatives, either specified explicitly using the alternation operator, or implicitly in such patterns as BAL and ARBNO. The pattern matching algorithm must examine all combinations of pattern elements, and do so in a standard order so that the programmer can specify the order of preference of a number of possible matches.

The pattern matching algorithm thus can work in the following way. A cursor is set to point to the beginning of the string, and then an attempt is made to match the first pattern element starting at the position specified by the cursor. If this fails, the cursor is moved forward, and the attempt repeated. If the end of the string is reached, the pattern match fails totally. If the first pattern element is matched successfully, the cursor is set to the position following the matched substring, and an attempt is made to match the next pattern element starting at the new cursor position. Each time an element is matched, the next element is tried, with success overall if all pattern elements are matched. Each time a pattern element does not match, an attempt is made to find an alternative match for the previous element. If these is one, then the process continues using this alternative and the first alternative of the following element; if there is not, the element before that is tried. As mentioned above, overall success is obtained when there are no more elements to be matched, and overall failure is obtained when there are no more alternatives for the first element.

Let us consider an example in some detail. Suppose the pattern is:

```
(('A' | 'B') ('C' | 'D'))|(('E' | 'B') ('DG' | 'CH'))'I'
```

This will match any of the strings:

```
ACI ADI BCI BDI EDGI ECHI BDGI BCHI
```

and will attempt the matches in that order. If we represent the pattern as a tree of the form of Figure 16.1, and consider the string BCHI, then we see that the patterns actually attempted are:

```
A(fail)
B
 C
  I(fail)
  D(fail)
 E(fail)
B
 DG(fail)
 CH
  I(success)
```

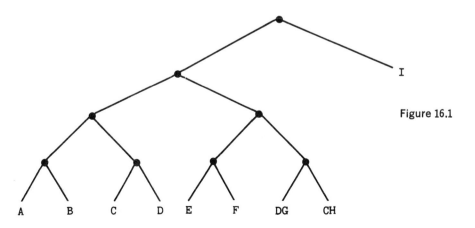

Figure 16.1

Each failure requires backing up and attempting the next alternative starting at the same position as the subpattern which failed.

It is clear that whenever a pattern element is matched, sufficient information must be kept to enable it to give the next alternative match if the subsequent pattern element fails. This next alternative may not be simply the next alternative in that pattern element, but rather the next alternative much lower in the tree. In the example above, for instance, after B and C match but I fails, it is not sufficient to look for the next top-level alternative to the pattern element preceding I, but to retrace down the tree to try the next alternative to C. This means that the standard method of processing a tree using recursion to provide backing-up information is not sufficient.

There are two different ways that we might keep this information. First, we might keep it in the pattern itself. This would require that the pattern be represented in such a way as to enable the matching routine to move forwards and backwards, downwards and upwards, which suggests that either a sequential structure or a two-way linked list be used. Of course even a sequential structure will require backwards pointers in it to permit backup. Second, we might keep it in an auxiliary structure which we could build and modify as necessary. In fact, because the object being matched is a string, we can use a push-down stack for this purpose, giving a rather efficient implementation.

If we assume a pattern representation in which each pattern consists of a sequential or linked list of pattern elements, and each pattern element consists of a sequential or linked list of patterns, then the following algorithm can be used:

1. Stack the first pattern element
2. Store the cursor position on the stack
3. Stack the first alternative
4. If it is not a string, go to 1
5. If there is a match, go to 8
6. If there are any alternatives left, replace the current alternative by the next, and go to 4
7. Otherwise, remove entries from the stack until there is a pattern element with an alternative; replace this by the next alternative, restore the cursor from the value specified, and go to 4; if there is no such pattern element, exit with failure.
8. Search the stack backwards until a pattern with an unmatched pattern element is found; if there is one stack it and the cursor value, and go to 2; if there is not, exit with success and details of the match on the stack.

Note that this algorithm needs only the ability to pass from each pattern element to its first alternative and the next pattern element, and from an alternative to its first pattern element and the next alternative.

For further discussion of pattern-matching, and in particular the algorithm used in the standard SNOBOL 4 implementation, see the paper by Gimpel (70).

STRING STORAGE

The standard SNOBOL 4 implementation uses a packed sequential structure for strings, and a plex representation for patterns. Whenever a new string is produced, it is looked up in the string table using hashing techniques. If it already exists, a reference to the existing string is returned. Otherwise a block of memory of appropriate size is requested from the storage allocator, the new string is constructed and entered into the table, and a reference to the new string is returned. The table has the structure shown in Figure 16.2. The effect of this is to ensure that strings are not duplicated in memory, but it is rather time consuming. As shown above, the representation of the string contains a field which can be used to specify the value of the variable whose name is the string. The value of a variable may be a number, a string, a pattern, an array, or a structure, and will carry flags to identify it as such.

This procedure is followed whenever a string is assigned as the value of a variable. Thus in the second of the two statements:

```
S = 'ABCDE'
S    LEN(1) =
```

which simply removes the first character from the string 'ABCDE' giving the string 'BCDE', the assignment to S is made by looking up 'BCDE' in the hash-table, and associating the result as the value of S. This rather simple operation thus appears highly time-consuming. The advantage is that all information associated with the string 'BCDE' is localized in memory, so that if it is used as a label in, for example:

```
A = B              : ($S)
```

the label information is readily available in the 'ABCD' memory block.

The string structure for a typical SNOBOL implementation is shown in Figure 16.3. The POINTER TO VALUE field contains a pointer to the value of the variable whose name is the string, while the VALUE TYPE field indicates what sort of an object is pointed to. The BUCKET POINTER field points to another string structure which falls

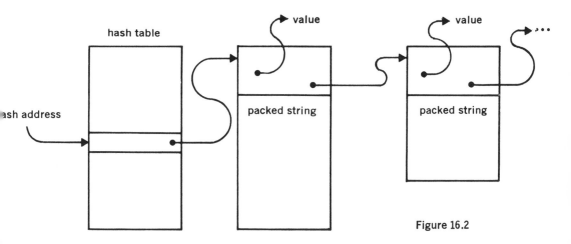

Figure 16.2

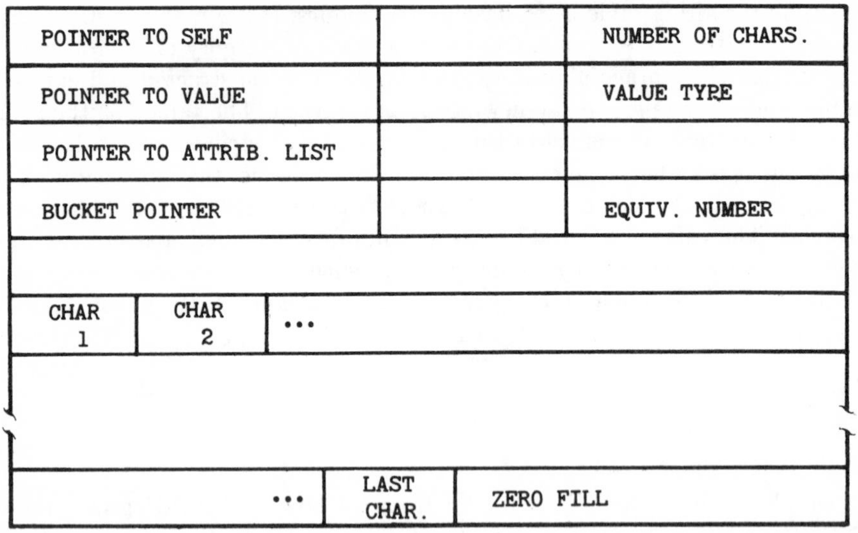

POINTER TO SELF		NUMBER OF CHARS.
POINTER TO VALUE		VALUE TYPE
POINTER TO ATTRIB. LIST		
BUCKET POINTER		EQUIV. NUMBER

CHAR 1	CHAR 2	...

| | ... | LAST CHAR. | ZERO FILL |

Figure 16.3

into the same hash bucket, while EQUIV. NUMBER holds another hash code of the string to allow fast string equality tests.

A basic data-item in SNOBOL is the *descriptor*, which essentially has the form of Figure 16.4. The type of data-object is identified by the contents of the TYPE field, and the VALUE field is used to contain the object itself, or be a pointer to it.

During execution, a substring is specified by a word pair called a *specifier*, of the form of Figure 16.5. This has a descriptor as its second word, and specifies a substring starting at the position starting at the WORD OFFSET word of the string and the BIT OFFSET bit in that word, and containing LENGTH characters. If WORK OFFSET and BIT OFFSET are both zero, the substring would start at the beginning of the string.

An array is implemented as a block of descriptors, and a programmer-defined data-type as a block of descriptors with components specified by names.

| VALUE | TYPE |

Figure 16.4

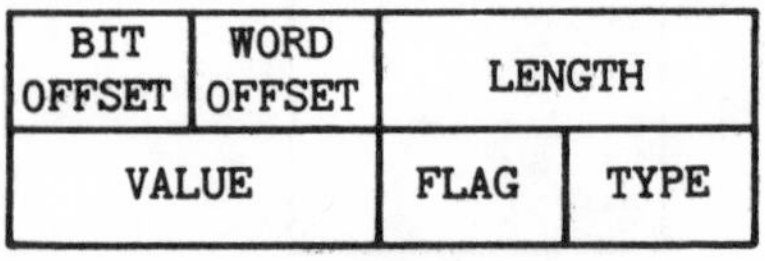

| BIT OFFSET | WORD OFFSET | LENGTH | |
| VALUE | | FLAG | TYPE |

Figure 16.5

ALTERNATIVE STRING REPRESENTATIONS

The simplest form of string representation uses sequential memory locations for successive characters in a string, and as we pointed out previously, allows efficient use of memory and fast processing in most cases. The disadvantages of this form are that it does not conveniently allow modifications of a string without moving the whole string. However, in Snobol the high-level nature of the language allows a large amount of analysis of existing strings to be done compared with the construction of new strings, so this disadvantage is less critical. Accordingly we will first consider this representation for strings.

Suppose a string is specified by the addresses of its first and last characters as shown in Figure 16.6. The effect of a Snobol statement on such a string can be to split it up into a number of (possibly overlapping) substrings which are assigned to variables, and also to change it to a new string (possibly the result of concatenation). It is clear that substrings can be specified in the same way, so that we might generate a picture such as Figure 16.7. When strings have to be concatenated to produce another string of this form, it is necessary that they be copied. This is most conveniently done if the length of the resulting string can be determined before any copying is done, so that a block of memory of the correct length can be requested from the storage allocator. Alternatively, if a push-down stack form of storage allocator is used, successive segments of the new string can be put on the top of the stack.

This can be improved somewhat by allowing a string to be specified explicitly as consisting of a sequence of substrings which are not stored in adjacent memory locations. See Figure 16.8. With this form of storage concatenation can be done by appending the pointers specifying the strings to be concatenated, which is more efficient as

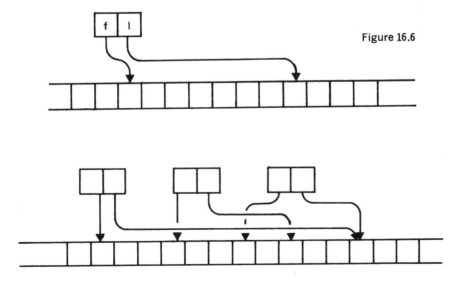

Figure 16.6

Figure 16.7

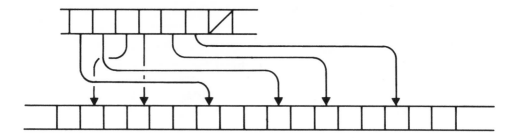

Figure 16.8

long as the storage taken up by the pointers is small compared with that occupied by the coded characters themselves. The general principal of such storage management would be to concatenate short strings by copying, but to concatenate long strings by copying pointers.

This type of storage works because an existing string is never changed, but merely has new strings constructed from its parts. Thus each statement can only use more storage, rather than releasing any, so eventually memory will become full. At this point a garbage collection phase can be initiated, which traces down all existing strings, marking all memory locations referenced, and collecting the remaining words into a storage pool. In the case of SNOBOL it is appropriate to consolidate those strings which have become fragmented during execution, and copy each string to a contiguous block of memory, leaving free memory locations in a contiguous block also. This form of garbage collection (or storage regeneration, as it is called in SNOBOL) can be used whether strings are always stored consecutively, or as a sequence of noncontiguous segments each stored consecutively.

17
APL AND SETL

INTRODUCTION

In this chapter we will consider two programming languages which have in common the fact that they use a single type of aggregate data-object, but provide a comprehensive set of very powerful operators. Both languages are well defined theoretically, but based on different notions. The first, APL, is based on the provision of a powerful set of operations on arrays, including the systematic extension of operations on scalars to arrays. The second, SETL, is based on the use of the set of mathematical set theory as the basic data-object, with the operations on sets including those developed by set theory to express the operations of mathematics.

The value of these languages is not that the facilities provided cannot be provided by other languages. An initial implementation of SETL and a version of APL is being done in BALM, for example, and it is likely that the essential facilities of APL and SETL could be written as a package of routines in ALGOL 68. The point is rather that an algorithm written in a language such as ALGOL 68 is often overspecified, in the sense that the programmer has been forced to make decisions which are in fact irrelevant to the correctness of the program. Such things as the order of execution of commands or evaluation of expressions, or the particular way chosen to represent a data-object, are often decisions which are made arbitrarily by the programmer. As such, they represent unnecessary information in the program which is potentially confusing to the reader (and sometimes to the programmer), and also inhibit the compiler from "understanding" the program sufficiently to translate it in the optimum way. This latter problem arises not only because the compiler has more information to process, but also because it is very difficult for the compiler to determine the theoretical properties of an operation which is defined by an algorithm. In fact in the general case it can be shown that it is not possible to find an algorithm which can determine the properties of an arbitrary program. While this should not be interpreted as suggesting that a compiler cannot determine, for example, that a procedure which computes the sum of two vectors is commutative, which might be necessary for the compiler to produce the optimum code, it is reasonable to assume that such determinations will be very difficult.

Because of the conciseness of the two languages, they have sometimes been used as a medium for communication of algorithms between programmers, and are sometimes referred to as *specification languages*.

In our description of these two languages we make no attempt at completeness, or even to express completely the flavor of these languages. The intention is merely to point out the major decisions which are implicit in their design. In Appendix C we give some examples which illustrate their use.

APL

APL is a programming language which was developed by Iverson in 1962, and has been implemented as a conversational system by a group at IBM. Its main characteristic is a very concise and powerful notation for manipulating arrays. The power of the language together with the convenience of the facilities provided in the implementation have made it a popular language for a number of applications areas.

DATA-OBJECTS

The primitive data-objects in APL are numbers and characters. Numbers carry with them information about their type, as in LISP and other languages, with type testing and conversion being done dynamically when necessary.

There is a single aggregate data-object in APL, the array. This can be regarded as a vector whose elements can be vectors or primitive data-objects. Arrays are constrained to be rectangular, and to have elements of the same type, and so lend themselves to the standard compact array representation.

Numerical constants are written in the usual notation. Constant vectors with numerical components are written by specifying the values of their components in order, separated by commas. Constant vectors whose elements are characters are specified by enclosing the sequence of characters in quote marks.

FORM OF LANGUAGE

The APL language form is a fairly conventional one, with variables, expressions, assignment statements, transfer statements, conditional statements, and functions. The value of a variable or an expression is in the general case an array of an arbitrary number of dimensions, and the assignment statement permits the array on the right-hand-side of the assignment operator to be assigned in one operation.

Operators are limited to having one or two arguments, called *monadic* and *dyadic*, and are used in expressions in prefix or infix form. Operators have no precedence, with the understood order of evaluation being right to left. Thus the expression $A \times B + C$ will be evaluated as $A \times (B + C)$. Parentheses can be used to change the order of evaluation if required. An expression containing the assignment operator $\leftarrow$ assigns the value of its right component to its left, but it can also be used as an expression which has the value of its right component.

DATA-STRUCTURES

Data-objects are represented by compact arrays which carry with them complete information about their dimensions and the type of their components. A single array can be the value of at most one variable, so assignment from one variable to another requires that a copy of the array be made and the copy be assigned to the variable on the left-hand-side. A variable is represented by an area of memory which contains, among other things, a pointer to the block of memory containing its current value. This block in turn contains a pointer to the variable whose value it is.

This permits a particularly simple form for storage allocation and reclamation. Allocation can be made from a stack in the standard way. When an array is assigned as the value of a variable, the variable pointer in the old array is erased, the variable pointer in the new array is set to point to the variable, and the variable is set to point to the array. Temporary arrays constructed as intermediate values during the evaluation of an expression are marked as in use, and the place from which they are referenced is stored. They are marked as freed when the evaluation of the expression is complete. Then when the storage allocator runs out of space, all arrays are examined, and the ones which are not in use, and not values of a variable, are released, and the remaining memory is compacted. When an array is moved, its unique reference is adjusted accordingly.

OPERATIONS

The simplest operation on arrays is the indexing operation. If I1, I2, I3, . . . , In are integers, the (I1, I2, I3, . . . , In)-th element of the n-dimensional array A is referred to as

A[I1;I2;I3; . . . ;In]

which can appear on the left-hand side of an assignment operator with its usual meaning. If any of the Is is left out, all the values in the corresponding dimension are selected; so, for example, M[J;] will select the J-th row of a two-dimensional array M, while M[;J] will select the J-th column. If, instead of being an integer, an I is a vector of integers, the corresponding elements in that dimension are selected. For example, if M is the matrix

$$1 \quad 2 \quad 3 \quad 4$$
$$5 \quad 6 \quad 7 \quad 8$$
$$9 \quad 10 \quad 11 \quad 12$$

and I is 2, 3 and J is 1, 4, then M[I;J] is the matrix whose elements come from the second and third rows and the first and fourth columns, so is

$$5 \quad 8$$
$$9 \quad 12$$

All these types of expression can be used on the left-hand-side of an assignment operator, and specify the subarray to be changed.

The first dimension of an array A is written as ρA. Thus, an array A may be regarded as a vector whose elements are

A[1],A[2],...,A[ρA].

There are a number of interesting operators for changing the "shape" of arrays. The compression operator / can be used to select certain elements of an array, regarded as a vector, and construct a new vector containing just the specified elements. The selection is done by a vector whose elements are either 1 or 0, depending on whether the corresponding element is to be retained. Thus the expression

(1,3,4)/(11,12,13,14, 15)

will have the value (11,13,14). In a similar way the expansion operator \ creates a larger vector by inserting the elements in positions corresponding to the 1's in the left-hand argument, and filling in the other elements with appropriately sized arrays containing zeros. Note that

L/L\A

gives A. Compression and expansion can also be specified along other dimensions than the first.

Logical vectors containing just ones and zeros can be created conveniently using the operators α and ω. The expression NαL creates a vector of length N with L leading ones, filled out with zeros, while NωL is similar, but with the ones being in the L trailing positions.

Cyclic left rotation of an array A by K places is written KϕA, while the reversal of A, the vector with the elements of the vector A but in the reverse order, is written ϕA.

All operations on numbers are generalised to arrays so that, for example, if B and C are arrays with the same dimensions, the assignment:

A← B + C

will assign to A an array such that A[I] has the value B[I] + C[I]. For example, if B and C are matrices this statement will assign their sum to A. In general, if $\oplus$ is an operator defined on scalars, the expression A $\oplus$ B will have its usual meaning if A and B are scalars, while if A and B are vectors its value will be a vector whose I-th element is A[I] $\oplus$ B[I]. If A is a scalar and B is a vector the result will be a vector whose I-th element is A $\oplus$ B[I].

If $\oplus$ is a dyadic operator then the $\oplus$-reduction of an array A, written $\oplus$/A, is defined as

A[1] $\oplus$ A[2] $\oplus$ ... $\oplus$ A[ρA]

The ⊕-scan of an array A, written ⊕\A, has as its i-th element

```
A[1] ⊕ A[2] ⊕ ... ⊕ A[i]
```

for $i = 1, 2, \ldots, \rho$A. The outer product of two vectors A and B whose (i, j)-th element is $A_i \oplus B_j$ for any dyadic scalar operator ⊕ is written Ao.⊕B, while the inner product whose [I:J]-th element is q/A[I;]p B[J;] for dyadic scalar operators p and q is written Aq.pB. The ordinary matrix product then becomes A+.×B. Both inner and outer products are generalizable to arrays of higher dimension. The reader is referred to more complete documentation for further details.

COMMENTS

APL, like LISP and SNOBOL, has a vigorous band of supporters who maintain that "this is the right way to do it." The power of the operators sometimes enables complex programs to be coded in highly concise ways, and the convenience of the operating system in which APL is embedded makes it one of the most convenient languages for on-line use. The operators have rigorous definitions which permit theoretical analysis, clearly useful in the future for optimisation of programs, and their high level sometimes permits a program to be written without much of the unnecessary specifications which must be given in lower level languages.

However, there are a number of serious disadvantages to APL as the ultimate language. Perhaps the most obvious of these is the restriction to arrays as data-structures. This often means that a program whose data-objects are not amenable to encoding as arrays will be distorted, and in fact the major programming effort is then directed to the necessary adaptation. This could be relieved if the elements of an array could be pointers to other arrays, but this would effectively create a different language. The garbage-collection process would then be complicated by the fact that an array could be referred to more than once. Also, the possible side effects of modifying an overlapping part of an array would destroy the rigorous definitions of the operators, so such occurrences would have to be detected, and the implementation of the operation modified. On the other hand, some mechanism would have to be provided to permit the programmer to modify common parts of arrays when necessary. It is not clear if the attractive characteristics of APL would survive such changes.

SETL

SETL is a language which is being developed at the time of writing by J. Schwartz at the Courant Institute, in which the basic data-object is a set. The specification of the language leaves open the question of the representation of a set, and in fact the initial implementation is being done in BALM, described in another chapter.

The form of the SETL language is based on the usual notions of expressions, statements, and procedures. A fairly large character set is used in the 'publication' form of the language, which we will use here. Actual implementations may use smaller character sets if necessary.

DATA-OBJECTS

Primitive data-objects in SETL include integers, logicals, character strings, bit strings, and labels. There is a single aggregate data-object, the set, which is considered to consist of an unordered collection of distinct data-objects. Elements of sets may be arbitrary data-objects, including other sets. Particular forms of sets are used to construct other useful data-objects, as in the mathematical development of set theory. These include the ordered set, the sequence, and the function, whose structure we will describe below.

The usual notation is used for numbers and strings, and the mathematical notation used for sets. Thus, the set whose elements are the integers 1 to 5 can be written

$$\{1,2,3,4,5\}$$

This set could also be defined as

$$\{1,3,5,2,4\}$$

or as

$$\{5,5,4,4,1,2,3\}$$

since the order of the elements is irrelevant, and duplicated elements are not permitted. The elements of the sets can be specified by arbitrary expressions, rather than integers as in these examples.

The ordered pair of elements x and y is written $\langle x, y \rangle$, and is defined to be the set

$$\{x, \{x, y\}\}$$

the usual mathematical definition. If p is an ordered pair $\langle x, y \rangle$, x is given by the expression hd p and y by tl p. Ordered sets of n elements, called n-tuples, are defined in terms of pairs, so that the ordered set with elements $x_1, x_2, \ldots, x_n$ is defined to be

$$\langle x_1, \langle x_2, \langle \ldots \langle x_{n-1}, x_n \rangle \ldots \rangle \rangle \rangle$$

Note that this is similar to the representation of a list used in LISP, with the minor difference that a list of n elements is like an $(n + 1)$-tuple whose last element is NIL.

Functions in SETL can be defined in two ways. The first is by an algorithm, as is done in other programming languages. The second is by giving specifically the correspondence between the arguments and the value of the function. Thus, a function of n arguments is a set of $(n + 1)$-tuples in which the last element of each tuple is considered to be the value of the function when applied to the arguments specified as the first n elements of the tuple. If f is such a set, the usual notation $f(x_1, x_2, \ldots, x_n)$ is provided for referring to the last element of the appropriate tuple if one exists, and an "undefined" value otherwise. Similarly, the notation

$$f(x_1, x_2, \ldots, x_n) = x_{n+1}$$

is used to define the value of f for the specified arguments.

The set-defined function can be very useful in a number of circumstances. The fact that values can be added or deleted means that it can be used in more dynamic ways than an algorithmically defined function, which is usually rather difficult to modify. Also, it is possible to specify a multivalued function simply by having many tuples specifying the same arguments.

OPERATIONS

A relatively small number of primitive operations on sets are provided in SETL, with the ability to define more elaborate operations in terms of them. These primitive operations include the following

$\#a$	the number of elements in the set a
$\ni a$	an arbitrary element of the set a
$x \in a$	true if x is an element of set a, false otherwise
a <u>with</u> x	the set containing the elements of the set a together with x
a <u>less</u> x	the set containing the elements of the set a with x removed if $x \in a$
a <u>eq</u> b	true if the sets a and b contain the same elements
a <u>lesf</u> x	the set containing the elements of the set a without those elements which are tuples whose first element is x

In addition to the above primitive operations, there are a number of more powerful operations. Amongst these is the operation for creating a set, which is written as follows

$$\{e(x_1, \ldots, x_n), x_1 \in e_1, x_2 \in e_2(x_1), \ldots, x_n \in e_n(x_1, \ldots, x_{n-1}) \mid c(x_1, \ldots, x_n)\}$$

This contains elements $e(x_1,\ldots, x_n)$ for the specified values of x_i for which the condition c is true. For example, the intersection of two sets a and b can be written

$$\{x, x \in a \mid x \in b\}$$

although an operator will usually be available for this purpose. If the range is a numerical one, alternate forms such as

$$\min(y) \leq x \leq \max(y)$$

can be used instead of $x \in a(y)$, and similarly in other operations outlined below. In the numerical case the iteration will proceed from the left limit to the right limit.

Boolean expressions on the elements of sets can be written as

$$\mathbf{\forall} x \in a \mid c(x) \qquad \mathbf{\exists} x \in a \mid c(x)$$

If in the second case the x is enclosed in square brackets an assignment will be made to x, the first element satisfying c if one exists, and undefined otherwise. These forms can be extended to search over more than one set simultaneously in the obvious way.

There is also a form of iterative loops, with iteration being over the elements of a set. This is written as

$$(\mathbf{\forall} x_1 \in a_1,\ x_2 \in a_2(x_1),\ \ldots,\ x_n \in a_n(x_1,\ \ldots,\ x_{n-1}) \mid c(x_1,\ \ldots,\ x_n))\ block$$

which means that *block* is executed for x_1 through x_n ranging over the specified sets.

Several operations are available for use with set-defined functions. These can be defined in the following way:

```
f{a}    {tl p, p∈f | (hd p) eq a}
f(a)    if # f{a} eq 1 then ∋f{a} else undefined
f[a]    {tl p, p∈f | (hd p)∈a}
```

Thus $f\{a\}$ will give the set of all x such that $\langle a, x \rangle \in f$, while $f(a)$ will give the unique x such that $\langle a, x \rangle \in f$ and *undefined* otherwise.

A number of other expressions are available in SETL, providing facilities for procedure and operator definitions, generalised extraction and replacement operations, multiple assignment statements, and a variety of control statements. However, the language is still under development, and the above description should give some flavour of the language.

IMPLEMENTATION

The implementation of SETL poses some very interesting problems, many of which stem from the fact that the language describes an algorithm at a high conceptual level which must be translated into concrete terms appropriate for machine representation. This is a different situation from that in APL, since the basic data-object of APL, the array, has a fairly obvious implementation, while that of SETL, the set, does not. There are many different ways of implementing a set in memory, some of which are appropriate for some operations while being grossly inefficient on others. In a sense a SETL program is only half programmed, since the all-important choice of data-structures is not expressed in the program, but left to the compiler. A programmer looking at a SETL program might have considerable difficulty in determining which was the optimum form of data-structure—the amount of work on sorting algorithms indicates the possible difficulties in even the simplest cases.

A number of possible representations are suggested by the basic operations which are provided on sets. For example, if the membership test $x \in a$ was executed frequently, the best representation for a would probably be some form of sorted or hashed structure. Frequent use of the a <u>less</u> x operation would in general require a similar form, but which would be amenable to removal of an element, such as a sorted chain or a hash table of chains. On the other hand, if the a <u>less</u> x operation is used simply to remove an arbitrary element from a after processing it, a much simpler representation would suffice.

Because it seems unlikely that a SETL compiler will be able to choose the optimum representation for the sets, a further development of SETL is in the direction of permitting the user to specify this representation. Such specifications are interesting because they have a different character from the type of declarations found in other languages in the sense that the compiler is perfectly at liberty to ignore them. They thus take on the character of hints to the compiler, rather than rigid specifications.

18
ALGOL 68

In previous chapters we have made reference to the notion of an *extendable* language—that is, a language which can be extended or modified to meet the user's needs. In this and the following chapter we will pursue this topic a little further by describing two extendable languages, ALGOL 68 and BALM. First, however, we will consider in more general terms some of the important questions which arise in connection with extendable languages.

As we have pointed out in the introduction, the programming process is similar in a number of respects to the language design process, particularly in connection with large and complex algorithms. In such cases the limiting factor on our ability to write and debug such programs is the human capacity for dealing with such complexity, and so our efforts are often addressed to the problem of reducing the complexity of the program to manageable proportions. The structure of the programming language plays a large part in determining the success of such an effort.

The main technique used to reduce complexity is that of modularity, which permits a large program to be broken into a number of smaller modules whose interaction is well-defined and easily specified. We made an informal distinction between hierarchical modularity, which permits an algorithm to be described in several levels of detail, and horizontal modularity, which permits different parts of the algorithm to be described independently. It is the objective of an extendable language to permit the programmer to construct hierarchically modular programs conveniently. This is done by providing features in the language which permit it to be extended so that it becomes adapted to the particular application. The final program can then take the form of a sequence of definitions of the language extensions, together with the algorithm stated in a much more concise and understandable form. For example, if the base language is B, then there might be one set of definitions c which effectively extend the language to the language C, and another set of definitions d which extend the language C to language D, in which the algorithm is written. If the extensions are well designed, the language D may be useful for many different applications, and may be made available as a library "package." Further, it may be that the language C can be used not only as an intermediate language for the language D, but also for other useful languages.

Thus we see the possibility of a single language with a network of extension packages replacing the rapidly expanding set of special-purpose languages which are in use.

At the time of writing, this idea has not been realized, and there is some doubt that it is possible in practice. The objections stem mainly from the requirement for efficiency, both in translation time and execution time. It is clear that the translator for an extendable language cannot be as efficient when translating a particular language as a translator specially designed for that language, particularly if efficient object code is required. However, it may be that in many cases this inefficiency can be tolerated—there are numerous examples where inefficient languages have been preferred for the convenience they offered the programmer, and it seems likely that as programs get larger and machines get faster there will be an increasing demand for special-purpose, easy-to-use languages, with less emphasis on efficiency.

EXTENDABILITY MECHANISMS

There are a number of general requirements which must be satisfied by a language for it to be considered extendable. The most important it that it be able to represent data-objects and operations which are appropriate to the area in which the extended language is to be used, permitting a form of expression which is close to the way in which the programmer thinks of the algorithms. There seems to be no precise prescription for ensuring this, but it certainly requires that the language provide a rich data-structure mechanism, together with the ability to construct procedures which can operate on such data-structures and return them as values. Control over memory allocation is of course necessary to permit such data-objects to be created when required. Also, the construction of a higher level language often requires that certain computations hidden from the programmer require data-structures of their own, so it is usually convenient to provide garbage collection as the basic memory-reusing mechanism rather than the explicit memory-freeing operations. It seems to be this latter requirement which prevents PL/1 from being a suitable language for extending, for example. In PL/1 most experiments in extendability seem to founder because it is not possible to hide from the higher-level programmer the details of what is going on underneath.

Assuming that the language permits the necessary data-objects and operations, the other requirement is a convenient mechanism to permit the user to define the ones which are appropriate for his application. Here there is a broad distinction which can be made between these mechanisms which require considerable knowledge of the translator, and those which do not. In the first category fall the systems which are sometimes called *compiler writing systems*, or *compiler compilers*. These provide the user with the tools for writing his own compiler, and vary considerably in power and sophistication. Such systems have been available for many years, but generally have not had the success which had been hoped for. The main reason for this was that they provided good facilities for the part of the translator involving syntax analysis, which can easily be mechanized, but only rather rudimentary facilities for code generation. The result was usually a system which could be a powerful tool in the hands of someone who knew it well, but which was too complicated for the ordinary programmer to use.

The second type of system, that which requires little knowledge to be extended by the user, is that which has come to be called an extendable (or *extendible* or *extensible*) language. Such languages provide a mechanism to specify extensions in terms of the unextended language. The usual subroutine or procedure mechanisms of FORTRAN and PL/1 are primitive examples of such extendability. However, the term is usually restricted to languages which permit a modification of the syntax of the language by the user. A good example is the operator definition which is permitted in ALGOL 68, described in this chapter, which allows the user to specify new operators, with their precedence. Below we will show how this mechanism can be used to construct languages with similar characteristics to LISP and SNOBOL.

This latter type of extendable language, though convenient for the novice user, can be too rigid a framework for some languages. In particular, some of the highly concise special-purpose languages make use of assumptions about the text which are not easily defined, or use a syntax which is not compatible with that used in the base language. In this case more powerful control is required over the translator than is provided by the more standardized form of extendable language. What is needed in this case is a more general-purpose mechanism for describing how the extended language should be translated. The language BALM described in a later chapter is an example of such a system. It attempts to provide both the novice-oriented types of extension as well as more powerful control if necessary. In the first case little knowledge is required of the mechanism used by the translator, while in the latter case the user has a wide range of choice, up as far as rewriting the whole translator if he requires and if he has the ability to do so.

INTRODUCTION TO ALGOL 68

ALGOL 68 is the latest in the series of programming languages whose design was commissioned by IFIP and which is currently documented by a series of reports describing the language. The objectives of the design were to provide a general purpose programming language and at the same time make significant contributions towards the field of programming. Its predecessor, ALGOL 60, had achieved some such objectives at a time when considerably less was known about programming languages and considerably less was expected. It was, in fact, the number of interesting theoretical and practical problems proposed by ALGOL 60 which generated much of the interest in programming languages.

There were a number of areas in which ALGOL 60 had obvious deficiencies. These included the inadequate set of data types which did not include character or bit strings, or pointers, the lack of facility for manipulating parts of words, no well defined I/0 operation, and a somewhat restrictive use of memory. In addition, a number of language characteristics such as the call by name feature turned out to have a rather unnatural implementation with the result that the language failed to represent in a satisfactory way the underlying machine language procedures.

As a very rough first approximation, ALGOL 68 should be regarded as similar to PL/1. However, there are a number of highly significant differences between the two languages which we will attempt to illustrate in this chapter. One of the important design principles of ALGOL 68 was that the facilities provided by the language should be constructed from as few basic ideas as possible, and that these should be general-purpose and interrelated in the language in a way which avoided special cases wherever possible. This general principle, called *orthogonal design*, has contributed significantly towards the clean lines and elegance of ALGOL 68. A second design principle was that the language should have an efficient machine language representation and that computations whenever possible would be done by the compiler rather than by the object program.

MODES

In ALGOL 68, as in PL/1, and unlike SNOBOL, LISP, and BALM, each variable identifier has a well-defined data type called its *mode*. Primitive modes include bit, character and real and integer numbers with varying precision. Aggregate modes include homogeneous arrays, and structures with named elements similar to PL/1. PL/1 bit and character strings in ALGOL 68 would be represented as arrays of bits and characters respectively. The most significant difference between PL/1 and ALGOL 68, and which has far-reaching consequences, is the fact that the equivalent of the PL/1 pointer, called a *reference* in ALGOL 68, is restricted so that it can only point to a data object of the specified mode. Thus the declaration

```
ref real a;
```

will declare the variable a to be a pointer to a real number. To be more precise, this declaration states that a will be used as the external representation of the place where a pointer to be a real number may be put. That is, the mode of a is actually <u>ref</u> <u>ref</u> <u>real</u>.

A simpler example should make it clear. Suppose we have the following declaration.

```
real x, y;
```

This declares that x and y are external representations of <u>ref</u> <u>real</u>s. In a simple assignment statement, such as

```
x := x + y;
```

which, of course, is meant to assign the sum of the values of x and y to x, the expression on the left hand side is a <u>ref</u> <u>real</u> specifying a place where a real can be put. On the right hand side, we have an expression which looks like the sum of two <u>ref</u> <u>real</u>s. However, the plus operator is not defined for <u>ref</u> <u>real</u>s but only for <u>real</u>s, so the compiler inserts a *dereferencing* operation before each <u>ref</u> <u>real</u>. That is, the x and y on the right-hand side are taken to represent values, not pointers. A more complicated example is the following:

```
x := y + i;
```

in which i is <u>ref</u> <u>ref</u> <u>int</u>. Here the right hand side shows the sum of a <u>ref</u> <u>real</u> and a <u>ref</u> <u>ref</u> <u>int</u> which is illegal as it stands but which is perfectly legal if the y is dereferenced once, the i is dereferenced twice, and the code appropriate to the addition of a real quantity with an integer quantity is used. Dereferencing is thus seen to be a simple extension of the usual type conversion rules such as is found in FORTRAN. Note that since the mode of a real variable is actually <u>ref</u> <u>real</u>, the mode <u>real</u> is available to be applied to constants or parameters. Thus, for instance, the declaration:

<u>real</u> pi = 3.1416;

declares pi to be of mode real and to have the value 3.1416. That is, pi is simply an external representation of the quantity 3.1416, not a variable with this value, so it cannot appear on the left-hand side of an assignment statement.

As we have seen in previous chapters, it is often necessary to permit one of a number of types of data-object to occupy the same storage. This is done by means of a <u>union</u> declaration:

<u>union</u> <u>list</u> = (<u>ref</u> <u>int,</u> <u>ref</u> <u>real,</u> <u>ref</u> <u>node</u>);

This declares mode <u>list</u> to be a pointer to either an <u>int</u> or a <u>real</u> or a <u>node</u>, whatever that might be. An identifier can be declared as mode <u>list</u> by:

<u>list</u> l;

Since it is necessary for the type of every data-object to be available to the compiler in one way or another, storage for l will include flags to distinguish which of the three types of <u>list</u> is actually stored there. All operations on l which may depend on this must be compiled with appropriate tests of these flags. We will see later how this facility can be used to simulate LISP with considerable ease.

PROCEDURES

A procedure in ALGOL 68 is another type of data object which can be assigned as the value of a variable or passed as a parameter to another procedure. A procedure may or may not have parameters and may or may not return a value. If it does, the mode of each parameter and of the returned value must be declared explicitly in the procedure definition.

It is possible to declare an identifier of a procedure without actually giving it any value. This is useful when the program is to be compiled separately from the routine, or when the identifier is to be assigned a number of different procedures. An identifier whose value can be a procedure with two real parameters and an integer result can be declared by:

<u>proc</u> (<u>real,</u> <u>real</u>) <u>int</u> ppp;

The identifier can then be given a value by assignment:

ppp := (<u>real</u> x, <u>real</u> y) <u>int</u> <u>round</u>(x * x + y * y);

Subsequent applications of ppp are written in the usual way. Thus the expression

ppp(2.0, 3.0)

requires that the procedure which is currently the value of ppp be applied to the <u>real</u> quantities 2.0 and 3.0, giving an <u>int</u> result, in this case 13. If however we had written

<u>real</u> xx, yy; <u>int</u> i; xx := 2.0; yy := 3.0; i := ppp(xx,yy);

then the arguments of ppp would have been <u>ref</u> <u>real</u>s. However, ppp requires <u>real</u> arguments, so the compiler would have dereferenced xx and yy to provide their <u>real</u> values as expected, and i would have received the value 13.

A more interesting example is obtained if we define qqq by

<u>proc</u> (<u>ref</u> <u>real,</u> <u>ref</u> <u>real</u>) <u>int</u> qqq; qqq :=
(<u>ref</u> <u>real</u> x, <u>ref</u> <u>real</u> y) <u>int</u> <u>round</u> (x * x + y * y);

This looks similar to ppp, but with <u>ref</u> <u>real</u> arguments instead of <u>real</u>s. Then the portion of program

<u>real</u> xx, yy; <u>int</u> i; xx := 2.0; yy := 3.0; i := qqq(xx,yy);

will still assign 13 to i, but will work slightly differently. That is, qqq requires, and is given, <u>ref</u> <u>real</u> s as arguments, so no dereferencing is necessary. However, when evaluating the defining <u>expr</u>, we find that x and y are now <u>ref</u> <u>real</u>s, so that they must be dereferenced before the multiplications and additions can be done. The main effect of using <u>ref</u> <u>real</u> parameters of a procedure is of course that it is then legal to make assignments to them. Thus if qqq were changed to

qqq := (<u>ref</u> <u>real</u> x, <u>ref</u> <u>real</u> y)
<u>int</u> <u>expr</u> (x := x + y; x * x +y * y);

and the same statements were executed, the value of xx would be changed to 5.0, and i would be given the value 34. The same body assigned to ppp would be illegal, since it would involve an assignment to a <u>real</u>.

The reader should note that ALGOL 68 arguments are not really called by value, since assignments could be made (in ALGOL 60) to such parameters. The ALGOL 60 call-by-name feature is not available directly either, but can be accomplished by using a parameter of <u>proc</u> mode, which represents the way the call-by-name feature was actually implemented. However, the use of <u>ref</u> parameters gives similar effects to the standard FORTRAN calling sequence. The main advantage of the ALGOL 68 calling mechanism in simple situations would appear to be that simple quantities such as numbers or pointers can be passed in high-speed registers rather than being stored in main memory and their addresses being passed in registers, which is very useful for simple procedures like sine, cosine, or square root.

A procedure in ALGOL 68 can deliver a value of an arbitrary type, including <u>proc</u> and <u>ref</u>. In particular, this allows a procedure to be used on the left-hand side of an assignment statement if it delivers a <u>ref</u> mode value. For example, the PL/1 SUBSTR function and pseudo-function can be implemented within ALGOL 68 without any special provisions.

ARRAYS

An array in ALGOL 68 is an aggregate data-object whose elements are of the same type, and which can be referred to by indexing operations. Each dimension of the array is specified by a lower bound and an upper bound, and only indices between these values are legal. Elements of an array can be of arbitrary type, including <u>procs</u>, arrays, <u>ref</u> arrays, etc. The representation of the array in memory is dependent on the extent to which its parameters can vary. If, for instance, the array is known to be [1:10] <u>int</u> then a simple block of 10 words of memory each capable of holding one integer. With the declaration

[1:10] <u>int</u> a;

the memory allocation shown in Figure 18.1 can be made, and references to the array a can simply be made by machine instructions which refer to the address marked b. That is, the <u>ref</u> [1:10] <u>int</u> which is represented by a will actually be the address shown as b.

However, if the declaration is:

[1:0 <u>flex</u>] <u>int</u> c;

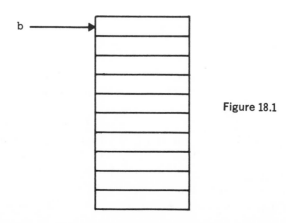

Figure 18.1

that is, c is an array of <u>int</u>s whose upper and lower bound is flexible, fixed memory locations cannot easily be reserved for c, and indirect reference is more appropriate. A reasonable representation for c is then simply a "dope vector" which gives the location and bounds of the array, as shown in Figure 18.2. Assignment to c may thus require a request to the storage allocator for memory in which to store the array. Subsequent assignments to c can return this space to the storage allocator (or in cases where the new array is smaller, just the superfluous space). References to elements of such an array will be considerably less efficient than to a fixed array, requiring access to the array address and the lower bound before the address of the element can be computed.

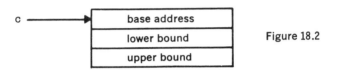

Figure 18.2

Considerable flexibility for referring to portions (or *slices*) of arrays is provided by the use of *trimmers*. Given the following declaration:

[1:10 , 1:10] <u>real</u> aaa;

we can refer to the third row of aaa by:

aaa[3,]

the third column of aaa by:

aaa[,3]

and the fourth to eighth elements of the third column by:

aaa[4:8,3]

That is, for each dimension we can either select a single element by specifying one index, or a sequence of elements by specifying two indices separated by a colon. By following the second subscript by <u>at</u> followed by a third subscript the slice is effectively renumbered from this subscript. Thus

aaa[4:8 <u>at</u> 2,3]

is of mode [2:6] <u>ref</u> <u>real</u>. Note that a slice of a <u>ref</u> <u>ref</u> [ ] <u>real</u> is also a <u>ref</u> <u>ref</u> [ ] <u>real</u>, a very reasonable choice.

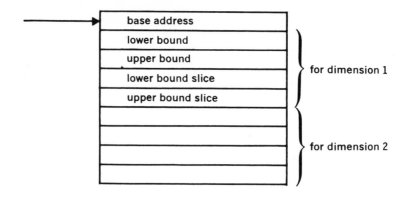

Figure 18.3

In general, a slice will require more information to specify than an array. For instance:

```
aaa[5:6, 5:6]
```

will require information such as Figure 18.3 shows. This is necessary because we can no longer assume a tightly packed array. A slice of a slice is of course legitimate.

Figure 18.4 is a representation of an array which can also be used to represent a slice. *Stride* is the amount of memory required by an element in that dimension.

STRUCTURES

A structure in ALGOL 68 is similar to its equivalent in PL/1 except for minor notational differences. A declaration of the form:

```
struct tree=([1:8] char name, ref tree father,
ref tree lson,ref tree rsib);
```

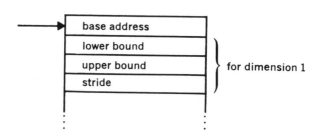

Figure 18.4

defines a new mode called `tree` which has 4 components called `name`, `father`, `lson`, and `rsib` of modes `[1:8]` `char`, `ref` `tree`, `ref` `tree`, and `ref` `tree` respectively. Subsequently the declaration:

    tree t;

will declare t to be of mode `ref` `tree` in an analogous way to declarations of other modes. Components of t are referred to as:

    father of t

This will be of type `ref` `ref` `tree`, so can be used in an expression on the left-hand side if necessary. Multiple uses of `of` are allowed, such as:

    name of father of t

Here `father` `of` t will have mode `ref` `ref` `tree`, so one level of dereferencing is necessary to give `ref` `tree` which does have a name component.

STORAGE ALLOCATION

Storage allocation in ALGOL 68 is done by what are called generators. These are of two types. Local generators can be thought of as allocating space on a stack, which is automatically freed when control leaves the innermost block in which the generator was invoked. Heap generators on the other hand can be thought of as allocating space on the "heap," and this remains allocated until it is no longer accessible to the program, when it may be freed by garbage collection.

All the allocation we have done so far has been local allocation. In fact the notation

    int x;

is an abbreviation for the form

    ref int x = loc int;

which says that x is of mode `ref` `int`, and that space on the stack should be allocated by the generator `loc` `int` for it. However, we could have allocated space in the heap for y as follows:

    ref int y = heap int;

In a similar way we can use any mode indicator combined with `loc` or `heap` as a generator. Note that we could also have abbreviated the declaration of y to

    heap int y;

That is, the default for declarations is effectively `loc` rather than `heap`.

The most common way of using generators in addition to the abbreviated <u>loc</u> forms is to allocate memory dynamically from the heap for variables of mode <u>ref</u> something. For example, if we have declared:

```
ref real p;
```

which allocates space to hold a pointer to a <u>real</u>, we can allocate space for such a <u>real</u> by writing

```
p := heap real;
```

The most significant difference between PL/1 and ALGOL 68 storage allocation is that there is no equivalent of the FREE command. Instead ALGOL 68 will rely on garbage collection for storage which was created by heap generators and which is no longer accessible. This can be done in a way quite similar to that used in LISP, namely by tracing down all variables which reference linked data-structures, and collecting the remaining storage. The reason this is possible is that the type of every data-object is known to the compiler, and if it contains any <u>ref</u>s, so is the type of object pointed to. Accordingly the compiler can compile itself a garbage collector capable of handling arbitrary data-structures. This is no mean problem, and the success of ALGOL 68 will probably depend on it.

OPERATORS

In ALGOL 68 a procedure is usually invoked in a form such as

```
p(a,b)
```

However, it is also possible to define new prefix and infix operators and associate a procedure with them. For instance, if we want an operator which will calculate the inner product of two vectors, we can write:

```
op dot = ([int i:int j] real a,b) real:
        begin int k; real s := 0;
        for k :=i to j do s := s + a[k] * b[k]
        end;
```

which declares the infix operator <u>dot</u> to be associated with the specified procedure. To specify the precedence of the operator <u>dot</u>, the declaration:

```
priority dot = 7;
```

can be used. Thus

```
[1:10] real x, y;
v = x dot y;
```

will assign the inner product of the vectors x and y to v.

In a similar way, prefix operators can be defined. Note that the procedure associated with an operator is dependent on the mode of its arguments.

In the Appendix we give some of the operators which are effectively predefined in the "standard prelude" of ALGOL 68, and which are thus automatically available to the user.

EXAMPLE: THE PL/1 SUBSTR PSEUDO-FUNCTION

A string in ALGOL 68 is implemented as a character array using the declaration:

```
mode string = [1:0 flex] char;
```

This has a virtual upper bound, so the declaration:

```
string s;
```

declares s to be of mode ref [1:0 flex] char with initial length 0. To define a procedure substr which when used as:

```
substr(s,i,l)
```

will give the string of length l starting at character number i of string s we can write:

```
proc substr =
([ ] char s, int i, int l) [ ] char
expr s[i: i+l−1];
```

However, this will not allow it to be used on the left-hand side of an assignment, since it yields mode [ ] char rather than ref [ ] char. To allow this we should change the definition to:

```
proc substr = (ref [ ] char s, int i, int l) ref [1: ] char
                            s[i: i+l−1 at 1];
```

This receives the string in mode ref [ ] char and returns mode ref [1:] char.

Note that the substr pseudo-function is in fact unnecessary in ALGOL 68 because of the availability of slices. If we have a declaration:

```
string s;
```

then it is perfectly all right to use expressions such as:

```
s[i:j]
```

in an expression to extract the characters between i and j, and also statements like:

s[i: j] := *expression*;

which will replace the characters of s between i and j by the characters of the string given by the *expression*. Similarly the i-th character of s can be referred to as s[i] either in an expression or on the left-hand side of an assignment.

EXAMPLE: LISP IN ALGOL 68

The sophisticated storage allocation features of ALGOL 68 allow a rather straight-forward implementation of the features of LISP within it. By this we mean more than simply the writing of a LISP translator and interpreter in the language. By "within the language" we mean that we can write LISP-like (or BALM-like) routines in ALGOL 68 itself. The main reason for this is the availability of garbage-collection for complex linked structures.

The implementation we will use is quite close to that used in BALM. For reasons associated with the necessity for specifying the number of arguments taken by a procedure, the internal structure will be somewhat different, however, and as a result somewhat less efficient. This disadvantage will be overcome by the fact that ALGOL 68 routines will be compiled rather than interpreted. A BALM compiler would not be as efficient as an ALGOL 68 compiler, simply because the type information available to the compiler allows considerable simplification of a number of processes. In addition, the ALGOL 68 programmer can take advantage of more efficient representations of numbers and arrays whenever it is possible.

We will start out by defining the basic binary mode of BALM as:

struct binode = (item hd, item tl);

This has two components, both of mode item, referred to as hd and tl respectively. An item is defined as:

union item =(ref int, ref real, ref string, ref bits,
            bool, ref lproc, ref [ ] item,
            ref binode, ref varb);

that is, one of nine types of object, each of which can be contained within an address-length quantity. These will be distinguished by the setting of at least 4 bits. Thus in an IBM/360 with a 24-bit address, an item could occupy 28 bits, and in the 6600 with a 17 bit address, 21 bits. The mode will be defined as:

struct varb = (item val, ref binode props);

The word lproc is of course used to refer to procs. We cannot do this directly because we want to be able to refer to procedures with an arbitrary number of arguments, so we define lproc as follows:

```
struct lproc = (bool type, vproc prc)
union vproc  = (proc item, proc (item) item,
                proc (item, item) item, ... etc.);
```

putting in as many alternatives as we will need. This is obviously a fake, and an unsatisfactory one at that, but it will work.

The standard LISP functions can then be written as follows.

```
CAR(x)      hd of x
CDR(x)      tl of x
CONS(x,y)   binode := (x,y)
ATOM(x)     ¬([ ] item :: x or binode :: x)
NULL(x)     x:=:nil
```

Of course they can also be defined as procedures, or as prefix or infix operators as in BALM, but this is mainly a matter of taste. The expressions shown will probably be most efficient, if not least space consuming. Note that hd of x and tl of x can appear on the left-hand side of an assignment.

All the standard LISP functions, including the interpreter, can be written to operate on such data-structures. Most of the user's programs, such as the following version of the reverse procedure, are quite straightforward.

```
proc reverse = (item l) item:
                 begin item t: :=nil; item ll:= l;
         next:   if ll:=:nil then goto fin;
                 t := binode := (referse(hd of ll),t);
                 ll:= tl of ll; goto next;
         fin:    t end;
```

This bears a remarkable similarity to BALM, as it happens, but some other operations, such as use of variables and expressions involving them will require the setting up of an association between variable names and the corresponding atoms, and the writing of the EVAL procedure.

The EVAL procedure similar to that used in BALM can be defined as follows:

```
proc eval =
  (item e) item:
    if atom(e) then if varb :: e then val of e
             else e fi
    else begin item f, args; lproc p;
         f := eval(hd of e); args := tl of e;
         if lp := f then
             if type of lp= fsubr then prc of lp(args)
```

```
                else begin [1:3] item evargs; int i:=1;
                    while args ≠ nil do
                        (evargs[i]:=eval(hd of args);
                         args := tl of args; i:=i+1);
                    case i in prc of lp,prc of lp(evargs [1]),
                             prc of lp(evargs[1], evargs [2])esac
            else prc of hd of lp(hd of tl of f,
                hd of tl of tl of lp,ars) fi
            end
    fi;
```

Note that this will only handle procedures requiring up to two arguments, but this can be arbitrarily extended. Note also that the compiler may insert code to check that the procedure is given the correct number of arguments.

EXAMPLE: SNOBOL IN ALGOL 68

There are a number of aspects of SNOBOL which require separate consideration. We shall concentrate on the basic pattern-matching process, and the use of strings as names of variables. First of all let us consider how we will write the equivalent of the SNOBOL statement:

```
L1 S 'AB' ARB . X 'CD' = 'CD' X 'AB'    :S(L2)
```

This can be written as a simple conditional statement of the form:

```
l1: if s contains 'ab' + arb(x) + 'cd' then
            (substitute ('cd' + x + 'ab'); goto l2) fi
```

We can use this form if contains is an infix operator associated with a proc (strong, pattern) bool and having side effects which set indicators which are used by the substitute procedure.

First the reader should note that we are using the infix operator + to concatenate strings, and also to join successive components of a pattern. This can be done by a number of definitions such as:

```
op + = (string s, pattern p) pattern: ... ;
op + = (pattern p1, pattern p2) pattern: ... ;
etc.
```

A pattern will be some sort of tree structure, which we will leave undefined here. For disjunction of patterns we can define:

```
op V = (string s1, string s2) pattern: ... ;
op V = (string s, pattern p) pattern: ... ;
etc.
```

The variable x can be an ordinary <u>string</u> variable declared by:

    <u>string</u> x;

while the pattern ARB will be implemented by a procedure arb defined as:

    <u>proc</u> arb = (<u>ref</u> <u>string</u> s) <u>pattern</u>: ... ;

This will require a <u>ref</u> <u>string</u> as argument, so that arb can return a pattern which will contain a pointer to the variable given as its argument. When arb is successful, assignment of the slice of the string can thus be made to the variable. Occurrence of the variable elsewhere will invoke the string which is its value in the usual way.

19
BALM

In this chapter we will describe in some detail an extendable language developed by the author and his colleagues at the Courant Institute. This is somewhat less ambitious than ALGOL 68, and has somewhat different aims. First of all, it attempts to provide the programmer with more extensive control over the translation of his program than is provided in ALGOL 68. Although the facilities of ALGOL 68 are powerful, in some cases it is necessary to permit the programmer to have access to the translator itself, so that he can make more fundamental modifications to its operation. For this reason we felt that the translator should be made sufficiently simple to permit the experienced user to understand its operation without undue effort. This required sacrifices in efficiency in a number of ways, but we felt that in a number of cases this would not be too much of a restriction. A listing of a version of the system, written in BALM, is given in Appendix B.

SYSTEM ORGANIZATION

In the BALM system the user is given control over the operation of the translator by making it one of the utility routines which form the basis of the system. The linkage to these routines is flexible, so that the user can replace the standard version of the translator, or any other utility routines, with his own. The system thus consists initially of a set of procedures, including translator and I/O routines and an executive routine, to which the user adds his own by executing commands which define procedures. These new procedures may be part of the users program, or they may be an addition to or a modification of the translator. Thus there is no real distinction between the users' program and the translator—both are written in BALM. The overall organization is illustrated below in Figure 19.1. A BALM program consists of a sequence of commands each one of which is translated and executed before the next one is read, thus permitting the execution to modify the translator.

In order to permit the user strong control over the translation process, while not requiring him to get too deeply into representations of his program in machinelike languages, an intermediate language is used in the BALM system. This is a well-defined simple but powerful language with a very simple syntax, which makes it easy to

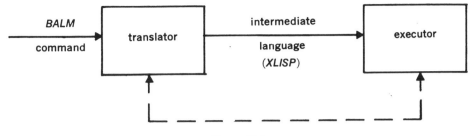

Figure 19.1

process when necessary. Thus the user who wanted to, say, print out the new value assigned to selected variables would be able to add a routine to the compiler to process the intermediate form of the language to make the necessary modifications to the code. The intermediate language is a slightly modified form of LISP, which we call XLISP.

The system has been implemented in several different ways. In the original implementation the executor was a slightly modified version of the standard LISP interpreter. In subsequent implementations a compiler was added to the executor. However, language extensions are normally done to the part of the translator which translates from BALM into XLISP with the executor usually being kept fixed. Below we will concentrate mainly on the extendable part of the translator.

The version of BALM given in Appendix B is a compiler-based implementation with the compiler producing code for a hypothetical machine which we call the MBALM. The MBALM machine can be realized by microprogramming on machines such as the IBM 360 and the Standard 9000, or by simulation. MBALM simulators are available for the CDC 6600, IBM 360, Univac 1108, and other machines.

DATA-STRUCTURES

Our objective in choosing data-structures was to include the minimum number which would permit the logical implementation of most common data-objects without too much inefficiency. To simplify garbage collection all data-structures are flagged with their type, so can be traced without requiring elaborate mapping information. A uniform format for a data-structure, or *item*, is used to permit handling all types similarly. This has the effect of permitting any variable in the language to have any item as its value, as in SNOBOL and LISP. The format chosen has two fields, a type field, and a pointer field, and in some implementations a third flag field for the user's use is also provided. In the case of some primitive items such as integers or logical quantities the pointer field is used to contain the information directly, but in the case of more elaborate data-structures the pointer field contains a pointer to other information.

The two main data-structures chosen were the *vector* and the *pair*. The first permits the use of arrays and indexing operations, while the second is essentially the basic data-structure of LISP and permits the construction of arbitrary branching structures. The elements of a vector or a pair can be arbitrary items, including other vectors and pairs, of course. From the logical point of view we could dispense with the pair and use a vector of length two, but in practice this would use up a little more space, and we felt that a distinction between vectors and lists (constructed from pairs) would more often than not be useful to the programmer. For the sake of economy of memory space we also provide a *string* of characters as a separate data-structure, stored sequentially in memory. Procedures represented as machine code are stored in a fourth data-structure called a *code block*. Vectors, strings, and code blocks may be of arbitrary size, but once allocated their length is fixed and stored in memory so that the programmer can determine the length if he requires.

To permit the user to manipulate programs, *identifiers* are also provided as a type of item. These can be thought of as represented by a pointer into a symbol table, in which is stored the name of the identifier, its current value, and another entry which we refer to as its property-list. These correspond very closely to the nonnumeric atoms of LISP, and similar operations are provided to manipulate them. In a similar way, there is a type of item called a *label*, which can be manipulated by a program to permit programmed switching of control.

OUTLINE OF THE BALM LANGUAGE

As we have pointed out, BALM is an extendable language, so it is not possible to give a complete definition of it. However, the system, if not modified by the user, defines a "standard" BALM language which permits a fairly convenient use of most of the basic features of XLISP. It is this "standard" BALM which we will describe below. The reader should note that nearly all features of the "standard" language are translated according to three lists which guide the translator, and which can thus be changed if necessary.

A BALM program consists of a sequence of commands separated by semicolons. Each command is read, translated, and executed before the next one is read. The program can be submitted either as a deck of cards, or typed in directly from a teletype terminal. In the first case, the card images will be printed, and will be followed by any printed output requested by the command. In the case of teletype input, only printed output will be typed. Note that a semicolon will always terminate a command, even if it occurs within parentheses or brackets (though not if it occurs as part of a string), so it acts as a sort of insurance that syntactic errors will not continue into the next command.

Commands in BALM include the usual type of assignment, written with an "equals" sign as in other languages. Thus

    A = 12.3;

will assign to the variable A the value 12.3, while

    B = C;

will assign to B whatever is currently the value of C. The right hand side of an assignment can be any expression, which can be written using infix notation and the usual functional notation for procedure applications. The usual arithmetic operators are available, and will accept numerical arguments of arbitrary type, doing execution-time conversion when necessary.

A command is just an expression which is evaluated, and whose value is ignored. An assignment command is simply an expression whose evaluation has the side effect of assigning the value of the right-hand side to the variable on the left, and as such it has a value, which in this case is the value of the right-hand side. Thus the command

```
A = B = 1.2;
```

will be executed as though it had been written:

```
A = (B = 1.2);
```

Here the right-hand side is an assignment, whose value is 1.2, which will thus be assigned to A as well as B. We will use the term "command" for such expressions merely to indicate this type of usage, rather than to imply some nonexistent distinction. Expressions such as assignments and transfers will usually though not always occur as commands, while those whose evaluation will produce no effect other than to calculate a value will not.

One use of commands will be as main components of a program as described above. However, they will also be used as the main constituent in programmer-defined functions, as we will see below. Expressions often used as commands include assignment, transfer, conditional, procedure invocations, and pattern matching and repetitive or looping operations.

A vector of n elements, but whose values are undetermined, can be written

```
MAKVECTOR(n)
```

This will dynamically allocate space for the vector, which will be collected automatically by the garbage collector when no longer accessible to the program. If the values of the vector are known, VECTOR can be used, so that the expression

```
VECTOR(1,2,3,4)
```

would represent a vector of length 4 whose elements were 1, 2, 3, and 4.

Indexing can be used to refer to the elements of a vector in the usual way, so that

```
v[i]
```

will refer to the i-th element of vector v, and

```
v[j] = x
```

will change the value of the j-th element of the vector v to x. Here v can be an arbitrary expression whose value is a vector, and i and j can be arbitrary expressions whose values are integers of appropriate size. This means that a two-dimensional array M represented as a vector of vectors can have its elements referred to as

$$M[i][j]$$

and so on. The length of a vector v is written SIZE v, and the expression VECTQ(x) will have the value TRUE if x is a vector and NIL otherwise.

The vector which is obtained by concatenating the two vectors x and y can be written

$$CONCATV(x,y)$$

A vector which has as its elements the j elements of the vector v starting at the i-th can be written

$$SUBV(v,i,j)$$

while these elements can be changed to the first j elements of the vector w by

$$SUBV(v,i,j) = w$$

A string can be converted to a vector whose elements are integers which are the internal representations of the characters in the string, and vice versa, by the operations

$$VFROMS(s) \qquad SFROMV(v)$$

The operations on pairs are essentially those provided in LISP for manipulating lists. A pair whose first component is x and whose second component is y is written $x:y$, and if p is a pair the first component is HD p and the second component is TL p. A list whose elements are the numbers 1, 2, 3, 4, for example, could be written

$$(1:(2:(3:(4:NIL))))$$

or, since the precedence of the colon is arranged appropriately, as

$$1:2:3:4:NIL$$

Here NIL is the logical item used to represent false, and by convention is used to terminate a list. This list could also be written as

$$LIST(1,2,3,4)$$

Components of a pair p may be changed by commands of the form

$$HD \ p = x \qquad TL \ p = y$$

but these should be used with caution, since the pair could be an element of other data-objects. The expression PAIRQ(x) will have the value TRUE if x is a pair, and NIL otherwise, and is the operation usually used for detecting the end of a list.

An identifier whose name is n is written as

"n

as long as n has the appropriate syntax for a name. In the current system names are sequences of letters and digits starting with a letter, or single special characters (with certain exceptions mentioned below). Note that "n does not refer to the value of the identifier named n, but to the data-structure which contains a pointer into the symbol table. If id is an identifier, the expression

VALUE(id)

gives the value of id, and

VALUE(id) = x

resets this value to x. Similarly

PROPL(id)

refers to the property-list of id, and

PROPL(id) = x

changes this property-list to x. The name of id is written

SFROMID(id)

which returns a string. If s is a string, then

IDFROMS(s)

refers to the identifier whose name is the characters of the string.

The quote can also be used for specifying constant vectors and lists. The notation used is essentially that of LISP. VECTOR(1,2,3,4), for example, could be written as

"[1 2 3 4]

while LIST(1,2,3,4) could be written

"(1 2 3 4)

Nesting is permitted, so expressions such as

```
"[[1 2] 3 [ABC $] (ZZZ)]
```

are also permitted. Note that such expressions do not have memory allocated during execution time, but during translation time, so if assigned to a variable and then modified, the "constant" will also be modified.

The above notation is also the one used by the utility I/O routines READ, WRITE, and PRINT. PRINT(x) will examine x and print it on the standard output medium, without the leading quote. READ(f) will read from file f the next complete item in the above notation, continuing reading until brackets and parentheses are balanced.

A whole vector or list can be assigned from one variable to another variable in a single statement, of course, but then any operation which changes a component of one will change a component of the other. If this is not desired, the vector or list should be copied, and the copy assigned.

A list or vector can be broken up into its constituent parts by the procedure BREAKUP. This takes two arguments, an item whose elements are constants or variables, and an item to be broken up. Parts of the second structure corresponding to variables are assigned as the values of those variables, while constants must match. If the structures cannot be matched, the BREAKUP procedure is terminated and gives the value NIL. Otherwise it has the value TRUE. For example

```
BREAKUP ("(A B), "((C C) (D D)));
```

will have the value TRUE and will assign (D D) to A and (D D) to B. Either structure can involve vectors, and constants in the first structure are specified by preceding them with the quote mark ". Thus

```
BREAKUP("[A "B C], "[[X X] B [Y Y]]);
```

will have the value TRUE and will assign [X X] to A and [Y Y] to C. The converse of BREAKUP is CONSTRUCT, which is given a single structure whose elements are variables, and which will construct the same structure but with variables replaced by their values. Thus

```
X = "(A B); Y="[C D]; PRINT(CONSTRUCT("(X Y)));
```

will print ((A B) [C D]).

A procedure in BALM is simply another kind of item which can be assigned as the value of a variable. The variable can then be used to invoke the procedure in the usual way. The statement

```
SUMSQ = PROC(X,Y),X*2+Y*2 END;
```

assigns a procedure which returns as its value the sum of the squares of its two arguments. The translator translates the PROC...END part into the appropriate internal form, which is assigned to SUMSQ. The procedure can subsequently be applied in the usual way, so

```
PRINT(5 + SUMSQ(2,3) + 0.5);
```

would print

```
18.5
```

Instead of assigning a procedure as the value of a variable, we can simply apply it, so that

```
X = 5 + PROC(X,Y), X*2+Y*2 END(2,3) + 0.5;
```

would assign $5 + 13 + 0.5 = 18.5$ as the value of X. Note that a procedure can accept any data-object as an argument, and can produce any data-object as its result, including vectors, lists, strings, and procedures. Procedures can be recursive, of course.

A procedure is simply an expression with certain variables specified as arguments. The most useful expression for procedure definitions is the block, which permits the declaration of local variables, and which is similar to that used in ALGOL but can have a value. Thus

```
REVERSE = PROC(L),
          BEGIN(X),
          COMMENT 'FIRST TEST FOR ATOMIC ARGUMENT'
          IF ¬PAIRQ(L) THEN RETURN(L),
          COMMENT 'OTHERWISE ENTER REVERSING LOOP'
          X = NIL,
          COMMENT 'EACH TIME ROUND REMOVE ELEMENT
              FROM L, REVERSE IT, AND PUT AT BEGINNING OF X'
NXT,      IF NULL(L) THEN RETURN (X),
          X = REVERSE(HD L):,
          L = TL L, GO NXT
          END END;
```

shows the use of a block delimited by BEGIN and END in defining a procedure REVERSE which reverses a list at all levels. The X following BEGIN indicates that X should be considered local to the block, while NXT is a label. The COMMENT operator can follow any infix operator, and will cause the following item to be ignored.

As well as an IF...THEN... statement there is an IF...THEN...ELSE... as well as an IF...THEN...ELSEIF...THEN..., etc. Looping statements include a FOR...REPEAT... as well as a WHILE...REPEAT.... A compound statement without local variables or transfers can be written DO..,..,..END. Of course any of these statements can be used as an expression, giving the appropriate value.

USER-DEFINED LANGUAGE EXTENSIONS

The TRANSLATE procedure used by BALM to translate statements into XLISP is particularly simple, consisting of a precedence analysis pass followed by a macroexpansion pass. Built-in syntax is provided only for parenthesized subexpressions, comments, the quote operator, the unary operator NOOP, procedure calls, and indexing. All other syntax information is provided in the form of three lists which are the values of the variables UNARYLIST, INFIXLIST, and MACROLIST. The user can manipulate these lists as he wishes by adding, deleting, or changing operators or macros.

Operators are categorized as unary, bracket, or infix, and have precedence values and a procedure (or macro) associated with them. Examples of unary operators are − (minus), HD, and IF, while infix operators include +, THEN, and ELSE. Bracket operators are similar to unary operators but require a terminating infix operator which is ignored. Examples of bracket operators are BEGIN and PROC, which both can be terminated by the infix operator END.

New operators can be defined by the procedures UNARY, BRACKET, or INFIX. These add appropriate entries onto UNARYLIST or INFIXLIST. For example the statement

UNARY("PR,150, "PRINT);

would establish the unary operator PR with priority 150 as being the same as the procedure PRINT. Thus we could subsequently write PR A instead of PRINT(A). Similarly we could define an infix operator by

INFIX("AP,49,50,"APPEND);

to allow an infix append operation. The numbers 49 and 50 are the precedences of the operator when it is considered as a left-hand and right-hand operator respectively, so that an expression such as A AP B AP C will be analyzed as though it were A AP (B AP C).

The output of the precedence analysis is a tree expressed as a list in which the first element of each list or sublist is an operator or macro. For example, the statement

SQ=PROC(X),X*X END;

would be input as the list

(SQ = PROC (X) , X * X END)

and would be analyzed into:

```
(SETQ SQ (PROC (COMMA X (TIMES X X))))
```

This would then be expanded by the macro-expander, giving

```
(SETQ SQ (QUOTE (LAMBDA (X) (TIMES X X))))
```

the appropriate internal form. This would then be evaluated, having the same effect as the statement

```
SQ = "(LAMBDA(X) (TIMES X X)),
```

which would in fact be translated into the same thing.

The macro-expander is a function, EXPAND, which is given the syntax tree as its argument. If the top-level operator of the syntax tree has a macro associated with it, the macro is applied to the whole tree. Otherwise EXPAND is applied to each of the subtrees recursively. Most operators will not require macros because the output of the precedence analysis is in the correct form. However, operators such as IF, THEN, FOR, PROC... etc., require their arguments to be put in the correct form for execution. For instance, the IF macro, MIF, uses recursive calls to EXPAND to transform subtrees in the appropriate way. The statement

```
MACRO("IF,MIF);
```

would associate the macro MIF with the operator IF.

One particularly useful outcome of this expansion procedure is the ability to write expressions on the left-hand side of assignment statements. These can be handled by a macro associated with the assignment operator, which tests for particular expressions on the left-hand side and makes appropriate modifications. For instance, the HD operator used on the left allows

```
HD X = Y;
```

to be written instead of

```
RPLACA(X,Y);
```

which the SETQ macro will in effect produce. Similarly, we can write

```
MACRO(IF) = PROC(IF) ... ;
```

as a more concise way of defining the IF macro, as long as the SETQ macro were prepared for this left-hand side form.

To provide this flexibility, the macro for the assignment operator, MSETQ, looks up top-level operators on the left-hand side on the list LMACROLIST, which can be extended by the user. The statement

    LMACRO(NAME,LMAC);

adds macros to LMACROLIST in a way analogous to MACRO.

THE TRANSLATOR

The BALM-to-XLISP translator is very simple and uses the technique known as precedence analysis. The BALM language is designed in such a way that it consists of "phrases" and "operators," and each phrase is preceded and followed by an operator. In theory this imposes certain limitations on the language, but we feel that in practice these are not serious, and in fact are insignificant compared with the ease of the translation.

To give an example, the expression

    IF A ≡ B+C THEN GO L

contains the operators IF, ≡, +, THEN, GO, and the phrases A, B, C, L. The analysis determines for each triple consisting of an operator, a phrase, and an operator, which operator has precedence. Thus in the expression

    A = B + C

the + has higher precedence than the =, so the expression should be analyzed as

    A = (B + C)

The bracketed version of the above statement would be

    (IF ((A ≡ (B + C)) THEN (GO L)))

from which we see that the operators =, +, THEN require two arguments, and the IF and GO require a single argument. For consistency we will change the order of the bracketed elements whenever necessary so that the operator always comes first. Thus the final version of the above statement would be

    (IF (THEN (≡ A (+ B C)) (GO L)))

We will refer to operators like THEN and + as infix, and to operators like IF and GO as unary.

A slight extension of this scheme is necessary to allow the use of functional notation such as

```
A = B + FF(C, D-E) + G
```

where FF is a function. In this case (can be regarded as an infix operator, but) does not fall into either the infix or unary class. Other similar examples are BEGIN and its associated END.

In the BALM version given in Appendix B, the parentheses will already have been removed by the BALM input routine, which will have made a sublist out of the intervening elements. The program will recognize such sublists and treat them accordingly. Note that if a simplified input routine which does not recognize parentheses is used, then only slight modifications need to be made to the program.

The function FNOTN which does this syntax analysis takes as its argument a list which is the program to be translated, and has as its value the tree structure which represents its syntax. The routine recognizes three types of operators, infix, unary, and bracket, and for each element on the list determines if it is such an operator. Associated with each operator is a list which gives appropriate information about it. Thus associated with the operator + is the list

```
(INFIX PLUS lpr rpr)
```

with PLUS being the atom which will be used in the tree structure, and *lpr* and *rpr* being the precedence of + when used as the left hand and right hand of two operators respectively.

The following input

```
LNGTH = PROC(X),
        BEGIN(U,V),
        U = 0, V = X,
LOOP, IF NULL(V) THEN RETURN(U),
        U = U+1, V = CDR(V), GO LOOP
        END
        END;
```

will be translated into

```
(SETQ LNGTH (LAMBDA (, X
  (PROG (, (, U V)
        (, (SETQ U 0)
        (, (SETQ V X)
        (, (LOOP
        (, (IF (THEN (NULL V) (RETURN U)))
        (, (SETQ U (PLUS U 1))
        (, (SETQ V (CDR V)) (GO LOOP)) ))))))) )))
```

which is easily translated into XLISP during macro-expansion.

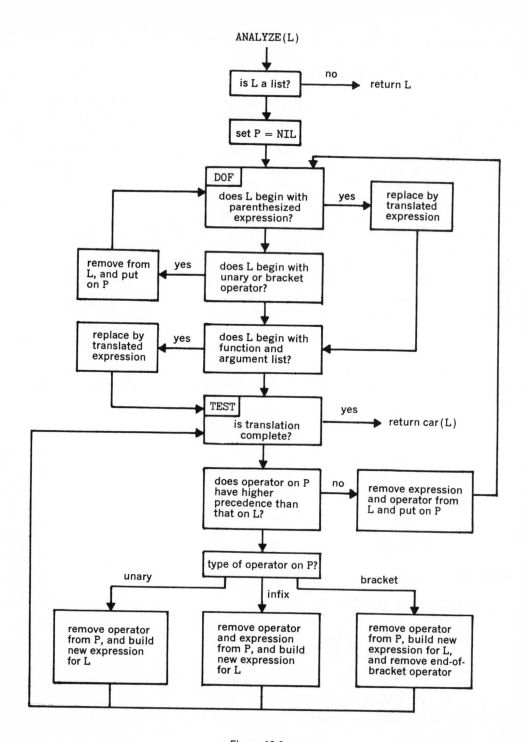

Figure 19.2

AN XLISP INTERPRETER

An XLISP interpreter can easily be written in BALM. It is a little different from the standard LISP interpreter. The main difference arises from the fact that only one form of binding is used. Rather than binding values of variables on an association list, and functions on the property list, all bindings are made in a cell associated with the variable called the *value cell*. This is more efficient than the association-list method, since access to the value cell for removal or insertion of bindings is immediate, and does not require any searching. When a procedure is entered, the current contents of the value-cells of local variables are saved and the new values inserted; the old values are restored on exit from the procedure.

A second difference is the fact that a machine-coded procedure in BALM is referenced by a recognizable data-type. This consists of a pointer to the first instruction of the procedure, together with flags to indicate what types of procedure it is. A function can be bound to a name simply by posting this data-object in the value cell, where it is accessible to the interpreter. Because of this uniform binding, the interpreter EVAL can look up the function bound to a name by simply evaluating it. This is conveniently generalized, so that when EVAL is given an argument of the form:

```
(FN ARG1 ARG2 ... )
```

the expression FN is evaluated, and the result, which should be either an entry point or a list structure representing a procedure such as a LAMBDA-expression applied to the arguments. This allows arbitrary expressions to be used as functions in an expression, but there are no tests for particular names in this position. Thus the form

```
((LAMBDA ... ) ... )
```

is not legal since the (LAMBDA ...) expression will not evaluate correctly. Instead the form

```
((QUOTE (LAMBDA ...)) ... )
```

should be used.

After evaluating the functional part of an expression the interpreter expects either a code block, which can be simply transferred to after processing the argument list, or an expression such as (LAMBDA ...) or (LABEL ...). These are conveniently evaluated by assuming them all to be of the form

$$(l \ e_1 \ e_2)$$

where l evaluates to a function which expects e_1, e_2 and the arguments list as its arguments. Thus the evaluation of

```
((QUOTE (LL AL EX)) ARG1 ARG2 ...)))
```

will be the same as

```
(LL AL EX (QUOTE (ARG1 ARG2 ...)))
```

This permits the user to provide his own versions of LAMBDA.

Three types of code block are used. These are called SUBR, FSUBR, and NSUBR, and can be distinguished by the setting of bits in the flag field. A SUBR, as in standard LISP, expects its arguments to be evaluated, and is the preferred type. An FSUBR expects a single argument which is the list of expressions supplied as arguments to the procedure, and, like LISP, is used to implement nonstandard operations such as SETQ, COND, and PROG. An NSUBR expects a single argument which is a list of the evaluated expressions supplied to the procedure as arguments. This is used for procedures which are standard except for the fact that they can have an arbitrary number of arguments, such as PLUS, LIST, VECTOR and PROGN. This last is a generalization of the LISP PROG2 procedure, and is used to implement the

```
DO ... END
```

type of compound expression. In fact PROGN is simply a procedure which returns the last element of a list.

The EVAL function takes a single argument which is the expression to be evaluated. It could be coded in BALM as follows:

```
EVAL = PROC(X)
        BEGIN(FN,ARGS),
        IF IDQ(X) THEN RETURN VALUE(X),
        IF ¬PAIRQ(X) THEN RETURN(X),
        FN=EVAL(HD X), ARGS=TL X,
        IF SUBRP(FN) THEN RETURN (XEQ(FN,EVLIS(ARGS))),
        IF FSUBRP(FN) THEN RETURN(XEQ(FN,ARGS:NIL))
        IF NSUBRP(FN) THEN RETURN(XEQ(FN,EVLIS(ARGS):NIL)),
        IF ¬PAIRQ(FN) THEN ERROR(FN:"(IS NOT A FUNCTION)),
        RETURN(XEQ(EVAL(HD FN),HD TL FN:HD TL TL FN:ARGS:NIL))
        END END;
```

Here XEQ executes the machine-coded function specified by the code block given as its first argument, with the elements of the list given as its second argument as arguments. Note that the version of EVAL given above can be generalized by changing the last command from:

```
RETURN(XEQ(EVAL(HD FN):HD TL FN:HD TL TL FN:ARGS:NIL))
```

to:

```
RETURN(EVAL(HD FN:HD TL FN:HD TL TL FN:ARGS:NIL))
```

which would permit a LAMBDA-like function to be written as a LAMBDA-expression. The procedure LAMBDA can be written in BALM as follows:

```
LAMBDA = PROC(VL,X,ARGL),
         BEGIN(PREVALS,RESULT),
         PREVALS=EVLIS(VL),
         BREAKUP(VL,EVLIS(ARGS)),
         RESULT=EVAL(X),
         BREAKUP(VL,PREVALS),
         RETURN(RESULT)
         END END;
```

Here we are using BREAKUP to do multiple assignment. The procedure EVLIS is the usual one defined as:

```
EVLIS=PROC(L),MAPX(L,EVAL)END;
```

EXAMPLES

As an example of the extendibility facilities provided in BALM, we give below a set of routines which permits a convenient form for introducing new expressions or commands. The aim is to permit the user to specify the meaning of these forms without needing to know the characteristics of the intermediate language. This is done by accepting a definition in terms of BALM itself, in the form

x MEANS y

where x and y are expressions in BALM. For example, the ALGOL 68 form of conditional could be defined as

```
X1 | X2 | X3 MEANS IF X1 THEN X2 ELSE X3;
```

The method requires that all operators in the new expression be declared as such before the MEANS definition. X1, X2, X3 can be any valid expressions as long as the precedence of the operators is higher than that of the operator. As usual, parentheses can be inserted to ensure the appropriate parsing. Other examples include the following

```
STEP X1 MEANS X1=X1+1;
FOR X1 = X2 STEP X3 UNTIL X4 DO X5 MEANS
     FOR X1 = (X2,X3,X4) REPEAT X5;
```

These would require the previous definition of the precedences of the operators STEP(unary), STEP(infix), UNTIL(infix), and DO(infix).

The technique used to implement MEANS uses the fact that the parse tree of a command of the form x MEANS y, where MEANS is an infix operator of very low precedence, contains the parse trees which will result from the expressions x and y. If, therefore, a macro is associated with MEANS, it can examine these trees and construct a macro which will transform any subtree which matches x into the equivalent tree of the form y. This macro will be associated with the top-level operator in the tree of x. The code to define MEANS is given below. The procedure SUBST, not given, is assumed to substitute its first argument for occurrences of its second in its third. Note that the code is written to permit multiple macros to be associated with the same operator.

`MMEANS = PROC(L),`	define procedure with argument L
`   BEGIN(LS,RS,M,OP,PREVM),`	define local variables
`   LS = HD TL L, RS = HD TL TL L,`	extract operands of MEANS
`   M=SUBST(LS,"L,TMAC),`	substitute for L and
`   M=SUBST(RS,"R,M),`	R in TMAC
`   OP = HD LS,`	extract top operator
`   PREVM = LOOKUP(OP,MACROLIST),`	retrieve any previous macro
`   IF PREVM≡NIL THEN`	and substitute it or EXLIS
`      M = SUBST("EXLIS,"E,M)`	for E in the modified TMAC
`   ELSE M = SUBST(PREVM,"E,M),`	
`   MACRO(OP,TRANSLATE(M)),`	associate new macro with operator, and return
`   RETURN NIL`	
`   END END;`	
`TMAC="(PROC(S),`	define untranslated procedure to process tree S
`   BEGIN(X1,X2,X3,X4,X5,X6),`	
`   IF MATCH("L,S) THEN`	if tree matches L then rebuild
`      RETURN BUILD("R)`	according to R
`   ELSE RETURN E(S)`	otherwise process as before
`   END END);`	
`MATCH=PROC(L,S),`	define procedure to match
`   IF PAIRQ(L) THEN`	trees
`    (IF PAIRQ(S) THEN`	
`     (IF MATCH(HD L,HD S) THEN`	return false if trees don't
`        MATCH(TL L,TL S)`	match
`      ELSE FALSE)`	
`     ELSE FALSE)`	
`   ELSEIF L≡"X1 OR L≡"X2 OR L≡"X3`	X1...X6 are assigned the
`      OR L≡"X4 OR L≡"X5 OR L≡"X6`	value of any corresponding
`   THEN DO VALUE(L)=S,RETURN TRUE`	subtree
`                           END`	
`   ELSEIF L≡S THEN TRUE`	
`   ELSE FALSE`	
`   END;`	

```
BUILD=PROC(R),
   IF PAIRQ(R) THEN
      BUILD(HD R);BUILD(TL R)
   ELSEIF R≡"X1 OR R≡"X2 OR R≡"X3
      OR R≡"X4 OR R≡"X5 OR R≡"X6
   THEN VALUE(R)
   ELSE R
   END;

INFIX("MEANS,0,0,"MEANS);
MACRO("MEANS,MMEANS);
```

define procedure to rebuild tree

replace X1...X6 with their current values

define MEANS as infix operator
define macro for MEANS

APPENDIX A:

ALGOL 68
STANDARD PRELUDE

The standard prelude in ALGOL 68 specifies those objects and operations which are to be regarded as provided in the standard system without being defined by the user. These illustrate a number of the more significant properties of the language. It contains the following declarations.

ENVIRONMENT INQUIRIES

a) <u>int</u> int lengths = <u>c</u> the number of different lengths of integers <u>c</u>;

b) <u>L</u> <u>int</u> L max int = <u>c</u> the largest L integral value <u>c</u>;

c) <u>int</u> real lengths = <u>c</u> the number of different lengths of real numbers <u>c</u>;

d) <u>L</u> <u>real</u> L max real = <u>c</u> the largest L real value <u>c</u>;

e) <u>L</u> <u>real</u> L small real = <u>c</u> the smallest L real value such that both <u>L</u>1 + L small real > <u>L</u>1 and <u>L</u>1 − L small real <<u>L</u>1 <u>c</u>;

f) <u>int</u> bits widths = <u>c</u> the number of different widths of bits <u>c</u>;

g) <u>int</u> L bits width = <u>c</u> the number of elements in L bits; see L <u>bits</u> <u>c</u>;

h) <u>op</u> <u>abs</u> = (<u>char</u> a) <u>int</u> : <u>c</u> the integral equivalent of the character 'a' <u>c</u>;

i) <u>op</u> <u>repr</u> = (<u>int</u> a) <u>char</u> : <u>c</u> that character 'x', if it exists, for which <u>abs</u> x = a <u>c</u>;

j) <u>int</u> bytes widths = <u>c</u> the number of different widths of bytes <u>c</u>;

k) <u>int</u> L bytes width = <u>c</u> the number of elements in L bytes; see L <u>bytes</u> <u>c</u>;

l) <u>char</u> null character = <u>c</u> some character <u>c</u>;

STANDARD PRIORITIES

a) <u>priority</u> <u>minus</u> = 1, <u>plus</u> = 1, <u>times</u> = 1, <u>overb</u> = 1,
    <u>div</u> = 1, <u>modb</u> = 1, <u>prus</u> = 1, ∨ = 2, ∧ = 3, = = 4,
    ≠ = 4, < = 5, ≤ = 5, ≥ = 5, > = 5, − = 6, + = 6, × = 7,
    ÷ = 7, ÷ : = 7, / = 7; <u>elem</u> = 7, ↑ = 8, <u>lwb</u> = 8,
    <u>upb</u> = 8, <u>lws</u> = 8, <u>ups</u> = 8, ⊥ = 9;

ROWS AND ASSOCIATED OPERATIONS

a) <u>mode</u> % <u>rows</u> = <u>c</u> an actual−declarer specifying a mode
    united from all modes beginning with 'row of' <u>c</u> ;

b) <u>op</u> <u>lwb</u> = (<u>int</u> n, <u>rows</u> a)<u>int</u> : <u>c</u> the lower bound in the
    n−th quintuple of the descriptor of the value of 'a', if
    that quintuple exists <u>c</u> ;

c) <u>op</u> <u>upb</u> = (<u>int</u> n, <u>rows</u> a)<u>int</u> : <u>c</u> the upper bound in the
    n−th quintuple of the descriptor of the value of 'a', if
    that quintuple exists <u>c</u> ;

d) <u>op</u> <u>lws</u> = (<u>int</u> n, <u>rows</u> a)<u>bool</u> : <u>c</u> true (false) if the lower
    state in the n−th quintuple of the descriptor of the
    value of 'a' equals 1(0), if that quintuple exists <u>c</u> ;

e) <u>op</u> <u>ups</u> = (<u>int</u> n, <u>rows</u> a)<u>bool</u> : <u>c</u> true (false) if the upper
    state in the n−th quintuple of the descriptor of the
    value of 'a' equals 1(0), if that quintuple exists <u>c</u> ;

f) <u>op</u> <u>lwb</u> = (<u>rows</u> a)<u>int</u> : 1 <u>lwb</u> a;
g) <u>op</u> <u>upb</u> = (<u>rows</u> a)<u>int</u> : 1 <u>upb</u> a ;
h) <u>op</u> <u>lws</u> = (<u>rows</u> a)<u>bool</u> : 1 <u>lws</u> a ;
i) <u>op</u> <u>ups</u> = (<u>rows</u> a)<u>bool</u> : 1 <u>ups</u> a;

OPERATIONS ON BOOLEAN OPERANDS

a) <u>op</u> ∨ = (<u>bool</u> a, b)<u>bool</u> : (a | <u>true</u>| b);
b) <u>op</u> ∧ = (<u>bool</u> a, b)<u>bool</u> : (a | b | <u>false</u>) ;
c) <u>op</u> ¬ = (<u>bool</u> a)<u>bool</u> : (a | <u>false</u> | <u>true</u>) ;
d) <u>op</u> = = (<u>bool</u> a, b)<u>bool</u> : (a ∧ b) ∨ (¬ a ∧ ¬ b) ;
e) <u>op</u> ≠ = (<u>bool</u> a, b)<u>bool</u> : ¬ (a = b) ;
f) <u>op</u> <u>abs</u> = (<u>bool</u> a)<u>int</u> : (a | 1 | 0) ;

OPERATIONS ON INTEGRAL OPERANDS

a) <u>op</u> < = (<u>L</u> <u>int</u> a, b)<u>bool</u> : <u>c</u> true if the value of 'a' is
    smaller than that of 'b' and false otherwise <u>c</u> ;
b) <u>op</u> ≤ = (<u>L</u> <u>int</u> a, b)<u>bool</u> : ¬(b < a) ;
c) <u>op</u> = = (<u>L</u> <u>int</u> a, b)<u>bool</u> : a ≤ b b ≤ a ;
d) <u>op</u> ≠ = (<u>L</u> <u>int</u> a, b) <u>bool</u> : ¬ (a = b) ;

e) $\underline{op} \geq = (\underline{L}\ \underline{int}\ a,\ b)\underline{bool} : b \leq a;$

f) $\underline{op} > = (\underline{L}\ \underline{int}\ a,\ b)\underline{bool} : b < a\ ;$

g) $\underline{op} - = (\underline{L}\ \underline{int}\ a,\ b)\ \underline{L}\ \underline{int} : \underline{c}$ the value of 'a' minus that
    of 'b' $\underline{c}$;

h) $\underline{op} - = (\underline{L}\ \underline{int}\ a)\ \underline{L}\ \underline{int} : \underline{L}0 - a\ ;$

i) $\underline{op} + = (\underline{L}\ \underline{int}\ a,\ b)\ \underline{L}\ \underline{int} : a - - b\ ;$

j) $\underline{op} + = (\underline{L}\ \underline{int}\ a)\ \underline{L}\ \underline{int} : a\ ;$

k) $\underline{op}\ \underline{abs} = (\underline{L}\ \underline{int}\ a)\ \underline{L}\ \underline{int} : (a < \underline{L}0\ |\ -a\ |\ a);$

l) $\underline{op} \times = (\underline{L}\ \underline{int}\ a,\ b)\ \underline{L}\ \underline{int} : (\underline{L}\ \underline{int}\ s := \underline{L}0,\ i := \underline{abs}\ b;$
    $\underline{while}\ i \geq \underline{L}1\ \underline{do}\ (s := s + a;\ i := i - \underline{L}1);$
    $(b < \underline{L}0\ |\ -s\ |\ s));$

m) $\underline{op} \div = (\underline{L}\ \underline{int}\ a,\ b)\ \underline{L}\ \underline{int} :$
    $(b \neq \underline{L}0\ |\ \underline{L}\ \underline{int}\ q := \underline{L}0,\ r := \underline{abs}\ a;$
    $\underline{while}\ (r := r - \underline{abs}\ b) \geq \underline{L}0\ \underline{do}\ q := q + \underline{L}1\ ;$
    $(a < \underline{L}0\ \wedge\ b \geq \underline{L}0\ \vee\ a \geq \underline{L}0\ \wedge\ b < \underline{L}0\ |\ -q\ |\ q))\ ;$

n) $\underline{op} \div: = (\underline{L}\ \underline{int}\ a,\ b)\ \underline{L}\ \underline{int} : a - a \div b \times b +$
    $(a < 0\ |\ \underline{abs}\ b\ |\ 0);$

o) $\underline{op}\ / = (\underline{L}\ \underline{int}\ a,\ b)\ \underline{L}\ \underline{real} : (\underline{L}\ \underline{real} : a)\ /\ (\underline{L}\ \underline{real} : b)\ ;$

p) $\underline{op} \uparrow = (\underline{L}\ \underline{int}\ a,\ \underline{int}\ b)\ \underline{L}\ \underline{int} :$
    $(b \geq 0\ |\ \underline{L}\ \underline{int}\ p := \underline{L}1;\ \underline{to}\ b\ \underline{do}\ p := p \times a;\ p);$

q) $\underline{op}\ \underline{leng} = (\underline{L}\ \underline{int}\ a)\ \underline{long}\ \underline{L}\ \underline{int} : \underline{c}$ the long L integral
    value equivalent to the value of 'a' $\underline{c}$;

r) $\underline{op}\ \underline{short} = (\underline{long}\ \underline{L}\ \underline{int}\ a)\ \underline{L}\ \underline{int} : \underline{c}$ the L integral value,
    if it exists, equivalent to the value of 'a' $\underline{c}$;

s) $\underline{op}\ \underline{odd} = (\underline{L}\ \underline{int}\ a)\underline{bool} : \underline{abs}\ a \div: \underline{L}2 = \underline{L}1\ ;$

t) $\underline{op}\ \underline{sign} = (\underline{L}\ \underline{int}\ a)\underline{int} : (a > \underline{L}0\ |\ 1\ |: a < \underline{L}0\ |\ -1\ |\ 0)\ ;$

u) $\underline{op} \perp = (\underline{L}\ \underline{int}\ a,\ b)\ \underline{L}\ \underline{compl} : (a,\ b)\ ;$

OPERATIONS ON REAL OPERANDS

a) $\underline{op} < = (\underline{L}\ \underline{real}\ a,\ b)\underline{bool} : \underline{c}$ true if the value of 'a' is
    smaller than that of 'b' and false otherwise $\underline{c}$;

b) $\underline{op} \leq = (\underline{L}\ \underline{real}\ a,\ b)\underline{bool} : \neg(b < a);$

c) $\underline{op} = = (\underline{L}\ \underline{real}\ a,\ b)\underline{bool} : a \leq b\ \ b \leq a;$

d) $\underline{op} \neq = (\underline{L}\ \underline{real}\ a,\ b)\underline{bool} : \neg(a = b);$

e) $\underline{op} \geq = (\underline{L}\ \underline{real}\ a,\ b)\underline{bool} : b \leq a\ ;$

f) $\underline{op} > = (\underline{L}\ \underline{real}\ a,\ b)\underline{bool} : b < a;$

g) $\underline{op} - = (\underline{L}\ \underline{real}\ a,\ b)\ \underline{L}\ \underline{real} : \underline{c}$ the value of 'a' minus
    that of 'b' $\underline{c}$;

h) $\underline{op} - = (\underline{L}\ \underline{real}\ a)\ \underline{L}\ \underline{real} : \underline{L}0 - a\ ;$

i) $\underline{op} + = (\underline{L}\ \underline{real}\ a,\ b)\ \underline{L}\ \underline{real} : a - - b\ ;$

j) $\underline{op} + = (\underline{L}\ \underline{real}\ a)\ \underline{L}\ \underline{real} : a\ ;$

k) $\underline{op}\ \underline{abs} = (\underline{L}\ \underline{real}\ a)\ \underline{L}\ \underline{real} : (a < \underline{L}0\ |\ -a\ |\ a)\ ;$

l) $\underline{op} \times = (\underline{L}\ \underline{real}\ a,\ b)\ \underline{L}\ \underline{real} : \underline{c}$ the value of 'a' times
    that of 'b' $\underline{c}$;

m) <u>op</u> / = (<u>L</u> <u>real</u> a, b) <u>L</u> <u>real</u> : <u>c</u> the value of 'a' divided
    by that of 'b' <u>c</u> ;
n) <u>op</u> <u>leng</u> = (<u>L</u> <u>real</u> a) <u>long</u> <u>L</u> <u>real</u> : <u>c</u> the long L real value
    equivalent to the value of 'a' <u>c</u>;
o) <u>op</u> <u>short</u> = (<u>long</u> <u>L</u> <u>real</u> a) <u>L</u> <u>real</u> : <u>c</u> the L real value, if
    it exists, equivalent to the value of 'a' <u>c</u> ;
p) <u>op</u> <u>round</u> = (<u>L</u> <u>real</u> a) <u>L</u> <u>int</u> : <u>c</u> a L integral value, if one
    exists, equivalent to a L real value differing by not
    more than one—half from the value of 'a' <u>c</u> ;
q) <u>op</u> <u>sign</u> = (<u>L</u> <u>real</u> a)<u>int</u> : (a > <u>L</u>0 | 1 |: a < <u>L</u>0 | −1 | 0);
r) <u>op</u> <u>entier</u> = (<u>L</u> <u>real</u> a) <u>L</u> <u>int</u> : (<u>L</u> <u>int</u> j := <u>L</u>0 ;
    <u>while</u> j < a <u>do</u> j := j + <u>L</u>1 ;
    <u>while</u> j > a <u>do</u> j := j − <u>L</u>1 ; j) ;
s) <u>op</u> ⊥ = (<u>L</u> <u>real</u> a, b) <u>L</u> <u>compl</u> : (a, b) ;

OPERATIONS ON ARITHMETIC OPERANDS

a) <u>op</u> <u>P</u> = (<u>L</u> <u>real</u> a, <u>L</u> <u>int</u> b) <u>L</u> <u>real</u> : a <u>P</u> (<u>L</u> <u>real</u> : b) ;
b) <u>op</u> <u>P</u> = (<u>L</u> <u>int</u> a, <u>L</u> <u>real</u> b) <u>L</u> <u>real</u> : (<u>L</u> <u>real</u> : a) <u>P</u> b ;
c) <u>op</u> <u>R</u> = (<u>L</u> <u>real</u> a, <u>L</u> <u>int</u> b) <u>bool</u> : a <u>R</u> (<u>L</u> <u>real</u> : b) ;
d) <u>op</u> <u>R</u> = (<u>L</u> <u>int</u> a, <u>L</u> <u>real</u> b) <u>bool</u> : (<u>L</u> <u>real</u> : a) <u>R</u> b ;
e) <u>op</u> ⊥ = (<u>L</u> <u>real</u> a, <u>L</u> <u>int</u> b) <u>L</u> <u>compl</u> : (a,b) ;
f) <u>op</u> ⊥ = (<u>L</u> <u>int</u> a, <u>L</u> <u>real</u> b) <u>L</u> <u>compl</u> : (a, b);
g) <u>op</u> ↑ = (<u>L</u> <u>real</u> a, <u>int</u> b) <u>L</u> <u>real</u> : (<u>L</u> <u>real</u> p := <u>L</u>1 ;
    <u>to</u> <u>abs</u> b <u>do</u> p := p × a ; (b ≥ 0 | p | <u>L</u>1 | p)) ;

OPERATIONS ON CHARACTER OPERANDS

a) <u>op</u> < = (<u>char</u> a, b) <u>bool</u> : <u>abs</u> a < <u>abs</u> b ;
b) <u>op</u> ≤ = (<u>char</u> a, b) <u>bool</u> : ¬ (b < a) ;
c) <u>op</u> = = (<u>char</u> a, b) <u>bool</u> : a ≤ b b ≤ a ;
d) <u>op</u> ≠ = (<u>char</u> a, b) <u>bool</u> : ¬ (a = b) ;
e) <u>op</u> ≥ = (<u>char</u> a, b) <u>bool</u> : b ≤ a ;
f) <u>op</u> > = (<u>char</u> a, b) <u>bool</u> : b < a ;
g) <u>op</u> + = (<u>char</u> a, b) <u>string</u> : (a, b) ;

COMPLEX STRUCTURES AND ASSOCIATED OPERATIONS

a) <u>struct</u> <u>L</u> <u>compl</u> = (<u>L</u> <u>real</u> re, im) ;
b) <u>op</u> <u>re</u> = (<u>L</u> <u>compl</u> a) <u>L</u> <u>real</u> : re <u>of</u> a ;
c) <u>op</u> <u>im</u> = (<u>L</u> <u>compl</u> a) <u>L</u> <u>real</u> : im <u>of</u> a ;
d) <u>op</u> <u>abs</u> = (<u>L</u> <u>compl</u> a) <u>L</u> <u>real</u> : L sqrt
    (<u>re</u> a ↑ 2 ÷ <u>im</u> a ↑ 2) ;
e) <u>op</u> <u>conj</u> = (<u>L</u> <u>compl</u> a) <u>L</u> <u>compl</u> : <u>re</u> a ⊥ − <u>im</u> a ;
f) <u>op</u> = = (<u>L</u> <u>compl</u> a, b) <u>bool</u> : <u>re</u> a = <u>re</u> b ∧ <u>im</u> a = <u>im</u> b ;

g) op ≠ = (L compl a, b) bool : ¬ (a = b) ;
h) op + = (L compl a) L compl : a ;
i) op − = (L compl a) L compl :− re a ⊥ − im a ;
j) op + = (L compl a, b) L compl :
      (re a + re b) ⊥ (im a + im b) ;
k) op − = (L compl a, b) L compl :
      (re a − re b) ⊥ (im a − im b) ;
l) op × = (L compl a, b) L compl :
      (re a × re b − im a × im b) ⊥ (re a × im b + im a ×
      re b) ;
m) op / = (L compl a, b) L compl :
      (L real d = re(b × conj b) ; L compl n = a × conj b ;
      (re n / d) ⊥ (im n / d)) ;
n) op leng = (L compl a) long L compl : leng
      re a ⊥ leng im a ;
o) op short = (long L compl a) L compl : short
      re a ⊥ short im a ;
p) op P = (L compl a, L int b) L compl : a P (L compl : b) ;
q) op P = (L compl a, L real b) L compl : a P (L compl : b) ;
r) op P = (L int a, L compl b) L compl : (L compl : a) P b ;
s) op P = (L real a, L compl b) L compl : (L compl : a) P b ;
t) op ↑ = (L compl a, int b) L compl : (L compl p := L1;
      to abs b do p := p × a ; (b ≥ 0 | p | L1 / p)) ;

BITS STRUCTURES AND ASSOCIATED OPERATIONS

a) struct L bits = ([1 : L bits width] bool L F) ;
      The field−selector is hidden from the user in order that
      he may not break open the structure; in particular, he
      may not subscript the field.
b) op = (L bits a, b) bool :
      (for i to L bits width do
      ((L F of a)[i] ≠ (L F of b)[i] | 1); true . 1 : false) ;
c) op ≠ = (L bits a, b) bool : ¬ (a = b) ;
d) op ∨ = (L bits a, b) L bits :
      (L bits c ; for i to L bits width do
      (L F of c)[i] := (L F of a)[i] ∨ (L F of b)[i] ; c) ;
e) op ∧ = (L bits a, b) L bits :
      (L bits c ; for i to L bits width do
      (L F of c)[i] := (L F of a)[i] ∧ (L F of b)[i] ; c) ;
f) op ≤ = (L bits a, b) bool : (a ∨ b) = b ;
g) op ≥ = (L bits a, b) bool : b ≤ a ;
h) op ↑ = (L bits a, int b) L bits : if abs b ≤ L bits width
      then L bits c := a ; to abs b do (b > 0 | for i from 2
      to L bits width do (L F of c)[i−1] := (L F of c)[i];

```
        (L F of c)[L bits width] := false | for i from L bits
        width by −1 to 2 do (L F of c)[i] := (L F of c)[i−1];
        (L F of c)[1] := false) ; c fi ;
i)  op abs = (L bits a) L int : (L int c := L0; for i to L bits
        width do c := L2 × c + abs(L F of a)[i] ; c) ;
j)  op bin = (L int a) L bits : if a > L0 then L int b := a;
        L bits c ; for i fromL bits width by −1 to 1 do
        ((L F of c)[i] := odd b ; b := b ÷ L2) ; c fi ;
k)  op elem = (Int a, L bits b) bool : (L F of b)[a];;
l)  op L btb = ([1:] bool a) L bits : (int n = upb a;
        (n ≤ L bits width | L bits c ; for i to L bits width
        do (L F of c)[i] := (i ≤ L bits width −n|false| a
        [i − L bits width + n]) ; c)) ;
```

BYTES AND ASSOCIATED OPERATIONS

```
a)  struct L bytes = ([1: L bytes width] char L F) ;
b)  op < = (L bytes a, b) bool : (string : a) < (string : b) ;
c)  op ≤ = (L bytes a, b) bool : ¬ (b < a) ;
d)  op = = (L bytes a, b) bool : a ≤ b ∧ b ≤ a ;
e)  op ≠ = (L bytes a, b) bool : ¬ (a = b) ;
f)  op ≥ = (L bytes a, b) bool : b ≤ a ;
g)  op > = (L bytes a, b) bool : b < a ;
h)  op elem = (int a, L bytes b) char : (L F of b)[a] ;
i)  op L ctb = (string a) L bytes : (int n = upb a;
        (n ≤ L bytes width | L bytes c ; for i to L bytes width
        do (L F of c)[i] := (i ≤ n | a[i] | null character) ;
        c)) ;
```

STRINGS AND ASSOCIATED OPERATIONS

```
a)  mode string = [1 : flex] char ;
b)  op < = (string a, b) bool : (int m = upb a, n = upb b ;
        int p = (m < n | m | n), int i := 1 ; bool c ;
        (p < 1 | n ≥ 1 | e : (c := a[i] = b[i] |:
        (i := i + 1) ≤ p | e) ; (c | m < n | a[i] < b[i]))) ;
c)  op ≤ = (string a, b) bool : ¬ (b < a) ;
d)  op = = (string a, b) bool : a ≤ b ∧ b ≤ a ;
e)  op ≠ = (string a, b) bool : ¬ (a = b) ;
f)  op ≥ = (string a, b) bool : b ≤ a ;
g)  op > = (string a, b) bool : b < a ;
h)  op R = (string a, char b) bool : a R (string : b) ;
i)  op R = (char a, string b) bool : (string : a) R b ;
j)  op + = (string a, b) string : (int m = upb a, n = upb b ;
        [1 :m + n] char c ; c[1 : m] := a;
        c[m + 1 : m + n] := b ; c) ;
```

k)   <u>op</u> + = (<u>string</u> a, <u>char</u> b) <u>string</u> : a + (<u>string</u> : b) ;
l)   <u>op</u> + = (<u>char</u> a, <u>string</u> b) <u>string</u> : (<u>string</u> : a) + b ;

The operations defined in b, h, and i imply that if <u>abs</u> "a" < <u>abs</u> "b", then
"" < "a"; "a" < "b"; "aa" < "ab"; "aa" < "ba"; "ab" < "b".

OPERATIONS COMBINED WITH ASSIGNATIONS

a)   <u>op</u> <u>minus</u> = (<u>ref</u> L <u>int</u> a, L <u>int</u> b) <u>ref</u> L <u>int</u> : a := a − b;
b)   <u>op</u> <u>minus</u> = (<u>ref</u> L <u>real</u> a, L <u>real</u> b) <u>ref</u> L <u>real</u>
       : a := a − b ;
c)   <u>op</u> <u>minus</u> = (<u>ref</u> L <u>compl</u> a, L <u>compl</u> b) <u>ref</u> L <u>compl</u>
       : a := a − b ;
d)   <u>op</u> <u>plus</u> = (<u>ref</u> L <u>int</u> a, L <u>int</u> b) <u>ref</u> L <u>int</u> : a := a + b ;
e)   <u>op</u> <u>plus</u> = (<u>ref</u> L <u>real</u> a, L <u>real</u> b) <u>ref</u> L <u>real</u>
       : a := a + b ;
f)   <u>op</u> <u>plus</u> = (<u>ref</u> L <u>compl</u> a, L <u>compl</u> b) <u>ref</u> L <u>compl</u>:
       a := a + b ;
g)   <u>op</u> <u>times</u> = (<u>ref</u> L <u>int</u> a, L <u>int</u> b) <u>ref</u> L <u>int</u> : a := a × b ;
h)   <u>op</u> <u>times</u> = (<u>ref</u> L <u>real</u> a, L <u>real</u> b) <u>ref</u> L <u>real</u> :
       a := a × b ;
i)   <u>op</u> <u>times</u> = (<u>ref</u> L <u>compl</u> a, L <u>compl</u> b) <u>ref</u> L <u>compl</u> :
       a := a × b ;
j)   <u>op</u> <u>overb</u> = (<u>ref</u> L <u>int</u> a, L <u>int</u> b) <u>ref</u> L <u>int</u> : a := a ÷ b ;
k)   <u>op</u> <u>modb</u> = (<u>ref</u> L <u>int</u> a, L <u>int</u> b) <u>ref</u> L <u>int</u> : a := a ÷: b ;
l)   <u>op</u> <u>div</u> = (<u>ref</u> L <u>real</u> a, L <u>real</u> b) <u>ref</u> L <u>real</u> :
       a := a / b ;
m)   <u>op</u> <u>div</u> = (<u>ref</u> L <u>compl</u> a, L <u>compl</u> b) <u>ref</u> L <u>compl</u> :
       a := a / b ;
n)   <u>op</u> Q = (<u>ref</u> L <u>real</u> a, L <u>int</u> b) <u>ref</u> L <u>real</u> :
       a Q (L <u>real</u> : b) ;
o)   <u>op</u> Q = (<u>ref</u> L <u>compl</u> a, L <u>int</u> b) <u>ref</u> L <u>compl</u> :
       a Q (L <u>compl</u> : b) ;
p)   <u>op</u> Q = (<u>ref</u> L <u>compl</u> a, L <u>real</u> b) <u>ref</u> L <u>compl</u> :
       a Q (L <u>compl</u> : b) ;
q)   <u>op</u> <u>plus</u> = (<u>ref</u> <u>string</u> a, <u>string</u> b) <u>ref</u> <u>string</u> :
       a := a + b ;
r)   <u>op</u> <u>prus</u> = (<u>string</u> a, <u>ref</u> <u>string</u> b) <u>ref</u> <u>string</u> :
       b := a + b ;
s)   <u>op</u> <u>plus</u> = (<u>ref</u> <u>string</u> a, <u>char</u> b) <u>ref</u> <u>string</u> : a := a + b ;
t)   <u>op</u> <u>prus</u> = (<u>char</u> a, <u>ref</u> <u>string</u> b) <u>ref</u> <u>string</u> : b := a + b ;

STANDARD MATHEMATICAL CONSTANTS AND FUNCTIONS

a)   L <u>real</u> L pi = <u>c</u> a L real value close to π ; see Math. of
       Comp. v. 16, 1962, pp. 80–99 <u>c</u> ;

b) <u>proc</u> L sqrt = (<u>L real</u> x) <u>L real</u> : <u>c</u> if x ≥ <u>L</u>0, a L real
     value close to the square root of 'x' <u>c</u> ;
c) <u>proc</u> L exp = (<u>L real</u> x) <u>L real</u> : <u>c</u> a L real value, if one
     exists, close to the exponential function of 'x' <u>c</u> ;
d) <u>proc</u> L ln = (<u>L real</u> x) <u>L real</u> : <u>c</u> a L real value, if one
     exists, close to the natural logarithm of 'x' <u>c</u> ;
e) <u>proc</u> L cos = (<u>L real</u> x) <u>L real</u> : <u>c</u> a L real value close
     to the cosine of 'x' <u>c</u> ;
f) <u>proc</u> L arccos = (<u>L real</u> x) <u>L real</u> : <u>c</u> if <u>abs</u> x ≤ <u>L</u>1, a L
     real value close to the inverse cosine of 'x',
     <u>L</u>0 ≤ L arccos(x) ≤ L pi <u>c</u> ;
g) <u>proc</u> L sin = (<u>L real</u> x) <u>L real</u> : <u>c</u> a L real value close to
     the sine of 'x' <u>c</u> ;
h) <u>proc</u> L arcsin = (<u>L real</u> x) <u>L real</u> : <u>c</u> if <u>abs</u> x ≤ <u>L</u>1, a L
     real value close to the inverse sine of 'x',
     <u>abs</u> L arcsin(x) ≤ L pi / <u>L</u>2 <u>c</u> ;
i) <u>proc</u> L tan = (<u>L real</u> x) <u>L real</u> : <u>c</u> a L real value, if one
     exists, close to the tangent of 'x' <u>c</u> ;
j) <u>proc</u> L arctan = (<u>L real</u> x) <u>L real</u> : <u>c</u> a L real value close
     to the inverse tangent of 'x',
     <u>abs</u> L arctan(x) ≤ L pi / <u>L</u>2 <u>c</u> ;
k) <u>proc L real</u> L random = L last random := <u>c</u> the next pseudo-
     random L real value after L last random from a uni-
     formly distributed sequence on the interval (<u>L</u>0, <u>L</u>1) <u>c</u> ;
l) <u>L real</u> L last random := <u>L</u> . 5 ;

SYNCHRONIZATION OPERATIONS

a) <u>op down</u> = (<u>ref int</u> dijkstra) : (<u>do</u>(<u>if</u> dijkstra ≥ 1 <u>then</u>
     dijkstra <u>minus</u> 1 ; 1 <u>else c</u> if the closed–statement
     replacing this comment is contained in a unitary–phrase
     which is a constituent unitary–phrase of the smallest
     collateral–phrase, if any, beginning with a parallel–
     symbol and containing this closed–statement, then the
     elaboration of that unitary–phrase is halted otherwise,
     the further elaboration is undefined <u>c</u> <u>fi</u>) ; <u>1</u> : <u>skip</u>) ;
b) <u>op up</u> = (<u>ref int</u> dijkstra) : (dijkstra <u>plus</u> 1 ; <u>c</u> the
     elaboration is resumed of all phrases whose elaboration
     is not terminated but is halted because the name pos–
     sessed by 'dijkstra' referred to a value smaller than
     one c) ;

For insight into the use of *down* and *up*, see E. W. Dijkstra (65).

APPENDIX B:

BALM LISTING

Given below is a listing of a version of the BALM system written in BALM. This is actually a minimal version of the system used to bootstrap itself, and does not include certain features described in the text. In particular, BREAKUP and CONSTRUCT are not included, the semicolon is not detected as an absolute terminator, bit-strings and reals are not supported, operators for manipulating strings are rather primitive, and the compiler is badly deficient in error detection. Also, arguments and local variables are usually compiled as stack locations, and so are not accessible inside another procedure or block respectively. If preceded in the declaration by a $, the compiler compiles references to the symbol table, thus permitting access to the value from other blocks or procedures. Thus in general any argument or variable whose scope is not strictly local should be preceded by $.

COMMENT

```
( ***************************************************************
                         MAIN PROGRAM
  ***************************************************************)
    BALM=PROC(), BEGIN( ),
         INITIATE( ),
         EXECUTE(INPUT,OUTPUT),
         STOP()
         END END;
EXECUTE=PROC($INPUT,$OUTPUT),
         BEGIN(ST,LS,$CURCOM,$PREVCOMMAND),
    MOR, PRINT(),
         ST=RDSEMI(INPUT),
         LS=TRANSLAT(ST),
         IF TALKATIVE EQ 2 THEN DO
             PRINT(=SYNTAX,=TREE), PRINT(LS) END,
         IF ¬ZR ERCOUNT THEN GOTO ERR,
```

```
        IF LS EQ =RESUME THEN RETURN NIL,
        IF LS EQ =STOP THEN RETURN NIL,
        LS = =LAMBDA:NIL:LS:NIL,
        CODEGEN(=CURCOM,LS),
        CURCOM(),
        GOTO MOR,
   ERR, PRINT(LIST(ERCOUNT,=ERRORS)),
        PREVCOMMAND=ST, GO MOR
        END END;

 RDSEMI=PROC(I), BEGIN(B,E,TOK), B=E=NIL:NIL,
   MOR, TOK=READ(I), IF TOK EQ IEOS THEN RETURN TL B,
        E=ADDON(E,TOK), GOTO MOR  END END;
COMMENT

(*************************************************************
                    UTILITY ROUTINES
*************************************************************)
 VFROML=PROC(L),BEGIN(N,V,I),
        N=0, V=L,
        WHILE V REPEAT DO N=N+1, V=TL V END, V=MAKVECTOR(N),
        FOR I=(1,N) REPEAT DO V[I]=HD L, L=TL L END,
        RETURN V  END END;
  ADDON=PROC(X,Y), TL RPLACD(X,Y:NIL) END;
 LOOKUP=PROC(X,L), BEGIN(P),
   MOR, IF IDQ(L) AND IDQ(X) THEN DO P=L, L=PROPL(X), X=P END,
        IF ¬PAIRQ(L) THEN RETURN NIL,
        IF X EQ HD HD L THEN RETURN HD TL HD L,
        L=TL L, GOTO MOR  END END;
ORDINAL=PROC(A,L),ORD1(A,L,1) END;
   ORD1=PROC(A,L,I),
        IF NULL(L) THEN NIL ELSEIF A EQ HD L THEN I
            ELSE ORD1(A,TL L,I+1)  END;
 LENGTH=PROC(X),IF PAIRQ(X) THEN 1+LENGTH(TL X)
        ELSEIF VECTQ(X) OR STRQ(X) OR CODEQ(X) THEN OLENGTH(X)
        ELSE 0  END;
IFROMID=PROC(X),X+0 END;
 GENSYM=PROC(), BEGIN(I),
        I=5, GENSYMB[I]=GENSYMB[I]+1,
        WHILE GENSYMB[I] GT NINE REPEAT DC
            GENSYMB[I]=ZERO,I=I-1,GENSYMB[I]=GENSYMB[I]+1 END,
        RETURN IDFROMS(SFROMV(GENSYMB))  END END;
   MAPX=PROC(X,P), IF PAIRQ(X) THEN MAPL(X,P)
        ELSEIF VECTQ(X) THEN MAPV(X,P)
        ELSE P(X)  END;
```

```
    MAPL=PROC(L,P), BEGIN(B,E), B=E=NIL:NIL,
    MOR, IF ¬PAIRQ(L) THEN RETURN TL B,
          E=ADDON(E,P(HD L)), L=TL L, GOTO MOR  END END;
    MAPV=PROC(V,P), BEGIN(N,VV,I), N=OLENGTH(V),
            VV=MAKVECTOR(N),
          FOR I=(1,N) REPEAT VV[I]=P(V[I]), RETURN VV  END END;
     SET=PROC(ID,X), IF IDQ(ID) THEN SETVALUE(ID,X)
          ELSE PRINT(ID:=IS:=NOT:=AN:=ID:NIL)  END;
  MEMBER=PROC(X,L), BEGIN(),
    MOR, IF PAIRQ(L) THEN
              (IF X EQ HD L THEN RETURN TRUE
               ELSE DO L=TL L, GOTO MOR END)
          ELSE RETURN NIL  END END;
 LFROMV=PROC(V), BEGIN(L,N,I),
          N=OLENGTH(V), L=NIL,
          FOR I=(N,1,-1) REPEAT L=V[I]:L,
          RETURN L  END END;
COMMENT

( ****************************************************************
                     INITIATION ROUTINES
  ****************************************************************)
  INITIATE=PROC(), BEGIN(),
            INITIO(),
            INITUNARY(),
            INITINFIX(),
            INITEXP(),
            INITCODG(),
            INITOPL(),
            INITMISC(),
            RETURN NIL  END END;
    INITIO=PROC(), BEGIN(LIN),
       LIN=RDLINE(1),
       LIN=VFROMS(LIN),
      BLANK=LIN[1], PERIOD=LIN[2],
       ZERO=LIN[3],   STAR=LIN[4],
      MSIGN=LIN[5],   STRQU=LIN[6],
       LPAR=LIN[7],   RPAR=LIN[8],
        LBR=LIN[9], RBR=LIN[10],
       NINE=LIN[11],   LETTB=LIN[12],
      SEMIC=LIN[13],   IEOS=IDFROMS(SFROMV(VECTOR(SEMIC))),
     IDTRUE=IDFROMS(SFROMV(VECTOR(LIN[14],LIN[15],LIN[16],
              LIN[17]))),
      IDNIL=IDFROMS(SFROMV(VECTOR(LIN[18],LIN[19],LIN[20]))),
      LPVAR=IDFROMS(SFROMV(VECTOR(LPAR))),
```

```
    RPVAR=IDFROMS(SFROMV(VECTOR(RPAR))),
    LBVAR=IDFROMS(SFROMV(VECTOR(LBR))),
    RBVAR=IDFROMS(SFROMV(VECTOR(RBR))),
  PERVAR=IDFROMS(SFROMV(VECTOR(PERICD)))),
   INPUT=MAKFILE(1,72),
  OUTPUT=MAKFILE(2,72),
BLANKLINE=MAKVECTOR(72),
           FOR I=(1,72) REPEAT BLANKLINE[I]=BLANK,
           RETURN NIL  END END;
INITUNARY=PROC(), BEGIN(),
UNARYLIST=LIST(
           LIST(≥DO,LIST(≥BRCKT,≥PROGN,100,100)),
           LIST(≥BEGIN,LIST(≥BRCKT,≥PROG,100,100)),
           LIST(≥PROC,LIST(≥BRCKT,≥LAMBDA,100,100)),
           LIST(≥IF,LIST(≥UNARY,≥IF,200,200)),
           LIST(≥RETURN,LIST(≥UNARY,≥RETURN,500,500)),
           LIST(≥WHILE,LIST(≥UNARY,≥WHILE,500,500)),
           LIST(=FOR, LIST(=UNARY,=FOR,500,500)),
           LIST(≥GOTO,LIST(≥UNARY,≥GO,500,500)),
           LIST(≥GO,LIST(≥UNARY,≥GO,500,500)),
           LIST(≥-,LIST(≥UNARY,≥NILQ,1200,1200)),
           LIST(=NOT,LIST(=UNARY,=NILQ,1200,1200)),
           LIST(≥NULL,LIST(≥UNARY,≥NILQ,1200,1200)),
           LIST(=PL,LIST(=UNARY,=IPOSQ,1200,1200)),
           LIST(=ZR,LIST(=UNARY,=IZEROQ,1200,1200)),
           LIST(≥-,LIST(≥UNARY,≥INEG, 1700,1700)),
           LIST(=SIZE,LIST(=UNARY,=OLENGTH,1900,1900)),
           LIST(≥$,LIST(≥UNARY,≥EVAL,1900,1900)),
           LIST(≥TL,LIST(≥UNARY,≥TL ,2000,2000)),
           LIST(≥HD,LIST(≥UNARY,≥HD ,2000,2000))
           ),
           RETURN NIL  END END;
INITINFIX=PROC(),BEGIN(),
INFIXLIST=LIST(
           LIST(≥TERMINATOR,LIST(≥INFIX,≥TERMINATOR,0,-1)),
           LIST(≥END,LIST(≥INFIX,≥END,0,0)),
           LIST(≥,,LIST(≥INFIX,≥COMMA,100,100)),
           LIST(≥ELSEIF,LIST(≥INFIX,≥ELSEIF,300,300)),
           LIST(≥ELSE,LIST(≥INFIX,≥ELSE,300,300)),
           LIST(≥THEN,LIST(≥INFIX,≥THEN,400,400)),
           LIST(≥REPEAT,LIST(≥INFIX,≥REPEAT,600,600)),
           LIST(≥=,LIST(≥INFIX,≥SETQ,700,701)),
           LIST(≥:,LIST(≥INFIX,≥PAIR,800,801)),
           LIST(≥OR,LIST(≥INFIX,≥OR,1000,1001)),
           LIST(≥AND,LIST(≥INFIX,≥AND,1100,1101)),
```

```
          LIST(=NE,LIST(=INFIX,=NE,1200,1200)),
          LIST(=LT,LIST(=INFIX,=LT,1200,1200)),
          LIST(=GE,LIST(=INFIX,=GE,1200,1200)),
          LIST(=GT,LIST(=INFIX,=GT,1200,1200)),
          LIST(=LE,LIST(=INFIX,=LE,1200,1200)),
          LIST(=SIM,LIST(=INFIX,=SIMQ,1200,1200)),
          LIST(≥-,LIST(≥INFIX,≥ISUB   ,1501,1500)),
          LIST(≥+,LIST(≥INFIX,≥IADD,1501,1500)),
          LIST(≥*,LIST(≥INFIX,≥IMPY ,1601,1600)),
          LIST(=≡,LIST(=INFIX,=IDENTQ,1400,1400)),
          LIST(≥/,LIST(≥INFIX,≥IDIV   ,1601,1600)).
          LIST(≥↑,LIST(≥INFIX,≥IEXP,1800,1800)),
          LIST(=EQ,LIST(=INFIX,=IDENTQ,1400,1400))
          ),
          RETURN NIL  END END;
  INITEXP=PROC(), BEGIN(),
MACROLIST=LIST(
          LIST(=IF,MIF),
          LIST(=THEN,EXPERR),
          LIST(=ELSE,EXPERR),
          LIST(=ELSEIF,EXPERR),
          LIST(=LAMBDA,MXLMBDA),
          LIST(=PROG,MPROG),
          LIST(=PROGN,MPROGN),
          LIST(=QUOTE,DUMMY),
          LIST(=SETQ,MSETQ),
          LIST(=REPEAT,EREMSPS),
          LIST(=COMMA,EREMSPS)   ),
LMACROLIST=LIST(
          LIST(=HD,LCAR),
          LIST(=TL,LCDR),
          LIST(=EVAL,LEVAL),
          LIST(=INDEX,LINDEX),
          LIST(=SUBV,LSUBV),
          LIST(=QUOTE,LQUOTE)   ),
          RETURN NIL  END END;
 INITCODG=PROC(),BEGIN(),
CODGENLIST=LIST(
          LIST(=LAMBDA,GLAMBDA),LIST(=PROG,GPROG),
          LIST(=RETURN,GRETURN), LIST(=PROGN,GPROGN),
          LIST(=GO,GGO), LIST(=COND,GCOND),
          LIST(=AND,GAND), LIST(=OR,GOR),
          LIST(=QUOTE,GQUOTE), LIST(=SETG,GSETG),
          LIST(=WHILE,GWHILE), LIST(=FOR,GFOR),
          LIST(=LIST,GLIST), LIST(=VECTOR,GVECTOR)
```

```
      KCALL=27B,  KRETPROC=115B,
   KNVARS=36B,  KRETPROG=131B,  KSETSTK=137B,  KPOP=35B,
      KARG=33B,  KVAR=31B,  KGLOB=5B,
KASTORE=34B,  KVSTORE=32B,  KGSTORE=6B,
          KNUM1=26B,  KNUM2=4B,  KNUM3=37B,
          KNIL=136B,  KTRUE=135B,
          KJMP=3B,  KJMPT=1B,  KJMPF=2B,
          KLBL=11B,  KJMPI=52B,
          KLIST=44B,  KVECTOR=56B,
          KTLOOP=14B,  KSTEPLOOP=15B,
          KINEG=76B,  KMAKVAR=41B,
          RETURN NIL    END END;
INITOPL=PROC(),BEGIN(),
 OPLIST=LIST(
          LIST(=PAIR,61B),  LIST(=HD,123B),  LIST(=TL,124B),
          LIST(=RPLACA, 121B),  LIST(=RPLACD,122B),
          LIST(=OLIST,44B),
          LIST(=MAKVECTOR,140B),  LIST(=OVECTOR,56B),
          LIST(=INDEX,117B),  LIST(=SETINDEX,120B),
          LIST(=SUBV,163B),  LIST(=SETSUBV,164B),
          LIST(=CONCATV,165B),
          LIST(=OLENGTH,114B),  LIST(=OSTRING,55B),
          LIST(=INTQ,77B),  LIST(=STRQ,101B),
          LIST(=CODEQ,104B),
          LIST(=IDQ,105B),  LIST(=LBLQ,107B),LIST(=VECTQ,102B),
          LIST(=PAIRQ,103B),  LIST(=LOGQ,161B),
          LIST(=IDENTQ,113B),  LIST(=SIMQ,162B),
          LIST(=IPOSQ,111B),  LIST(=IZEROG,112B),
          LIST(=NILQ,132B),  LIST(=OAND,134B),  LIST(=OOR,133B),
          LIST(=VFROMS,46B),  LIST(=SFROMV,45B),
          LIST(=IDFROMS,60B),  LIST(=SFROMID,130B),
          LIST(=CFROMV,150B),
          LIST(=IADD,71B),  LIST(=ISUB,72E),  LIST(=INEG,76B),
          LIST(=IMPY,73B),  LIST(=IDIV,74E),  LIST(=IEXP,75B),
          LIST(=PROPL,160B),  LIST(=SETPROPL,110B),
          LIST(=VALUE,50B),  LIST(=SETVALUE,51B),
          LIST(=MODE,152B),  LIST(=SETMODE,151B),
          LIST(=RDLINE,141B),  LIST(=WRLINE,142B),
          LIST(=REWIND,143B),  LIST(=BACKSPACE,144B),
          LIST(=GARBCOLL,153B),
          LIST(=SAVEALL,145B),  LIST(=RESLMEALL,146B),
          LIST(=ENDFILE,147B),LIST(=PROTECT,155B),
          LIST(=TIME,154B),
          LIST(=NUMARGS,47B),  LIST(=ARGUMENT,42B),
          LIST(=NE,LIST(113B,132B)),
          LIST(=LT,LIST(72B,111B,132B)),
```

```
                LIST(=GE,LIST(72B,111B)),
                LIST(=GT,LIST(72B,76B,111B,132B)),
                LIST(=LE,LIST(72B,76B,111B)),
                LIST(=STOP,116B)    ),
                RETURN NIL  END END;
   INITMISC=PROC(),BEGIN(),
                FALSE=NIL,
                SYSLIST=NIL,
                TTYFLAG=NIL,
                TALKATIVE=0,
                GENSYMB=VECTOR(STAR,ZERO,ZERO,ZERO,ZERO),
                RETURN NIL
                END END;
COMMENT

(*************************************************************
                         I/O ROUTINES
*************************************************************)

 MAKFILE=PROC(FN,LLEN),
            BEGIN(LIN,I),
            LIN=MAKVECTOR(LLEN), FOR I=(1,LLEN) REPEAT
               LIN[I]=BLANK,
            RETURN VECTOR(FN,LIN,LLEN,2)
            END END;
    READ=PROC(FIL),
              BEGIN(ITM,$LIN,$LLEN,$NEXT,$TERMLINE),
            FN=FIL[1], LIN=FIL[2], LLEN=FIL[3], NEXT=FIL[4].
               TERMLINE=READIN,
            ITM=RDITEM(),
            FIL[2]=LIN, FIL[4]=NEXT, FIL[3]=LLEN, RETURN ITM
            END END;
RDTOKEN=PROC(FIL), BEGIN(ITM,$LIN,$LLEN,$NEXT,$TERMLINE),
            FN=FIL[1], LIN=FIL[2], LLEN=FIL[3], NEXT=FIL[4],
               TERMLINE=READIN,
            ITM=LXSCAN(), FIL[2]=LIN, FIL[4]=NEXT, FIL[3]=LLEN,
            RETURN ITM  END END;
  RDITEM=PROC(),
            BEGIN(ITM),
            ITM=LXSCAN(),
            IF ITM EQ LPVAR THEN ITM=GETLIST()
            ELSEIF ITM EQ LBVAR THEN ITM=GETVECT(),
               IF ITM EQ IDTRUE THEN RETURN TRUE,
               IF ITM EQ IDNIL THEN RETURN NIL,
            RETURN ITM
            END END;
```

```
GETLIST=PROC(),
        BEGIN(ITM),
        ITM=RDITEM(),
        IF ITM EQ RPVAR THEN RETURN NIL
        ELSEIF ITM EQ PERVAR THEN RETURN HD GETLIST()
        ELSE RETURN ITM:GETLIST()
        END END;
GETVECT=PROC(), VFROML(GETV()) END;
   GETV=PROC(),
        BEGIN(ITM),
        ITM=RDITEM(),
        IF ITM EQ RBVAR THEN RETURN NIL
        ELSE RETURN ITM:GETV()
        END END;
 LXSCAN=PROC(),
        BEGIN(C,J,E),
   NXT, IF NEXT GT LLEN THEN TERMLINE(),
        C=LIN[NEXT], NEXT=NEXT+1,
        IF C EQ BLANK THEN GOTO NXT,
        J=NEXT- 1,
        IF C LT ZERO THEN GO SYMB
        ELSEIF C LE NINE THEN GO NUMB
        ELSEIF C EQ STRQU THEN GO STR,
        RETURN IDFROMS(SFROMV(VECTOR(C))),
   SYMB, WHILE NEXT LE LLEN AND LIN[NEXT] LE NINE REPEAT
            NEXT = NEXT+1,
        RETURN IDFROMS(SFROMV(SUBV(LIN,J,NEXT-J))).
   NUMB, E=C-ZERO,
        WHILE NEXT LE LLEN AND (C=LIN[NEXT]) GE ZERO AND C LE
            NINE REPEAT
            DO E=E*10+C-ZERO, NEXT=NEXT+1 END,
        IF C EQ LETTB THEN DO NEXT=NEXT+1, RETURN  MAKOCT(E)
            END,
        RETURN E,
    STR, E=MAKVECTOR(0),
   MSTR, IF NEXT GT LLEN THEN DO
            E=CONCATV(E,SUBV(LIN,J+1,LLEN-1)), J=0,
            TERMLINE()  END,
        IF ¬IDENTQ(LIN[NEXT],STRQU) THEN DO NEXT=NEXT+1.
            GOTO MSTR END.
        E=CONCATV(E,SUBV(LIN,J+1,NEXT-J-1)),
        NEXT=NEXT+1, RETURN SFROMV(E)
        END END;
 MAKOCT=PROC(I), BEGIN(B,M,J), M=1, B=0,
    MOR, IF I EQ 0 THEN RETURN B,
```

```
              J=I/10, I=I-J*10, B=B+M*I, I=J, M=M*B, GOTO MOR
                 END END;
   READIN=PROC(), DO LIN=RDLINE(FN), LIN=VFROMS(LIN),
              IF FN EQ 1 AND ¬TTYFLAG THEN
                 WRLINE(SFROMV(CONCATV(VECTOR(BLANK),LIN)),
                 OUTPUT[1])
              ELSE NIL,
              LLEN=OLENGTH(LIN), NEXT=1,  END  END;
    WRITE=PROC(L,FIL),
              BEGIN($FN,$LIN,$LLEN,$NEXT,$BPCNT,$TERMLINE),
              FN=FIL[1], LIN=FIL[2], LLEN=FIL[3], NEXT=FIL[4].
                 TERMLINE=WRITOUT,
              BPCNT=0, PUTITEM(L), TERMLINE(),
              FIL[2]=LIN, FIL[4]=NEXT, RETURN L
              END END;
    PRINT=PROC(),
              BEGIN($FN,$LIN,$LLEN,$NEXT,$BPCNT,$TERMLINE,I.N,
                 FIL,TR),
              TR=TRACE, TRACE=0,
              N=NUMARGS(), FIL=OUTPUT, TERMLINE=WRITOUT,
              FN=FIL[1], LIN=FIL[2], LLEN=FIL[3], NEXT=FIL[4],
              BPCNT=0, FOR I=(1,N) REPEAT PUTITEM(ARGUMENT(1)),
                 TERMLINE().
              FIL[2]=LIN, FIL[4]=NEXT, TRACE=TR,
              RETURN ARGUMENT(N)  END END;
  WRITOUT=PROC(), BEGIN(I),
              WRLINE(SFROMV(LIN),FN), NEXT=BPCNT+2,
                 SETSUBV(LIN,1,LLEN,BLANKLINE)
              END END;
PUTBLANK=PROC(), IF NEXT GT LLEN THEN TERMLINE() ELSE
                 PUTCH(BLANK) END;
 PUTITEM=PROC(L),
              IF VECTQ(L) THEN PUTVECT(L)
              ELSEIF PAIRQ(L) THEN DO
                 IF NEXT GT LLEN-10 THEN TERMLINE() ELSE NIL,
                    BPCNT=BPCNT+1,
                  PUTCH(LPAR), PUTLIST(L)  END
              ELSEIF STRQ(L) THEN PUTSTR(L)
              ELSEIF IDQ(L) THEN PUTCHV(VFROMS(SFROMID(L)))
              ELSEIF INTQ(L) THEN PUTINT(L)
                 ELSEIF IDENTQ(L,TRUE) THEN PUTCHV(VFROMS(SFROMID
                    (IDTRUE)))
                 ELSEIF IDENTQ(L,NIL) THEN PUTCHV(VFROMS(SFROMID
                    (IDNIL)))
              ELSE PUTCHV(VECTOR(STAR,STAR,STAR))
              END;
```

```
PUTVECT=PROC(L), BEGIN(N,I),
            IF NEXT GT LLEN-10 THEN TERMLINE(), PUTCH(LBR),
        N=OLENGTH(L), BPCNT=BPCNT+1,
        FOR I=(1,N) REPEAT PUTITEM(L[I]),
        NEXT=NEXT-1, PUTCH(RBR), BPCNT=BPCNT-1,
            PUTBLANK()
        END END;
PUTLIST=PROC(L),
        IF NULL L THEN DO NEXT=NEXT-1, PUTCH(RPAR),
            BPCNT=BPCNT-1,
                PUTBLANK()   END
        ELSEIF PAIRQ(L) THEN DO PUTITEM(HD L), PUTLIST(TL L)
            END
        ELSE DO PUTCHK(PERIOD), PUTCHK(BLANK), PUTITEM(I),
            NEXT=NEXT-1, PUTCH(RPAR), BPCNT=BPCNT-1,
                PUTCHK(BLANK) END
        END;
 PUTSTR=PROC(S), BEGIN(N,I),
        S=VFROMS(S), N=OLENGTH(S),
        PUTCHK(STRQU), FOR I=(1,N) REPEAT PUTCHK(S[I]),
        PUTCHK(STROU), PUTCHK(BLANK)
        END END;
 PUTCHV=PROC(S), BEGIN(N,I),
        N=OLENGTH(S), IF N GE LLEN-NEXT THEN TERMLINE().
            SETSUBV(LIN,NEXT,N,S), NEXT=NEXT+N, PUTBLANK()
        END END;
  PUTCH=PROC(C), DO LIN[NEXT]=C, NEXT=NEXT+1 END END;
 PUTCHK=PROC(C), DO IF NEXT GT LLEN THEN TERMLINE() ELSE NIL,
        LIN[NEXT]=C, NEXT=NEXT+1   END END;
 PUTINT=PROC(N), BEGIN(S,NN,Q), S=NIL,
        IF NEXT GT LLEN-10 THEN TERMLINE(),
        IF PL N THEN NN=N ELSE DO PUTCH(MSIGN), NN=-N END,
   MOR, Q=NN/10, S=(NN-Q*10+ZERO):S, NN=Q,
        IF ¬ZR NN THEN GOTO MOR,
        WHILE S REPEAT DO PUTCH(HD S), S=TL S END,
            PUTCH(BLANK)
        END END;
COMMENT

(***************************************************************
                    TRANSLATOR ROUTINES
***************************************************************)

TRANSLAT=PROC(B1),BEGIN(X),
        ERCOUNT=0,
        X=FNOTN(B1),
        IF ZR ERCOUNT THEN RETURN EXPAND(X),
```

```
            RETURN(X)
            END END;
  MACDEF=PROC(B1,B2),
            MACROLIST=LIST(B1,B2):MACROLIST END;
  LMACRO=PROC(B1,B2),
            LMACROLIST=LIST(B1,B2):LMACROLIST END;
   INFIX=PROC(B1,B2,B3,B4),
            INFIXLIST=LIST(B1,LIST(≥INFIX,B4,B2,B3)):INFIXLIST
               END;
   UNARY=PROC(B1,B2,B3),
            UNARYLIST=LIST(B1,LIST(≥UNARY,B3,B2,B2)):UNARYLIST
               END;
 BRACKET=PROC(B1,B2,B3),
            UNARYLIST=LIST(B1,LIST(≥BRCKT,B3,B2,B2)):UNARYLIST
               END;
COMMENT


(**************************************************************
                    PARSER ROUTINES
**************************************************************)

   FNOTN=PROC(B1),
         BEGIN(P,I1,I2,U,P1,$LST,UL,INFL,TERM),
         IF ¬PAIRQ(B1) THEN RETURN(B1),
         LST=B1, TERM=≥TERMINATOR,
         UL=UNARYLIST, INFL=INFIXLIST,
         P=NIL,
   DOF, I1=GETOKEN(),
         IF PAIRQ(I1) THEN DO I1=FNOTN(I1), GOTO TEST END,
         IF I1 EQ =COMMENT THEN DO GETOKEN(), GOTO DOF END,
         IF I1 EQ =NOOP THEN DO I1=GETOKEN(), GOTO NOTU END,
         IF I1 EQ == OR I1 EQ =≥ THEN
             DO I1 = =QUOTE:GETOKEN():NIL, GOTO NOTU END,
         IF U =LOOKUP(I1,UL) THEN DO P=U:P, GOTO DOF END,
   NOTU, I2=GETOKEN(),
         IF VECTQ(I2) THEN
             DO I1=LIST(≥INDEX,I1,FNOTN(LFRCMV(I2))),GOTO NOTU
             END,
         IF PAIRQ(I2) THEN DO
             I2=REMCOM(FNOTN(I2)),
             IF NULL(I2) THEN I2=I2:NIL ELSE NIL,
             I1=I1:I2, GOTO NOTU END,
         IF NULL(12) THEN DO I1=I1:I2, GOTO NOTU END,
         GOTO TEST1,
   TEST, I2=GETOKEN(),
```

```
  TEST1,  IF PAIRQ(I1) THEN NIL ELSEIF LOOKUP(I1, INFL) THEN
              PRINT(=WARNING:I1:=IS:=AN:=INFIX:=OPERATOR:
                 NIL),
          U=LOOKUP(I2,INFL),
          IF NULL(U) THEN DO OPERROR(I2), GOTO TEST END.
  TEST2,  IF NULL P AND I2 EQ TERM THEN RETURN I1,
          IF NULL(P) THEN GOTO PSH,
          IF HD TL TL HD P GT HD TL TL TL U THEN GOTO PIL,
    PSH,  P=U:(I1:P), GOTO DOF,
    PLL,  IF HD HD P EQ =UNARY THEN GOTO UNRY,
          IF HD HD P EQ =BRCKT THEN GOTO BRCKT,
          I1=LIST(HD TL HD P,HD TL P,I1),
          P=TL TL P, GOTO TEST2,
   BRKT,  I1=LIST(HD TL HD P,I1), P=TL P, GOTO NOTU,
   UNRY,  I1=LIST(HD TL HD P,I1), P=TL P, GOTO TEST2
          END END;
 GETOKEN=PROC(), BEGIN(TOK),
          IF ¬PAIRQ(LST) THEN RETURN =TERMINATOR,
          TOK = HD LST, LST = TL LST,
          RETURN TOK   END END;
  REMCOM=PROC(B1),BEGIN(), IF NULL(B1) THEN RETURN(NIL),
          RETURN(REMSEP(B1,≥COMMA)) END END;
  REMSEP=PROC(B1,B2),BEGIN(),
          IF ¬PAIRQ(B1) THEN RETURN B1:NIL,
          IF HD B1 EQ B2 THEN RETURN
              HD TL B1:REMSEP(HD TL TL B1,B2),
          RETURN B1:NIL   END END;
 OPERROR=PROC(B1),BEGIN(),
          ERCOUNT=ERCOUNT+1,
          PRINT(B1:LIST(≥IS,≥NOT,≥AN,≥OPERATOR)),
          RETURN(NIL) END END;
COMMENT

(***************************************************************
                    SYNTAX TREE PROCESSORS
***************************************************************)

  EXPAND=PROC(B1), BEGIN(OP,M),
          IF ¬PAIRQ(B1) THEN RETURN(B1),
          IF PAIRQ(OP=HD B1) THEN GOTO NOTM,
          M=LOOKUP(OP,MACROLIST),
          IF NULL(M) THEN GOTO NOTM,
          RETURN(M(B1)),
   NOTM,  RETURN(EXLIS(B1)) END END;
   EXLIS=PROC(B1),BEGIN(),
          IF NULL(B1) THEN RETURN(NIL),
```

```
            RETURN(EXPAND(HD B1):EXLIS (TL B1)) END END;
    EXPERR=PROC(B1),BEGIN(), PRINT(B1),
            PRINT(LIST( ≥SYNTAX,≥ERROR,≥IN,≥ABOVE,≥-,≥PASS,≥TWO
            )),
            ERCOUNT=ERCOUNT+1,RETURN(NIL) END END;
   EREMSPS=PROC(B1),EREMSP(B1,HD B1) END;
    EREMSP=PROC(B1,B2),BEGIN(),
            IF ¬PAIRQ(B1) THEN RETURN LIST(B1),
            IF HD B1 EQ B2 THEN RETURN
                EXPAND(HD TL B1):EREMSP (HD TL TL, B1,B2),
            RETURN(EXPAND(B1):NIL) END END;
      LCAR=PROC(B1),  LIST(≥RPLACA,
            EXPAND(HD TL HD TL B1),EXPAND(HD TL TL B1)  ) END;
      LCDR=PROC(B1),   LIST(≥RPLACD),
            EXPAND(HD TL HD TL B1),EXPAND(HD TL TL B1))  END;
     LEVAL=PROC(B1),   LIST(≥SET,
            EXPAND(HD TL HD TL B1),EXPAND(HD TL TL B1) ) END;
    LINDEX=PROC(B1),BEGIN(F), F=TL HD TL B1,
            RETURN(LIST(=SETINDEX,EXPAND(HD F),
                EXPAND(HD TL F), EXPAND(HD TL TL B1) )) END END;
     LSUBV=PROC(X), BEGIN(L,R), L=TL HD TL X, R=HD TL TL X,
            RETURN EXLIS(=SETSUBV:HD L:HD TL L:HD TL TL L:R:NIL)
            END END;
   MXLMBDA=PROC(L), BEGIN(P), P = TL HD TL L,
            RETURN LIST(=QUOTE,LIST(HD L,REMCOM(HD P),EXPAND(HD
            TL P)))
            END END;
     DUMMY=PROC(X),X END;
   MELSEIF=PROC(B1,B2,B3),BEGIN(P),
            IF B1 EQ=THEN THEN RETURN(
                LIST(LIST(EXPAND(B2),EXPAND(B3)),LIST(TRUE,NIL))),
            IF ¬ HD B2 EQ =THEN THEN GOTO IFERR,
            P=LIST(EXPAND(HD TL B2),EXPAND(HD TL TL B2)).
            IF B1 EQ =ELSE THEN RETURN(
                LIST(P,(LIST(TRUE,EXPAND(B3)))))),
            IF ¬PAIRQ(B3) THEN GOTO IFERR,
            IF B1 EQ =ELSEIF THEN RETURN(
            P:MELSEIF (HD B3,HD TL B3,HD TL TL B3)),
    IFERR, RETURN(EXPERR(LIST(B1,B2,B3))) END END;
     MPROG=PROC(B1),BEGIN(P,Q),
            Q=HD (P=EXPAND(HD TL B1)),
            IF Q AND ¬PAIRQ(Q) THEN RPLACA(P,LIST(Q)),
            RETURN((HD B1):P) END END;
    MPROGN=PROC(B1),
            (HD B1):EREMSP(HD TL B1,≥COMMA) END;
```

```
      MIF=PROC(B1)BEGIN(X),X=HD TL B1,
          IF ¬PAIRQ(X) THEN RETURN(EXPERR(E1)),
          RETURN(≥COND:MELSEIF(HD X,HD TL X,HD TL TL X)) END
             END;
    MSETQ=PROC(B1),BEGIN(F1,F2,U),
          F1=HD TL B1, F2=HD TL TL B1,
          IF ¬PAIRQ(F1) THEN GOTO NOTLM,
          U=LOOKUP(HD F1,LMACROLIST),
          IF NULL(U) THEN GOTO NOTLM,
          RETURN(U(B1)),
   NOTLM, RETURN(LIST(HD B1,EXPAND(F1),EXPAND(F2))) END END;
COMMENT

(*************************************************************
                    MAIN CODE GENERATOR
*************************************************************)

 CODEGEN=PROC(NAM,X),
         BEGIN($ERRCNT,$LIST2,$END2,LIST3,
            $GLOBL,$LBLVALS,$NBYTE,$LBLNO,
            I,CODEV),
         ERRCNT=0, GLOBL=NIL, NBYTE=3, LBLNO=1, LBLVALS=NIL,
         LIST2=END2=(0:NIL), END2=ADDON(END2,GREFS(NAM)),
         COMP(X),
         IF TALKATIVE GE 1 THEN PRINT(=GLOBAL,=VARS,GLOBL),
         IF TALKATIVE EQ 2 THEN DO
            PRINT(=BINARY,=CODE), PRINT(LIST2) END,
         IF TALKATIVE EQ 2 THEN PRINT(=LABEL,=LIST,LBLVALS),
         LIST3=LIST2,  WHILE LIST2 REPEAT DO
            HD LIST2=SUBLBLS(HD LIST2), LIST2=TL LIST2 END,
         IF ZR ERRCNT THEN DO
            NBYTE=NBYTE-1, CODEV=MAKVECTOR(NBYTE),
            FOR I=(1,NBYTE) REPEAT DO
               CODEV[I]=IFROMID(HD LIST3), LIST3=TL LIST3 END,
            FOR I=(NBYTE,2,-1) REPEAT
               IF CODEV[I] GT 177B THEN DO
                  CODEV[I-1]=CODEV[I]/200B,
                  CODEV[I]=CODEV[I]-200B*CODEV[I-1]  END,
               ELSE NIL,
            $NAM=CFROMV(CODEV), RETURN NAM  END,
         PRINT(ERRCNT:COMP:ERRORS:NIL),
         RETURN NAM
         END END;
  SUBLBLS=PROC(X), IF ¬PAIRQ(X) THEN X ELSE
         BEGIN(Y),
         Y=LOOKUP(HD X,LBLVALS),
```

```
                IF Y THEN RETURN Y,
                ERRCNT=ERRCNT+1,
                PRINT(X:=IS:=UNDEF:=LABEL:NIL),
                RETURN NIL
                END END;
        COMP=PROC(X), BEGIN(FN,ARGL,GENR),
                IF IDQ(X) THEN RETURN GVAR(X),
                IF ¬PAIRQ(X) THEN RETURN GCON(X),
                FN=HD X, ARGL=TL X,
                IF IDQ(FN) THEN DO
                    GENR=LOOKUP(FN,CODGENLIST),
                    IF GENR THEN RETURN GENR(X) ELSE NIL
                    END,
                RETURN CALLS(X)
                END END;
        GVAR=PROC(ATM),
                BEGIN(Y),
                IF Y=ORDINAL(ATM,ARGS) THEN ASS(KARG,Y)
                ELSEIF Y=ORDINAL(ATM,VARS) THEN ASS(KVAR,Y)
                ELSEIF MEMBER(ATM,LBLIST) THEN ASS(KLBL,O,LIST(ATM))
                ELSE ASS(KGLOB,O,GREFS(ATM)),
                RETURN NIL
                END END;
        GCON=PROC(X), BEGIN(N),
                IF NULL(X) THEN ASS(KNIL)
                ELSEIF X EQ TRUE THEN ASS(KTRUE)
                ELSEIF INTQ(X) THEN
                    (IF X LT O THEN DO GCON(-X), ASS(KINEG) END
                     ELSEIF X LE 177B THEN ASS(KNUM1,X)
                     ELSEIF X LE 37777B THEN ASS(KNUM2,O,X)
                     ELSE ASS(KNUM3,O,O,X)   )
                ELSEIF IDQ(X) THEN DO
                    ASS(KNUM2,O,GREFS(X)), ASS(KMAKVAR) END
                ELSEIF HD X EQ =LAMBDA THEN DO
                    N=GENSYM(), CODEGEN(N,X), ASS(KGLOB,O,GREFS(N))
                        END
                ELSE DO N=GENSYM(), SN=X, ASS(KGLCB,O,N) END
                END END;
        CALLS=PROC(X), BEGIN(ARG,FN,ARGL,SARGL,CP),
                FN=HD X, ARGL=TL X, SARGL=ARGL,
                WHILE ARGL REPEAT DO COMP(HD ARGL), ARGL=TL ARGL END,
                IF OP=LOOKUP(FN,OPLIST) THEN
                    (IF INTQ(OP) THEN RETURN ASS(OP)
                     ELSE RETURN MAPX(OP,ASS)   ),
                COMP(FN),
```

```
            ASS(KCALL,LENGTH(SARGL))
            END END;
    GREFS=PROC(A),
            DO  IF MEMBER(A,SYSLIST) THEN
                DO A=VFROMS(SFROMID(A)),
                A=CONCATV(VECTOR(STAR),A),  A=IDFROMS(SFROMV(A))
                  END
                ELSE NIL,
            IF MEMBER(A,GLOBL) THEN NIL ELSE GLOBL=A:GLOBL,
            A   END END;
        ASS=PROC(),  BEGIN(I,OP),
            NBYTE=NBYTE+NUMARGS(),
            FOR I=(1,NUMARGS()) REPEAT END2=ADDON(END2,
                ARGUMENT(I))
            END END;
        LBL=PROC(X),  LBLVALS=(X:NBYTE:NIL):LBLVALS END;
    GENLBL=PROC(),  LBLNO=LBLNO+1 END;
    COMMENT
(***********************************************************
                        CODE GENERATORS
***********************************************************)
 GLAMBDA=PROC(X),
            BEGIN($ARGS,$VARS,EXPX,SARGS,$LBLIST),
            VARS=NIL, LBLIST=NIL,
            ARGS=HD TL X, EXPX=HD TL TL X,
            IF  HD ARGS EQ =GLOBAL   THEN ARGS=ARGS:NIL.
            SARGS=ARGS,  ARGS=EXCHANGE(SARGS,1),
            COMP(EXPX),
            EXCHANGE(SARGS,1),
            ASS(KRETPROC)
            END END;
EXCHANGE=PROC(L,I),  IF NULL(L) THEN NIL
            ELSEIF ¬PAIRQ(HD L) THEN HD L : EXCHANGE(TL L.I+1)
            ELSE DO ASS(KARG,I),  ASS(KGLOB,0,HD TL HD L),
            ASS(KASTORE,I),  ASS(KPOP,1),
            ASS(KGSTORE,0,HD TL HD L),  ASS(KPCP,1),
            I : EXCHANGE(TL L,I+1) END END;
    GPROG=PROC(X),
            BEGIN($VARS,PROGRAM,T1,$LBLIST,$RET,SVARS),
            IF HD VARS EQ =GLOBAL THEN VARS=VARS:NIL,
            VARS=HD TL X, PROGRAM=TL TL X,
            ASS(KNVARS,LENGTH(VARS)),
            SVARS=VARS,  VARS=SAVLOCS(SVARS,1),
            RET=GENLBL(),
            X=PROGRAM,
```

```
          WHILE PROGRAM REPEAT DO
             T1=HD PROGRAM, PROGRAM=TL PROGRAM,
             IF ¬PAIRQ(T1) THEN LBLIST=T1:LBLIST ELSE NIL END,
          PROGRAM=X,
          WHILE PROGRAM REPEAT DO
             T1=HD PROGRAM, PROGRAM=TL PROGRAM,
             IF ¬PAIRQ(T1) THEN LBL(T1)
                ELSE DO ASS(KSETSTK), COMP(T1) END END.
          ASS(KNIL), LBL(RET),
          RESTLOCS(SVARS,1),
          ASS(KRETPROG)
          END END;
  SAVLOCS=PROC(L,I), IF NULL(L) THEN NIL
          ELSEIF ¬PAIRQ (HD L) THEN HD L : SAVLOCS(TL L.I+1)
          ELSE DO ASS(KGLOB,O,HD TL HD L), ASS(KVSTORE,I),
          I:SAVLOCS(TL L,I+1) END END;
  RESTLOCS=PROC(L,I), IF NULL(L) THEN NIL
          ELSEIF ¬PAIRQ(HD L) THEN RESTLOCS(TL L,I+1)
          ELSE DO ASS(KVAR,I), ASS(KGSTORE,O,HD TL HD L),
             ASS(KPOP,1), RESTLOCS(TL L,I+1) END END;
  GRETURN=PROC(X),
          DO COMP(HD TL X), ASS(KJMP,O,LIST(RET)) END END;
  GPROGN=PROC(L), BEGIN(E),
          L=TL L, COMP(HD L), L=TL L,
          WHILE L REPEAT DO
             E=HD L, L=TL L, ASS(KPOP,1), COMP(E) END
          END END;
    GGO=PROC(X), BEGIN(ARG),
          ARG=HD TL X,
          IF MEMBER(ARG,LBLIST) THEN ASS(KJMP,O,LIST(ARG))
          ELSE DO COMP(ARG), ASS(KJMP1) END
          END END;
  GCOND=PROC(X), BEGIN(P,E,NTRUE,LAST),
          LAST=GENLBL(),
          X=TL X,
          WHILE X REPEAT DO
             E=HD X, X=TL X, P=HD E, E=HD TL E,
             IF P EQ TRUE THEN DO COMP(E), X=NIL END
             ELSEIF HD E EQ=GO AND MEMBER(HD TL P,LBLIST) THEN
                DO COMP(P), ASS(KJMPT,O,LIST(HD TL E)) END
             ELSE DO COMP(P), NTRUE=GENLBL(),
                ASS(KJMPF,O,LIST(NTRUE)), COMP(E),
                IF HD E NE=GO AND HD E NE =RETURN AND X THEN
                   ASS(KJMP,O,LIST(LAST)) ELSE NIL,
                LBL(NTRUE)  END  END,
```

```
        LBL(LAST)
        END END;
   GAND=PROC(X), BEGIN(L),
        L=GENLBL(), ASS(KNIL),
        COMP(HD TL X) ,ASS(KJMPF,0,LIST(L)),
        ASS(KPOP,1), COMP(HD TL TL X),
        LBL(L)  END END;
    GOR=PROC(X), BEGIN(L),
        L=GENLBL(), ASS(KTRUE),
        COMP(HD TL X) ,ASS(KJMPT,0,LIST(L)),
        ASS(KPOP,1), COMP(HD TL TL X),
        LBL(L)  END END;
 GQUOTE=PROC(X), BEGIN(ARG),
        ARG=HD TL X,
        GCON(ARG)
        END END;
  GSETQ=PROC(X), BEGIN(ATM,VAL),
        ATM=HD TL X, VAL=HD TL TL X,
        COMP(VAL), ASSIGN(ATM)
        END END;
 ASSIGN=PROC(ATM), BEGIN(X),
        IF ¬IDQ(ATM) THEN DO
           ERRCNT=ERRCNT+1,
           PRINT(ATM:===:VAL:NIL),
           PRINT(=ASSIGN:=ERROR:NIL),
           RETURN NIL
           END,
        IF X=ORDINAL(ATM,ARGS) THEN ASS(KASTORE,X)
        ELSEIF X=ORDINAL(ATM,VARS) THEN ASS(KVSTORE,X)
        ELSE ASS(KGSTORE,0,GREFS(ATM))
        END END;
 GWHILE=PROC(X), BEGIN(MORE,NTRUE,P,E),
        X=TL X,
         X=HD X, P=HD X, E=HD TL X,
         ASS(KNIL),
         MORE=GENLBL(),
        LBL(MORE),
        COMP(P),
         NTS(KNIL),
         MORE=GENLBL(),
        LBL(MORE),
        COMP(P),
         NTRUE=GENLBL(),
         ASS(KJMPF,0,LIST(NTRUE)),
         ASS(KPOP,1),
```

```
            COMP(E),
             ASS(KJMP,0,LIST(MORE)),
            LBL(NTRUE)
             END END;
     GFOR=PROC(X),
            BEGIN(E,I,J,K,L,LAST,FORL),
            X=HD TL X, L=TL HD X, E=HD TL X,
            I=HD L, L=HD TL L, J=HD L, K=HD TL L, L=TL TL L,
            IF NULL(L) THEN L=1 ELSE L=HD L,
            LAST=GENLBL(),
            COMP(K), COMP(L), COMP(J),
            ASS(KNIL), ASS(KPOP,1),
            FORL=GENLBL(), LBL(FORL),
            ASSIGN(I),
            ASS(KTLOOP,0,LIST(LAST)),
            COMP(E),
            ASS(KSTEPLOOP,0,LIST(FORL)),
            LBL(LAST)
            END END;
    GLIST=PROC(X), BEGIN(),
            X=TL X, MAPX(X,COMP),
            GCON(LENGTH(X)), ASS(KLIST)    END END;
  GVECTOR=PROC(X), BEGIN(),
            X=TL X, MAPX(X,COMP),
            GCON(LENGTH(X)), ASS(KVECTOR)    END END;
```

APPENDIX C:
COMPARATIVE EXAMPLES

Below are given examples of a single algorithm coded in a number of different programming languages. The algorithm is the Huffman algorithm for encoding symbols which occur with a given frequency in a set of messages as sequences of zeros and ones, in such a way that the length of the messages is minimized. The input of the algorithm is the set of frequencies, and the output is a binary tree with the terminal nodes specifying the frequencies, and such that the encoding of a symbol can be found by tracing down the tree from the root, counting a zero when a left branch is taken, and a one when a right branch is taken. For example, if the frequencies are 2, 4, 5, and 7, the tree would be of the form of Figure C.1 which would indicate that the symbols with frequencies 7, 5, 4, and 2 should be represented by the binary sequences 0, 10, 111, and 110 respectively.

The algorithm builds the tree from the bottom upwards. The representation at each stage of the algorithm consists of a set of disjoint subtrees whose terminal nodes are the initial frequencies, with the frequency of a subtree being considered to be the sum of the frequencies of its terminal nodes. Each stage of the algorithm then consists of removing the two subtrees with the smallest frequencies and replacing them with a new subtree whose branches are the two subtrees. Initially the subtrees are just the initial frequencies, and the algorithm terminates when only one subtree remains, which is then the final tree.

In the programs given below, the algorithms used in the BALM, LISP, ALGOL 68, PL/1, and SNOBOL versions are substantially the same. In each case the argument is a chain whose elements represent degenerate subtrees specifying the frequencies, with

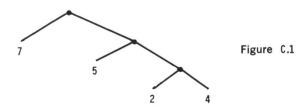

Figure C.1

the elements in the chain being in increasing order of frequency. The algorithm then removes repeatedly the first two elements of the chain, constructs a new subtree, and inserts it in position in the chain by comparing the sum of the two frequencies with the other frequencies in the chain. The algorithm terminates when only one element is left on the chain.

The SETL algorithm is similar, but a set is used instead of a chain, with the next two elements to be coalesced being found by searching. The FORTRAN version simulates a chain by indexing within an array, while the APL version constructs a new array with the elements always in increasing order.

SETL

```
definef huffman(a);
   more: if #a eq 1 then return a;
         ∃[s1]∈a | (∀x∈a|hd s1 le hd x);
         a = a less s1;
         ∃[s2]∈a | (∀x∈a|hd s1 le hd x);
         a = a less s2;
         a = a with ⟨hd s1 + hd s2, s1, s2⟩;
         goto more;
         end huffman;
```

This takes an argument a which is a set of tuples, with the hd of each tuple being the frequency of a symbol. In each iteration s1 and s2 are the subtrees with the smallest frequencies, and each new subtree is a 3-tuple.

BALM

```
HUFFMAN = PROC(L), BEGIN(LL,L1,L2,V,X),
   NEXT, L1=HD L, L2=HD TL L, L=LL=TL TL L,
         X = VECTOR(V=L1[1]+L2[1],L1,L2),
         IF NULL L THEN RETURN X,
         WHILE V GT (HD LL)[1] REPEAT
             IF NULL TL LL THEN DO TL LL=X:NIL, GOTO NEXT END
             ELSE LL=TL LL,
         TL LL=HD LL:TL LL, HD LL=X, GOTO NEXT
         END END;
```

The argument L is a list whose elements are vectors whose first elements are the frequencies.

LISP

```
(LAMBDA (L) (PROG (LL L1 L2 V X)
   NEXT   (SETQ L1 (CAR L))   (SETQ L2 (CADR L))
          (SETQ L (SETQ LL (CDDR L)))
          (SETQ V (ADD (CAR L1) (CAR L2)))
```

```
       (SETQ X (LIST V Ll L2))
       (COND ((NULL L) (RETURN X)))
 NXT    (COND ((NOT (GREATERP V (CAAR LL)))
              (PROGN (RPLACD LL (CONS (CAR LL) (CDR LL)))
                     (RPLACA LL X) (GO NEXT) ))
             ((NULL (CDR LL))
              (PROGN (RPLACD LL (CONS X NIL)) (GO NEXT)) ))
       (SETQ LL (CDR LL))  (GO NXT)  ))
```

This is essentially the same program as the BALM version, except the elements of the lists are themselves lists, not vectors.

ALGOL 68

```
mode tree = struct(ref tree left, ref tree right,
                   int val, ref tree next);
proc huffman = (ref tree p) ref tree:
        begin ref tree p1, p2, q, pp;
  more: p:=next of (p2:=next of (p1:=next of p));
        q:=tree:=(p1,p2,val of p1 + val of p2,nil);
        if p :=: nil then goto fin fi;
        if val of q le val of p then
           (next of q:=p; p:=q; goto more) else pp:=p fi;
   gr:  if next of pp :=: nil then
           (next of q:=nil; next of pp:=q; goto more) fi;
        if val of q le val of next of pp then
           (next of q:=next of pp; next of pp:=q; goto more)
              fi;
        pp:=next of pp; goto gr;
  fin: q end;
```

The argument is a chain of elements of mode tree, linked by their "next" components.

PL/1

```
HUFFMAN: PROCEDURE(P) RETURNS PTR;
         DCL 1 NODE BASED(Q), 2 LEFT PTR, 2 RIGHT PTR,
              2 VAL FIXED BIN, 2 NEXT PTR;
         DCL (P,P1,P2,Q,PP) PTR;
   MORE: P1=P; P2=P->NEXT; P=P2->NEXT;
         ALLOCATE NODE; Q->LEFT=P1; Q->RIGHT=P2;
         Q->VAL = (P1->VAL)+(P2->VAL);
         IF P=NULL THEN RETURN(Q);
         IF Q->VAL LE P->VAL THEN DO;
            Q->NEXT=P; P=Q; GOTO MORE; END;
         PP = P;
```

```
GR:  IF PP->NEXT=NULL THEN DO;
        Q->NEXT=NULL; PP->NEXT=Q; GOTO MORE; END;
     IF Q->VAL LE PP->VAL THEN DO;
        Q->NEXT=PP->NEXT; PP->NEXT=Q; GOTO MORE; END;
     PP=PP->NEXT; GOTO GR;
     END;
```

This is essentially the same program as that given in ALGOL 68.

SNOBOL

```
          DEFINE('HUFFMAN(P)V,P1,P2,PP')
          DATA('TREE(LEFT,RIGHT,VAL,NEXT)')
          ...
          ...
HUFFMAN  P1 = NEXT(P); P2 = NEXT(P2); P = NEXT(P2)
         V = VAL(P1) + VAL(P2); HUFFMAN = TREE(P1,P2,V)
         IDENT(P)  :S(RETURN)
         PP = P; LE(V,VAL(P))  :F(GR)
         NEXT(HUFFMAN) = P; P = HUFFMAN  :(HUFFMAN)
GR       IDENT(NEXT(PP))  :F(NEND)
         NEXT(HUFFMAN) = ; NEXT(PP) = HUFFMAN  :(HUFFMAN)
NEND     LE(V,VAL(PP))  :F(NLE)
         NEXT(HUFFMAN) = NEXT(PP); NEXT(PP) = HUFFMAN
             :(HUFFMAN)
NLE      PP = NEXT(PP)  :(GR)
          ...
          ...
```

This uses a programmer-defined data-type TREE similar to that used in the ALGOL 68 and PL/1 routines. The end of the chain is indicated by a NEXT component equal to the null string.

FORTRAN

```
     FUNCTION HUFFMAN(K,N)
     DIMENSION K(4,2)
     DO 1 L=1,N
     K(2,L)=0
     K(3,L)=0
   1 K(4,L)=L+1
     K(4,N)=0
     I=1
     M=N
   7 I1=I
     I2=K(4,I1)
     I=K(4,I2)
```

```
      IF (I.EQ.0) RETURN(I1)
      KSUM=K(1,I1)+K(1,I2)
      II=I
      M=M+1
    5 IF (KSUM.GT.K(1,II)) GOTO 3
      DO 6 J=1,4
    6 K(J,M)=K(J,II)
      K(1,II)=KSUM
      K(2,II)=I1
      K(3,II)=I2
      K(4,II)=M
      GOTO 7
    3 IF (K(4,II).EQ.0) GOTO 4
      II=K(4,II)
      GOTO 5
    4 K(4,II)=M
      K(1,M)=KSUM
      K(2,M)=I1
      K(3,M)=I2
      K(4,M)=0
      GOTO 7
      END
```

This takes as an argument a 4 by 2N array K with the frequencies in increasing order in the first column. The rows of K are used as nodes of the tree, with the fourth column being used to link the nodes together in increasing order of frequencies. The algorithm is similar to the ALGOL 68 and PL/1 algorithms in other respects.

APL

```
      ∇T ← HUFF L
  [1] T ← ((ρL,3)0) [;I←1] <- L
  [2] SUM ← T[I;1]+T[I+1;1]
  [3] T ← T[(iN ←+/∼S),1,(S←SUM>T[;1])/iρT;]
  [4] T[1+N;] ← SUM,I,I+1
  [5] →((I←I+2)<(ρT)[1])/2
  [6] ∇
```

The argument L is an array of nonzero frequencies in ascending order. Statement 1 creates from this a three-column matrix T whose first column is L, with zeros elsewhere. The main loop of the algorithm takes rows I and I+1, constructs a new row from them, and inserts it in order in T. Note that statement 3 computes a vector S with ones corresponding to rows of T with larger frequencies than the new row, and zeros elsewhere. This is used to compute N, the position for the new row, and to construct the new T with a duplicate of row 1 temporarily in position N. The new row is inserted in statement 4, and statement 5 increments and tests I, transferring to statement 2 if not finished.

REFERENCES
AND BIBLIOGRAPHY

BOOKS

Barron, D. W., *Recursive Techniques in Programming* (New York: American Elsevier Publishing Co., Inc., 1968).

Cocke, J., and J. T. Schwartz, *Programming Languages and Their Compilers* (New York: Courant Institute, New York University, 1970).

Feller, William, *An Introduction to Probability Theory and Its Applications*, 2nd Edition (New York: John Wiley & Sons, Inc., 1957).

Foster, John M., *List Processing* (New York: American Elsevier Publishing Co., Inc., 1967).

Gries, David, *Compiler Construction for Digital Computers* (New York: John Wiley & Sons, Inc., 1971).

Griswold, Ralph E., J. F. Ponge, and I. P. Polansky, *The SNOBOL 4 Programming Language* (Englewood Cliffs, New Jersey: Prentice-Hall, Inc., 1968).

Iverson, Kenneth E., *A Programming Language* (John Wiley & Sons, Inc., 1962).

Knuth, Donald E., *The Art of Computer Programming*, Vol. 1 (Reading, Massachusetts: Addison-Wesley Publishing Co., Inc., 1968).

Maurer, W. D., *Programming* (San Francisco: Holden-Day, Inc., 1968).

McCarthy, John, et al., *LISP 1.5 Programming Manual* (Cambridge, Massachusetts: MIT Press, 1962).

Newell, Allen, et al., *IPL-V Manual* (Englewood Cliffs, New Jersey: Prentice-Hall, Inc., 1964).

Pollack, Seymour V., and T. D. Sterling, *A Guide to PL/1* (New York: Holt, Reinhart & Winston, Inc., 1969).

Randell, Brian, and L. J. Russell, *ALGOL 60 Implementation* (New York: Academic Press, Inc., 1964).

Schwartz, Jacob T., *SETL Notes* (New York: Courant Institute, New York University).

Wegner, Peter, *Programming Language, Information Structures and Machine Organization* (New York: McGraw-Hill Book Company, 1968).

COLLECTIONS OF PAPERS

Berkeley, Edmund C., and D. G. Bobrow, eds., *The Programming Language LISP* (Cambridge, Massachusetts: MIT Press, 1964).

Bobrow, D. G., ed., *Symbol Manipulation Languages and Techniques* (Amsterdam: North-Holland Publishing Company, 1968).

Michie, Donald, et al., *Machine Intelligence* 1–5 (New York: American Elsevier Publishing Co., 1967–1970).

Rosen, Saul, ed., *Programming Systems and Languages* (New York: McGraw-Hill Book Company, 1967).

PAPERS

Abrahams, P., et al., *The LISP 2 Programming Language and System*, FJCC, 1966.

Arden, B. W., B. A. Galler, and R. M. Graham, *The MAD Definition Facility*, CACM, August 1969.

Arora, S. R., and W. T. Dent, *Randomized Binary Search Technique*, CACM, February 1969.

Belady, L. A., and C. J. Kuehner, *Dynamic Space-Sharing in Computer Systems*, CACM, May 1969.

Bell, J. R., *The Quadratic Quotient Method: A Hash Code Eliminating Secondary Clustering*, CACM, February 1970.

Bobrow, D. G., and B. Raphael, *A Comparison of List-Processing Computer Languages*, in Rosen (67).

Bookstein, Abraham, *On Hamson's Substring Test*, University of Chicago Library School (unpublished).

Burstall, R. M., and R. J. Popplestone, *POP-2 Reference Manual*, in Michie (67–70), Vol. 2.

Busam, V. A., and D. E. Englund, *Optimization of Expressions in FORTRAN*, CACM December 1969.

Cheatham, T. E., *The Introduction of Definitional Facilities into Higher-Level Programming Languages*, FJCC, 1966.

Coffman, Jr., E. G., and J. Eve, *File Structures Using Hashing Codes*, CACM, July 1970.

Cohen, J., *A Use of Fast and Slow Memories in List-Processing Languages*, CACM, February 1967.

Daley, R. C., and J. B. Dennis, *Virtual Memory, Processes, and Sharing in Multics*, CACM, May 1968.

Day, A. C., *Full Table Quadratic Searching for Scatter Storage*, CACM, August 1970.

Dennis, J. B., *Segmentation and the Design of Multiprogrammed Computer Systems*, JACM, p. 589, 1965. Also in Rosen (67).

Dijkstra, E. W., *Cooperating Sequential Processes*, EWD123, Tech. Univ. Eindhoven, 1965.

Dijkstra, E. W., *Recursive Programming*, Numerische Mathematik 2, p. 312, 1960. Also in Rosen (67).

Dodd, G. G., *Elements of Data Management Systems*, Computing Surveys, June 1969.

Fateman, R. J., *Optimal Code for Serial and Parallel Computation*, CACM, December 1969.

Feldman, J., and D. Gries, *Translator Writing Systems*, CACM, February 1968.

Fenichel, R. R., and J. C. Yochelson, *A LISP Garbage Collector for Virtual-Memory Computer Systems*, CACM, November 1969.

Galler, B. A., and A. J. Perlis, *A Proposal for Definitions in ALGOL*, CACM, April 1967.

Hansen, W. J., *Compact List Representation: Definition, Garbage Collection, and System Implementation*, CACM, September 1969.

Hoare, C. A. R., *Record Handling*, in Bobrow (68).

Irons, E. T., *Experience with an Extensible Language*, CACM, January 1970.

Jodeit, A., *Storage Organization in Programming Systems*, CACM, November 1968.

Johnson, W. L., et al., *Automatic Generation of Efficient Lexical Processors Using Finite State Techniques*, CACM, December 1968.

Jones, B., *A Variation on Sorting by Address Calculation*, CACM, February 1970.

Kain, R. Y., *Block Structures, Indirect Addressing, and Garbage Collection*, CACM, July 1969.

Laski, J., *The Morphology of Prex—An Essay in Meta-Algorithmics*, in Michie (67–70), Vol. 3.

Lawson, Jr., H. W., *PL/1 List Processing*, CACM, July 1967.

Lindsey, C. H., *Algol 68 with Fewer Tears*, Algol Bulletin, 1969.

Lowry, E. S., and G. W. Medlock, *Object Code Optimization*, CACM, January 1969.

Luccio, F., *A Comment on Index-Register Allocation*, CACM, September 1967.

Lum, V. Y., P. S. T. Yuen, and M. Dodd, *Key-to-Address Transform Techniques*, CACM, April 1971.

McIlroy, M. D., *Macro Instruction Extensions of Computer Languages*, CACM, March 1960. Also in Rosen (67).

McKellar, A. C., and E. G. Coffman, *Organizing Matrices and Matrix Operations for Paged Memory Systems*, CACM, March 1969.

Madnick, S. E., *String Processing Techniques*, CACM, July 1967.

Maurer, W. D., *An Improved Hash Code for Scatter Storage*, CACM, January 1968.

Mooers, C. N., *TRAC, a Procedure-Describing Language for the Reactive Typewriter*, CACM, March 1965.

Morris, R., *Scatter Storage Techniques*, CACM, January 1968.

Nakato, Ikuo, *On Compiling Algorithms for Arithmetic Expressions*, CACM, August 1967.

Patt, Y. N., *Variable-Length Tree Structures Having Minimum Average Search Time*, CACM, February 1969.

Radke, C. E., *The Use of the Quadratic Residue Research*, CACM, February 1970.

Randell, B., and C. J. Kuehner, *Dynamic Storage Allocation Systems*, CACM, May 1968.

Raphael, B., *The Structure of Programming Languages*, CACM, February 1966.

Redziejowski, R. R., *On Arithmetic Expressions and Trees*, CACM, February 1969.

Rochfeld, A., *New LISP Techniques for a Paging Environment*, private communication.

Ross, D. T., *A Generalized Technique for Symbol Manipulation and Numerical Computation*, CACM, March 1961.

Schorr, H., and W. M. Waite, *An Efficient Machine-Independent Procedure for Garbage Collection in Various List Structures*, CACM, August 1967.

Strachey, C., *A General-Purpose Macrogenerator*, Comp. Jour., p. 225, 1965.

Van Wijngarden, ed., *ALGOL 68*, IFIP, 1968.

Weber, H., *A Microprogrammed Implementation of EULER on IBM System/360 Model 30*, CACM, September 1967.

Weizenbaum, J., *Recovery of Reentrant List Structures in SLIP*, CACM, July 1969.

——, *Symmetric List Processor*, CACM, September 1963.

Wirth, N., and C. A. R. Hoare, *A Contribution to the Development of ALGOL*, CACM, June 1966.

Wirth, N., and H. Weber, *Euler*, CACM, January 1966.

INDEX